THE SCIENCE
OF CHARACTER

THINKING LITERATURE
A series edited by Nan Z. Da and Anahid Nersessian

The Science of Character

HUMAN OBJECTHOOD AND THE
ENDS OF VICTORIAN REALISM

S. Pearl Brilmyer

The University of Chicago Press
Chicago and London

The University of Chicago Press, Chicago 60637
The University of Chicago Press, Ltd., London
© 2022 by The University of Chicago
All rights reserved. No part of this book may be used or reproduced in any manner whatsoever without written permission, except in the case of brief quotations in critical articles and reviews. For more information, contact the University of Chicago Press, 1427 East 60th Street, Chicago, IL 60637.
Published 2022
Printed in the United States of America

31 30 29 28 27 26 25 24 23 22   1 2 3 4 5

ISBN-13: 978-0-226-81577-0 (cloth)
ISBN-13: 978-0-226-81578-7 (paper)
ISBN-13: 978-0-226-81579-4 (e-book)
DOI: https://doi.org/10.7208/chicago/9780226815794.001.0001

Library of Congress Cataloging-in-Publication Data

Names: Brilmyer, S. Pearl, author.
Title: The science of character : human objecthood and the ends of Victorian realism / S. Pearl Brilmyer.
Other titles: Thinking literature.
Description: Chicago : University of Chicago Press, 2022. | Series: Thinking literature | Includes bibliographical references and index.
Identifiers: LCCN 2021034811 | ISBN 9780226815770 (cloth) | ISBN 9780226815787 (paperback) | ISBN 9780226815794 (ebook)
Subjects: LCSH: English literature—19th century—History and criticism. | Characters and characteristics in literature. | Personality development.
Classification: LCC PR461 .B73 2021 | DDC 823/.809—dc23
LC record available at https://lccn.loc.gov/2021034811

So time passed on, changing all things greatly, or with infinitesimal changes, according to their nature.... The very faces of the streets were changing enlivened by plaster and paint and polish: the face of the land with the certain advance of the season; the faces of friends with something not to be named, but visible, strange, and, for the most part, disheartening. It was the old story for ever and ever; all things changed always; but the chime was immutable.

SARAH GRAND, "Proem," *The Heavenly Twins*

Contents

LIST OF FIGURES ix

INTRODUCTION · Ethology, or the Science of Character 1

As Much an External Thing as a Tree or a Rock 14
A Power of Observation Informed by a Living Heart; or, Involuntary, Palpitating 24
Inconsistency and Formlessness 33

CHAPTER 1 · Plasticity, Form, and the Physics of Character in Eliot's *Middlemarch* 42

Plastic Forms 45
Irregular Solids, Viscous Fluids 60

CHAPTER 2 · Sensing Character in *Impressions of Theophrastus Such* 75

Theophrastus Who? 79
Descriptive Minutiae 85
To Sketch a Species 88
The Natural History of Human Life 93
After the Human 97

CHAPTER 3 · The Racialization of Surface in Hardy's *Sketch of Temperament* and Hereditary Science 103

The Color of Heredity 110
On the Whiteness of the Ground 117
Accretions of Character 129

CHAPTER 4 · Schopenhauer and the Determination of Women's Character 144

An English Start 151
The Character of the Will 156
Impulsive Aesthetics 168

CHAPTER 5 · The Intimate Pulse of Reality; or, Schreiner's Ethological Realism   180

The Ethics of Nature   189
The Ethics of Description   201
The Ethics of Force   209

CODA · Spontaneous Generations of Character between Realism and Modernism   220

ACKNOWLEDGMENTS   245

BIBLIOGRAPHY   249

INDEX   275

Figures

1 Jens Nikolaus, Five Regular Solids (2015) 64
2 James Clerk Maxwell, Dynamical Top (1890) 65
3 Francis Galton, Diagram of White, Black, and Hybrid Grey Forms (1875) 126
4 Stan Celestian, Oolite (2018) 134
5 Grover Schrayer, Cross-section of Oolitic Limestone (2009) 135

Ethology, or the Science of Character

INTRODUCTION

In 1843, John Stuart Mill outlined a new science he hoped would gain traction in the coming years, which he termed "Ethology, or the Science of Character." This new field of research, proposed in his monumental contribution to the philosophy of science, *A System of Logic*, would investigate the forces—biological, environmental, and cultural—at work in the formation of character. Mill suggested that whereas psychology should concern the general principles governing subjectivity, ethology should attend to the particular and circumstantial processes through which character takes shape: "We employ the name Psychology for the science of the elementary laws of mind," he wrote, adding, "Ethology will serve for the ulterior science which determines the kind of character produced in conformity with those general laws, by any set of circumstances" (*System* 869).

Prior to Mill, the word *ethology* had been used to describe the study of ethical behavior, for instance, in ancient works on manners and morals, the Greek word *ethos* (ἔθος) being the root for *ethics*.[1] But Mill had in mind a different application for the term. His science would uncover how subjects acquired physical and mental traits through a complex interplay of causes. What causes one person's character to develop like this and another's to develop like that? What laws governed the transformation of subjectively experienced events (the unique sequence of which constitutes a life) into objectively observable traits (the unique combination of which

---

1. The roots of the term *ethology* can be traced to the Stoic doctrine of the first century BCE, where *ethologia* (ηθολογία) referred to the study of how particular virtues and vices manifested themselves in physical traits, differentiating people from one another. Ethology, Seneca explains, "gives the signs and marks which belong to each virtue and vice, so that by them distinction may be drawn between like things," noting that "this science Posidonius calls ethology (*ethologia*), while others call it characterization (*charactêrismos*)" (99). On ethology in antiquity, see Schurig.

constitute character)? Any attempt to uncover the laws of character would be forced to reckon with the contingencies of *circumstance*, the watchword for the particular science of character Mill envisioned (the Greek *ethos* also meaning "habitat" or "milieu").[2] He proposed that ethology should concern "not the principles of human nature, but results of those principles under the circumstances in which mankind have happened to be placed" (861–62). And circumstances, Mill observed, generate infinite differences. He continued, "Every individual is surrounded by circumstances different from those of every other individual, every nation or generation of mankind from every other nation or generation: and none of these differences are without their influence in forming a different type of character" (864).

Such a desire to account for the ever-specifying, ever-pluralizing force of circumstance placed Mill's science at odds with other, more essentializing sciences of character of the period—most notably physiognomy and phrenology. In contrast to these characterological sciences, which interpreted the shape and appearance of the body to reveal the inner truth of character, ethology arose from Mill's conviction that the body is an unreliable source of information about character. Given that all bodies respond differently to the same stimuli, Mill reasoned, the effect of "organic causes" on "mental phenomena" must be highly mediated, rendering the etiology of character a challenging affair (860).[3] If character were written in a kind of language, its sign system could not simply be decoded. The connection between cause and effect, signified and signifier, is far too weak.

---

2. Over a decade later, the French naturalist Isidore Geoffroy Saint-Hilaire would, independent of Mill, take up the term *éthologie* to envision a new science, the biological study of animals in relationship to their milieu, discussed at greater length in chapter 5 (Jaynes 602). On the interest of Geoffroy and his colleague Jean-Baptiste Lamarck on the formative power of milieu in evolution, see Canguilhem, "The Living and its Milieu."

3. On the characterological claims of physiognomy, see Pearl (93–97); and Hartley, *Physiognomy* (chap. 3). On phrenology's development of a biological basis for character, see Claggett. Mill had positioned ethology as an alternative to phrenology, claiming that phrenology failed to account for the determining force of circumstance, as well as how and why bodies responded differently to those circumstances. "It is certain that, in human beings at least," he wrote, "differences in education and in outward circumstances, together with physical differences in the sensations produced in different individuals by the same external or internal cause, are capable of accounting for a far greater portion of character than is supposed even by the most moderate phrenologists" (858). The Victorian psychologist Alexander Bain would extend and elaborate upon Mill's critique of phrenological science in *On the Study of Character: Including an Estimate of Phrenology* (1861).

Mill's attempt to make room for contingency in his science of the accretion of personal traits introduced a problem, however. How, if character forms contingently in particular subjects in response to particular circumstances, could one produce a systematic science of character? Mill's vision for ethology was that it would become an "Exact Science of Human Nature" (870); "its truths," he wrote, "are not like the empirical laws which depend on them, approximate generalizations, but real laws" (870). But what laws could possibly follow from this ontology of the incident—a science that, in its obsession with the accidents of circumstance, seemed ill equipped to outline anything so certain as a law? Even Mill, who at times expressed hope that an adequate knowledge of circumstances might allow scientists to eventually "positively predict the character that could be produced," wavered on the question of ethology's predictive power: were laws of character discovered, he admitted, "they should be hypothetical only, and affirm tendencies, not facts" (870). Were a science of character to be formulated, it would be an "ulterior science"—a science of the indeterminate, the unforeseen, and the not yet expressed (869).

The tension at the heart of Mill's science between necessity and contingency—between "universal or general rules" and "the circumstances of the particular case"—proved too great to sustain (877). While a few English scientists, most notably the psychologist Alexander F. Shand, attempted to implement Mill's ethological program, the attempt to establish ethology as a scientific discipline in England was by and large unsuccessful. At the turn of the twentieth century, psychology, anthropology, and sociology—all nascent disciplines in the nineteenth century—would become institutionalized fields of study with distinct methodologies and objects. "Ethology, or the Science of Character," on the other hand, remained unrealized, becoming, as one historian put it, "one of the many nineteenth-century proposals that did not pass the test of history" (Leary 153).[4]

This book arises out of a thought experiment turned proposition: although ethology failed to cohere into a systematic scientific practice, it took

---

4. On the rise and fall of ethology in the English context, see Leary, who notes that throughout the nineteenth century, "there was much discussion about character and character formation in England, but the major part of this discussion was couched in moralistic, educational, and inspirational works on how to raise and train children. Although some of these works made reference to Mill's Ethology, none of them constituted a real attempt to develop Mill's program" (157). In France, on the other hand, Mill's idea was better received, being publicized through the work of Théodule Ribot, Frédéric Paulhan, and Michel Foucault's uncle, Paulin Malapert. Leary speculates that "France's literary tradition of studying *le caractère*" provided fertile ground for the formulation of an ethological science there, "in more or less conscious imitation of Mill's original program" (157).

hold in the work of novelists who used fiction to explore the dynamic, material processes through which character is formed. I argue that although Mill's science of character faltered in its promise to reveal how unique, circumstantial experiences give rise to general and recognizable characterological forms, the novel, especially as transformed in the hands of realist authors at the turn of the twentieth century, rose to that challenge, cultivating its own narrative science of human nature.

What was this nature? To what extent could it be transformed? Such were the founding questions of the novel genre as it emerged throughout the eighteenth and nineteenth centuries in Europe to represent "man *in the process of becoming*" (Bakhtin 19).[5] Especially in its early manifestation as the *Bildungsroman*, the realist novel was premised upon the suggestion that character emerges, relationally and contingently, in response to circumstances. In 1853, Elizabeth Gaskell invoked this basic tenet of realism in her bildungsroman *Ruth*, when her narrator described herself as setting out to analyze "the circumstances which contributed to the formation of character" through close attention to "the daily life into which people are born, and into which they are absorbed before they are well aware" (4). But whereas Gaskell and other midcentury novelists sometimes celebrated the ability of certain extraordinary people to transcend their circumstances through supreme "moral strength" and "independent individual action," a new generation of realists would be far more uncompromising (4).[6] Doubling down on the ethological proposition that character is determined by milieu, feminist realists of the fin de siècle would reinvent character itself as a circumstance, an irreversible sequence of

---

5. In "The Bildungsroman and Its Significance in the History of Realism," Mikhail Bakhtin differentiates what he calls "the novel of human emergence" from earlier narrative fiction by arguing that here, the hero's transformation becomes the driving force of the plot. In this new form of novel, Bakhtin observes, "Time is introduced into man, enters into his very image, changing in a fundamental way the significance of all aspects of his destiny and life" (21). It is no accident, this study wagers, that a scientifically minded author like Goethe founded the bildungsroman tradition.

6. One of the first novels to feature a fallen woman as its protagonist, *Ruth* laid the groundwork for later feminist realists to show how circumstances influenced the development of a woman's character. Narrating how the "chains of daily domestic habit" stifled the expression and development of women, Gaskell's novel highlights the challenges to self-transformation faced by women without social and economic means (4). Mill likewise mobilized the discourse of circumstances toward feminist ends in "The Subjection of Women" (an essay likely coauthored by Harriet Taylor Mill). "Whatever any portion of the human species now are, or seem to be," it argued, "the most elementary knowledge of the circumstances in which they have been placed, clearly points out the causes that made them what they are" (277).

events that engender a person—unwillingly and irrevocably—and without their being "well aware."

The Science of Character began from a curiosity about how fiction, when it stages encounters between imaginary people in imaginary situations, produces knowledge about reality. As its initial conjectures cohered into hypotheses, it developed into a historically attuned account of a particular time and place, namely, late Victorian England, where a new generation of writers had begun to make powerful claims for the epistemological purchase of the literary. Scholars of nineteenth-century literature and science have shown how the representational aims of the realist novel were informed by the scientific discourse of the time, which likewise confronted problems of objectivity, reference, and mimesis.[7] But the realist endeavor to represent "people as they are," to invoke George Eliot's pithy phrase, although closely engaged with the sciences, proceeded according to a uniquely literary logic ("Natural History" 110). Uninterested in the achievement of "scientific certitude," foundational English realists such as Eliot employed narrative to study "the history of man, and how that mysterious mixture behaves under the varying experiments of Time" (*Middlemarch* 3). Bringing to life Mill's unrealized dream of ethology, they explored how characterological traits and behaviors emerge and develop across a person's life and how physical features—shapes, colors, and gestures—take on cultural meaning through categories such as race, class, and sex. The literary figure they used to do so was *character*, a term that, because it tracked across fields as various as natural history, metaphysics, ethics, and a nascent genetics, became the vehicle for the investigation of something beyond the pages of fiction: the elusive unity that renders a being distinct, an essence in transformation across space and time.

Deidre Shauna Lynch has powerfully argued that "novel writing's claim to a singular distinction among the disciplines would be founded on the promise that it was this type of writing that tendered the deepest, truest knowledge of character" (28). As the nineteenth century came to an end, realist novelists in England took up this characterological project with renewed enthusiasm, extending its claims and testing its limits. But if the aspiration of the novel remained at the century's close to offer "a full and authentic report of human experience," as Ian Watt once described the aim of the genre, the qualifications for such "fullness" and "authenticity" had changed completely (28). *The Science of Character* shows how what

---

7. On the shared epistemological aims of Victorian novelists and scientists, see Beer, *Open Fields* and *Darwin's Plots*; Levine, *Dying to Know*; Garratt, *Victorian Empiricism*; Herbert, *Victorian Relativity*; Griffiths, *The Age of Analogy*; and Tondre, *The Physics of Possibility*.

scholars have long recognized as the hallmarks of nineteenth-century realist character—individuality, interiority, and the capacity for intellectual and moral growth—would be replaced between the years of 1870 and 1920 with a much more materialist set of ideals: plasticity (discussed in chapter 1), impressibility (chapter 2), spontaneity (chapter 3), impulsivity (chapter 4), relationality (chapter 5), and vitality (coda). In the final decades of the nineteenth century, English, South African, and Irish writers such as Thomas Hardy, Olive Schreiner, and Sarah Grand emphasized the role of physical encounters and bodily impulses in character formation, transforming character from the hidden kernel of an individual personality into an impersonal phenomenon that formed though corporeal interactions. In so doing, they built on the foundational work of Eliot, whose late fiction presents character not as a special feature of the human psyche, but rather as something humans share with nonhuman animals and things. In cultivating a more materialist approach to the human, these novelists would do more than revise the qualifications for what counted as a realistic character. This book maintains that they would entirely redraw the lines according to which reality itself had been partitioned, insisting on the power of the literary to offer insight into the workings of nature, in addition to culture.

The Science of Character begins in the 1870s, at a moment when a progressively restricted and professionalized English scientific culture had staked its claim to a reality defined increasingly in materialist terms, and literature had come to assert greater cultural authority. Culture, Matthew Arnold wrote in 1869, "moves by the force, not merely or primarily of the scientific passion for pure knowledge, but also of the moral and social passion for doing good" (*Works* 6:7). More than the scientific endeavor "to see things as they are" (6:7), Arnold consistently argued that literature and its study are best able to answer the "question: How to live" (4:105).[8] The

---

8. Toepfer has traced the belief, expressed by Arnold here, that science is theoretical and observational, and art is practical and instructive back to the early eighteenth century ("Wissenschaft" 300). This view would persist throughout much of the nineteenth century, perpetuated not only by humanists such as Arnold, but also by scientists such as William Whewell. In his monumental study of the history and philosophy of science, *The Philosophy of the Inductive Sciences, Founded upon Their History* (1840), for example, Whewell writes, "Art and Science differ. The object of Science is Knowledge, and the objects of Art, are Works. In Art, truth is a means to an end; in Science, it is the only end" (xli). As with Arnold, Whewell implies that where science seeks to know the world in itself and for itself, art engages with the world with some other end in mind (namely, critique and improvement, in Arnold's view). The terms of the debate started to shift slightly in the final two decades of the nineteenth century, when advocates of science education began insisting on "the practical value of science" against the liter-

novelists at the heart of this study spurned the suggestion that while the sciences investigate the neutral and valueless world beyond the subject, literature concerns itself only with human action, speech, and meaning. What's more, they refused the notion that while the sciences describe the world as it is, literature imagines the world as it could or should be.

"Since Art is science with an addition, and some science underlies all Art," Thomas Hardy wrote in 1891, "there is seemingly no paradox in using the phrase 'the Science of Fiction'" (101). Hardy's 1891 essay "The Science of Fiction" represents one of several turn-of-the-century attempts to claim a fundamental stratum of ontology for literature at a time when the physical world was increasingly understood to be the province of the sciences. Positioning fiction as an authority on character, and character as the key to reality, Hardy argued that literature does more than illustrate social or moral principles: it produces "comprehensive and accurate knowledge of realities" ("Science" 101). Aligning his own aesthetic with that of the *New Realism* that had emerged in recent years, he proposed that, through close attention to the complexities of human perception and embodiment, fiction generates such a precise and vivid account of reality: "The particulars of this science," he contends, "are the generals of almost all others. The materials of Fiction being human nature and circumstances, the science thereof might be dignified by calling it the codified law of things as they really are" (101).[9]

---

ary arts (Huxley, "Science" 138). Advocating for the value of science-based education in 1880, T. H. Huxley countered Arnold's claims for the practical value of literary study by arguing that a man with an "exclusively literary education" (141) is as likely to enter "upon a criticism of life" as "an army, without weapons of precision and with no particular base of operations" is able to "enter upon a campaign on the Rhine" (144). In response to Huxley, Arnold continued to insist on the practical value of the humanities, as well as to make the case that humanistic study is itself scientific: "all learning is scientific which is systematically laid out and followed up to its original sources, [thus] a genuine humanism is scientific," he argues in an 1882 lecture (*Works* 4:324). While accusations of lack of practical value and coherent methodology are no doubt in part what disqualified literary studies in England and the United States from their claim to the status of a "science," this study wagers that beginning from the assumption that the value of any knowledge system corresponds to its utility is to lose the game before it begins. In insisting on the *theoretical* and *observational* capacities of the literary, the authors that I examine suggest that literary studies today may have something to learn from fields such as theoretical physics or animal ethology—fields do not appeal to utility in the same way that their counterparts in the applied and experimental sciences do.

9. Hardy is, of course, no conventional realist. Indeed, he once famously declared that "'realism' is not Art," because the goal of art should be "a disproportioning—(i.e., distorting, throwing out of proportion)—of realities" (*Life* 239). The aim of such disproportioning, however, he goes on to argue, indicating his investment in another, more

Hardy's suggestion that fiction not only *represents* reality but also *codifies its laws*, might appear naïve from our contemporary vantage. Poststructuralist theorists have taught us to be skeptical of the suggestion that literature simply "describes" reality, maintaining instead that realist novelists use language to create the "effect of the real" (Barthes, "Reality" 16). Rather than understanding realism as an act of deception or apparition, as this tradition does, however, I approach the reality effect of the nineteenth-century realist novel more literally—that is, as an effect of reality, as the place where reality's textures, surfaces, and forms are not merely reflected through language but amplified and added to through emergent processes.[10]

Literary scholars working within the theoretical framework of new materialisms such as Ada Smailbegović have called into question the assumption that "signs possess only an arbitrary, disembodied, and hence transposable relation to material substrates that passively underlie them," emphasizing how nonhuman animals and things themselves signify through color, shape, and movement ("From Code" 135).[11] These scholars' insights into what the physicist-philosopher Karen Barad has called "entanglement of matter and meaning" build upon a long tradition of feminist science studies to which this book is indebted in both content and approach (Barad, *Meeting* iii).[12] Where Donna Haraway, in her coinage of the

---

philosophical notion of realism, is "to show more clearly the features that matter in those realities" (239). On the metaphysical problems that inform Hardy's relationship to realism, see Wright, "Thomas." Plietzsch has likewise interpreted Hardy's 1891 essay to suggest that he "regards his fiction in light of the new realism" (184).

10. In asking to what extent the realist novel can be seen to succeed in its mission to describe physical reality, I share with Elaine Freedgood and Cannon Schmitt a desire to open up literary "textuality to other- and nontextuality" (8). To ask such a question, does not necessitate reinscribing transparency or stability to realist representation, as Freedgood demonstrates in *Worlds Enough*. As Freedgood argues there, the "novels that critics have perhaps helped us to homogenize into a recognizable realism" are more messy and multiple than we have led to believe: their "lack of unity, the intrusive omniscient author, and multiple plots militated against any positive sense of" formal coherence (xi).

11. As Smailbegović observes, while "the 'linguistic turn' [has] typically figured matter… as immutable and deterministic and hence as vulnerable to various forms of essentialism," much new materialist scholarship has often failed to "seriously consider that materiality and signification are complexly and perhaps irresolvably imbricated" (137). This book takes cues from Smailbegović's suggestion that "signification is imminent within materiality" itself (139).

12. For an introduction to feminist science studies, see Cipolla et al. On feminist materialism, see Alaimo and Hekman. On new materialism, see Dolphijn and van der Tuin; and Coole and Frost.

term "material semiotic," upends the suggestion that there exists a prediscursive "matter" to which language points, Elizabeth Grosz, in her analysis of Darwin's theory of sexual selection, reframes the aesthetic as a nonhuman semiotic that generates variation throughout the natural world.[13] To understand semiosis not only in terms of human language but also as "a material process occurring between bodies and environments—a phonetic and graphic outgrowth of corporeal existence," opens up the study of realism to new vistas (Brilmyer and Trentin 503). Fredric Jameson claims that all literature, especially realist literature, suffers from a "profound envy of the other arts" in its desire to "be a thing, as the objects of the other arts seem to be" (*Singular* 174). If matter is as semiotic as language is material, however—if humans are not the only ones to wield signs, and if all bodies are figures—then literature need not be understood as having to overcome some sort of vast epistemological gulf to represent, interact with, and be affected by (the rest of) the physical world.

Thus, where some scholars of nineteenth-century literature and science emphasize the power of fiction to construct alternative worlds, I follow Eliot's and Hardy's lead in asking to what extent literature teaches us about things "as they really are."[14] The philosopher Odo Marquard once defined fiction as "the sense of reality of the sense of possibility [*Wirklichkeitssinn des Möglichkeitssinns*]" (490). Such a definition encourages us to notice how fiction activates potentials immanent in the actual in order to generate figures "poised at the knife edge between the real and the unreal," as Michael Tondre has written (4). I approach character as a vector that bisects fiction and reality and, as such, the key figure for a realism that aspires to render "art [as] ... the nearest thing to life" (Eliot, "Natural" 110). In so doing, I shift the critical focus of character studies from the historical and formal conditions of character's production to the kinds of claims that the novels make in and through their construction of fictional figures. The driving questions of this study thus are not (or, at least, not only): How does the concept of literary character change historically?[15] What makes a literary character appear lifelike or sympathetic?[16] What role do flat or round (or, alternatively, minor or major) characters play in

13. See Haraway, "Promises"; and Grosz, *Chaos*.

14. Scholarship on Victorian science fiction understandably tends to take this approach (e.g., Philmus; Parrinder). The counterfactual has been another rich resource for thinking about the relationship between fiction and possibility, (e.g., Andrew Miller, *On Not Being*; Gallagher, *Telling It*; and Gallagher et al.). For some philosophical perspectives on the role of the imagination and possibility in fiction, see Nichols; and Walton.

15. On this question, see Lynch; and Gallagher, "Rise."

16. On this question, see Vermeule; Ward; Auyoung; as well as Felski's chapter in Anderson et al., *Character*.

the novel or other genres?[17] While I at times address such historical, psychological, and formal questions, my focus is on how the figure of character became the locus of a literary-philosophical inquiry into corporeal existence.

What indeed might character in fiction tell us about character in reality? Literary scholars have emphasized the extent to which we misunderstand character when we align it too closely with individual human psychology, highlighting how characters are discursively constructed to appear "as if" they were real people with feelings, thoughts, and aims.[18] As Mieke Bal reminds us, a "character is not a human being, but it resembles one. It has no real psyche, personality, ideology, or competence to act, but it does possess characteristics that make readers assume that it does" (113). Recognizing the fundamental "non-human-ness" of literary character, as Megan Ward encourages us to do, allows us to comprehend how characters are constructed to "seem human" through a range of formal techniques (Ward 2).[19] This work has served as an important corrective to the long-standing tendency to presume that characters—at least the most real-seeming and successful ones—are furnished with an individual and subjective dimension. But where the recent groundswell of character scholarship has focused on the "createdness of fictional character," show-

---

17. On this question, see Woloch.

18. Lynch has shown how the alignment of fictional characters with individual human subjectivity was neither natural nor inevitable; rather, it emerged during the eighteenth and nineteenth centuries as writers worked to distinguish public from private, inside from outside, and fiction from reality. Figlerowicz further complicates the narrative of character's inward turn by elucidating a long, if intermittent, history of "flat realism" that stretches from the seventeenth to the twentieth century, in which novelistic characters becomes "increasingly stereotypical and predictable" as the plot progresses (2). Focusing on the nineteenth century, moreover, Ward shows that that Victorian novelists did not always take psychological depth as a precondition for human likeness, but simulated intelligence using mechanical techniques similar to early artificial intelligence research. While both Ward and Bal encourage readers to abandon anthropomorphism in their approach to character, Auyoung is more forgiving of the cognitive "failure to recognize that literary characters are linguistic constructions rather than social beings" (38). At the same time, Auyoung shares with these scholars a commitment to understanding the formal mechanisms through which we "feel" that characters are like real humans, despite knowing that they are not. On "how the taboo on treating characters as if they were real people hardened into a dogma," see Moi's chapter in Anderson et al.'s *Character* (29). On the importance of the phrase "as if" itself for the simulation of characterological interiority in Victorian fiction, see Farina, "Dickens' 'As If.'"

19. On the formal construction of characters as "person-like entities," see Frow (2). Like many of the scholars cited in note 18, Frow seeks to keep the categories of "character and person distinct to the fields in which they operate" (viii).

ing how characters are constructed in order to "simulate" human life, this book takes a different tack, asking what fiction can tell us about how character works on and off the page (Ward 4).

Taking cues from nineteenth-century philosophers for whom the experience of character was grounded in the experience of the body and its physical activities, I suggest that what imaginary literary persons have in common with human beings is not an appearance of consciousness, individuality, nor even necessarily the ability to grow or change, but rather the expression of an aggregate of qualities that temporarily unify to create the sense of "character."[20] In literature, this temporary unity is produced through the arrangement of (textual) characters on a page; in life, it is produced through the arrangement of (corporeal) characters on a living body. Drawing on the ethological theory of the Victorian scientists A. F. Shand and James Sully, I maintain that the power of realism inheres less in its insights into the human mind or the value of sympathetic exchange than in its ability to both represent and theorize of the sensorial experience of encountering a human being in the flesh. While literary characters might seem like thinking subjects, they are in fact aesthetic *objects*—textual entities whose features and actions, while generated through language, give the impression of a living, breathing person.

Before moving on to discuss the significance of Shand and Sully's work for my theory of character as an ontological link between fictional and real humans, however, a small caveat is necessary here. What might be described as this book's post-constructivist approach to character arises neither from a conviction that characters are somehow outside of history or ideology nor from the assumption that they are direct or unmediated representations of actual people. Rather, in excavating from an archive of turn-of-the-century realist fiction a science of character—an ethological account of what, circumstantially, makes people who they are—I ask what fiction—precisely because it is not a scientific experiment with positivist aspirations to objectivity and facticity, but instead a historically and culturally mediated aesthetic phenomenon—might tell us about character that other modes of knowledge production cannot.

Today, if fiction is thought to teach us about life, it is typically thought to expose the workings of history, power, or ideology—forces that construct

20. To re-suture literary characters to their human analogs need not entail embracing a biblical approach to fiction as illustrative of moral principles, nor does it require abandoning the insights of literary studies into character as an aesthetic phenomenon. I thus remain skeptical of the lineage of philosophical ethics, cited approvingly by Anderson, Felski, and Moi, which turns to fiction "to exemplify forms of response to the conditions of human existence or the demands of moral life" because "productively unconstrained by the field conditions of literary studies" (Anderson et al. 7–9).

and discipline subjects whose individuality and autonomy constitute a fantasy to be dispelled.[21] And even this knowledge, it is sometimes implied, is not properly literature's own, generated as it is by the critic who reveals the novel's complicity in the production of the troubling fantasy of a "stable, centered subject in a stable, centered world" (Miller, *Novel* xi). Returning to a historical moment in which literature was thought to produce real knowledge about the real world, including the figure of the human at its center, *The Science of Character* encourages a reassessment of the novel's genre-founding claim to offer "a full and authentic report of human experience" (Watt 28). It does so, however, not via the notion of the subject that has grounded literary and cultural theory over the past half decade, but through the much older notion of character, a figure that decenters subjective experience at the same time that it takes the human as its focus.

In 1991, Jean-Luc Nancy provocatively asked, "Who comes after the subject?" (4). In response to this question, this book answers: character—a figure that is, however, less a "who" than a "what." The novelists analyzed here engaged materialist science and philosophy to transform character from the inner truth of an individual into a materially determined figuration produced through shifts in the boundaries between the body's interior and exterior. In so doing, they shift our attention from human subjecthood toward what I call *human objecthood*—physical and determined aspects of existence that humans share with nonhuman animals and things. In turning away from the *subject* toward *character*, these authors began with the presumption of a shared materiality between human beings and the world they describe, encouraging us to recognize the material-semiotic processes that knit together worlds.

In her work on the rise of fictionality, Catherine Gallagher argues that the invention of fiction consisted less in the attempt to produce a fantasy world, detached from this one, than in the reorganization of the semiotic relationship between literary personae and the real kinds of people they were thought to represent. Early novelists, she contends, often insisted that their characters did not refer to specific people but rather to types— this or that *kind* of person out there in the world. Gallagher invites her readers to think of the ontology of literary character "like a triptych, in which ontologically distinct categories of 'the particular' appear on either side of a category of 'the general'" ("George" 62). In a complex referential gymnastics, she contends, early novelists understood themselves to have *deduced* their fictional characters from abstract, ideational types, which they in turn *induced* from real and particular individuals. In so doing, Gal-

---

21. For a compelling argument about how novels both construct and dispel the myth of the individual, see Armstrong's *How Novels Think*.

lagher argues, they inverted "normal empirical ways of thinking about the relation between the real and the imaginary, the sensual or experiential, on the one hand, and the ideational, on the other" (62).

Gallagher's historically situated account of how early novelists came to understand themselves as producing knowledge about humans in general by referring to "nobody in particular" undergirds a key philosophical premise of this book: novels engage in induction and deduction in ways that the empirical and rational sciences cannot (*Nobody's* 283). While I examine the work of a much later generation of novelists, I do not so much track Gallagher's argument forward in time as I push it, logically, one step further: within the paradigm of realism that *The Science of Character* elucidates, fictional characters are understood not merely as representative of types, but as ciphers for the theorization of character as such.[22] I believe this is what Hardy meant when he wrote that "the particulars of this science are the generals of almost all others. The materials of Fiction being human nature and circumstances, the science thereof might be dignified by calling it the codified law of things as they really are" ("Science" 101).

To fiction's capacity to generalize—to its capacity to employ particular, imaginary figures to think through conceptual problems about the nature of reality—I sometimes give the name "theory," contending that when fiction attends to the observable, the particular, and the contingent—in a word, to circumstance—it theorizes. In 1896, Shand marveled at the "empirical generalisations concerning character which are stored in literature," suggesting that it was the mark of a great novelist to be able to portray in a realistic way the "feeling and conduct which will be produced in the characters he represents in the circumstances in which he places them" ("Character" 205, 213). Shand's turn-of-the-century reformulation of ethology shifted the study of character from its focus on static qualities (e.g., pride and cowardice) toward the affective encounters that give rise to patterns of behavior. In his influential 1896 essay "Character and the Emotions," Shand attacked the dogma of what he called the "dualism of Character and Circumstance," according to which "Circumstance is regarded as something external to Character and acting upon it from the outside" (210).[23] The realist novel was, for Shand, an ally in breaking down such

---

22. For another argument about how literary characters enable generalization, see Kunin.

23. Shand's critique of the "dualism of Character and Circumstance" anticipates the critique by the twentieth-century French philosopher Gilbert Simondon of the "duality of milieu and individual—the milieu having been deprived of the individual it no longer is, and the individual no longer possessing the wider dimensions of the milieu" (305). On how the concept of "milieu" is imported from mechanics to biology in the

dualisms insofar as it attended to the "dynamical" relation between character and milieu (*Foundations* 1).[24]

Novels, Shand maintained, are a source of scientific information about character, to the extent that they realistically narrate how character forms, relatively and specifically, in relation to circumstances, while at the same time conforming to more general characterological laws. The scientist thus has much to learn from the fiction writer, whose narratives immanently reveal these laws by employing induction and deduction in ways that experiments, among other scientific methods, do not. Our understanding of these laws, Shand proposed in his defense of reading as a path to knowledge of character, "derive as much from our own observation and thought as from books" (205).

While early novelists, as Gallagher shows, enlisted specific fictional individuals to make observations about real *kinds* of people, the Victorian novelists I examine dilate their characters yet further in order to make not merely ontic (i.e., specific and factual) but also ontological (i.e., general and theoretical) claims about what Shand called the "dynamical" relationship between character and circumstances (*Foundations* 1). Mobilizing the tension between the aesthetic and philosophical notions of character—character as a specific fictional personage and general ontological phenomenon—these writers staked a claim to a physical reality that many believed to be the property of the sciences but that, in this unique historical moment, became the province of the literary.

As Much an External Thing as a Tree or a Rock

In the nineteenth century, the word *character* encompassed a wide range of thinking about the relationship between sensation, perception, and the body—a much broader range than has been recognized in the field of Victorian studies, which has tended to focus on the emergence of liberal theories of character as a self-formed property or more deterministic notions

---

eighteenth century, transforming throughout the nineteenth century from that peripheral to the organism to a "system of relationships without supports," see Canguilhem.

24. Shand opens his 1914 study, *The Foundations of Character: Being a Study of the Tendencies of the Emotions and Sentiments*, with the suggestion that "the treatises on the science of Mind that have appeared up to recent times... have accomplished [little] toward the foundation of a science of character" because of the "small and subordinate place offered to the emotions" (1). In the empirical sciences, he laments, "they are treated in such a way as to deprive them of the living interest which they have in the drama and the novel" (1). Shand's thinking about the role of the emotions and the environment in character formation was influential for the formation of the fields of social psychology (Leary 157–59) and social anthropology (Stocking, *After* 155–57).

of character as the biological essence of a social group.[25] I began this introduction with a classic example of the former in my discussion of Mill, although there, I emphasized the extent to which Mill's never-realized science of ethology was premised on the assumption that character is radically open to circumstances. One of the founding fathers of modern liberalism, of course, Mill would go on to develop an understanding of character as ultimately autonomous and self-willed. Although he continued to maintain that circumstances greatly influence the development of character, he would go on to argue that "our own desires can do much to shape those circumstances; and that what is really inspiring and ennobling in the doctrine of free-will, is the conviction that we have real power over the formation of our own character" (*Autobiography* 177).

Whereas Mill believed that to let impersonal forces determine one's existence was to fail to exercise one's moral agency, a new generation of hereditary scientists and population scientists would argue that character is governed by immutable physical laws acting on the species.[26] While these late-century characterologists may have contested Mill's faith in the power of individual choice, however, they were no less invested in social change. If one could simply uncover character's fundamental laws, the English

---

25. On character in Victorian liberal political theory, see Collini (chap. 3); Goodlad (chap. 1); Hadley (98–106); Thomas (167–82); and Anderson, *The Powers of Distance* (especially the conclusion), and *The Way We Argue Now* (chap. 5). As Collini observes, the ideal of character "enjoyed a prominence in the political thought of the Victorian period that it has apparently not known before and that it has, arguably, not experienced since" (94). These notions of character were not always individualizing, however. Collini points out that the notion of "national character" was of great importance to Mill and other English political thinkers. The late nineteenth century, however, saw a new scientization of the notion of national character, transforming it from the spiritual *Geist* of a people to a material, and, ultimately, racial essence (an insight I owe to Sebastian Lecourt). Mill, for his part, approached national character as a cultural construct, describing it in 1843 as the "power by which all those of the circumstances of society which are artificial, laws and customs for instance, are altogether moulded" (*System* 905). By the time we get to Walter Bagehot's 1872 discussion of "nation building" in *Physics and Politics*, however, the process through which "national characters are formed is... not wholly mental," and the word "nation" is used interchangeably with "breed" (146). On racializing and typologizing discourses of character in the Victorian period, see Hartley, "Constructing"; Stocking, *Victorian* (chap. 3); and Beasley (chaps. 3–4). That these two poles have long formed (and still form) the focus of research on character in the Victorian period speaks to the continued influence of Foucault, who posits that the nineteenth century saw the emergence of (a) a new self-regulating, interiorized subject and (b) the rise of a new biopolitical regime concerned to regulate and mold the species.

26. On the Victorian novelists' engagement with population science, see Steinlight, *Populating*.

statistician and biologist Francis Galton proposed in a series of works that lay the foundation for a new science he called "eugenics," then one might alter the character of the species to develop a harmonious and "extraordinarily gifted race" ("Hereditary" 1:325).

While the birth of liberalism and the rise of eugenic science are two important nodes in the history of character tracked within these pages, the bifurcation of character into something either social or biological, individual or typological, chosen or predetermined, reproduces the dualisms that many late Victorian novelists challenged in their cultivation of what I describe as a *dynamic materialist* approach to character. Within the archive assembled here, I discover an understanding of character as the dynamic material substrate of subjectivity—the ever-changing product of physical processes through which subjectively experienced events are transformed into objectively perceivable traits and behaviors. While these works offer no coherent or unified characterological program, a few basic principles do emerge: Character inheres in the materiality of the body but is no more predictable or governable for that reason; it is the result of action but infrequently any action's intended effect; it is plastic yet determined. Indeed, character's inherent "spontaneity," as many Victorians referred to it, actively frustrates attempts to control its outcome.

If materialism consists in the belief that reality is fundamentally material, and dynamism entails the claim that matter results from the dynamic action of forces, then what I call *dynamic materialism* names the theory that reality consists not of static, individuated things but rather forces that generate characters through interactions. "Which was first, Matter or Force?" the physicist William Crookes asked in his 1860 preface to Michael Faraday's *The Forces of Matter* (1860). "If we think on this question," he answered, "we are unable to conceive of matter without force, or force without matter" (iii). As underlined by the scientist William R. Grove, in the 1874 edition of his widely read *On the Correlation of Physical Forces* (1846), to comprehend matter in terms of "the co-relation of forces" would be to abandon the search for "the ultimate causes or essences" of things (5). It would be to ask not what things *are* but rather how they *act*. In their descriptions of dynamical physical systems, nineteenth-century physicists such as Faraday and Grove held that the actions of forces generate differences between material entities that always exist in relation. Their scientific figures would be taken up in the coming decades by writers whose novels modeled how bodies—human and nonhuman—sensitively respond to one another to give rise to character.

In conceptualizing character as fundamentally material, and matter as fundamentally dynamic, the Victorians ushered in a new characterological paradigm, in which the human being no longer stood above the physical world but rather was a particularly complex knot in a webbed reality. Benjamin Morgan has shown how Victorian artists and aesthetic scientists had "a common grounding in a particular version of materialism" that centered "dynamic interactions" among bodies, minds, and texts (5–6). These "meditations on the shared materiality of human bodies and their surrounding environments," he argues, called into question the passivity of "the seemingly inert world of physical substance" (9). Not only did Victorian thinkers attribute sentience and agency to nonhuman things in their belief that "in aesthetic objects matter became spiritualized, animated, and enminded" (6), however; they also increasingly approached the human being itself as a kind of aesthetic object—a physical being on which forces acted to generate colors, shapes, and other qualities.

In his 1895 study of human development, James Sully highlighted the shared investment of the natural and the human sciences in uncovering the laws of character formation. He wrote, "The same kind of curiosity which prompts the geologist to get back to the first stages of the building up of the planet or the biologist to search out the pristine forms of life is beginning to urge the student of man to discover by a careful study of infancy the way in which human life begins to take its characteristic forms" (*Studies* 4). Between the 1870s and the 1890s, England saw a surge of scientific theories that reduced human thought and action to matter in motion and that therefore considered the possibility that the actions of human beings are as subject to natural law as those of their nonhuman animal counterparts. In the work that brought the human into the evolutionary schema, *The Descent of Man, and Selection in Relation to Sex* (1871), Charles Darwin took cues from his cousin, the abovementioned eugenicist Francis Galton, in arguing that mental and moral character in humans is not the result of some intangible spirit but rather has evolved and could be inherited in the same way as physical character. And yet, Darwin maintained—contesting Galton's faith that the physical appearance of the body could be read for signs of a person's social or moral superiority—indicators of sexual and racial differences, including body shape, skin color, and facial features, bear no necessary relation to fitness or survival but instead emerged as a result of a sometimes death-driven desire for sexual pleasure.[27]

"The variability of all the characteristic variations between the races," Darwin wrote in a reflection on the category of race in *The Descent*, "indicates that these differences cannot be of much importance; for, had they been important, they would long ago have been either fixed and pre-

---

27. For Darwin, Grosz has shown, sexual selection "not only works in cooperation with natural selection but at times functions in conflict with it, placing individuals and species in potential danger to the extent that they attract partners" (*Chaos* 29).

served, or eliminated. In this respect man resembles those forms, called by naturalists protean or polymorphic, which have remained extremely variable, owing, as it seems, to their variations being of an indifferent nature" (229). We will see in chapter 3 of this book, on Hardy and Darwin, how the theory of inheritance Darwin constructed to explain the physical transmission of characters was founded on the fundamental permeability not only of individual bodies but also of the concept of *race* itself—a concept always already a mixture in Darwin rather than a purity tainted through sexual encounters. In the face of nationalistic and eugenic projects aimed at insulating and perpetuating so-called "English character," both Darwin (from a scientific standpoint) and Hardy (from a literary one) advocated for an understanding of character as biologically resistant to human control as a result of its spontaneous variations.

A Darwinian faith in the "protean or polymorphic" quality of the human and the "indifferent nature" of its variations ("an indifference to difference," to borrow a phrase from Madhavi Menon) are two key tenets of the impersonal, non-subject-centered science of character this study tracks across the nineteenth and early twentieth centuries.[28] Another key tenet is a desire to comprehend the forces of determination that give rise to such differences in the first place. Forces of determination do not always constrain; they also activate, specify, and pluralize, enabling entities to attain predicates.[29] Many English readers interpreted *The Descent* to have finally accorded a place to human will in character formation, suggesting that in foregrounding sexual preference Darwin had introduced individual choice into the theory of evolution. However, in the second edition of *The Descent*, Darwin turned to the Romantic philosopher Arthur Schopenhauer to clarify that sexual selection is an entirely nonteleological and *unwilled* force—a force, as he put it in his mediation on the arbitrariness of

---

28. With regard to the context of contemporary identity politics, Menon argues against the imposition of a "universal regime of difference that fixes difference into identity" (5).

29. I use the word *determination* here and throughout to indicate not only how human subjects are limited in their ability to act but also how the character of all beings is produced through interactions through which they attain qualities. Aquinas uses the notion of determination in this way when he sets out to explain how and why there is so much diversity in the physical world: *determinatio*, he writes, "is the first principle of plurality" (80). Along similar lines, Spinoza uses the phrase "forces of determination" to describe how bodies are modified through productive constraints that specify "how and to what extent each thing brings about its own effects" (Sangiacomo 516). Within this scholastic lineage—which stretches from Aquinas, Descartes, and Spinoza through to Schopenhauer—one discovers an understanding of determination as "the modification of a predicate, the qualification of a quality" (Damerow et al. 109).

racial categories, that "acted as powerfully on man, as on any other animal" (229).[30]

The historian of science Rick Rylance has observed that "for many Victorians, the exercise of the will, particularly the ethical will, was the behavioural feature that most clearly distinguished humans from other species" (73). In his 1871 essay "The Physiology of the Will," to give just one example, the Victorian physiologist William Carpenter argues that while "in the lower tribes of animals a large part of the ordinary movements of Locomotion" are "executed in direct response to a stimulus," in the human, voluntary and eventually also "volitional power is gradually acquired" over such "automatic activity" through the "controlling power of the Will" (192–94). Revisiting an old Platonic analogy, Carpenter compares the human body to "a horse under the guidance and control of a skillful rider," a "well-trained steed" onto which man "impresses his mandates" (199). While human beings also are likewise subject to forces beyond their control—physiological drives and impulses such as the heartbeat, which "cannot be altered either in force or frequency by a *volitional* effort" (193)—it is in the realm of character, Carpenter argues, where humans obtain more power. "In proportion as the Will acquires domination over the Automatic tendencies," he writes, echoing Mill, "our characters are shaped *by* ourselves" (199).

Carpenter's suggestion that the human being is superior to other animals in its ability to shape its character through the control of its more "automatic tendencies"—figured here as the animal within—speaks to the enduring influence of dualist models of the subject in nineteenth-century England. Within this lineage, what distinguishes the human from the nonhuman is the possession of a soul, mind, or will, capable of directing the otherwise determined matter of the body. One can observe the legacy of this lineage in nineteenth-century thinkers as diverse as Mill and Galton, who, for all their differences, were united in their faith that the human being stands above the rest of nature as a result of its ability to actively form its own character. As Kyla Schuller has shown, faith in the malleability of human character undergirded not only nineteenth-century liberal discourse but also eugenic science, which sought to improve the human race through the "deliberate molding of hereditary material" (22). If matter is inert and predicable and the human will is active and sponta-

---

30. Darwin's emphasis on the individual organism's lack of agency in response to the formative power of milieu (a milieu viewed not as an imposition from the outside, but, dynamically, as a nexus of relations) is an important point of difference between him and Lamarck, for whom "the milieu provokes the organism to orient its own development," as Canguilhem has noted (23).

neous, such thinkers reasoned, the latter could be used to direct and control the former.

Unbeknownst to many Victorian scientists, this hylomorphic understanding of character had been called into question in the early years of the century by Schopenhauer. Chapter 4 of this book tracks how Schopenhauer rose to prominence in the final decades of the century in England thanks to the work of several British women translators, philosophers, and critics who were drawn to his creative solution to the problem of mind-body dualism. Read in conversation with field theorists, evolutionary scientists, and other materialist scientists, Schopenhauer's nonvolitional theory of *Wille* (Will) was thought to confirm recent scientific insights into the fundamentally dynamic nature of matter. As Schopenhauer argued, although matter "exhibits itself as a body [*als Körper*]," "its whole essence consists in acting [*im Wirken*]" (*WR* 2:302, 305).[31] Well before Faraday and Grove showed that objects are not bounded, contained units but rather concatenations of force, Schopenhauer had argued that matter and force are two sides of the same coin. One arrives at this insight, he proposes, through the experience of the human body itself, the single physical "object" to which we have "inside access."[32] From the recognition that Will is the essence or underlying nature of our own bodies, he argues, we can reason that Will is in fact the nature of all observable bodies. The growth of trees, the falling of rocks, magnetism, chemical attraction and repulsion, sexual desire, all these things—including human agency—are different "gradations" of Will. Thus, he concludes, "every object as thing-in-itself is Will, and as a phenomenon is matter" (*WR* 2:307, translation modified).

How is it that bodies can be part of a physical world, their actions determined by natural law, and yet also be experienced as acting of their own volition? This was the driving question of Schopenhauer's *The World as Will and Representation* (1819, 1844), a touchstone for my thinking throughout this book, not only for its import for many of the writers analyzed here, but also insofar as it informs my approach to character as human objecthood. Schopenhauer believed that although everyone *experiences* their actions as intentional, those actions are no more volitional than those of nonhuman animals and things. Rather than draw ontological distinctions between

31. All references to Schopenhauer's *The World as Will and Representation* are indicated throughout as *WR*.

32. Atwell helpfully glosses Schopenhauer's argument here as follows: "Only from a comparison with what goes on within me when my body performs an action from a motive that moves me, with what is the inner nature of my own changes determined by external grounds, can I obtain an insight into the way in which those inanimate bodies change under the influence of causes, and thus understand what is their inner nature" (100).

human subjects, which act of their own free will, and nonhuman objects, whose actions are determined, Schopenhauer approached "subject" and "object" as two perspectives from which a body can be experienced.[33] When a body is experienced from the inside, he suggests, it appears, "subjectively," as Will; when experienced from the outside, however, that Will crystalizes into a physical entity with shape, color, extension, and other "objectively" (i.e., externally) experienced qualities. "In the case of man," Schopenhauer writes of the latter, externalized experience, "this is called character [*Charakter*]; in the case of a stone, it is called a quality [*Qualität*]; but it is the same in both" (126).

Although elaborated with unrivaled sophistication by Schopenhauer, the theory that character concerns the experience of a body qua object crops up with surprising frequency in Victorian England. Jonathan Farina has observed that "Victorian writings about natural history, geology, architecture, painting, furniture and the decorative arts, sculpture, and fashion manifestly show that Victorians were as comfortable as we are ascribing 'character' to things other than people" ("Character" 609). And Athena Vrettos has shown that within much nineteenth-century thinking about character, "character consists of the cumulative process of taking in the outside world," such that not only "things are embodied in persons," but persons are "in danger of slipping into things" (411-12). As evidence of this claim, Vrettos cites Edwin P. Whipple's 1866 *Character and Characteristic Men*, which defines character as "the embodiment of things in persons," and characterization as the process through which the writer attempts to become the things she describes (Whipple 8). As he writes, "Balzac thought he could not describe a landscape, until he had turned himself for a moment into the trees, and grass, and fountains, and stars, and effects of sunlight, and thus entered into the heart and light of the objects he ached to reproduce" (7-8). For Whipple, realist fiction is a site in which the subject-object boundary is destabilized, arising as it does out of an aching desire to transform oneself into the objects one perceives.

The idea that literature, specifically realist literature, might be an aesthetic vehicle for comprehending "the intractable intimacy between being a person and being a thing," to borrow a phrase from Ann Anlin Cheng, motivates the work of Victorian England's foremost literary theorist of character, James Sully (*Ornamentalism* 17). "Every human being is not only a subjective mind; he is also, in regard to other minds, a part of the

---

33. Marx echoes Schopenhauer in this regard, in his preference for the more relational concept of *Gegenstand* (literally, "that which stands against") over that of *Objekt* or *Ding* in his 1844 manuscripts. On Marx's careful use of these terms, see Freitas-Branco.

objective world," remarks Sully in his 1871 essay "The Aesthetics of Human Character." For Sully, character was a material phenomenon, experienced first and foremost through the senses: "the feelings of others being known only to us through the external signs of his bodily movements and vocal sounds," he observes, every person appears to us "as much an external thing as a tree or a rock" ("Aesthetics" 505).[34] As with Schopenhauer (of whom Sully was a close reader), "character" was Sully's name for this external aspect of human existence.[35]

In his writing on character in fiction, Sully suggests that it is the novelist's unique capacity to generate—in the reader's mind, through language—the sensory experience of the human subject qua object that renders it such an important window into character's aesthetic workings: in suggesting "to the reader's mind... an intricate series of visual and other impressions, such as those conveyed by the person's gesture, dress and outward carriage, by the varying cadences of his voice, and so on," fiction constructs "transformed embodiments of character" out of the "sensuous medium of words" (*Sensation* 284). While a realist novelist might at various points choose to give the reader access to a character's thoughts (presenting them as a subject to which the reader is uniquely privy), it is the representation of a character's outwardly apparent traits, gestures, tone of voice, and so on (i.e., their objecthood) that most accurately mimics the experience of character in real life. This is because, when properly executed, aesthetic representations of character produce "impressions" that trigger memories of aesthetic encounters with persons whose thoughts we rarely have access to (*Sensation* 284).[36]

Sully's claim that fiction reproduces in the mind of the reader the colors, shapes, and sounds of the "objective world" might be met with suspicion from the contemporary reader. Are not the sensations "felt" in reading imagined and thus entirely subjective? Why should we think of them

---

34. Even a person's "internal mental states," Sully argues, when perceived by another, "become revealed by means of this material investiture," thus constituting "in reference to other minds, an object of contemplation" (505). The same can be said of the subject doing the contemplating: "the very consciousness which shares in the subjective feeling, may, in turn, be the cause or objective source of the feeling for others" ("Aesthetics" 505).

35. Sully discusses Schopenhauer at length in his 1877 study *Pessimism: A History and a Criticism*.

36. On the historicity of impressions, see Sully (*Sensation* 38) and Lewes (*Problems* 3.2:101–2). Before Lewes and Sully, the concept of *impression* had been central to the work of associationist philosophers such as David Hume and David Hartley. On the gendered and racial implications of the concept of impressibility, see Schuller, as well as chapter 3 of this study.

as "objective"—that is, as deriving from a world beyond the subject? In Sully's view, as Morgan rightly observes, "the perception of character (real or fictional) takes places in the same register as the perception of physical objects" (162). Far from a disembodied or solipsistic practice, the practice of reading was for Sully, as for many other Victorian thinkers, a "perceptual experience ... that folds together the actual sensory presence of words on a page with the virtual presence of the objects to which those words refer," as David Sweeney Coombs has written (9).[37] Further attention to the ways in which the Victorians themselves understood the phenomenological practice of reading, as provided by Coombs and others, opens up new possibilities for understanding the project of nineteenth-century realism as it used language to re-create the experience of encountering character in the flesh.[38] For Sully, words on a page, properly arranged, indeed reproduce the aesthetic experience of a person in reality. Realist fiction is especially adept at doing so, he implies, because it presents humans less as subjects and more as objects.

While many nineteenth-century novelists no doubt sought to present their characters as real-seeming subjects with minds, perspectives, and intentions, the authors examined here engaged the work of Sully and Schopenhauer to present the human being as a new kind of sensible object, a dynamic material body like any other. Chapter 2 of this book shows how George Eliot engaged Sully's thinking about the sensory basis of character, along with the descriptive traditions of natural history and the character sketch, to highlight the outwardly visible and embodied elements of character in her last published work of fiction, *Impressions of Theophrastus Such* (1879). In *Impressions*, Eliot emphasizes that human beings, like other animals, are conditioned by bodily frameworks and habitual responses that allow them to sense some things and not others. Her reflections in this late work on the role of outwardness and typology in realist worldbuilding can be read as a reflection on her novelistic practice, affirming Marta Figlerowicz's suggestion in her book *Flat Protagonists* that "we have never been as complex, or as deep, as the realist novel would have us believe" (20).

Read alongside Heather Love's work on description, Figlerowicz's thinking about the important role that flat characters play in the nineteenth-century realist novel directs us to understand the surprising ethical poten-

---

37. In *Readings with the Senses*, Coombs shows that for many Victorians, the mental image of an object conjured in the act of reading was thought to mirror the image of an object conjured in direct, perceptual experience.

38. On the phenomenology of reading in the Victorian period, see also Morgan; Auyoung; Dames; and Ablow.

tial of realism's objectifying tendency. If the ethical force of literature inheres not in its representation of characterological depth or roundness, but rather in its ability to carefully document and describe "surfaces, operations, and interactions," as Love has argued, then realism's attention to human objecthood might actually be an ethical mode of representation specifically because it refuses to grant the human special ontological status, privileging a less anthropocentric—and less self-centered—view of life ("Close but Not Deep" 375). The point is not that humans are not characterized by psychological complexity, but rather that there is something ethically valuable in obsessing less about it.

It might be argued here that in "objectifying" its characters, the late Victorian realist novel merely reinscribed the "secret subject" at its center: "if the Novel is the genre of 'secret singularity,'" D. A. Miller famously concludes his analysis of midcentury novels by Dickens, Wilkie Collins, and Anthony Trollope in *The Novel and the Police*, "it becomes so less by providing us with an intimate glimpse of a character's inner life than by determining this life in such a way that its limitations forcibly contrast with our own less specific, less violated inwardness" (208-9). As we will see, however, attention to the work of women and feminist realists of the turn of the century complicates Miller's assessment of the formal structure of the nineteenth-century novel at the same time that it affirms his underlying philosophical thesis: there is no subject who is not also an object—and as such, no "secret refuge" from the material determinations that make character, character (215).

A Power of Observation Informed by a Living Heart; or, Involuntary, Palpitating

In pausing to consider the value of realism's objectifying impulse, this book inverts the movement of much recent critical theory in which agency, depth, and autonomy are attributed to nonhuman things in concepts such as "thing-power" (Bennett 2), "realist magic objects" (Morton, *Realist*), and "the secret life of things" (B. Brown 49).[39] Of course, philosophers since Kant have worried that treating human beings as objects—whether through commodification, instrumentalization, or sexualization—fundamentally

39. In *Vibrant Matter* Bennett advocates for a politics in which "all bodies become more than mere objects, as thing-powers of resistance and protean agency are brought into sharper relief" (13). Focusing on the depth rather than the agency of things, in *Realist Magic* Morton argues that things are "bound up with a certain mystery, in these multiple senses: unspeakability, enclosure, withdrawal, secrecy" (17-18). Finally, in *Other Things*, Bill Brown centers his analysis on "the thingness of things in its unconditioned autonomy" (39).

diminishes their humanity.[40] Whereas feminist thinkers argue that objectification strips subjects of their personhood by denying them their autonomy, Marxist theorists critique the processes through which a "relation between people takes on the character of a thing" (Lukács, *History* 83).[41] The nineteenth-century realist novel is said to be especially guilty of such objectification in drawing "its momentum from representing bound women" (144), as Naomi Schor has powerfully contended, or using description to "debase characters to the level of inanimate objects," as György Lukács once argued ("Narrate" 133).

Whereas Lukács could see in Marx's concept of *objectification* only negative connotations, however, Marx himself elaborated a materialist ontology predicated on the ethical value of allowing "oneself to be object" (*Economic* 135).[42] Man "only creates or posits objects," the young Marx had argued, "because he is posited by objects—because at bottom he is *nature*" (134). In making such a claim, Marx built on the work of the philosopher Ludwig von Feuerbach, whose commitment "only to *realism*, to materialism" led him to proclaim: "I do not generate the object from the thought, but the thought from the object" (xiv). From Eliot's production of the first English translation of Feuerbach's *The Essence of Christianity* in 1854 to Schreiner's literary engagement of Marx in her posthumously published novel *From Man to Man* (1926), the novelists I analyze build on this philosophical lineage to question the notion that the "*subject* is always *consciousness* or *self-consciousness*" by presenting character as the object within

---

40. Nussbaum identifies seven features involved in the idea of treating a person as an object: instrumentality, denial of autonomy, inertness, fungibility, violability, ownership, and denial of subjectivity ("Objectification"). One of the earliest and most influential philosophical arguments against the objectification of persons is made by Kant, who worries that in sex, it is persons "themselves, and not their work and services, [that] are its Objects of enjoyment" (162).

41. A classic feminist critique of objectification is that of Dworkin. In a revision of Kant's argument against the use of others as means, Korsgaard has proposed that the problem with valuing a person solely on the basis of their physical qualities is that they are reduced to an "aesthetic object, something to enjoy" (186). Had I more space in this book, I would argue that although objectification might be a necessary condition for aestheticization, neither aestheticization nor objectification necessitate instrumentalization.

42. Lukács's misreading of Marx's concept of objectification (*Vergegenständlichung*) speaks to the fact that he was unaware of the existence of Marx's 1844 manuscripts until 1930. In his 1967 preface to *History and Class Consciousness* (1923), Lukács admits that he had previously mistakenly "identified alienation with objectification [*Entfremdung mit Vergegenständlichung*]" (xxiv), realizing only later that "objectification... can be either a positive or a negative fact" (xxxvi).

the subject (Marx, *Economic* 150).[43] The mechanism that animates their thought is dialectical but in the Marxist rather than the Hegelian sense of the term: the realist epistemology that I chart across fiction, science, and philosophy does not maintain a dialectical tension between subject and object, such that one ultimately maintains its dominance and control over the other (a framework iconically consolidated in Hegel's master-slave dialectic).[44] Rather, it evokes a pulsating material reality from the perspective of subjects, who—because they are also objects—find themselves implicated in that reality.

Let me underline here that coming to fuller terms with the objecthood of the subject need not entail spiraling into a cultural amnesia about the uneven and power-laden ways through which objectification has occurred and continues to occur. "I came into the world imbued with the will to find a meaning in things, my spirit filled with the desire to attain to the source of the world, and then I found that I was an object in the midst of other objects," writes Frantz Fanon in dialogue with Hegel in *Black Skin, White Masks* (82). Fanon's narrative of "crushing objecthood" teaches that the philosophical category of the subject is founded upon the repression of an object that—while immanent to being as such—is negatively projected onto some beings more than others (82). In the master-slave dialectic, the master notably achieves his self-consciousness by forcing the slave to occupy the position of "objecthood in general [*Dingheit überhaupt*]" (Hegel 115), while the slave clings to the remnants of his consciousness through work, a practice through which he "rids himself of his attachment to natural existence" by negating the objecthood foisted upon him (117). If, following Fanon, "ontology—once it is finally admitted as leaving existence by the wayside—does not permit us to understand the being of the black man," then only one option remains: to forestall the process through which

---

43. The materialist approach to character one discovers in Eliot's work can be traced, among other sources, to Feuerbach's claim in *The Essence of Christianity* that "the body is the basis, the subject of personality" (91). Marx's writings entered the purview of English intellectual culture later than those of Feuerbach and Schopenhauer, with the first English translations of *Capital* (1867) and *A Contribution to the Critique of Political Economy* (1859) appearing in 1887 and 1904, respectively.

44. In Hegel's section of *The Phenomenology of Spirit* on "Lordship and Bondage," the lord's "presentation of himself… as the pure abstraction of self-consciousness" is dependent upon forcing the bondsman into the position of "a thing as such, the object of desire [*ein Ding als solches, den Gegenstand der Begierde*]" (113, 115). In the section of his 1844 manuscripts on "Critique of the Hegelian Dialectic and Philosophy as a Whole," Marx rejects this oppositional framework, arguing, "*To be* objective, natural and sensuous and at the same time to have object, nature and sense outside oneself… is one and the same thing" (135).

that being is negated—the (white man's) crusade for an unassailable self-consciousness (Fanon 82).[45]

A desire to inhibit the processes of *Bildung* and recognition that had lent the novel genre its early shape characterizes much English fiction post 1870. In Eliot, such a desire erupts, metonymically, in Daniel Deronda's attempt to "shift his centre till his own personality would be no less outside than the landscape" in a "half-involuntary identification of himself with the objects he was looking at" (*Daniel* 160), as well as in Theophrastus's attempt to envision a subject without "the futile cargo of a consciousness" (*Impressions* 141). Scholars of literature and science have interpreted such passages as reflections on realist epistemology that appropriate and affirm nineteenth-century scientific models of objectivity, in which the fallible and all-too-embodied human self is seen as an impediment to knowledge and revelation must thus occur in the "negation of embodiment" (Levine, *Dying* 69). Drawing on the historians of science Lorraine Daston and Peter Galison, for instance, George Levine argues that, like their scientific contemporaries, the Victorian realist novel expresses a "willingness to repress the aspiring, desiring, emotion-ridden self and everything merely personal, contingent, historical, material that might get in the way of acquiring knowledge" (*Dying* 2). Just as nineteenth-century scientists attempted to erase every trace of the observer's embodied perspective through self-imposed rules and automated processes, realism is said to aspire to a disembodied and perspectiveless view of reality.[46]

Questioning the historical alignment of the realist novel with scientific ideals of bodily abnegation and self-restraint, I show how later Victorian

---

45. Others have argued that the only logical solution to the problem identified by Fanon is to abandon ontology entirely. See, for example, Rosenberg, who argues that the "ontological turn is a theoretical primitivism that presents itself as a methodological avant-garde" ("Molecularization"). Recent work in Black studies undertaken by Jackson, Weheliye, and A. Henry, among others, however, suggests otherwise. On how the objecthood attributed to Black subjects can be performatively transformed into a form of agency, see McMillan.

46. In Levine's reading of this cited passage from *Daniel Deronda*, "Deronda undergoes the very act of self-obliteration that would be taken as the ideal condition of scientific objectivity," metonymically embodying the realist desire to transcend the self (*Dying* 185). In his earlier book *The Realistic Imagination*, however, Levine questioned the notion that realism was "a solidly self-satisfied vision based in a misguided objectivity and faith in representation" (20). In *Victorian Empiricism*, Garratt likewise turns to Daston and Galison to draw parallels between the aims of Victorian novelists and scientists; however, he subtly pushes back on their argument by pointing out the investment of Victorian empiricists across the sciences and the arts in comprehending how the sensorium might serve as the basis for knowledge (27–29).

realists appropriated scientific research on sensation and perception to *account for* rather than *erase* the role of the body in knowledge production, supporting art historian Jonathan Crary's claim that the nineteenth century saw a radical rematerialization of the observer. Across the sciences, philosophy, and visual arts, Crary argues in *Techniques of the Observer*, one can witness "a new 'objectivity' accorded to subjective phenomena" (98).[47] This new objectivity looked different from objectivities of old, and it looks different from the "mechanical objectivity" that Daston and Galison attribute to the period, too (43). Crary shows that in experiments on the velocity of nerve impulses undertaken by the German psychophysicist Hermann von Helmholz, and in the dynamic metaphysics of Schopenhauer, objectivity inheres in a (feminized) state of sensory receptivity that, in Schopenhauer's words, "increases the attention and enhances the susceptibility of the central nervous system" (WR 2:367–68).

From Eliot's 1870s fiction to the New Realism that emerged in the hands of Hardy, Schreiner, and Grand, the lineage of realist aesthetics this book traces stresses the impressibility of observers and their sensory apparatus. In so doing, it cultivates a stance toward reality similar to what Donna Haraway, in a foundational moment for the field of feminist science studies, called "situated knowledge" ("Situated" 579). In 1988, Haraway famously called for scientists to reject the "doctrine of objectivity that promises transcendence" and to "reclaim the sensory system that has been used to signify a leap out of the marked body and into a conquering gaze from nowhere" (580). And yet, like Crary's nineteenth-century actors (who sought not to infinitely subjectivize knowledge but rather to rethink the object relations that were the conditions of knowledge's production), Haraway does not give up on the quest for truth. While her essay is remembered today largely as a critique of scientific practice, its actual aim is to inspire the cultivation of a "feminist objectivity" that would acknowledge the role of the body and emotions in science (583).[48] Counting herself as among those thinkers "who would still like to talk about *reality*," she encourages feminists to "to insist upon a better account of the world" (577, 579).

47. According to Crary, seventeenth- and eighteenth-century scientists and artists "sundered the act of seeing from the physical body of the observer" (39). But this model of perception faded in the early nineteenth century, Crary argues, as scientists and artists became interested in the physiology of perception. Crary's argument accords with that of scholars of the history of reading such as Dames and Coombs, who show how nineteenth-century authors and scientists came to understand reading as an embodied practice that could be empirically observed and studied.

48. My argument here is indebted to Love's reminder of Haraway's "dual investment in the anchoring and the destabilization of reality" ("Temptations" 53).

A better account of the world is precisely what realists of the 1880s and 1890s desired when they sought to differentiate their "new" realism from realisms of old. Let us return here to what is a pivotal moment in this book's redrawing of late Victorian literary history: Hardy's 1891 essay "The Science of Fiction," which denounces the aspiration of scientific realists to unfeeling, scientific ideals of objectivity. Emphasizing the impossibility of eliminating "discriminative choice" and "pleasure" in "telling a tale," Hardy identifies a contradiction in the attempts of certain naturalist writers to excise emotion from their literary-descriptive practice: while the "most devoted apostle of realism, the naturalist," might "subscribe to rules," Hardy contends, he cannot but "work by instinct" (101-2). In so doing, the literary naturalist "maintain[s] in theory what he abandons in practice," defining his "impartiality as a passion, and plan as a caprice" (101-2). Hardy's essay imagines a literary practice that is *attuned*, rather than averse, to the impulses of the body. Based on "the fruits of closest observation," literature elucidates the "vital qualities" of things (103). Distinguishing his own form of writing from that of Émile Zola, "the author of *Germinal* and *La Faute de l'Abbé Mouret*," Hardy calls for a realism driven by the "power of observation informed by a living heart" (104). The true "scientist of fiction" does not aspire to transcend his embodied perspective; he works to account for "our widened knowledge of the universe and its forces, and man's position therein" (101-2).

Hardy's critique of Zola's literary-experimental method in his 1891 essay renders salient an important distinction between the aims and ambitions of late Victorian realists and those of their French contemporaries, many of whom likewise centered the concept of character in their fiction. Whereas Zola recommended "the *application* of the experimental method to the novel" ("Experimental" 104; emphasis mine), the English realists of interest to me here echo Hardy in arguing "against such conformation of story-writing to scientific processes" ("Science" 102).[49] Literature, Hardy

---

49. In highlighting the power of bodily drives and causal forces over individual agency, the French naturalist tradition shares much with the character-centered lineage of British realism this book traces. Still, some differences are worth noting. The first, discussed previously, is concerned with method. As Furst and Skrine argue in their foundational 1971 study *Naturalism*, "true literary Naturalism is at least as much a question of method as of subject; only when the writer treats his subject with the objectivity of the analytical scientist, can we speak of Naturalism" (43). As the case of Hardy shows, the authors that I examine were by and large uninterested in applying scientific methods and models to their literary practice. The second difference concerns the treatment of character: the novels of French naturalists were often premised on the empirical existence of certain character types. The English writers that I examine were also interested in typology; however, most understood "character type" to be a con-

insists, does not take cues from science; it is itself a science: "In no proper sense can the term 'science' be applied other than in this fundamental manner" (101–3).

Another version of this book might have advocated the existence of a wider naturalist literary movement in England and in so doing claimed an expanded archive for that movement beyond those directly influenced by Zola and other French writers.[50] Hewing more closely to the terminology and context of Victorian England, however, I prefer the term *New Realism* for my archive, both for its historical accuracy and as a means of distinguishing between the aims and methods of turn-of-the-century English realists and those of their French and American contemporaries.[51]

I use "New Realism" broadly to refer to the wide-scale reinvention of realism in the late nineteenth century, and I situate the genre of the New Woman novel at the center of this movement. Literary scholars often distinguish between New Realism (an aesthetic typically associated with male writers such as George Gissing, George Moore, and Hardy) and the New Woman novel (a genre originating with female authors such as Schreiner, Grand, and George Egerton). This distinction is registered, among other places, in Volume 4 of *The Oxford History of the Novel in English: The Reinvention of the British and Irish Novel, 1880–1940*, in which an entry entitled "New Women and the New Fiction" centers on the social and political interventions of women realists, and an entry entitled "Realism and the Fiction of Modern Life: From Meredith to Forster" highlights the aesthetic innovations of male realists (Parrinder and Gasiorek v). Taking cues

ceptual abstraction, not an empirical reality. A third distinction is concerned with the role of experimentation. Zola had understood plot as the mechanism through which to experiment with character. In the preface to *Thérèse Raquin* (1867), for instance, he describes the novel as a study of "the strange union which may be produced between two different temperaments... a sanguineous nature coming into contact with a nervous one" (*Thérèse* 2). The works I analyze do not approach plot as a scientific method for deductively testing characterological hypotheses; rather, they exploit the formal tension between character and plot to immanently theorize the circumstantiality of character.

50. Such is the path taken, in the American context, by Fleissner. Where in the United States and France "naturalism" would come to denote a unified and systematically articulated aesthetic movement, in England, as Baguely points out, "all those usual indications for the existence of a literary movement (groups, manifestos, polemics, theoretical writings) seem to have been virtually nonexistent, such that one might be legitimately led to wonder, on the basis of the unusual evidence, if indeed there was any English naturalist literature at all" (29).

51. I take cues here from Arata, who observes that in the case of England, "it is more accurate to talk about the 'New Realism'... than about Naturalism, a term applied usually only to certain kinds of fiction produced on the Continent and in the United States" (186n5).

from recent scholarship on the role of women writers in transforming realist aesthetics in the late Victorian and Edwardian periods, I resist this gendered bifurcation.[52] Reading authors such as Hardy and Gissing alongside authors such as Schreiner and Grand allows us to see that realism at the turn of the twentieth century was bound up with questions of gender and sexuality, in particular the role of body in realist epistemology.

Paying closer attention to moments of epistemological intimacy and embodied knowledge in the work of women and feminist realists at the fin de siècle troubles the critical portrait of realism as a practice of self-mastery predicated on the suppression and control of bodily impulses. The most mature expression of this New Realist aesthetic emerges in Schreiner's last novel, posthumously published in 1926, *From Man to Man; or Perhaps Only*, the focus of my final chapter. Composed between 1870 and 1920—almost the entirety of the historical period this study covers—*From Man to Man* not only registers many of the shifts in thinking about character in this period of rapid social, intellectual, and economic change, it condenses them into a manifesto for a realism capable of comprehending the ethical responsibility of the human subject in relation to a "pulsating, always interacting whole" (181).

In the seventh chapter of her novel, Schreiner's protagonist, Rebekah, interrupts the narrative for over eighty pages to outline her metaphysical theory that the character of human and nonhuman beings is linked by "internetting lines of action and reaction which bind together all that we see and are conscious of" (*From Man* 180). This metaphysical theory undergirds her novel's pointed critique of social Darwinism and eugenic sciences aimed at facilitating the "characteristics of the to-be-preserved races" (160). Critical of atomized materialisms in which the universe is presented as "a thing of shreds and patches and unconnected parts," Rebekah advocates thinking in terms of interconnecting forces rather than separate organisms or entities. As she writes:

> Between mind and matter, between man and beast and plant and earth, between life that has been the life it is, I am able to see nowhere a sharp line of severance, but a great, pulsating, always interacting whole. So that at last it comes to be, that, when I hear my own heartbeat, I actually hear in

52. Youngkin has made a particularly powerful case against "pitting male and female novelists against each another" in her account of how turn-of-the-century feminist realism influenced modernist aesthetics (174–75). The foundational work of Ledger, Ardis, and Heilmann has demonstrated the substantial contributions of women and feminist writers to the transformation of realism at the fin de siècle. On the aesthetic innovations of turn-of-the-twentieth-century British women's fiction more broadly, see Dowling, J. E. Miller, Schaffer, and Showalter, *Literature*.

it nothing but one throb in that life which has been and is—in which we live and move and have our being and are constantly sustained. (181)

We saw earlier in this introduction how Victorian scientists and philosophers such as Carpenter insisted upon the supremacy of the human being over the nonhuman on account of its ability to control its more automatic activities (a tool mobilized by social Darwinists to justify the oppression of those races, classes, and genders deemed inherently less free and less than human). Schreiner, however, invokes the image of the heartbeat to make the case that all beings are linked in causal systems of "action and reaction." If all physical creatures are subject to nonvoluntary forces, her character Rebekah argues, and if all creatures "throb" with the beat of the pulse, then no one person, race, or species can be understood as being superior to, or autonomous from, all others. Rather than emphasizing the human's special ability to overcome or control its baser impulses, she seeks to comprehend the ethical consequences of the fact that the human, like any other animal, is driven by forces that are, in the words of George Eliot, "involuntary, palpitating."

In a well-known passage from Eliot's novel *Middlemarch* (1871-72), Dorothea, upon feeling her own heartbeat, realizes that she, too, is "a part of that involuntary, palpitating life" and cannot "look out on it as a mere spectator" (741). Neil Hertz has shown how the metaphor of the "pulse" erupts across Eliot's fiction in moments of self-extension, reading the image as "a small replicable unit of vitality," a "sign of life" that animates interaction and change (13). Relatedly, Ian Duncan has interpreted Dorothea's realization as "an intuition of the immanence of life as such, a dynamic material process exceeding human consciousness" (26).

Over and beyond the moments of pulsating vitality that Hertz and Duncan discover in Eliot, the pulse erupts across turn-of-the-century literature, science, and philosophy as a record of intimate relation—a mark of the dynamic materiality that ontologically binds the character of the human to the character of the nonhuman world. Tracing the dynamic materialist model of character emergent in Eliot's arch-document of realism, *Middlemarch*, forward to the New Realism of New Woman novelists such as Schreiner allows us to uncover a lineage of feminist realism in which matter is a site of aleatory transformation rather than a pliant (or obdurate) substance to be molded by (or resistant to) the will.[53] It also allows us

---

53. On the longer history of the alignment of the feminine with the pliancy and passivity of matter (and the masculine with the activity and power of form), see Bianchi, *The Feminine Symptom*, which discovers within Aristotle's natural philosophy a suppressed history of matter as aleatory and disruptive.

to appreciate how the attempts of authors of all genders to represent the dynamic material character of the New Woman gave rise to a crisis of representation that would indelibly alter the novel form.[54]

Inconsistency and Formlessness

The New Realism that emerged in the 1880s and 1890s aspired to produce a more complete account of character than realisms before it had done, generating modes of description and narration capable of representing what Eliot once described as the "inconvenient indefiniteness" of women's lives (*Middlemarch* 3). In *Human Forms: The Novel in the Age of Evolution*, Duncan argues that the perceived formlessness of the novel genre rendered it especially fit "to model the changing form of man" (1). In the final decades of the nineteenth century, the "variable, fluid, and fleeting" human form that Duncan identifies at the center of the realist project between 1750 and 1880 would be increasingly gendered as feminine. Her life marked by "inconsistency and formlessness," it was woman, not man, who was the ideal subject for the study of the determinative effect of circumstances on the formation of character (*Middlemarch* 3-4).

In using the term "woman," here and elsewhere, I do not indicate a biological category (nor also, by contrast, a performed one), but rather those persons who are feminiz*ed* in and through their association with a nonagential or otherwise determined materiality. Rather than attempt to claim agency and self-determination for women (or matter, for that matter, as is the strategy of many feminist materialist philosophers today), the New Woman authors I examine here exploited the longtime association of the feminine with an overdetermined materiality in order to disrupt the masculinist theories of the subject as that which stands over and against an object. Emily Steinlight has observed how in the late-century fiction of Hardy and Gissing, "character development and social mobility are curtailed by forces of resistance that no individual exertion can overcome" (170). Indeed, to the dismay of readers both Victorian and contemporary, the New Realism cultivated by New Woman authors would not showcase the individual's ability to overcome challenging circumstances; some went so far as to suggest that woman was "foredoomed by every circumstance of her life" (Grand, *Heavenly* 277). As I argue in chapter 4, the emphasis in this work on the determinative role of the environment points less to the affirmation of the passivity of the feminine than to the Schopenhauerian challenge to contemporaneous

---

54. On how "The New Woman frequently posed a representation problem," see Ledger (181).

accounts of character as self-determined, such as those given by Mill and Carpenter.

The New Woman who emerged in the final decades of the nineteenth century in England was unmarried (or had left her marriage), was sexually open, and refused to conform to Victorian ideals of femininity. To her critics, her biography appeared as a fallen arc, a broken line riddled with moral error and social embarrassment. In the preface to her debut novel, *Ideala: A Study from Life* (1888), the Irish novelist Grand defended the New Woman's failure to adhere to traditional life narratives, along with her own realist commitment to "exhibit the details of the process," by arguing that life is "in fact, not a perfect, but a transitional state... a state which has its repulsive features, but which, it may be hoped, would result in a beautiful deposit, when at last the inevitable effervescence had subsided" (5). Grand's mineral metaphor, in which life is figured as a "deposit," is introduced in an epigraph from Ruskin, in which life is characterized as "overlaid by the weight of things external to it, and is moulded by them... crystallised over with it" (Ruskin quoted in *Ideala* 5). But whereas the Ruskin quotation celebrates the capacity of subjects to break through their oppressive "frost-bitten" exteriors, "encumbered and crusted over with idle matter," as a demonstration of "their own inward strength," Grand's novel stresses the difficulty of transcending one's circumstances through sheer force of will (5). In *The Ethics of the Dust* (1865), Ruskin drew parallels between the crystallization of minerals and the Bildung of young schoolgirls to highlight how a person's character is influenced by their milieu.[55] In *Ideala*, however, Grand rewrites and in some cases abandons the Bildung project championed by Ruskin—a "project of self-formation," Ella Mershon has observed, that "triangulates the good, the beautiful, and the formed" (468).

Breaking down the opposition between character's inward kernel and its "circumstantial" surfaces, Grand's novel suggests that what Ruskin

---

55. In Ruskin's *The Ethics of the Dust*, crystals are said to be "wonderfully like human creatures," in that their colors, shapes, and textures are not entirely inherent to their respective types, but rather emerge in response to their environment or locality, as well as growth conditions such as heat, pressure, and space (334). Presenting a young girl with a "green Indian piece, in which the pillar is first disjointed, and then wrung round into the shape of an S," the "Old Lecturer" in Ruskin's dialogue remarks, "There are a thousand ways in which it may have been done; the difficulty is not to account for the doing of it; but for the showing of it in some crystals, and not in others" (326). As the lecturer implies, offering a compelling theory of how and why a particular trait has arisen is not especially challenging: the shyness of a child raised in isolation would seem to have an obvious cause. What remains much more difficult is to explain how another such child, raised in similar circumstances, grows up to be affable and loquacious.

thought of as externally imposed "encrustations" are as essential to a person or thing as anything else (Ruskin quoted in *Ideala* 5). In so doing, she can be seen to prefigure Shand's ethological critique of the "dualism of Character and Circumstance," in which, as we have already seen, "Circumstance is regarded as something external to Character and acting upon it from the outside" ("Character" 210). At one point in *Ideala*, a misguided Ruskinian architect seeking to impose his individual vision of the beautiful on a town is shocked to discover that after a long absence, his plot of land has become "crowded with wharves and human habitations," taking on new vernacular and collective uses he could not have foreseen (79). While Ruskin laments that life becomes layered with an "agglomeration of thoughts and habits foreign to it," which must be "crushed and broken to bits if it stands in our way," *Ideala* celebrates the "habitations" that proliferate unexpectedly on the surface (5).

Recent work in literary studies has turned to the surface as an alternative to ideology critique, which seeks to plumb the depths of texts in order to reveal their latent meaning.[56] In the novels of Hardy, however, as we will see in chapter 3, surfaces themselves perform a kind of critique when they draw attention the latent whiteness of Victorian ideals of femininity. In his last published novel, *The Well-Beloved: A Sketch of Temperament* (1897), Hardy tells the story of a neoclassical sculptor who overlooks the aesthetic variety of the women he encounters in his pursuit of an ethereal, colorless feminine ideal. Underlining the extent to which the novel form had absorbed England's imperial logic, the novel critiques aesthetic systems that strip character of its distinctive, localized markings, such that they conform to an Englishness increasingly understood to be exportable while at the same time inseparable from bodies perceived to be white. *The Well-Beloved* calls upon Darwin's writings on the fossil record and the characterological notion of *temperament* to conceptualize character otherwise—as a sedimented accumulation colored by one's surroundings—as well as to insist on the uncontrollable spontaneity of character in the face of eugenic attempts to mold the species by force of will.

In understanding character as the result of spontaneous bodily interactions, both Hardy and Grand moved in lockstep with the foundational

---

56. See especially Best and Marcus, "Surface Reading," in which the authors position the mode of literary interpretation that they call "surface reading" against ideology critique and the hermeneutics of suspicion. Toward the end of their essay, however, they suggest that "producing accurate accounts of surfaces is not antithetical to critique" (18). My thinking about surfaces proceeds from the assumption that the insights of critique—especially those elaborated in the fields of postcolonial studies, critical race studies, and gender and sexuality studies—are important for understanding how surfaces operate both to resist and produce meaning (18).

New Woman novelist, Olive Schreiner. Outlining the aesthetic and ethical principles behind her New Realist aesthetic in the iconic preface to the second edition of her pathbreaking *The Story of an African Farm* (1883), Schreiner famously declares, "Human life may be painted according to two methods." In the first method, "each character is duly marshalled at first, and ticketed; we know with an immutable certainty that at the right crises each one will reappear and act his part.... There is a sense of satisfaction in this, and of completeness. But there is another method—the method of the life we all lead." According to this method, "nothing can be prophesied. There is a strange coming and going of feet. Men appear, act and re-act upon each other, and pass away" (xxxix). Schreiner implies that the arc of a conventional plot, while it might provide the reader with a sense of completeness, smooths over the unevenness of real experience. Like Grand, whose effervescent bubbles likewise dissipate, leaving behind an uneven but beautiful deposit, Schreiner calls for the cultivation of literary forms that are adequate to the experience of modern womanhood, new narrative strategies for what feels not like growth or development, but diffusion.[57]

In insisting on character's incalculability, its propensity to swerve in unexpected directions, Schreiner heeded the call of Eliot to find characters "who found for themselves no epic life," whose "heart-beats and sobs" are "dispersed among hindrances, instead of centring in some long-recognizable deed" (*Middlemarch* 3–4). The life of Eliot's protagonist, Dorothea, does not culminate in the achievement of a fully formed identity like those of previous, male-authored bildungsromans but rather remains "incalculably diffusive" at the novel's end (785). Her literary figuration thus marks a pointed departure from a historic lineage of novel writing in which Eliot herself is sometimes uncomfortably situated, which aspired to produce characters as "original, discriminated, and individual person[s]," and narrate their forward-moving development toward self-realization or social recognition (Scott 549).

Chapter 1 of this book distinguishes Eliot's dynamic materialist conception of character in *Middlemarch* from conceptions of character in terms of individual personhood and personality by reading Eliot's character descriptions in conversation with works by English materialist scientists such as John Tyndall and Robert Brown. As I argue, *Middlemarch* develops a vocabulary for the plasticity of character that, while figural in

---

57. Esty has attributed Schreiner's formal challenges to the "accrued or conventional sense of teleological and masculinist destiny" of the Goethean bildungsroman to her experience of the contradictions of self, nation, and empire in colonial South Africa (75).

nature, exceeds the metaphorical in its consistent explanation of characterological traits and behaviors with reference to physical laws. This chapter, along with chapter 2 on *Impressions*, thus nudges studies of Eliot away from their longtime focus on humanist sympathy and the subject-centered ethics that emerges from it.

Attention to the material determination of character across the archive of nineteenth-century realism authored by women reveals a lineage that stretches from Dorothea's wayward feminine subjectivity to Schreiner's New Woman, lending force to Nancy Armstrong's claim that "the modern individual is first and foremost a woman" (*Desire* 8). But where Armstrong and other literary historians emphasize how this modern feminine subjectivity formed through an inward turn from "the surface of [the] body" toward "the depths of... private feelings" (112), the modern feminist characterology I track here often presents the matter of the objectified and feminized body as so dynamic and unpredictable that it resists subordination to the mind.

What might a literary history of character look like that did not trace the gradual movement inward, toward the production of subjective interiority (however fragmented), but rather outward, toward a still-unfolding history of realist characterization centered on the appearance and motions of the body? To do so would require resisting the narrative of realism's "reversal" (Levine, *The Realistic* 317) or "dissolution" (Jameson, *Antinomies* 11) in modernism and instead to reorient the discussion to account for the continued evolution of the realist project across its many ends.[58]

Should the title of my book be thought to imply that Victorian realism has an end, the coda of this book disabuses readers of this assumption by tracking the afterlife of the Victorian realist project forward to the American writer Gertrude Stein's focus on the shared texture of people's character in her 1925 experimental novel *The Making of Americans*. *The Science of Character* ends not, as some other literary histories of realism do, with Woolf's "movements within the consciousnesses of individual personages" (Auerbach 529), but with Stein's "grouping of men and women" in terms of "a kind of substance common to their kind of them, thicker, thinner, harder, softer, all of one consistency"—a perhaps surprising modernist inheritor of the realist science of character this book elucidates (*Mak-

---

58. Whereas Levine's *The Realistic Imagination* ends with an epilogue on the "reversal of realism" in modernism (317), Jameson's *The Antinomies of Realism* tracks the "dissolution" of realism in a modernism that will finally "exhaust and destroy it" (11). In his earlier study, *A Singular Modernity*, however, Jameson remarks that he "always thought it would be interesting... to show how, through the prism of realist innovation theory, all later modernisms can be revealed to be in reality so many unwitting realisms," a notion I take up in the coda (123–24).

ing 344–45). The coda trades the characterological dialectic between the "flat" and "round" born of twentieth-century literary criticism for an older, natural-philosophical binary, the "mechanistic" versus the "vital," in order to forge a series of unexpected links between Eliot and Stein. I argue that for both of these authors, realist character entails not the production of consciousness or individuality but rather the generation of what the Victorian physicist Robert Brown described as the "very unexpected fact of seeming vitality" in things neither alive nor organic (470).

In closing, let me remark that the science of character this book uncovers in realist fiction composed between 1870 and 1920 has perhaps been imperceptible to literary and cultural studies not only because of the way we tell our literary histories but also because of the scale at which our theory tends to unfold. Social-constructivist theories of identity emphasize the power of *macroscopic* discourses and ideologies to form subjectivities, highlighting how abstract norms materialize through performative acts that are enacted in response to ideals.[59] Responding to this work, more recent critical theory has scaled down to the *microscopic* to consider the way that inhuman or prehuman forces interact to generate bodies with identities like male or female, wave or particle.[60] The science of character that arises in late Victorian realist fiction, however, operates on an interstitial plane that the philosopher of science Isabelle Stengers has called the *meso*.

In a 2008 interview, Stengers distinguishes between the more familiar scales at which the physical sciences traditionally operate, the *micro* and *macro*, as well as what contemporary physics refers to as the *meso*:

> The idea of the meso is quite new in physics. Microphysics is well known—it's the stuff of physicists' dreams. The macro in physics is also familiar—it's crystals, liquids, and bodies that can be characterized by general, measurable properties. But the meso is neither of these. It concerns not matter, but material. Why does glue stick? Why do metals tend to stress and break? This is a science of the interstices and the cracks. It's a science of defects. It is the kind of science where it is always a question of *this* material, rather

---

59. As an exemplary instance of macroanalysis, see Butler's argument in *Gender Trouble* that "gender is… a set of repeated acts within a highly rigid regulatory frame that congeal over time to produce the *appearance* of substance, a natural sort of being" (*Gender* 43–44).

60. As an exemplary instance of microanalysis, see Barad, who makes the case that Butler's theory holds also on the level of atoms, arguing that "it is through specific agential intra-actions that the boundaries and properties of the 'components' of phenomena become determinate and that particular embodied concepts become meaningful" ("Posthumanist" 815).

than "matter," and which encounters "procedures," like those of metallurgy. Why must the iron be beaten as long as it is hot? The macro is matter in general. Gas is marvellously "in general." With the meso, on the other hand, the questions that must be asked are utterly specific—questions that bring characters into existence. What is a crack? How does this propagate? How is that encountered? What brings this to a threshold where it breaks? These are questions that demand the invention of beings. ("History")

Stengers's discussion of the meso offers a compelling posthumanist framework for comprehending what we might call the *circumstantiality* of character—the way that qualities and behavior patterns emerge in humans as a result of physical interactions. Macroanalysis concerns the general laws to which all bodies are subject. Microanalysis concerns the tiny, irreducible components into which the macro may be broken (and which are no less abstract for their minuteness). Mesoanalysis, on the other hand, concerns how materials enter into contingent situations that—sometimes temporarily, sometimes irrevocably—transform their natures.

What tools do we have for the investigation of human character on the mesoscopic scale? The questions of the meso, Stengers goes on to argue, "enter more into narratives than into deductions." This is because mesoanalysis, unlike macroanalysis and microanalysis, does not seek to deduce laws that apply far and wide to all bodies, but instead attempts to describe the behavior of specific bodies as they encounter specific situations: it asks how *this* liquid entered into contact with *this* rock, cooling to *this* temperature to become *this* crystal—and no other.[61]

This book arises out of the assumption that the late Victorian realist novel offer us one such tool. Founded on close attention to what Stengers calls character's "copresence with a milieu," realism, especially as it developed in the hands of women writers at the turn of the century, cultivates a science of character that is attentive to the way that subjects enter into encounters that leave them transformed ("History"). At the same time, these novelists' fascination with the accidents of circumstance does not prevent them from making generalizations about how people and things react to the environments they enter. Their focus on the particular and the contingent, in other words, does not prevent them from *theorizing*.

The twentieth-century American psychologist Silvan Tomkins coined the term "weak theory" to describe theoretical practices that, in their observational focus on the particular and the contingent, barely (but still do)

---

61. For a brilliant analysis of how deictic demonstratives such as "this" or "that" function as descriptive tools in modernist fiction, see Zhang, chap. 5.

rise to the status of a theory. "To the extent to which [a] theory can account only for 'near' phenomena," Tomkins writes, that theory "is a weak theory, little better than a description of the phenomena it purports to explain" (*Affect* 519). Since Eve Kosofsky Sedgwick introduced literary studies to Tomkins's term, literary critics have invoked the notion of weak theory to advocate for "weaker" modes of reading. In recalling Tomkins's term here, I am less interested in calling for new or better practices of textual interpretation than I am in observing what fiction already does on its own. I propose that what novels do when they narrate the formation of character—in particular imaginary beings in particular imaginary times and places—is theorize. Strong theory, Tomkins suggests, entails the formulation of abstract propositions that explain a wide range of phenomena. On the other end of the spectrum, description simply documents what is there, explaining nothing. While it might be "little better than a description," weak theory (as is often forgotten today) is not purely descriptive; it moves between the particular *and* the general, the micro *and* the macro, to trace loose causal links between what has occurred and what might occur. Committed to more than the elucidation of unrelated particulars, it is attuned to what Sedgwick, in a rather Eliotan turn of phrase, calls "the heartbeat of contingency" ("Paranoid" 147).[62]

In *A System of Logic*, Mill wondered whether the circumstantiality of character might present an obstacle to the elucidation of its general principles, fretting that "the peculiarities of circumstances are continually constituting exceptions even to the propositions which are true in the great majority of cases" (864). Mill's imagined science was predicated on

62. Sedgwick popularized Tomkins's concept of *weak theory* in an essay that called for literary critics to *weaken* their interpretive practice ("Paranoid"). I am invoking the term here, in a different way, to highlight the relative *strength* of the literary as a form of thought, a mode of theorizing that, I am arguing, happens in and through the construction of fictional worlds. This use of the term is more in line with the context in which it was originally formulated. When Tomkins coined the term, he did so in order to attribute value to the everyday kind of theorizing that people do in their lives in order to manage affect. He formulates the distinction between strong and weak theory with regard to the scene of clinic, distinguishing between the "strong" kinds of theories that an analyst (read: critic) generates when they explain the behavior of a patient and the "weak" kinds of theory that that patient herself (read: literary work) generates when she describes her experience of the world. Nowhere does Tomkins advocate for the analyst to weaken his theories. His point, rather, is that although the theoretical practices of the analyst and the analysand might operate at different levels of abstraction (the former widely recognized as "theory" and the latter perceived as "mere description"), *both are theory* insofar as they link one affective experience to another to explain patterns of behavior.

the opposition of circumstance to theory.[63] The science of character that would emerge in the hands of novelists after him, however, would mobilize aesthetic particularity in the service of theoretical generality. Mill was mistaken to claim that the laws of character could be deduced from the general laws of psychology and then applied to explain the formation of character in specific people. But if his fatal step was to place his faith in the rational and deductive sciences to outline how contingent, subjective experiences give rise to objective, observable traits, his sense that such an "ulterior science" might be formulated was not entirely misplaced. Mobilizing the critical tension between the necessary and the accidental, realist novelists at the turn of the century explored how such a wide variety of people could be generated by such a finite world, concluding, as Mill did, that "mankind have not one universal character, but there exist universal laws of the Formation of Character" (864).

63. On how Eliot's decision to take up the novel genre was inspired by Mill's critique of philosophy as unable to come to terms with situational particularity, see Dodd, who argues that Eliot's novels, "in testing philosophical truths against an intuitively apprehended reality, made a contribution to philosophical debate" (146).

Plasticity, Form, and the Physics of Character in Eliot's *Middlemarch*

[CHAPTER ONE]

...the way in which your life presses on others, and their life on yours...

GEORGE ELIOT, *Daniel Deronda*

George Eliot's novel *Middlemarch* is famously said to both thematize and foster intersubjectivity through its psychologically rich and detailed portrait of human life.[1] However, to elide the distinction between subjectivity and what I have been referring to as its dynamic material substrate—character—risks overlooking the extent to which human life in *Middlemarch* is presented as taking shape not only through intentions, thought, or speech, but through physical actions and reactions as well. Deidre Lynch has shown how the protocols of interiority attributed to the novelistic modes of characterization were not endemic to the novel genre but rather emerged in attempts to "validate and naturalize a concept of character as representational" (3). Building on the work of Lynch, Catherine Gallagher, and other character historians and theorists, this chapter shows how *Middlemarch* engages Victorian materialist science to produce not only sympathetic and real-seeming minds but also lively and reactive characterological bodies, cultivating an ethological approach to the human that models the dynamic, material processes through which character takes shape.

Closer attention to the representation of character in Eliot's novel troubles the suggestion that as the nineteenth century progressed, the representation of character became increasingly inward-oriented and psychologized. Narrating "how it came to be that novels, to be good novels, had to be *about* character," Lynch suggests that as the nineteenth century

---

1. According to Kay Young, for instance, the fundamental problematic of *Middlemarch* is "the problem of other minds," and the "solution" it proposes is "a physiology of empathy" (4). In a different vein, Palmer has suggested that *Middlemarch* presents readers with a unity of collectively thinking subjects whose communal cognitive processes mirror their own. See Palmer, "Social Minds in Fiction," and *Social Minds in the Novel*.

turned, character cleaved from the body and its materiality, transforming character from an "outer" to an "inner" quality (29). In *Middlemarch*, however, character appears not as a hidden or buried kernel of personhood but instead as an empirically observable, materially determined figuration produced through shifts in the boundaries between the body's inside and outside. As we will see, even the most notoriously "brainy" of Victorian novels—on the level of its descriptions—resist a too-easy alignment of its characters with the individual human personality.[2]

The characterological bodies that form the focus of my analysis are not verisimilitudinous human anatomies, with faces and limbs. Where Eliot certainly describes her characters with regard to their phenomenal appearances—Dorothea has "dark-brown hair" (81); Celia is "amiable and innocent looking" (9)—the more ontological characterology I elucidate in what follows presents characters less in terms of particular, observable traits than with regard to *general states of matter*, drawing upon knowledge of how materials in different physical states respond differently under different circumstances. So doing constitutes an example of what in the introduction to this book I referred to as "weak theory"—theory that immanently unfolds through close attention to situational particularities, straddling the descriptive and the theoretical.

Consider, as an initial example, the narrator's description of Rosamond Vincy's persistence as that which "enables a white soft living substance to make its way in spite of opposing rock" (*Middlemarch* 324). This description of Rosamond's tenacity relies on the reader's corporeal awareness of the general properties of matter—in this case, soft matter, which has the capacity to envelop harder bodies thanks to its looser molecular structure. The descriptive force of the figure inheres in the lively materiality of this "white soft living substance"—its soft texture, plastic form, and unexplained animacy. Notice also how the figure presents Rosamond's ability to overpower her father not in terms of an individual or conscious intention but rather as a nonintentional affordance of the materiality of her character. Much later in the novel, the narrator describes Rosamond's behavior with a maxim that harkens back to her plastic quality:

> We cannot be sure that any natures, however inflexible or peculiar, will resist this effect from a more massive being than their own. They may be taken by storm and for the moment converted, becoming part of the soul which enwraps them in the ardor of its movement. (714)

---

2. Puckett riffs on Henry James's observation that "a marvelous *mind* throbs in every page of *Middlemarch*," using James to explore the paradox of *Middlemarch*'s simultaneous desire for the cerebral and fascination with the visceral (293).

As we will see, few natures in *Middlemarch* are so inflexible; most are like Rosamond in their affinity to a soft, plastic substance. Arthur Brooke, for example, is described as "glutinously indefinite" (8). He is "a very good fellow, but pulpy; he will run into any mould, but he won't keep shape" (65). Sir James Chettam, likewise, is made of a kind of "human dough"; he has but the "limpest personality," furnished "with a little gum or starch in the form of tradition" (20). Taken separately, such descriptors might read as metaphors for particular personality traits (Brooke is fickle; Chettam, lacking in substance). Taken together, however, they develop a vocabulary for the plasticity of character that—while certainly figural in nature—exceeds the metaphorical in its consistent explanation of characterological traits and behaviors with reference to fundamental physical laws.

A metaphor sets up a comparison between two distinct concepts or objects, highlighting similarities between two apparently unrelated things; Eliot's character descriptions, however, often assume no categorical difference between the "stuff" of human character and that of nonhuman physical things. Both are presented as the product of what J. S. Mill, A. F. Shand, and other Victorian ethologists called "circumstances"—interactions between bodies that lend shape to their being. To return to my initial example, notice that Rosamond is not *compared to* a "white soft living substance... mak[ing] its way in spite of opposing rock." Rather, she is said to derive her forcibility from the *very same quality* that allows this plastic substance to envelop rigid structures. To quote the passage in full: "The circumstance called Rosamond was particularly forcible *by means of* that mild persistence which, as we know, enables a white soft living substance to make its way in spite of opposing rock" (324, emphasis mine).

In revealing the characterological link between the behavior of these two beings—one nonhuman, one human—Eliot might be said to produce what the feminist science studies scholar Donna Haraway calls a *figure*. "Figures," Haraway writes, "are not representations or didactic illustrations, but rather material-semiotic nodes or knots in which diverse bodies and meanings coshape one another" (*When Species* 135). "For me," she continues, "figures have always been where the biological and literary or artistic come together with all of the force of lived reality. My body itself is just such a figure, literally" (135). Haraway's body is a figure in the same way that Eliot's "white soft living substance" is: both signify meaning to those who encounter them. Rather than understand this "white soft living substance" as a metaphor "for" Rosamond, then, we might follow Haraway in considering how "the circumstance called Rosamond" and this imaginary substance "coshape one another" via the node that is their "mild persistence."

It is one of the driving arguments of this book that late Victorian realist fiction offers special insight into the workings of character. This story begins with Eliot, whose 1870s fiction laid the conceptual and formal groundwork for the later realists I analyze. Her fiction did so by shifting the reader's attention from human subjecthood toward what I have called *human objecthood*—physical aspects of existence that humans share with nonhuman animals and things. The objecthood of the human is rendered in Eliot's novel through figural, descriptive language that pushes past the metaphorical to generate theories about how character emerges, physically and relationally, across scales.

Elucidating what I call Eliot's *physics of character*—a figural characterology that represents human life in terms of its physical limitations and potentials—this chapter tests two hypotheses in two sections. The first hypothesis is that the plasticity of Eliot's characters in *Middlemarch* records the capacity of bodies for relation and thus for change as well. The second hypothesis is that throughout *Middlemarch*, rigidity signals the apparent autonomy of character, the phenomenal experience of characters as stable, individuated entities that remain consistent throughout time. Phrased differently, I will argue that where soft matter for Eliot embodies the interactivity and transformability of character as an impersonal substrate that takes form only through its relations, solids emerge as figures in the production of fictional worlds populated by individual persons with self-possessed natures. While the fictional world of the realist novel might be imaginary, as I go on to suggest in tracing Eliot's historical ties to the English philosophical tradition known as *emergentism*, its apparent reality is no mere illusion but rather an emergent property of the matter of fiction: language. Aiding me in making this argument will be a diverse set of thinkers—from nineteenth-century scientists such as Robert Brown, Michael Faraday, and William James to present-day feminist materialist philosophers, including Catherine Malabou and Elizabeth Grosz. My analysis will focus on how Eliot exploits certain formal elements of descriptive language and realist worldbuilding in order to explore the limits and potential of characterological change and to theorize the role of character in mediating fiction and reality.

Plastic Forms

"Character," the narrator of *Middlemarch* explains, is "a process and an unfolding" (140). This process is one of neither passive imprintation nor heroic self-formation but rather one that emerges from the *plasticity* of matter itself.[3] Incorporating nineteenth-century research into the activ-

---

3. Newby has likewise highlighted the tension of activity and passivity at work in this line, noting that "To *unfold* is to open up and spread out, as with paper or a flower: the

ity of matter into her weak-theoretical descriptions of characters, Eliot develops a physics of character in which matter both figures *and* participates in characterological transformation.

In the nineteenth century, the extent to which the matter of character could be intentionally transformed was a subject of great debate. Where pseudosciences like phrenology and physiognomy understood character to be biologically inherent, if also manipulable, many political and educational theorists by contrast held that character, even if materially conditioned, was a direct product of the will—a thing crafted through individual practices and man-made social institutions. In the introduction, I noted that scholarship in Victorian studies has tended to focus on the overlapping binaries of the predetermined and the chosen, the biological and the social, as well as the typological and the individual. Athena Vrettos, for example, has tracked anxieties about the "potential rigidification of human character" in Victorian psychological discourse, showing how "biologically based theories of the mind" often called into question the possibility of "individual reformation, spiritual growth, or free will" (400, 404). Where Vrettos paints a portrait of rigid, mechanized minds, "driven to repetitive, automatic behaviors in order to conserve energy for more difficult or novel tasks" (400), Sara Ahmed, writing from a different critical perspective, describes the simultaneously occurring liberal dream of self-transformation in which character was thought by Mill and other Victorians to be "amenable to [the] will" (Mill, *William Hamilton* 466). As she remarks, in the nineteenth century, character was often presented as a pliable substance given shape by either individuals or social institutions like schools. "If a character can be thought of as a will product," Ahmed writes in reference to this liberal political tradition, "then character might even be the material, or provide the material, that is given form through will, in the sense of given an end, shape, or purpose" (234).

Eliot's novel circumvents the binary in Victorian characterological thinking elucidated by Vrettos and Ahmed (as well as by Amanda Anderson, elsewhere), refusing both the discourse of biological fixity and that of willed flexibility.[4] In so doing, she cultivates what I have been describing as a *dynamic materialist* approach to character. While for some Vic-

---

extension of a material body whose once-veiled contents are newly and vulnerably exposed. It's a word that has passivity built deep into its fabric—not a passivity of resignation or inertia, but of expectation, attunement, pliancy, generosity. It's a willingness to be transformed by the environment: to come apart at the seams through contact with the other that will radically remake the self" (Newby).

4. I treat Anderson's account of the opposition in Victorian characterological discourse between "an illusory ideal of autonomy" and "an extreme determinism characteristically gendered as feminine" (*Tainted* 19) at greater length in chapter 4.

torians, materialism entailed a mechanism whereby the actions of all physical things were thought to obey a simple set of causal laws, for Eliot, along with New Realist authors that followed in her footsteps, the dynamic forces that act in and on matter were understood to be no less predictable and determined than the human will. In the dynamic materialist characterology that emerges in *Middlemarch*—and which this book tracks forward across the turn of the century through the late fiction of Thomas Hardy to the New Woman novel—character traits and behaviors arise neither through the unfolding of a preformed nature nor through the expression of the individual mind, but circumstantially as a result of material affordances like the dynamic responsiveness of organic tissue to outside force. Borrowing a term from recent new materialist philosophy and tracking its use back to contemporaries of Eliot such as William James, I suggest that character for Eliot is fundamentally *plastic*.

In contemporary philosophy, the term *plasticity* has recently resurfaced as a keyword in theories of the brain and body. Such philosophies have aimed, broadly speaking, to conceive of bodily matter as more than a precultural given, a fixed constant that is "inscribed" or passively molded by culture or society.[5] As Catherine Malabou has pointed out, the word *plasticity* implies an active principle. Its etymology can be traced to the Greek *plassein* (πλάσσειν), which "means at once the capacity to *receive form* (clay is called 'plastic,' for example) and the capacity to *give form* (as in the plastic arts or plastic surgery)" (*What Should We Do* 5).[6] Plasticity theory is an expression of dynamic materialism insofar as it understands matter broadly to be an active producer of form rather than merely its passive recipient. This is because, as Malabou underlines, plasticity connotes the *active* potential of transformation—the idea that a thing is simultaneously susceptible to *and* can cause change. It does not mean that something is infinitely modifiable but rather that impressions and forces that act on a body from the outside are consolidated and transformed to produce intentions, desires, and thoughts that sometimes appear to originate solely from within.

For Malabou, such actions and reactions are not governed by the same causal laws that apply to the inorganic world. Far more complex in structure, life is defined by the potential for discontinuity between action and reaction. Put otherwise, the plasticity of life consists in the ability of an

---

5. See Malabou, *What Should We Do*, and *Plasticity*; Grosz, *Volatile*, and *Time*; and P. Brush.

6. Malabou contrasts the notion of "plasticity" with that of "flexibility," which she views as purely passive. Both Malabou and Emily Martin critique the notion of "flexibility" as it is used in neoliberal economic discourse.

organism to introduce spontaneous delays and shifts into nexuses of force. (This definitional distinction between life, which is plastic, and nonlife, which is not, will be called into question by Eliot, as we will see in the second part of this chapter, as well as in the coda.) The turn to plasticity in cultural studies and critical theory, which is initiated largely through the innovations of feminist science studies, though now unfolding outside this arena, has afforded thinkers new ways of conceiving of identity formation. Rather than perceiving matter as the passive background to social formations, critics have increasingly come to understand matter, as well as nature, as an active force at work in the production of culture, identity, and agency.[7] Contemporary plasticity theory thus emerges as a particular instantiation of the dynamic materialism that this book traces to the work of nineteenth-century novelists, philosophers, and scientists such as William James and Eliot.

In line with present-day theorists of plasticity such as Malabou, these nineteenth-century thinkers challenge our tendency to understand character solely as the product of human forces, be they individual wills or sociocultural norms. They challenge this tendency not from the present, of course, but from their historical moment, a moment in which the assumptions that matter was static and reactive, and the human mind, dynamic and active, were increasingly being called into question. In *The Outward Mind*, Benjamin Morgan argues that "a nineteenth-century fascination with matter occasioned new speculation about the agencies of physical things that had previously seemed still and inert" (6). A watershed moment in this history was the Irish physicist John Tyndall's 1874 address to the British Association for the Advancement of Science at Belfast, which drew on a long history of materialist philosophy and science to argue that movement and power were immanent to matter. What in 1874 Tyndall referred to as the "structural power of matter" had been recognized by previous Victorian thinkers, including field theorists such as Michael Faraday and William Grove (*Address* 56). Less widely recognized at the time was the work of the botanist Robert Brown, whose observations of pollen earlier in the century had suggested that the irregular movements of particles he witnessed under his microscope had a *physical* rather than biological cause. Brown's contemporaries had a difficult time believing him when he claimed to have observed a "very unexpected fact

---

7. Grosz, for instance, has proposed that we view nature "in terms of dynamic forces, fields of transformation and upheaval, rather than as a static fixity, passive, worked over, transformed and dynamized only by culture" (*Time* 7). Relatedly, Barad described a world in which objects, including humans, emerge through interactions between material agencies always already imbued with meaning.

of seeming vitality" in things that were neither alive nor organic (R. Brown 470). As a result, his theory that matter was not fundamentally inert but rather composed of microscopic dancing particles went unnoticed for over thirty years—that is, until the late 1860s, when Eliot began composing *Middlemarch*.[8]

Setting her novel in 1828 (the year Brown's pamphlet "A Brief Account of the Microscopical Observations on the Particles Contained in the Pollen of Plants" first appeared in print), Eliot turns to Brown to imply the prescience of her character Tertius Lydgate.[9] "I have some sea-mice—fine specimens—in spirits," Lydgate tells Camden Farebrother, adding, "and I will throw in Robert Brown's new thing—'Microscopic Observations on the Pollen of Plants'—if you don't happen to have it already" (163). I will return later to the significance of Brown's observation for Eliot's representation of the plasticity of character across human and nonhuman worlds. For now, however, let me just remark that although at the time of *Middlemarch*'s composition, Eliot was likely unaware of the major impact Brown's research would have on the field of physics (this would not be fully apparent until the early twentieth century), nor had she heard Tyndall's address (delivered three years after the publication of *Middlemarch*), her representation of the matter of character in the novel aligns with these physicists' attempts to reveal, in the words of Tyndall, "the error... in ascribing fixity to that which is fluent" (*Address* 380). In this, her novel can be seen actually to prefigure advancements in materialist science—especially as it would come to be applied to the study of character in the late nineteenth century.

Six years after the first installment of *Middlemarch*, the American psychologist William James published an essay that drew upon principles derived from physics and chemistry to develop a new theory of character formation.[10] This essay, entitled "The Laws of Habit" (1877), begins with the suggestion that "the moment one tries to define what habit is, one is led to the fundamental properties of matter" (*Principles* 104). A basic proneness to habit formation, the essay goes on to suggest, seems to be ingrained in the very structure of matter itself. Indeed, James went so far as to suggest that "the laws of Nature are nothing but the immutable habits which

---

8. According to Stephen Brush, "after the initial flurry of excitement caused by Brown's publications in 1828 and 1829, interest in Brownian movement dropped off to almost nothing for about thirty years" (7).

9. Brown's pamphlet was initially intended for private circulation and was technically never officially published. In 1828, however, it was printed in the *Edinburgh Journal of Science* (S. Brush 3).

10. James would later minimally revise this essay to include in *The Principles of Psychology* (1890), from which I quote.

the different elementary sorts of matter follow in their actions and reactions upon each other" (104). These habits are yet more variable in organic matter. A piece of paper, for example, once folded, folds more easily the second time; likewise, an ankle once sprained is more likely to be reinjured; joints once afflicted by rheumatism are more prone to relapse. And so, James formulated the hypothesis that "the phenomena of habit in living beings are due to the plasticity of the organic materials of which their bodies are composed" (105). For James, *plasticity*, "in the wide sense of the word, means the possession of a structure weak enough to yield to an influence, but strong enough not to yield all at once" (105). James's suggestion that human character is essentially "plastic" is more than a metaphor to describe the responsiveness of a personality to influence or willed intent. Rather, he argues, the basic responsiveness of organic matter, especially nervous tissue, to applied force makes possible characterological transformation as such. Like Eliot, James does not describe humans as if they were plastic material substances; his writing explores the nature of the plastic matter of which human beings are composed.

Prefiguring James, Eliot attributes the potential for characterological change not to the power of the human psyche or will but to the plasticity of organic matter. Take the example of Dorothea's uncle, Arthur Brooke, who is described in the first few pages of *Middlemarch* as "glutinously indefinite" (8), and later, as "a very good fellow, but pulpy" (65). Such descriptions of the soft matter of Brooke's character assist, on one level, in the characterization of his particular behavioral tendencies. Brooke, we are told, has "an acquiescent temper, miscellaneous opinions, and uncertain vote"; his conclusions are "as difficult to predict as the weather" (8). Despite his wavering opinions on most issues, however, in some things Brooke is fastidious. He is thrifty, for instance, always "spending as little money as possible." The narrator explains what might initially seem a characterological contradiction—Brooke's general fickleness about most things and his extreme particularity about others—with the pithy remark: "Even the most glutinously indefinite minds enclose some hard grains of habit" (8). On this level of characterization, it seems, the narrator can explain any given character strictly through reference to physical laws.

Closer attention to Eliot's descriptive language here, however, shows that she may have had a particular kind of plasticity in mind: that of the protein gluten. A basic physiological guide from 1869 suggests that "nearly all [nutritious grains] are composed of two principles, the glutinous and the farinaceous, mingled together" (*Elementary* 34). In fact, according to the guide, one might reduce *all* organic substances to these two basic principles. For what concerns food, the more farinaceous (or grainy) substances are "*warming*," and those more glutinous (or proteinous), "*plas-*

tic" or "building." An example of the latter compound is meat, which "has a large abundance of albuminous or plastic principle (*the fibre of the flesh*) in a condensed state" (35). Proteins, early examples of which included wheat gluten and albumen (egg white), are polymers—chains of compounds known for their extreme plasticity. Recognized as a distinct class of molecules in the late eighteenth century, proteins take their name from Proteus, the Greek god who was able to change his shape at will. More than 80 percent water and protein, the human body could be described as "glutinously indefinite." We thus might read Eliot's maxim—"Even the most glutinously indefinite minds enclose some hard grains of habit"— more straightforwardly as a description of all minds, which, consisting of proteins (and, to a much lesser extent, carbohydrates) are composed of both plastic and rigid molecules. Brooke's mind, in this sense, is literally part glutinous, part grainy, and his capacity for characterological shape-shifting is tied to his body's proteinous base.

It has long been a tendency of literary studies to approach references to material substances in literature as projections of cultural meaning or as symbolic of sociocultural shifts. Jules Law's book, *The Social Life of Fluids: Blood, Milk, and Water in the Victorian Novel*, for instance, considers how developments in the manipulation of fluids produced "fantasies of control and anxieties of identity" within the pages of Victorian fiction, approaching novels as a reflection of shifts in the social meaning of material substances (ix). Law asserts in his introduction: "Victorian obsession with liquids had little to do with the ostensibly intrinsic properties of water, blood, alcohol or milk" (2). But Law's contention that Victorians were little concerned with the "ostensibly intrinsic properties" of fluids speaks less to the actual relationship of Victorians to the fluids they described than to his own critical method, which merely *attends* to the cultural meanings of fluids like blood, milk, and water.

I suggest, *pace* Law, that the force of meaning of material substances for Eliot emerges not only from how they are arbitrarily made to signify but also from how they more basically *act*. As close attention to *Middlemarch*'s character descriptions demonstrates, Victorians were in fact concerned with the "intrinsic properties" of matter as well as their role in the construction of social and cultural formations. Some, like Eliot, even looked to literature as a mode of exploring their role in the formation of human character.

A certain irreverence for the categorical distinction between specific persons and more general physical phenomena, as well as the literal and the figurative, can be seen in Eliot's descriptions of humans as material substances and geometrical forms, which operate both as metaphors for specific personalities and—more literally—as weak-theoretical descriptions of how character generally functions. Elaine Freedgood has described the "intense commingling of the literal and the figurative" in Eliot's research notebook, which lists under the entry for "M" interests like "Milton, Medusa, moisture, mist," placing persons (real and fictional) on the same plane as fluid states of matter (*Ideas* 111). Indeed, the material and semiotic occur simultaneously and inseparably in Eliot's novel, such that glutinous materiality does not only signify or symbolize Brooke's fickleness but also harbors it, makes it possible. As Freedgood reminds, to reduce nonhuman things in novels to what they tell us about a character's personality is to view them as "indentured to the subject" (12). While things often function as metaphors, she explains, they can also function as metonymies tied to histories outside "the novel's manifest or dominant narrative—the one that concerns its subjects" (12). While Freedgood cultivates a new mode of historicism that tracks literary objects to their real-world referents and back again, I approach Eliot's materialist descriptors more theoretically, as interventions in the history of thinking about the impersonal forces at work in the formation of character. As scholars have often remarked when drawing parallels between Eliot and Darwin, Eliot's approach to character in *Middlemarch* speaks to the emergence of a new evolutionary paradigm, according to which species characteristics were themselves not fixed but rather changing over time as the result of chance variations and encounters with the environment. What Elizabeth Grosz has described as Darwin's "dynamic and open-ended understanding of the intermingling of history and biology" (*Time Travels* 17) can be witnessed in the opening lines of *Middlemarch*'s prelude, in which man is described as a "mysterious mixture... under the varying experiments of Time" (3). Eliot investigates the composition of this "mysterious mixture" and its capacity for change in her characterizations, which explore the bodily sensitivity, impressionability, and propensity toward habit formation that enable characterological change throughout time.

As in James's writings, in Eliot, habits are described as rigid kernels emerging out of otherwise plastic compounds. Walter Vincy, for instance, "was not a rock: he had no other fixity than the fixity of alternating impulses sometimes called habit" (324). Such descriptions anticipate how James would later theorize changes in habit in terms of changes in material structure. In the natural world, James argues, what we think of as the "laws of Nature" are really "nothing but immutable habits which different elementary sorts of matter follows in their actions and reactions upon each other" (*Principles* 105). For James, as Philip Fisher has put it, "stones fall by habit, birds build nests by habit" (6). But not all habits are as "immutable" as these physical actions and reactions. As James points out, although the structure of a single particle may be difficult to change, the structures of *larger compounds* are far more plastic. In other words, "either outward forces or inward tensions can, from one hour to another, turn that structure into something different from what it was," James writes, proposing that we think of "each relatively stable phase of equilibrium in such a structure" in terms of the "new set of habits" that marks its change (*Principles* 105).

Like James, Eliot prefers to draw parallels rather than distinctions between the structure and behaviors of humans and those of nonhuman material formations. But where James sometimes suggests that character, "like plaster" (144), will eventually set, Eliot—here more akin to Malabou—emphasizes the extent to which character harbors unforeseen possibilities, responding unpredictably to the forces that impress upon it.[11] In *Middlemarch*, "character is not cut in marble—it is not something solid and unalterable. It is something living and changing, and may become diseased as our bodies do" (694). This line, delivered by Farebrother in reference to the questionable behavior of Lydgate, draws upon the moral valence of the word *character* in the Victorian period. Having taken money from Nicholas Bulstrode around the time of John Raffles's death, Lydgate is suspected of having been bribed by Bulstrode to ensure the removal of Bulstrode's blackmailer, Raffles. As a result, as Lydgate puts it, his character is "blighted—like a damaged ear of corn" (719). Blight is a botanical disease "of atmospheric or invisible origin, that suddenly blasts, nips, or destroys plants."[12] It is a bad encounter between the molecules inside and molecules outside of the plant that leads to an insufficient production of chlorophyll; it "arrests their growth, or prevents their blossom from 'setting.'"

Lydgate's run-in with Bulstrode is a similarly bad encounter, a loss of integrity that results in a damage in structure—a concept I will return to in a moment.[13] First, however, let us take a closer look at the scene in which Lydgate is publicly shamed for his connection to Bulstrode, noticing that Eliot describes Lydgate's loss of integrity not in terms of a moral failure but as an unexpected change in the compound of his character.

"Bulstrode's character has enveloped me," Lydgate laments to Doro-

11. As Malabou writes, "If being was able to change once, in the matter of contracting a habit, it can change again. It is available for change to come. Certainly, change generates habit, but in return habit is actualized as a habit of changing" ("Addiction" viii).

12. *OED Online*, Oxford University Press, s.v. "blight," accessed October 11, 2011.

13. Since at least the fifteenth century, the word *integrity* has indicated soundness of structure, the "condition of not being marred or violated; unimpaired or uncorrupted." It came to take on its more metaphorical sense of "freedom from moral corruption" a century later. *OED Online*, Oxford University Press, s.v. "integrity," accessed October 11, 2011.

thea after a fateful scene at the town hall, "the business is done and can't be undone" (719). More than a public defaming, what occurs at the town meeting is the forging of an affective connection through which Lydgate is overtaken by both Bulstrode's feelings and character—further proof of the maxim stated just a few pages earlier with regard to Rosamond: "We cannot be sure that any natures, however inflexible or peculiar, will resist this effect from a more massive being than their own" (714). Having been publicly accused not only of philandering his way into fortune but also of Raffles's murder, Bulstrode begins to experience "a crisis of feeling almost too violent for his delicate frame to support" (683). Worried for Bulstrode's well-being, Lydgate reaches out his arm, guiding the tottering man out of the room. As if enacted by the touch itself, the character of "this man who was leaning tremblingly on his arm" becomes associated with Lydgate's own, as Bulstrode's misdeeds taint Lydgate's reputation in the eyes of the public (686). In a quick turn of mood, "this act which might have been one of gentle duty and pure compassion" becomes for Lydgate "unspeakably bitter to him." Not only do Bulstrode's wrongdoings become magnetized to Lydgate's moral character in the eyes of those present, but Bulstrode's susceptibility and nakedness also become his. Within the span of a few pages, Lydgate's characterological transformation is complete. He goes from feeling like "the Healer which thinks first of bringing rescue or relief to the sufferer" (683) to "the sufferer" himself (695), cringing from a "sense of exposure" similar to that which afflicted Bulstrode's "susceptible nerve" (683).

In this scene, Eliot portrays how interacting through touch can affectively transform a person's character. Her descriptive focus is not so much on the ethical consequences of their interaction (Lydgate is not "corrupted" by Bulstrode, although his reputation might be damaged), but rather on the way that emotion travels, tremblingly, through Bulstrode's "delicate frame" to introduce a change in Lydgate's constitution. Her concern, we might say, is not so much ethical as it is ethological. In 1843, as we saw in the introduction, John Stuart Mill proposed the construction of a science of human character called *ethology*, which would reveal "not the principles of human nature, but results of those principles under the circumstances in which mankind have happened to be placed" (*System* 861–62). Writing in 1970 about the seventeenth-century Dutch philosopher Benedict de Spinoza, Gilles Deleuze would likewise turn to the notion of ethology to describe Spinoza's project in his 1677 treatise *Ethics: Demonstrated in a Geometrical Order*. In Deleuze's reading, Spinoza's ethics is less concerned with the difference between right and wrong than with the affective relations and capacities of bodies, human and nonhuman. Where morality tends to foreground individual choices, ethology, as Deleuze conceptualizes it in relation to Spinoza's writings, tracks the "relations of speed and slowness, of the capacities for affecting and being affected that characterize each thing," as well as how those "capacities can compound" into new relations (*Spinoza* 125–26).[14]

Eliot's physics of character might be read as a conceptual link between these two ethologies—Mill's human-centered science and Spinoza's posthumanist ethics. If *Middlemarch* can be seen to implicitly answer Mill's call for "a science of the formation of character," the science of character it develops does afford an exceptional status to the human. Whereas Mill, as we have already seen, emphasized the special capacity of the human to willfully transform its character, Spinoza—whose *Ethics* and *Tractatus* Eliot translated throughout the 1840s and 1850s—approached "human actions and appetites" more geometrically, "as if the subject were lines, surfaces, or solids" (*Spinoza* 162). In presenting the human as a material creature determined in and through its relations, Eliot can be seen as building on the work of both Spinoza and Mill to show how the dynamic materiality of the body endows it with causal powers that allow it to affect others, as well as how those circumstantial encounters in turn transform the structure of its being.[15]

Let us return here to the notion of structure, or as Eliot calls it, *form*, to better comprehend the role of affect in Eliot's physics of character. For Eliot, it is the form-taking quality of the matter that enables character's affectability. "What is a structure but a set of relations?" she inquires in her essay "Notes on Form in Art" (c. 1868), composed the year before she began writing *Middlemarch*. In both poetry and life, she argues there, form is "a limit determined partly by the intrinsic relations or composition of the object, & partly by the extrinsic action of other bodies upon it" ("Notes" 234).[16] "This is true," the essay continues, "whether the object is a rock or a man."

Eliot's essay highlights the way that form enables affection across human and nonhuman worlds. "Fundamentally, form is unlikeness," Eliot defines her key term, "and in consistency with this fundamental meaning, every difference is form" (232). If "Matter" is what is common between all beings, she proposes, "Form" is the site of their difference. Such differences are neither essential nor unchanging, however. For Eliot, all

---

14. As Hasana Sharp articulates the distinction, for Deleuze, where morality is "the doctrine of what rational beings *ought* to do," ethology is "the liberation of what 'a body can do'" (211).

15. On Eliot's translations of Spinoza, see Gatens; Carlisle.

16. Eliot's remarks here echo Spencer's definition of life as "the continuous adjustment of internal relations to external relations" (374).

forms are temporary compounds, not immutable unities; they are nexuses of relations open to change as their relations change.[17] This is because all boundaries enable affection, which in turn allows for the possibility of change. Our most basic understanding of form, she suggests, is "derived principally from touch," emerging from the tactile "perception of separateness" (232). Where James traces the transformability of character to responsiveness of organic matter to applied force, Eliot traces the affective capacity of people as well as things to the fact that they are composed of a formative matter from which the very possibility of interconnection (and thus also sensation) arises.[18] Recall here Malabou's definition of plasticity as "the capacity to *receive form* (clay is called 'plastic,' for example) and the capacity to *give form* (as in the plastic arts or in plastic surgery)." Rather than employ a hylomorphic understanding of form as that which imposes itself upon a passive matter, Eliot suggests that character can never be conceived without form because the matter of character is formative activity.

Eliot's "Notes on Form in Art," while little cited, is integral to understanding the quest of both Edward Casaubon and Lydgate in *Middlemarch* for "fundamental knowledge of structure" (139). Where Casaubon, in his search for "the Key to All Mythologies," hopes to uncover a singular, unchanging structure, in his quest for "the primitive tissue," Lydgate imagines a more dynamic form, a plastic material that, in its ability to take on new forms, renders life, in all its diversity, possible. Scholars have long suggested that Lydgate's research into tissue is implicitly misguided, pointing to the fact that cell theory had emerged by the time Eliot began composing *Middlemarch*.[19] But Lydgate's attempt "to demonstrate the more inti-

17. Eliot's argument here might on first glance resemble that of certain Romantic thinkers about the nature of "organic form." Like many poets and philosophers of organic form, Eliot proposed that forms emerge as a result of the properties of the materials from which they are composed. But her theory of form differs in significant ways from the traditional Romantic conception of organic form. Samuel Taylor Coleridge, for instance, suggests that organic form is "innate. It shapes, as it develops itself from within, and the fullness of its development is one & the same with the perfection of its outward form" (495). Not only does Eliot never imply belief in an intrinsic "formative force," she also stresses repeatedly the power of actions that are "extrinsic" to the body and its biology on organic formation. On the organicism implicit in Eliot's famous notion of the web, see Eagleton. In contrast to Eagleton, who suggests that Eliot's web preserves "the essential unity of the organic mode," I read this figure as a difference engine in which the friction between a multiplicity of parts makes change itself possible (120).

18. Mill also once defined matter as "the Permanent Possibility of Sensation" (*William* 183).

19. See, for instance, Harvey; Tambling; Menke; and Rothfield.

mate relations of living structure" is actually consistent with advances in the biological sciences around the time of *Middlemarch*'s composition. Indeed, there is little evidence to suggest that the phrase "primitive tissue" is anything other than Eliot's way of imagining what a good scientist in 1829 would be looking for; "such missing of the right word befalls many seekers," we are told (132).

Lydgate's quest for the primitive tissue is supposed to build on the legacy of Xavier Bichat, a real-life French anatomist who died in the year the fictional Lydgate would have been born.[20] Eliot's characterization of Bichat's innovations in histology is telling, given her own thoughts on form as she expressed them just three years earlier in "Notes on Form in Art." As the narrator of *Middlemarch* explains:

> That great Frenchman first carried out the conception that living bodies, fundamentally considered, are not associations of organs which can be understood by studying them first apart, and then as it were federally; but must be regarded as consisting of certain primary webs or tissues out of which various organs—brain, heart, lungs, and so on—are compacted, as the various accommodations of a house are built up in various proportions of wood, iron, stone, brick, zinc, and the rest, each material having its peculiar composition and proportions. No man, one sees, can understand and estimate the entire structure or its parts—what are its frailties and what its repairs, without knowing the nature of the materials. (138–39)

Like Eliot herself, whose novel presents character as being composed of a plastic, organic matter common to all beings, Bichat is said to have approached the living body as being composed of "primary webs or tissues," as opposed to "associations of organs which can be understood by studying them first apart, and then as it were federally." His line of inquiry jolts anatomy out of its obsession with identifying and studying a fundamental and limited set of body parts to consider the "peculiar composition and proportions" of the materials of which those parts (as well as the whole) are made. As Eliot's narrator suggests in closing, in order to understand such a complex, compound structure as the human body, one must understand "the nature of the materials" of which it is composed.[21] An impor-

20. As Tambling has pointed out, Lydgate is twenty-seven in 1829, meaning he was born in 1802.
21. Almost twenty years earlier, Lewes had described Bichat's "grand philosophical device" as "decomposing the organism into its various elementary tissues." As he wrote, "We must commence with the study of the tissues, and thence proceed to the

tant aspect of the nature of this material is its dynamic ability to sustain and produce changes in form. Such plasticity is the precondition for what I have been calling character's *circumstantiality*—the ability of character to transform, contingently and unpredictably, through external relations.

Lydgate's instinct to conceive of the fundamental basis of life in terms of plastic matter in 1828 can be seen to anticipate developments in the life sciences between the 1840s and 1860s. While the emergence of cell theory in the early nineteenth century consolidated many scientists' sense that life was best conceived in molecular terms, as the century progressed, new research by botanists on the European continent called into question the structural emphasis of cell theorists who, in focusing largely on the cell walls and nucleus, had treated the plastic substance between the two as mere filler. Instrumental to this shift were the objections to cell theory raised by the botanists Hugo von Mohl and Carl Nägeli, who drew attention to the important role of what Mohl in 1846 called "Protoplasma" (protoplasm) in sustaining the physiological activities of the cell.[22] Nägeli and Mohl's insights were popularized in England by T. H. Huxley's 1868 lecture "On the Physical Basis of Life," which followed these Swiss and German scientists in redirecting the scientific quest for the fundamental basis of life away from the unit of the cell and toward the "striking uniformity of material composition in living matter" (142). Huxley argued there: "Protoplasm, simple or nucleated, is the formal basis of all life. It is the clay of the potter; which, bake it and paint it as he will, remains clay, separated by artifice, and not by nature, from the commonest brick or sundried clod" (142). His suggestion that—despite the myriad of forms that life takes—all organisms are united in their basis in this plastic *matter* implies that Lydgate's focus on "the nature of the materials" in his research is far from misguided. Indeed, Eliot's character descriptions themselves would seem to draw attention to that idea of "one kind of matter which is com-

---

analysis of the laws of their combination into organs, and finally, to the consideration of the grouping of those organs into system" (*Comte* 181). Not only does it seem unlikely that Eliot would be mocking Lydgate's quite similar approach but, as Duncan has recently noted, the foundational cell theorist Theodor Schwann himself also had "acknowledged Bichat's tissue theory as laying the foundation for his identification of the nucleated cell as the fundamental unit of life, so a commitment to it would not necessarily disqualify Lydgate's project" (181).

22. Geison notes that "Nägeli and von Mohl attacked the emphasis placed by Schleiden and Schwann on the cell wall by suggesting that it was really the cellular contents which sustained the physiological activities of the plant cell and which were particularly important in the formation of new cells and in the formation of the cell wall itself" (274).

mon to all living beings," the complex "proteinaceous" substance Huxley called "protoplasm" (5, 12).[23] While they might take different forms, Huxley argued, "all living forms are fundamentally of one character" (138).

We have seen throughout this section how Eliot's novel constructs a physics of character in which matter both figures and participates in characterological transformation. A certain ontological proposition undergirds this physics: character has its basis in a plastic matter that is able not only to take on new forms but also to affect changes in form. This proposition raises a few philosophical questions. First, if the truth of character is that it is soft and relational, then why does it so often appear rigid and autonomous? Certainly, both real and fictional people *appear* as individuated entities with characters that persist throughout time for the most part unchanged. Are their autonomy and stability mere illusions? If so, do these illusions paper over a more flowing or changeful reality? To maintain that, in Huxley's words, there is "one kind of matter which is common to all living beings" is to raise the question not only of how such differences in form emerge but also whether the boundaries between organisms are somehow less real than the plastic matter that unites them. Here, a second question arises: to what extent is the matter of character plastic because it is living?

So far, most of the figures I have tracked have been organic: Brooke's gluten, Lydgate's blight, Rosamond's soft white living substance. In her work on plasticity, Malabou has stressed the special plasticity of organic matter, a plasticity that is especially fundamental to the operation of brain and stem cells. Varying slightly, James held that *all physical things* obey the laws of habit, though as compounds become more complex (in organic beings, for example), they are seen to express greater plasticity.

Taking a page from James, my next section reads Eliot's treatment of character in *Middlemarch* less as "a chapter in physiology or psychology" than as "a chapter in physics" (James, *Principles* 105). To understand the role of character in Eliot's realism entails close attention to the way she engages with the physical sciences in order to represent nonliving, literary characters as *inorganic* relational forms capable of rapidly taking on new shapes.[24] An analysis of how Eliot uses literary characters to mediate fiction and reality will thus get us some way toward answering the philosophical questions posed above.

23. Duncan likewise draws parallels between Huxley's protoplasmic theory of life and "the formal horizon of totality that the novel lays claim to" (185).

24. I am grateful to Anna Henchman for identifying a tension between the organic and the inorganic in the previously published version of this argument, which inspired deeper thought.

Irregular Solids, Viscous Fluids

In his foundational 1937 study in rheology, *Elasticity, Plasticity, and Structure of Matter*, the Dutch physicist Roelof Houwink defines plasticity as a middle point between two extremes of physical behavior: the pure elasticity of a solid and the pure viscosity of a fluid. The atoms of most solids are arranged in a regular, latticelike structure held together by strong intermolecular forces (i.e., microscopic units that do not easily change in their pattern). Fluids, on the other hand, are composed of larger structural units, heterogeneously organized and held together by weaker forces (i.e., mesoscopic units that easily change their position), allowing them to undergo Brownian motion (irregular molecular movements that take place over small distances) to a greater degree. As Houwink explains, while a perfectly elastic solid will return to its original form after force is no longer applied, a purely viscous fluid will continue to flow after the release of a stressor. "Where both effects are simultaneously involved," he writes, "the deformation is said in certain schools to be visco-elastic... also frequently referred to as plastic" (3).

In the last section, we saw how Eliot describes her characters as if they were composed of plastic matter—materials capable not only of sustaining but introducing changes in form. This section considers how she mobilizes the tension between the two extremes of physical behavior with which plasticity intercedes—the elasticity of the solid and the viscosity of the liquid—to reflect upon the production of real-seeming characters in literature. Throughout *Middlemarch*, solids often indicate the perceived autonomy of character, such as in the passage in which Dorothea's realization of Casaubon's "equivalent centre of self" is described as "an idea wrought back to the directness of sense, like the solidity of objects" (198). This characterological autonomy, however, is often revealed to be less solid than meets the eye: characters initially characterized by "rocky firmness" will appear, at another scale, to be fluid, "presenting new aspects in spite of solidity, and altering with the double change of self and beholder" (88). In aligning "the solidity of objects" with "the directness of sense," Eliot's novel explores the affective dynamics of realist fiction, which—in producing characters that *feel* like autonomous and individuated human beings—generates a sense of solidity through the novelist's manipulation of what the character Will Ladislaw calls the "liquid flexibility" of words (510).

In her work on Victorian conceptions of space, Alice Jenkins has suggested that when Eliot's novels criticize the notion that physical objects have definite form and extension, they reflect the insights of the most innovative physics of their day. In the 1840s, the inventor of classical field theory, Michael Faraday, called into question the idea of space as an empty container filled with rigid, self-contained bodies. His experiments with the behavior of forces suggested that objects are not bounded, contained units, as they appear to the naked eye, but rather concatenations of force that produce a sense of solidity.

Consistent with field theory, *Middlemarch* implies that what appear, at one scale, to be bounded and unified objects are, at another scale, dynamic fields of force. As Jenkins as well as Michael Tondre have highlighted, Eliot was deeply engaged with the physical sciences, having read widely on the subject in preparation for *Middlemarch* and having attended a lecture course on experimental physics in Geneva with Arthur Auguste de la Rive (an expert in electromagnetic theory and close friend of Faraday).[25]

Expanding on a recent wave of scholarship on the affective dynamics of Eliot's fiction, I show how throughout *Middlemarch* solids emerge as a means of reflecting on how novelists produce the feeling of reality through language, a medium no less real for its lack of physical extension. Summer J. Star has suggested that Eliot's aim in *Middlemarch* is to both "evoke and investigate what gives one the feeling of 'reality'" (850). And Elaine Auyoung has argued that Eliot's novels work to bring her "readers' experience as close as possible to the experience of firsthand perception" (80). I turn to early philosophies of emergence such as that elaborated by Eliot's longtime partner, the philosopher and physiological psychologist, George Henry Lewes, to outline the metaphysical theory that implicitly informs such claims, exploring how *Middlemarch* uses language to produce fictional characters that *feel like* real human beings with shape, color, and extension.

Throughout *Middlemarch*, descriptions of characters as "solid" often indicate the limits of subjective perception, implying that there is more to the experience of human objecthood than initially meets the eye. Consider, for example, Casaubon's description of Dorothea in his proposal letter as "a rare combination of elements both solid and attractive" (40). In contrast to fluids, which flow into the shape of any container they enter as a result of their loose molecular structure, solids, as noted earlier, are

---

25. Eliot's reading list for the years she was preparing for *Middlemarch* (1868–71) included two general physics texts, a biography of Faraday, an essay on the atomic theory of Lucretius, and Tyndall's *Fragments of Science for Unscientific People* (1871) (Eliot, Middlemarch *Notebooks* 41). Both Eliot and Lewes were personally acquainted with Tyndall, who began to visit the couple in the 1860s. Eliot also read extensively about thermodynamic theory, including works by Hermann von Helmholz (whom she had met in Germany in the 1850s) and William Grove, whom, as Tondre notes, she describes as rereading "with renewed interest after a lapse of years" in 1870 (Eliot, quoted in Tondre 212).

defined by their rigid, crystalline pattern. Their elasticity results from the strength of the intermolecular and intramolecular forces that hold their atoms, molecules, and ions in a stable state of attraction. Based on this knowledge, we might read Casaubon's description of Dorothea as "a rare combination of elements both solid and attractive" as something of a jest. Given that solids are actually *defined* by the strong forces of attraction that render them resistant to deformation, the "combination" of these qualities should be anything but rare.[26] The joke is on Casaubon, it seems, as Eliot undermines his fictional authority with the power of her all-too-real pen. Were Dorothea not so absorbed in the fantasy of her future life, we are told, she might have looked at Casaubon's flattering description more "critically as a profession of love" (41).[27] Instead, the reader is guided to take this critical stance through Casaubon's inaccurate description of Dorothea as "solid."

Dorothea is again described as "solid" with reference to her uncle Brooke's failed attempt to understand her desire to marry a scholar twenty-seven years her elder—and here again a rift emerges between Dorothea's appearance to the human eye and her reality on another scale. Holding Casaubon's letter anxiously in his pocket, Brooke attempts to subtly dissuade his niece from marrying Casaubon should he propose. Faced with his niece's resolve to accept the proposal, however, Brooke reluctantly hands her the letter as she leaves the room. "In short," the narrator closes the chapter, "woman was a problem which, since Brooke's mind fell blank before it, could be hardly less complicated than the revolutions of an irregular solid" (39).

As in the former case, ignorance and misrecognition are associated with the identification of Dorothea as solid. Though she does not examine this specific passage, Jenkins has suggested that in Victorian literature generally, geometry tends to crop up in moments of sexual maturation

---

26. In 1866, an article in *All the Year Round* described the phenomenon as follows: "In imagining the ultimate composition of a solid body, we have to reconcile two apparently contradictory conditions. It is an assemblage of atoms which do not touch each other—for we are obliged to admit intermolecular spaces—and yet those atoms are held together in clusters by so strong a force of cohesion as to give the whole the qualities of a solid" ("Atoms" 236).

27. Casaubon's failure as a lover is likewise explained with reference to physical laws: "It is true that he knew all the classical passages implying the contrary, but knowing classical passages, we find, is a mode of motion, which explains why they leave so little force for their personal application" (78–79). S. Brody has interpreted this passage as a reference to Tyndall's account of the kinetic theory of gases, according to which the more motion occurs, the less force remains. In reading too much about love thus, the narrator implies, Casaubon has dissipated his erotic energy (46–47).

"to signify the clarity and order of the presexual mind which must be lost or renounced if maturity is to be reached" ("George" 83).[28] As she points out, within the Victorian educational system, the study of Euclid (a staple in the narrow curriculum for boys) often coincided with puberty—a fact that might explain why geometrical metaphors often contrast mathematical certainty with the murkiness and ambiguity of sexual adulthood (83). Along these lines, the description of Dorothea as a "woman" who "could be hardly less complicated than the revolutions of an irregular solid" could be read as a reference to her increasing maturity as an adult. Indeed, both here and in the aforementioned passage, Dorothea's womanhood is the thing of confusion and complexity to men especially, whose perspectives are revealed to be limited. References to her solidity thus might be read to signal the misguided perceptions of male characters to whom women appear opaque—the masculinist desire for concrete and totalizing knowledge troubled by the epistemologically disruptive force of the feminine. But they do something else too: they indicate that what appears on one scale to be recalcitrant and stable might, on another scale, be flexible and motile.

But let us further unpack this multidimensional phrase, which inspires reflection on the affective dynamics of realist fiction. A regular solid (Figure 1) is a polyhedron (or three-dimensional figure), the faces of which are all identical regular polygons. The number of faces that meet at each corner is also the same. A regular solid is easily described in basic terms—by measuring, say, the length of a side of a cube. An irregular solid, on the other hand, is defined precisely by the difficulty one encounters in mathematically describing it. Because of their complex shape, irregular solids pose a problem for mathematical description; calculating such a body in rotation would require finding its moments of inertia—which in the case of an irregular solid would be a real challenge without the aid of a computer. The description of Dorothea as more "complicated than the revolutions of an irregular solid" thus not only signals her opacity to Brooke, it also signals the complexity of the *process of describing her*, producing her as a human object that exists beyond the text and that which the text describes.

In fiction, the word *description* typically refers to the process of constructing a fictional entity through (often nonnarrative) language; but in physics, to *describe* a body usually means to give an account of its being using mathematics, models, or both. In the history of mechanics, the

28. Eliot attended Francis Newman's lectures on geometry at the Ladies College in January of 1851 (Jenkins, "George" 73). Frustrated with geometric traditionalism, Newman argued that the field should move forward from Euclid's "unbending" theories (Newman, quoted in "George" 80).

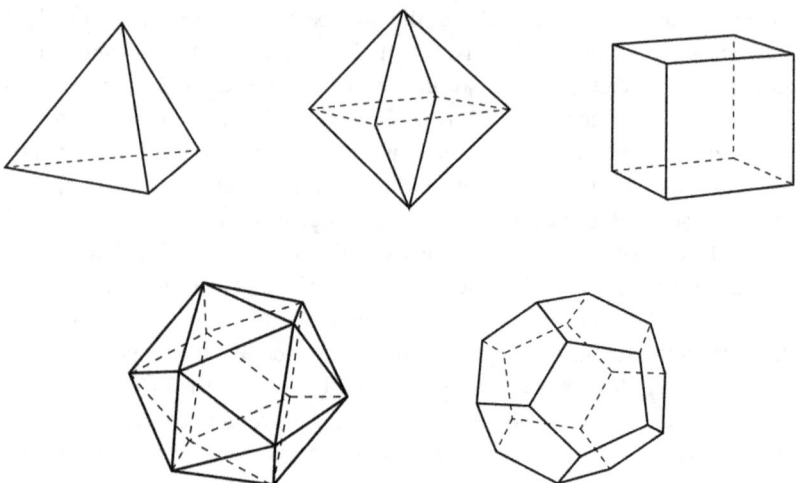

1. Jens Nikolaus, Five Regular Solids (2015).

description of the rotation of rigid bodies is a classic problem, often modeled by tops. In 1857, the Scottish physicist James Clerk Maxwell observed that the "problem of the rotation of a solid body" was so difficult "that it had never been thoroughly understood by any but the most expert mathematicians" (249). This difficulty did not stop Maxwell, however; he would go on to formulate classical electromagnetic theory. By age twenty-six, he had created a "dynamical top" (Figure 2) that validated his calculations of the dynamics of a rotating solid body. The creation of the dynamical top followed on the heels of his groundbreaking work on Saturn's rings. As Maxwell showed in 1856, the rings of Saturn were not uniformly solid, as others had suggested.[29] Rather, they were a rotating mass of *irregular solid* particles. His prizewinning paper "On the Stability of the Motion of Saturn's Rings" (1856) demonstrated his hypothesis that the "theory of an Irregular Solid Ring leads to the result that to ensure stability the irregularity must be enormous" (289). In other words, what appeared to be the stable, concentric circles of Saturn's rings were really the strange and distant motions of irregular particles.

In his 2012 book, *Ends of Enlightenment*, John Bender proposes that the realist novel is "apparitional" in its "capacity... to give us the impression

---

29. Most influentially, in his four-volume magnum opus, *Traité de Mécanique Céleste*, Pierre-Simon, marquis de Laplace, proposed that a single solid ring rotated around Saturn's main body.

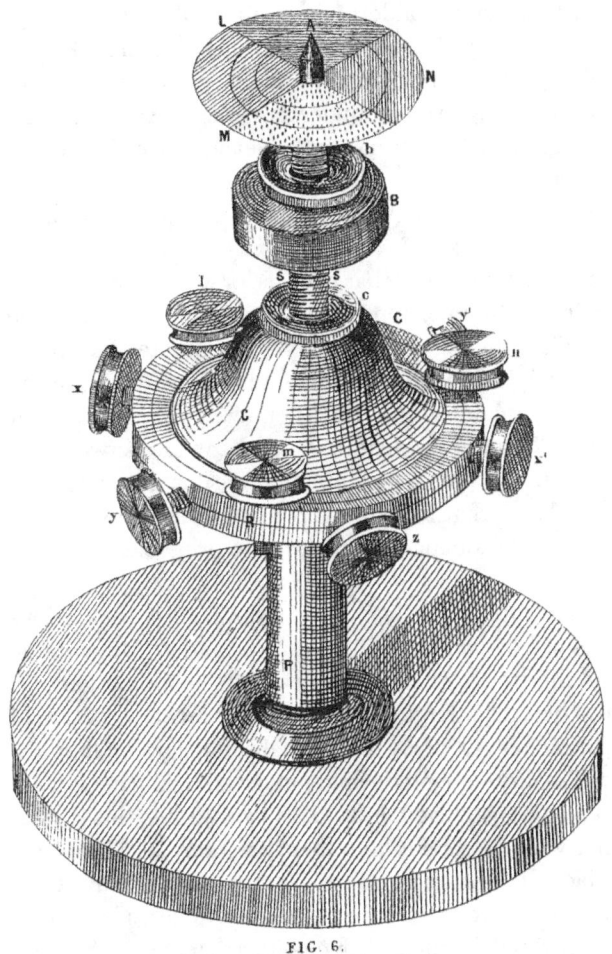

FIG. 6.

2. James Clerk Maxwell, Dynamical Top (1890). From James Clerk Maxwell, *The Scientific Papers of James Clerk Maxwell*, vol. 1, edited by W. D. Niven (Cambridge: Cambridge University Press, 1980), plate III.

of real things—to use means other than direct, sensory apprehension of the real in order to project a reality" (104). Along these lines, one might read Eliot's fiction as performing something like Saturn's rings: characters like Dorothea appear as individual people with specific traits and centers of self; in reality, however, they are loosely structured material systems, concatenations of words (themselves composed of letters) that, when combined, produce the "effect" of human life. In fact, a previously published version of this chapter undertook such a reading.[30] As I suggested there, the analogy introduced between Dorothea's fictional being and Maxwell's dynamical top implies that the stability and autonomy of character is illusory. In coming to better understand the physical and philosophical theories that inform Eliot's analogy, however, I have come to believe this was a misstep.

When Bender argues that "through its neutrality of style, its profusion of detail, and its causal sequences of action, realism produces a coherent, linguistic version of the real that never has been, is, or will be," he extends a long poststructuralist tradition of approaching the fictional world of the realist novel as a "reality effect"—a reality only ever connoted, never denoted. "Expect the principles of realist fiction to apply in everyday life and you get delusion at best, madness at worst," Bender cautions his reader (105). While undoubtedly there are distinctions to be made between the laws that govern fiction and those of everyday life, such critics are too quick to dismiss the claims that realist novels make when they use descriptive detail and causal sequences to explore the principles that govern character.

Taking these claims more seriously, in what follows, I ask what Eliot's novel can tell us about how character functions in reality. Drawing on nineteenth-century philosophical accounts of ontological emergence—the theory that novel objects emerge as a result of the causal structure of reality—I approach the "reality effect" of the realist novel more literally, that is, as an effect *of* reality—the place where material reality itself is casually registered, if also transformed. Indeed, as I will argue, this is what *Middlemarch* teaches when it implies both that character has a basis in a plastic matter capable of taking on new forms (as we have already seen), and (as we shall see here) that character emerges and appears to observers in the form of individuated bodies, with qualities that persist throughout time.

Since 1875, the word *emergence* has indicated the belief that genuinely novel properties and entities arise from when matter is organized in different ways. The origins of the term can be traced to G. H. Lewes, whose *Problems of Life and Mind* built on Mill's discussion of causality in *A System of Logic* to distinguish between what Lewes called "resultants" and "emergents" (*Problems* 1.2:412–13). Resultants, Lewes proposed in his chapter on causality in *Problems*, are nothing more than the sum of their component parts; emergents, on the other hand, possess qualities that are not to be found in their parts. Tracing the concept of emergence forward from Mill and Lewes to that of more recent English philosophy, the historian of phi-

---

30. See Brilmyer, "Plasticity."

losophy Brian McLaughlin argues that the tradition of British Emergentism is defined by a few basic principles: the belief that reality is fundamentally material, that matter is composed of elementary particles, that the movement of these particles generates change, and these particles are organized differently at different scales—all principles that likewise characterize the ontology of character I have been tracking in *Middlemarch* (49–50). "What is especially striking about British Emergentism, however," McLaughlin observes, "is its view about the causal structure of reality" (50). For many emergentist thinkers, the physical structure of matter endows it with certain causal powers that affect change at different scales, giving rise to "emergent laws" that govern reality at different orders of complexity (51).[31]

Maxwell's account of Saturn's rings is emergentist insofar as it posits that the stability of Saturn's rings is not an illusion but another layer of reality that *emerges* from the motions of particles which are themselves unstable. As his calculations and subsequent dynamical top demonstrated, the stability of Saturn's rings is produced by the random movements of subvisible particles. Maxwell might have dismissed this stability as an optical illusion; instead, however, he argues that it is the irregular motions of particles that actually "*ensure* stability" (289, emphasis mine).

The implications of Maxwell's emergentist theory would be wide-ranging. As the contemporary condensed matter physicist Piers Coleman has noted, Maxwell's theory of Saturn's rings would go on to form the basis of his theory of atomic movement.[32] In the case of Maxwell, what was initially conceived as a description of a specific, local phenomenon (to wit, the rings of Saturn) would provide the model for a theory of physical reality generally: all matter, he later posits, is composed of tiny particles move in such an irregular way that stability is ensured.

I approach Eliot's character descriptions in *Middlemarch* in a fashion similar to that which physicists such as Coleman understand Maxwell's dynamical top: as a description of the workings of character in general. Within contemporary physics, Maxwell's dynamical top—although it was

31. Bivona has recently also taken up the framework of emergence in his analysis of *Middlemarch*, arguing that "the novel's treatment of character formation is closely linked to emergent concepts" ("Emergence" 73).

32. As Coleman explains: "Maxwell understood that the properties of Saturn's rings were a collective consequence of collisions between its constituent particles. Later, when he moved from Aberdeen to London, he used the astronomic inspiration from Saturn's rings as a model to develop his molecular theory of gases. At a time where the concept of an atom was as controversial as modern string theory, his particulate model for Saturn's rings provided a valuable launching pad for his derivation of the kinetic theory of molecular motion" (301).

constructed to explain the motions of Saturn's rings—is believed to have revealed something about dynamic structure of material reality. That historians of science situate Maxwell's theories in relation to his social milieu, predecessors, or followers does not take away from his model's scientific insight. Likewise, that Eliot's fictional figures are the product of historical and cultural contingencies does not mean that they do not also reveal any truth about the nature of character, too. Let us return to the concept of emergence to comprehend how.

In his foundational theorization of the term, Lewes suggests that emergence signals an unpredictable element in a physical system, a causal leap between scales that introduces a change between scales. In an emergent system, "we cannot always trace the steps of the process, so as to see in the product the mode of operation of each factor," he writes (*Problems* 1.2:412). This is because the causal laws that govern one scale of reality do not apply at another scale.

Picture now a hard, purple crystal. This crystal obeys certain laws, such as gravity, that its constituent parts (colorless atoms and molecules, arranged in a motile, latticelike structure) do not to the same degree. A change in that crystal's constituent parts (say, in their arrangement) might effect a change on another scale (say, the crystal could turn brown or become less rigid). In such a case, the change is an emergent rather than a resultant effect; a change at one scale of an entity (arrangement) has effected a change at another scale of that entity (color, rigidity).[33]

Lewes's theorization of emergence as the generation of new qualities through changes at different scales offers a compelling framework for understanding Eliot's characters. Here, characters, which are observed at one scale to possess certain qualities ("brown hair," "innocent looking" faces), are composed at another scale of smaller components (letters, words, sentences) that when properly arranged combine to give rise to those qualities. Is one of these scales more "real" than the other? "Which of the objects in front of us is the real table," asks the contemporary philosopher of emergence Paul Humphreys, "the familiar, middle-sized object possessing rigidity, solidity, brownness, and woodenness, or the extraordinarily complex collection of atoms that make up the table?" (16). The concept of emergence offers a unique solution to this problem insofar as it holds that "the emergent properties of rigidity and solidity exist in addition to the micro properties" (16). For the emergentist, the table does not "appear"

---

33. On the relationship between emergence and quality, see Silver, who shows how the concept of emergence explains "how a world rich in varied forms and qualities might be explained simply through the disposition of simple particles with almost no properties at all" (169).

to be unified and rigid while "really" being multiple and motile. Rather, it is both at the same time.

In allowing us to hold more than one reality to be real simultaneously, emergence offers a useful framework for understanding "different orders of being" that the realist novel sutures together in its "hetero-ontology," to borrow a term from Freedgood (*Worlds* 99).[34] These different orders are not just *fiction* and *reality*—two terms often hierarchized when not simply opposed—but multiple scales of perception. It is not that characters in realist fiction *appear* real when they are *really* fictional. (Does a wall *appear* pink when it is *really* colorless?) Rather, as *Middlemarch*'s character descriptions help us to see, fiction has the capacity of solidifying and individuating entities that, observed at another scale or through a different apparatus, are fluent and dynamic.

The emergent quality of realist character is nowhere more apparent than in Eliot's description of Dorothea, who is often depicted as hard and solid, only to be later dissolved into a soft, viscous substance. Dorothea's fluid quality is first alluded to in the novel's prelude, which suggests that *Middlemarch* will narrate nothing so "coherent" as an "epic life," but will rather tarry with lives characterized by "inconsistency and formlessness" (3–4). This line is typically read as foreshadowing Dorothea's failure to achieve the status of a "Saint Theresa," a historically influential figure recognized as having achieved a certain level of success or fame. But it also gestures toward the preoccupation of the novel with feminine figures that do not always cohere into solid, individuated entities. Privileging the logic of dispersion ("loving heart-beats and sobs... dispersed among hindrances") over the heroic concentration of potential into "some long recognizable deed" (4), *Middlemarch* explores the connection not only between affection and boundedness (as theorized in "Notes on Form in Art") but also affection and unboundedness—that is, between the potential of a substance to affect and be affected and its potential to loosen or become flexible in form. Notably, at the end of the novel, Dorothea's great achievement is thus not the solidification of an initially pliable subject into a fully formed identity (as it might have been in a typical bildungsroman), but rather her continued ability to scatter the self in such a way as to widen its field of effects.

Although Dorothea is sometimes perceived by other characters as solid, by the time the reader has reached the novel's final lines, this solidity has

---

34. Freedgood has suggested that the realist novel is characterized by an "ontological flexibility" that "allows us to decide what is historically accurate and what is purely or only fictional on a case-by-case basis," by setting its fictional murders in real cities, for example (*Worlds* 99).

dissolved into the much looser molecular structure of a fluid, in which everything is in motion. Her "nature" is described as a "river" having "spent itself in channels," implying a connection between her viscosity and her high capacity for relation (785). It does not matter, we are told, that these channels "had no great name on earth"; what matters is "the effect of her being on those around her." As the novel's final lines affirm, "the effect of her being on those around her was incalculably diffusive" (785).[35]

With connotations of the sprawling and vague, the abstract and unformed, the word "diffusive" alludes to the physical process of *diffusion*, in which molecules intermingle as a result of their kinetic energy. If one dissolves small particles into a solution, the molecules of both substances will mix due to Brownian motion—a phenomenon to which, as we have already seen, *Middlemarch* elsewhere makes explicit reference. We saw in the first part of this chapter that Brown's major contribution to the history of physics was not the observation of moving particles under the microscope (this had been observed before) but rather his proposition that these irregular motions were a structural property of matter itself. After observing the same motion not only in pollen, but also in rocks, glass, and other substances, Brown concluded, as the historian of science Stephen Brush relates: "that almost any kind of matter, organic or inorganic, can be broken into fine particles that exhibit the same kind of dancing motion; thus, he removed the subject from the realm of biology to the realm of physics" (3). I noted earlier that the impact of Brown's theory would not be recognized until much later in the century. As Brush underlines with regard to Maxwell's theory of atomic motion, elaborated throughout the 1860s in his work on gas, the concept of Brownian motion "was generally ignored even by the physicists who developed the kinetic theory of gases, though it is now frequently remarked that Brownian movement is the best illustration of the existence of random molecular motions" (1).

To what extent might Eliot's novel itself be seen to make the theoretical connection between the random motions of particles observed by Brown in 1828 and the kinetic theory of gases that emerged from Maxwell's work on Saturn's rings in the 1850s and 1860s? This link would not be made scientifically, as Brush notes, until 1905 when Albert Einstein published his famous paper on Brownian motion. In referencing both Brown's pamphlet and Maxwell's paper, however, *Middlemarch* implicitly associates the two theories—both of which, as we have seen, were constructed to explain

---

35. Soon after completing *Middlemarch*, Eliot composed a notebook entry entitled "'A Fine Excess': Feeling Is Energy." On *Middlemarch*'s dialogue with energy science, see Tondre, who argues that "the language of diffusion in *Middlemarch* represents a moral and aesthetic vision rooted in unproductive expenditure" (205).

how what appears macroscopically as solid and unified is fluid and dynamic on the microlevel.

In a reading of the novel's final lines, the philosopher Martha Nussbaum has observed that the ending of *Middlemarch* is "extremely and frustratingly vague," seeming to "parry the supposed claims of realism to presence, solidity" (*Subversion* 303). Indeed, as I have been arguing, Eliot's interest in solidity as a foundation for realist aesthetics is in fact limited. Indefiniteness and even generality are equally central to her mode of realism, which mobilizes the tension between the soft and the hard, as well as that between the general and the particular, to comment on the capacity of realist fiction, *like reality itself*, to generate bodies that on one scale appear to be unique and individual and on another, general and multiple. Attention to the surprisingly central role of generalization to Eliot's mode of realism allows us to reassess the oft-made claim that her great innovation as a realist stems from her production of characters as specific and particularized individuals, in contrast to the tradition of presenting characters as types, a topic I will address at greater length in chapter 2.[36]

In a powerful essay on characterization in *Middlemarch*, Catherine Gallagher suggests that Eliot's novel marks an important shift from the fictional paradigm in which characters were presented as fictional instantiations of classes or species of persons. As I noted in the introduction, Gallagher argues that earlier novelists positioned their characters as representative of kinds of people existing in the world (reversing the commonsense empiricism that presumed that types are ideational and particulars real things-in-the-world). Eliot's characters, however, she argues, are presented as "category defiers," instantiations of types that nonetheless always deviate from the type they are supposed to exemplify ("George" 64). As Gallagher argues with regard to *Middlemarch* specifically, "Classification, foreknowledge, and reference are the inevitable framework of the novel, but the dynamic impulse established here is toward fiction, unpredictability, and particular realization" (68).

I will have more to say about unpredictability as a characterological ideal as it functions in the work of both Eliot and Lewes in the coda. For now, though, I want to underline that what is so distinct about Eliot's mode of characterization is not that her characters always exceed types, but that in describing her characters in terms of states of matter—fluids, solids,

---

36. A case made most frequently with regard to Dorothea, cf. I. Armstrong's claim that Eliot "subtracts from Dorothea's situation what is common, what can be recognized, and then goes on to describe what is not, the things which make her situation unique and pitiable" ("A Note" 128), or Gallagher's claim that Eliot is "the nineteenth-century novelist who is most skeptical about categorical thought" ("George" 16).

plasmas, and other types of condensed matter—her descriptions can be read as offering its readers something yet more general: a general theory of character as an impersonal material structure.

Eliot once wrote: "A correct generalization gives significance to the smallest detail, just as the great inductions of geology demonstrate in every pebble the working of laws by which the earth has become adapted for the habitation of man" ("Rev. of *The Progress*" 271). How might *Middlemarch*'s descriptive generalizations about the operations of character broadly "give significance" to its more detailed descriptions of fictional individuals? The answer to this question lies in what the philosopher of science Isabelle Stengers calls the *meso*. As we saw in the introduction to this book, Stengers defines the meso as that which negotiates micro- and macroscales to ask "questions which bring characters into existence." Where microanalysis breaks matter down into subvisible entities (particles that compose larger structures), and macroanalysis scales up to consider general states of matter (liquids or gases, for example), mesoanalysis proceeds, as Stengers puts it, "par le milieu" (through the middle, through the environment) to investigate how matter reacts and behaves to its surrounds ("History"). "The macro," Stengers explains, "is matter in general":

> Gas is marvellously "in general." With the meso, on the other hand, it is necessary in each instance to redefine topically how the relations between the micro and the macro are assembled. In other words, it's about everything that the macro does not allow to be said, and everything that the micro does not permit to be deduced. ("History")

Eliot's physics of character is a similarly mesological project: her weak-theoretical descriptions of characters in terms of plastic matter (i.e., matter organized at a mesoscopic scale) consistently emphasize how character is intimately intertwined with milieu. More than this, however, in dialectically engaging the two extremes of behavior the plasticity intercedes—the pure viscosity of the liquid and the pure elasticity of the solid—she reveals how realist character (rather than being *either* fluent *or* fixed) manifests itself differently at different scales—micro- and macrolevels that all realist literature negotiates between in its construction of characters that are simultaneously specific and general. In their possession of certain specific qualities, all characters are to some extent rigid. (Dorothea's hair remains "brown" not only for the duration of the novel, but for all readers, for all eternity.) At the same time, certain gaps in their being—let us call this property, following Stengers, their "gaseous generality"—allow them to remain fluid enough to transform as they enter different contexts. (While her hair color might remain the same, other aspects of Dorothea change, not only throughout the duration of the novel but also historically, as different readers encounter her.)[37]

Middlemarch, as I pointed out at the start of this chapter, is often upheld as the paragon of a novelistic paradigm in which characterization corresponds to the representation of the individual human personality. By contrast, what I have been tracking is a mode of description in which characters often appear as loosely structured material formations, softly bounded forms that are open to reconfiguration or change. This does not mean that there are not aspects of *Middlemarch* that at times conform to the narrative of the emergence of literary characters as "original, discriminated, and individual person[s]," to cite Sir Walter Scott (549). Indeed, through references to solidity, Eliot signals how such formed individuality—like the stability of Saturn's rings—is an emergent property of realist fiction. In so doing, she reveals something about the nature of *literary* character, an inorganic yet still plastic material formation that, irrespective of time and place, attains form in and through its relations.

Compare here the characterization in *Middlemarch* of the fictional Mr. Brooke as a character who "will run into any mould" with Eliot's description in a letter to her friend Maria Lewis of an actual person, a certain "Mr. Henslowe," as "evidently a character made up of natural crystallization instead of one turned out of a mould" ("To Maria Lewis" 98). In contrast to the fictional Brooke—who is said to be able to take on any shape at any time—this actual person, Henslowe (perhaps John Henslow, the botanist who recommended that the young Charles Darwin set sail on the HMS *Beagle*) is said to attain his form though the much more linear and finite process of crystallization.

Importantly, Henslowe is not Brooke's structural opposite; had Brooke been described as *produced from* a mold, we might assume the relation between Brooke and Henslowe is a relation of type to instance. Rather, he is a person who emerges according to a different logic and tempo than that of Brooke. Crystals are surprisingly plastic forms, with structural dislocations that allow them to transform more than many other solids. (They thus are situated in the middle of the two extremes of physical behavior Houwink described: viscous and elastic.) Where Henslowe takes shape according

37. The tension between the rigid and the fluid I am tracking here maps to some extent onto what Gallagher elsewhere describes as the finished/unfinished quality of literary character. As Gallagher observes, characters are "are at once utterly finished and also necessarily incomplete" ("Rise" 358). Unlike material objects and real humans, she remarks, characters are "exhaustible" in terms of what we can know about them; at the same time, though, their necessarily "incomplete" status means that there is much that remains indeterminate and unknowable about them (358).

to the logic of crystallization, a mode of becoming in which traits accrete along the arrow of time, receiving and giving form in response to the pressures of his environment, the more fluid Brooke exists in a much more open temporal space that allows him to remain much more consistently open to a range of reconfigurations. Depending upon whom he encounters and when—that is, depending on circumstances—the more malleable Brooke will take on a slightly different form.

"Form," Eliot writes, "as an element of human experience, must begin with the perception of separateness" ("Notes on Form" 232). But this appearance of separateness fades, she argues, upon the realization that all "wholes [are] composed of parts more & more multiplied and highly differenced," and thus that all forms are sites of "mutual dependence." Literary characters, we might then venture in closing, despite being nonliving, are themselves plastic. They are dynamic, material forms capable of engaging readers not because they appear (like humans) to have consciousness or intentionality but because, as "relations and groups of relations," they are "not only determined by emotion, but intended to express it" (233). Where human beings accrete and express traits due to structural changes in the plastic matter of which they are composed, literary characters are *yet more fluid figures*, capable of rapidly taking on new shapes in response to the circumstances they encounter. This special viscosity of literary character might be said to emerge from what the narrator calls the "liquid flexibility" of words—a phenomenon Ladislaw describes as the capacity of language to create forms strategically "vague" in boundary (*Middlemarch* 510). Reflecting on the difference between painting and literature, Ladislaw suggests that where painting risks presenting its subjects as "mere coloured superficies..., language gives a fuller image, which is all the better for being vague" (179). Might language's particularite, recombinatory nature render it especially capable of recording how a person changes, in Ladislaw's words, "from moment to moment," allowing for the possibility of "movement"?[38] Eliot's descriptive technique throughout *Middlemarch* would seem to affirm such a thesis: as a demonstration of the power of language to produce the dynamic, material experience of human objecthood, her novel exhibits the capacity of fiction to generate characters that can be formed and reformed by readers because their natures are soft.

---

38. For an argument about the significance of vagueness to Eliot's conception of language that dovetails with my own, see Wright, "George."

Sensing Character in *Impressions of Theophrastus Such*

[CHAPTER TWO]

Dorothea had no such defence against deep impressions.
GEORGE ELIOT, *Middlemarch*

"Will not a tiny speck very close to our vision blot out the glory of the world, and leave only a margin by which we see the blot?" asks the narrator of *Middlemarch*. Indeed it will, comes the answer; and in this regard, there is "no speck so troublesome as self" (392). Metaphors of sensory failure in Eliot's fiction seem to capture the self-absorption of characters who discount empirical knowledge in favor of their own straightened worldviews. In *Middlemarch*, Casaubon's shortsightedness is tied to his egocentric attempts to "understand the higher inward life" (21). Dorothea, who marries Casaubon in an effort to attain this kind of understanding, is correspondingly "unable to see" the right conclusion (29), can "never see what is quite plain" (34), "does not see things" (52), and is "no judge" of visual art, which is composed in "a language [she does] not understand" (73). When Eliot describes obstacles to sensation, however, she does more than provide a critique of egoism in which the corrective is a sympathetic exchange. More basically, Eliot's fascination with the limits of perception points to an issue of increasing epistemological concern in her work: that every subject's faculties illuminate but a sliver of the world, leaving vast swaths of the universe dark and unfelt.

What would it feel like to see outside one's own subjectivity or, yet further, to step outside the human altogether and look on the world with a nonhuman range of faculties? "[I]t would be like hearing the grass grow and the squirrel's heart beat, and we should die of that roar which lies on the other side of silence" (182). To have "a keen vision and feeling of all ordinary human life," the narrator of *Middlemarch* implies in this oft-cited passage, would be to sense what a human being cannot sense, to feel more than the human body allows one to feel (34).[1] This chapter proceeds from

---

1. This trope first appears in Eliot's novella *The Lifted Veil* (1859), in which her protagonist's ability to "participat[e] in other people's consciousnesses" is compared to his

a literal interpretation of this fantastical line, tracking Eliot's interest in realism as a path to enhanced sensation.[2] From her early description of art in "The Natural History of German Life" (1856) as "a mode of amplifying experience" to her investigation of the emergent quality of character in *Middlemarch*, Eliot's career is marked by a concern with understanding how language impresses itself upon subjects to generate feeling (110). This concern would culminate in her last published work, *Impressions of Theophrastus Such* (1879), a text much neglected in Eliot scholarship.[3]

Although often dismissed as inaccessible and overly allusive, Eliot's collection of fictional character sketches and essays provides important insights into her concern with the limits of human subjectivity, as well as the relation of this problematic to her realist aesthetic. A theory of realism as much as it is an instantiation of it, *Impressions* explores an activity foundational to Eliot's practice as a fiction writer: how sense impressions that originate in our experience of the physical world might be both reproduced and heightened through literature. Impressions are physical marks, inscriptions that signify meaning to those who encounter them, catapulting persons and things into sign systems that are used to interpret their bodies and histories. In ancient Greek, *kharaktēr* (χαρακτήρ) referred to both the tool for writing as well as the impression made in wax writing tablets.[4] Likewise, not only is character *produced* through impressions, character also *produces* impressions, leaving its mark on those subjects who observe and interpret its markings. Eliot's 1870s fiction explores this dual meaning of impressibility: whereas *Middlemarch*, as we saw in the previous chapter, emphasizes the capacity of people to be impressed by others through interactions that fundamentally transform their characters, *Impressions* develops a theory of knowledge (and, as such, reading and writing) as sensitive encounter.

Character's special intimacy with language was perhaps one reason why Victorian scientists of character believed fiction to be a privileged

---

having "a preternaturally heightened sense of hearing, making audible to one a roar of sound where others find perfect stillness" (15, 18). For a powerful reading of this passage attentive to Eliot's curiosity about sensory expansion, see Hertz 39–41.

2. Here, I follow the lead of Dames, Ablow, and Coombs, each of whom explore how Victorians conceived the effect of reading on the sensorium.

3. Despite Henry's groundbreaking edition from 1994, *Impressions* has attracted little scholarly attention. Given the book's robust engagement with Victorian natural-historical, biological, and psychological discourse, it is especially disappointing to discover its absence from book-length studies of Eliot and science (e.g., Shuttleworth; M. Davis, *George*).

4. For an excellent discussion of the relationship between semiosis and materiality in antiquity with respect to the question of impressions, see Bianchi (90–91).

site for its study. The same year that *Impressions* was published, the mathematician and philosopher William Kingdon Clifford suggested that, in attending closely to the influence of circumstances on character, the novel revealed something about the nature of character itself—its fundamental impressibility:

> Is it not regarded as the greatest stroke of the novelist that he should be able not merely to draw a character at any given time, but also sketch the growth of it through the changing circumstances of life? In fact, if you consider a little further, you will see that it is not even true that a character remains the same for a single day: every circumstance, however trivial, that in any way affects the mind, leaves its mark, infinitely small it may be.... And the sum of all these marks is precisely what we call character, which is therefore continually being added to, continually growing, continually in a state of change. (205)

Clifford's 1879 remarks affirm this book's most basic argument: that in the late Victorian period, scientists and writers alike understood fiction not only as modeling but also as revealing something true about how character operates in reality. In highlighting the semantic connection between "character" and "mark," Clifford gestures toward a possible reason why. If human character is to some extent a semiotic system—a set of physical "marks" interpretable by "readers"—then its literary analog, *that other character*, might actually be the ideal figure for its investigation.

I noted in chapter 1 that Eliot has long been read in support of the claim that literature inspires moral action by portraying characters as "containing a rich inner life," the hidden contents of which are essential to "defining a creature as fully human" (Nussbaum, *Cultivating* 90). While I acknowledge Eliot's concern with the value and agency of human beings, my reading of her late-career sketches in this chapter builds upon the last to push against the humanist interpretation of Eliot in two ways. First, I suggest that her late-career turn to the descriptive tradition of the character sketch asserts a critical distance from what Heather Love has called "the traditional humanist categories of experience, consciousness, and motivation" that ground the modern notion of character ("Close" 375). If we can distill a literary ethics in Eliot's final work, I argue, it is an ethics, to cite Love's distinction, "grounded in documentation and description, rather than empathy and witness" (375). As we will see, Eliot's naturalistic investment in describing people in terms of the characterological traits they share not only with other members of their species but also with nonhuman animals calls into question the human exceptionalism of certain modes of novelistic characterization.

Rather than crafting characters as uniquely psychological beings, Eliot's sketches put them on the same plane as other creatures; like fish, sea lions, or even microscopic *Vorticellae*, human beings are conditioned by bodily frameworks and habitual responses that allow them to sense and experience some things and not others. In so doing, she continues to both represent and theorize what, drawing on Schopenhauer, I have termed *human objecthood*—physical aspects of existence that humans have in common with nonhuman animals and things. As I elaborate in chapter 4, Schopenhauer understood character as the "objectification" of Will, a dynamic but nonintentional force thought to motivate not only human agency but also earthly movement and change. In its "objectified" form (i.e., perceived from the outside, in another's body), the Will manifests itself as character—a nexus of traits, behaviors, and qualities that lends a person or thing its characteristic quality. Likewise, in *Impressions*, persons are not presented as uniquely conscious or intentional subjects but rather as dynamic material formations with "objective" qualities similar to those of nonhuman organisms, such as touchwood or *Vorticella*—the namesakes of characters I unpack as this chapter unfolds.

Second, by taking inspiration from Love's postulate that literature accounts for the variation and complexity of life, as well as for its richness and depth, I highlight Eliot's interest in literature not as a medium for intersubjective understanding but as an amplificatory technology, a tool for the sensation of multifarious realities. "How many conceptions & fashions of life have existed to which our understanding & sympathy have no clue!" Eliot writes in a notebook dated from the 1870s (quoted in Collins, "Questions" 390).[5] Her task in *Impressions* is not to penetrate the depths of the human psyche but rather to sketch a vast characterological landscape, to put humanity into perspective by zooming out until the human being appears as a mere speck in an array of sensitive life forms. Situating Eliot's 1879 sketches and essays in a longer history of the character sketch, a history beginning with the ancient Greek naturalist and sketch writer Theophrastus of Eresus, I show how the observation-based methodology Eliot develops in her mature work draws on her longtime interest in the practice of natural history.[6] In aligning *Impressions* with the descriptive traditions of natural history and the character sketch, I argue, Eliot puts pressure on

---

5. In this late notebook, Eliot calls for further exploration of the nonhuman and nonlinguistic worlds: "we are the better off for knowing better the nature of fishes & storms & acting according to that knowledge" (quoted in Collins, "Questions," 392).

6. On the nineteenth-century sketch genre, see Sha; Garcha; Hamilton; and Lauster. On the relationship between the nineteenth-century sketch form and natural history, see King, *Divine*, chap. 1.

the modern association of character with individual human psychology. She does so by retaining the interest in these traditions with the notion of the "type," a theoretical abstraction based in empirical observation.

Theophrastus Who?

Impressions of Theophrastus Such chronicles the attempts of a curmudgeonly London bachelor named Theophrastus to catalog and describe members of the human genus in order to better understand the species to which he belongs. Eliot's Theophrastus calls his project "the natural history of my inward self," a phrase that brings into strange harmony the expansive, outward-oriented practice of natural-historical description and the inward-oriented quest for self-knowledge that is characteristic of novelistic narrative (104). The path to knowledge, however, at least for this character-narrator, is not inward to the self but rather outward; it entails describing the members of one's own species to discern "the figure the human genus makes in the specimen which I myself furnish" (104). Amassing descriptions of various unperceptive and unsympathetic human beings, many of whom are writers like him, Theophrastus tries to illuminate that which escapes his subjective awareness: the general form of the species of which he is but one instance. Through his sketches we meet characters such as Touchwood, whose touchy temper repeatedly interrupts his quest for knowledge (56–62); Merman, a comparative historian who drives his career into the ground by forgoing historical accuracy to maintain his pride (28–40); and Spike, a "political molecule" who, having none of his own opinions, votes always unwaveringly for "Progress" (63–66). Attentive to the prominent and distinctive qualities of people, Theophrastus's character descriptions echo those of the historical Theophrastus, the ancient Greek naturalist and writer whose *Characters* (c. 322–317 BCE) is considered the first attempt at systematic character description.[7] Like the sketches of this other Theophrastus (which I will return to), Eliot's sketches try to record aspects of human character that impress themselves upon the senses. These sketches thus inhabit the latter side of a distinction Eliot once made between "'psychological' novels (very excellent things in their way)" and works that provide "genuine description of external nature… flowing from spontaneous observation" ("Rev. of 'Westward Ho!'" 288).

---

7. Eliot had considered titling her book *Characters and Characteristics: Impressions of Theophrastus Such*, a more direct reference to the ancient text (Henry, "Introduction" xxxvin11). At the time *Impressions* was composed, the most recent English translation of *Characters* was that of Richard Jebb (1870), whom Eliot met had five years before she began working on *Impressions* (Millett 122n3).

In presenting character as something empirically observable, *Impressions* risks the biological essentialism of Victorian pseudosciences that sought to correlate physical traits with moral or psychological ones. Physiognomy and phrenology, for instance, like other nineteenth-century epistemologies that linked the visible and the invisible, imagined that one could read surfaces for their deep, characterological meaning. Unlike such discourses of character, however, *Impressions* stays on the surface of the body, implying that the feel of a person's character is significant and deserves to be examined. In the first chapter of the book, Theophrastus makes clear his disdain for physiognomic logic. Although he believes that "direct perceptive judgment is not to be argued against," he critiques the tendency of observers to draw correlations between a person's "physical points" and "mental" ones: "With all the increasing uncertainty which modern progress has thrown over the relations of mind and body, it seems tolerably clear that wit cannot be seated in the upper lip, and that the balance of the haunches in walking has nothing to do with the subtle discrimination of ideas" (7). As a rule, Eliot's fiction warns against forms of knowledge that situate a "key to all mythologies" in symbolic systems of the visible and invisible.[8] Instead of seeing character as a hidden signified of which "physical points" are apparent signifiers, Eliot indicates that character is a material-semiotic system in which meaning is not transcendent, but immanent to the body.

As we saw in chapter 1, for Eliot, character inheres in the body; and like the body, it "is a process and an unfolding" (140). In *Impressions*, too, character sticks in the living body and its interactions, not in its intentions. It inheres in the subject's position in space and time, in the fact that one has an embodied perspective and cannot but look out of it. Character is neither voluntary nor essential; rather, it unfolds according to the same logic and temporality afforded to bodies.

How, then, does one describe a human being, as a novelist must—through language? Eliot's philosophical reflections on the representational challenge of literary characterization in her last published work of fiction would seem to answer a question posed in the novel published just prior to *Impressions*, *Daniel Deronda*. Beginning to describe the character Henleigh Grandcourt, the narrator of *Deronda* remarks: "Attempts

---

8. In *Middlemarch*, the "Key to All Mythologies" is Casaubon's unfinished magnum opus. Logan has shown how Eliot's fiction responds to new scientific models of the body as decentralized, arguing that "whereas in the early part of the century observers face the problem of misconstruing the body's truthful signs or of being misled by deliberately false signs, in the new body they face the problem of signs that, although they have meaning, are inherently ambiguous" (*Nerves* 169).

at description are stupid, for who can all at once describe a human being? Even when he is presented to us we only begin that knowledge of his appearance which must be completed by innumerable impressions under differing circumstances. We recognize the alphabet; we are not sure of the language" (160). "Attempts at description are stupid," it is implied here, not only because character itself is constantly changing, but because circumstances in which we encounter character are changing too, making it difficult to get at the truth of the thing. What's more, if human character is written in a "language," this language is not a sign system that can be decoded easily.

In *Reading with the Senses*, David Coombs (53-59) interprets this passage with reference to the epistemological distinction formulated by G. H. Lewes between "the Logic of Feeling" and "the Logic of Signs" in his work *Problems of Life and Mind* (1874-79). According to Lewes, the Logic of Feeling is what governs a subject's direct experience of a thing; it concerns the faculties of sensation, perception, appetite, and emotion, and is a logic possessed both by humans and nonhuman animals. The Logic of Signs, by contrast, is particular to humans; it concerns the operations of the intellect, conscience, and will; and it allows subjects to produce indirect knowledge of things using concepts and language (*Problems* 3.2:227).[9] In Coombs's interpretation, Eliot's narrator invokes Lewes's distinction in order to explore to what extent "reading a novel's descriptions of the world differs from experiencing the world firsthand" (Coombs 38). For what concerns character at least, this passage implies, this is no small difference. Much is lost, the narrator suggests, in the attempt to translate *sensory* impressions into *linguistic* impressions. This is because, one might venture, in reality character unfolds according to the Logic of Feeling, a material-semiotic language whose alphabet we can recognize but which is not easily translatable into the Logic of Signs in which fiction is written. Under this rubric, curiously, human language would seem to be an obstacle to, rather than a facilitator of, knowledge of character: "Attempts at description are stupid." And yet, this is precisely the task of the realist novelist: to mediate between these two Logics, one (non)human, and one all too human.

Throughout *Impressions*, Theophrastus's attempts to describe the character of others underline the ontological impossibility of shedding his all-too-human perspective. In the book's first chapter, "Looking Inward," Theophrastus expresses a frustrated desire to overcome his humanity—a desire akin to the wish to have one's "squint or other ocular defect" cor-

---

9. Thompson has stressed the interdependence of these forms of knowledge in Lewes, explaining that for Lewes, "Feeling and thought are two renderings of the same process (like the concave and convex aspects of a lens)" (131).

rected with spectacles (9). Lamenting the impossibility of remedying his "inward squint," he continues: "Perhaps I have made self-betrayals enough already to show that I have not arrived at that non-human independence. My conversational reticences about myself turn into garrulousness on paper—as the sea-lion plunges and swims the more energetically because his limbs are of a sort to make him shambling on land" (12). Here, we find another metaphor of sensory failure similar to that with which I began and another suggestion that the self somehow "blots out" the world as a result of an egoism figured as a defect of vision.

Literary scholars have tended to read Eliot's fascination with perceptive limits in terms of what the historians of science Lorraine Daston and Peter Galison have called the "moralization of objectivity" of the late nineteenth century (*Objectivity* 81): the tendency of nineteenth-century scientists to equate objectivity with ideals of self-abnegation or self-restraint.[10] To read Eliot's concern about the failures of human perception under this modern epistemological rubric, however, risks reducing her affective vision to one in which the central problem is human access to a nonhuman natural world. On the contrary, *Impressions*—in part by invoking ancient Greek knowledge systems—contravenes the anthropocentrism of modern epistemology and its focus on the singularity of the human knower. While I agree with George Levine that for Eliot, "personality is an obstruction to perception," I want to stress first that the character of both human and nonhuman beings provides such obstacles, and second, that the overcoming of such obstructions through the achievement of a godlike omniscience is not presented as the goal of realism in *Impressions* ("George" 1). In *Impressions*, character is framed broadly and philosophically as that which gives rise to the conditions of perception by delimiting what can be sensed and how it is sensed. It is an ontological problem that gives rise to epistemological problems. The solution to these problems, however, is neither the repression nor the elimination of the basis for sensation: the body.

In a notebook passage thought to have been composed around 1874, Eliot turns to a German proverb to underline the material finitude of every being: "'Es ist dafür gesorgt [sic] dass die Bäume nicht in den Himmel wachsen,'" she writes, adding, "in other words, everything on this Earth has its limits which may not be overpassed" (quoted in Collins, "Questions" 387). I translate this quotation, the epigraph to part 3 of Goethe's *Autobiography*, as "it has been arranged that trees do not grow into the sky." While many of her contemporaries might have placed humankind in the sky in this schema, thereby contrasting the infinite potential of humanity to the limited nature of nonhuman life, Eliot extends this proverb to cap-

---

10. See, for example, Levine, *Dying* 171–99; Garratt 27–37.

ture the limits of the human as well, arguing that "a being like man, having a certain shape, certain modes of movement, certain forms of movement sense, & certain unchangeable wants must continue to be determined & limited by these in all his invention" (quoted in Collins, "Questions" 387–88). In Eliot's *scala naturae*, human beings are no more exempt from limits imposed by nature than is any other creature. They have great potential, yes, but they have bodies, forms, sense capacities, and modes of desiring and moving. They have, like any other physical thing, character.

Aligning human observers with nonhuman observers and actors, *Impressions* treats the problem of character as a (species-specific) universal. Theophrastus's observations result in what might be read as a more basic and open-ended claim that all sensitive bodies, by virtue of "seeing," are also "blind" to many things. Recall here the passage from *Middlemarch* with which I began, in which there is said to be "no speck so troublesome as self." Consider also the previously cited passage in which Theophrastus describes the correction of his "inward squint" as the achievement of a certain "non-human independence" (12). Significantly, Theophrastus express a desire to experience the world not from an objective, bodiless god's-eye view but rather from a "non-human" perspective. As Theophrastus reminds us, the body of the sea lion, while perfect for swimming, renders him "shambling on land" (12). The materiality of the sea lion's body limits his ambulatory capacity. Similarly, Theophrastus cannot overcome the limits of his sign-centered humanity and the gaps in (self-)perception that frustrate his writerly existence. And like the sea lion whose frustration on land inspires him to swim with vigor, Theophrastus puts pen vigorously to paper, hoping to find nonhuman extension through the affective medium of the text.

Theophrastus's desire to transcend his all-too-human perspective prompts a consideration of his descriptive project in terms of the desire to achieve narratorial omniscience. In an illuminating comparison of Theophrastus to the narrator of Eliot's novella *The Lifted Veil* (whose heightened sense capacities are less a boon than a stumbling block), Rae Greiner has observed that "Theophrastus isn't omniscient, but he is too knowing for his own good" (129). At the same time, she notes, "his status *as* a character is continually scrutinized, as he seems a being unlike the rest" (129). Following Greiner, who sees Theophrastus as straddling the character-narrator binary, I read *Impressions* as insisting on the limits of the epistemological reach of the realist narrator, who is revealed to be as much a "character" as the fictional people he describes. In an analysis of Eliot's narrative techniques across her literary corpus, Cristina Griffin has suggested that Eliot's narrators "do not solely peer into the worlds they narrate or directly address the reader from a disembodied vantage point…

but rather metaleptically materialize alongside... their fellow characters" (Griffin 475-76).[11] Especially in moments of "rhetorical intrusion," Griffin writes, "her omniscient narrators assume the same level of corporeality that they attribute to their characters" (475-76).

Impressions pushes this narratorial materialization to a new extreme. Not only is Theophrastus characterized as much as the characters he characterizes, but also his perceptive powers are presented as being equally limited as those people and animals he perceives. As such, the work opens up the possibility of reassessing the project of realism as practiced by Eliot, specifically for what concerns the role of the realist narrator.

Nineteenth-century realism, Jonathan Crary observes, has long been understood as "part of the continuous unfolding of a Renaissance-based mode of vision," centered on "a self-present beholder to whom a world is transparently evident" (4, 6). In scholarship on Victorian fiction, the locus of this transparent mode of vision is often said to be the third-person narrator, whose disembodied viewpoint perpetuates ideologies of objectivity, interiority, and privacy. In *The Novel and the Police*, to cite one influential example, D. A. Miller argues that the Victorian novel interpolates its readers as autonomous, interiorized subjects by instituting an ontological distinction between its (overly embodied) characters and its (disembodied) narrator, the latter "so shadowy and indeterminate a figure that it scarcely seems right to call him a person at all" (209). By insisting on its narrator's status as both an *object* and a subject of knowledge, however, *Impressions* troubles the "rigid opposition" between "subject and object or narrator and character" that Miller believes structures nineteenth-century fiction, including the character sketch genre (211).[12] According to Miller, "the most fundamental value" of the Victorian novel and sketch forms "is privacy, the determination of an integral, autonomous 'secret' self" (162). But the "secrets" possessed by Eliot's character-narrator are no more hidden from others than they are from himself: "while there are secrets in me unguessed by others," Theophrastus writes, "others have certain items of knowledge about the extent of my powers and the figure I make with them, which in turn are secrets unguessed by me" (*Impressions* 4). In insisting

---

11. Along similar lines, Star proposes that Eliot's novels "redefine realism" by "locating her characters' access to reality in moments that specifically defy a totalizing vision" (840).

12. Taking Dickens's *Sketches by Boz* (1833-36) as his case study, Miller argues that the character sketch genre functions as a testing ground for the production of narratorial omniscience by rehearsing the narrator-character distinction that structures the novel genre. On the omniscient narrator's "refusal of character" and the subject-object distinction in Dickens's fiction, see also Jaffe, *Vanishing* (13).

that the perceptions others have of us are often more accurate than those we have of ourselves, *Impressions* asks what is to be gained by turning the microscope on that creature who believes himself the world's great observer—to shift our attention from human subjecthood to human objecthood. To have "a keen vision and feeling of all ordinary human life," Eliot suggests, thus entails treating the human being not as a *subject* to which the author—or narrator—has special access but as a new kind of sensible *object*, a dense and complex material body like any other. And she turns to the science of natural history to issue this challenge.

Descriptive Minutiae

That Eliot names her protagonist after the ancient Greek naturalist Theophrastus of Eresus (c. 371-287 BCE) situates *Impressions* in a lineage of natural-historical practice that begins in the fourth century BCE. Her explicit and implicit references to processes of species identification tie the text to the long history of biological classification and taxonomic ranking that has allowed scientists to understand the phylogenetic interrelation of life forms. Around 335 BCE, Theophrastus had helped Aristotle, his teacher and friend, found the Peripatetic school in Athens's Lyceum—the school that instigated the shift in Greek philosophy away from Plato's theory of forms and toward a mode that more highly valued sense experience as a foundation of knowledge. Sensation and affect played crucial roles in Theophrastus's philosophy, as can be seen most clearly in his treatise *On Sensation* (Baltussen 71-94). In his best-known work, *Characters*, he applies the Peripatetic methodology to the study of human behavior, producing the first systematic attempt at character description.

Theophrastus also wrote treatises on the nature of stones as well as on ethics, and he is said to have inaugurated the field of botany in the West with his many detailed studies of plants (Sharples 126-27). Like his colleague Aristotle, whom he succeeded as head of the Peripatetic school, he composed an array of philosophical and naturalistic studies based on careful observations of the natural world. The two friends' approaches to the organization of this world differed, however. Whereas in Aristotle's ordered universe, the base and the monstrous are deviations from ideals, in Theophrastus's *Metaphysics*, baseness and monstrosity are the rule, and harmony and beauty the exceptions. Likewise, *Characters* focuses on ignorance and other negative aspects of human life, describing such types as the thankless man, the coward, and the bore. In Theophrastus's philosophy, this relegation of the noble and the ignoble to the same ontological plane comprehends the relation of the human to the nonhuman. Instead of according the human a special or high place in the natural order, he grants people, rocks, and trees the same ontological status.[13]

Eliot's Theophrastus is also interested in exploring lateral rather than hierarchical relations between forms of life. Characters crystallize in descriptions, thick with zoological reference, that draw parallels between human and nonhuman behavior. The character Merman, a scholar who reacts aggressively when his arguments are challenged, is said to resemble a walrus, which, "though not in the least a malignant animal, if allowed to display its remarkably plain person and blundering performances at ease in any element it chooses, becomes desperately savage and musters alarming auxiliaries when attacked or hurt" (34). The name of another character, Vorticella, a writer, recalls the parasitic single-celled organisms *Vorticellae*, which encase themselves in a cystic covering for reproduction. Dismissing all criticism of her writings, Vorticella allows vanity to overtake her like a "polypus, tumour, fungus, or other erratic outgrowth, noxious and disfiguring in its effect on the individual organism that nourishes it" (126). Consumed by the success of her only book, Vorticella brings it up at every possible moment, driving away her company, to live the life of solitude to which her name seems to have destined her. In an article on the zoophyte in Victorian natural history, Danielle Coriale has suggested that the polyp "resisted, repulsed, or confused sympathetic attachment, human identification, and intelligibility in the Victorian imagination" (19). Consistent with this view, Eliot uses the *vorticella* to portray an unsympathetic, gothic character, self-absorbed and self-enveloping.

Readers of *Middlemarch* will remember that the *vorticella* is a favorite figure for Eliot. It crops up in the novel in a parable that, like the sketch form, grants priority to the minutiae of everyday experience over the drama of narrative action. In *Middlemarch*, Eliot attends to the characteristic of the *vorticella* from which its name derives: the vortex formed in its mouth through the simultaneous beating of the small hairs, called *cilia*, that surround the oral cavity:

> Even with a microscope directed on a water-drop we find ourselves making interpretations which turn out to be rather coarse; for whereas under a weak lens you may seem to see a creature exhibiting an active voracity into which other smaller creatures actively play as if they were so many animated tax-pennies, a stronger lens reveals to you certain tiniest hairlets which make vortices for these victims while the swallower waits passively at his receipt of custom. (55)

13. On the decentered position of the human in Theophrastus's philosophy, see Hughes; Cole.

This parable serves to explain the actions of Mrs. Cadwallader, whose attempts at matchmaking, the narrator implies, might at first appear like the workings of some masterly and premeditated plot. On closer inspection, however, one finds that her actions stem not from "any ingenious plot, any hide-and-seek course of action," but rather from "a play of minute causes producing what may be called thought and speech vortices to bring her the sort of food she needed" (55).

Scholars have typically understood this passage to comment on the interpretive nature of knowledge. But it does something else too: it places human and nonhuman organisms on the same plane as a strategy to describe human behavior as no more rational or intentional than that of other organisms. What might appear to be the willing actions of a subject are shown to be the passive compulsions of a hungry animal. "Thought and speech"—ostensibly characteristic of human behavior—are reduced to a "play of minute causes," like those that allow the lowly *vorticella* to eat. Eliot's language in this *Middlemarch* passage echoes that of Lewes, whose discussion of the *vorticella* in his *Studies in Animal Life* (1860) begins with a call for a more sustained study of life's "minuter or obscurer forms" (3).[14] *Impressions* puts what Lewes called the "Philosophy of the infinitely little" into literary practice, looking to the sketch form in order to render visible the microscopic (*Animal Life* 1). If plot, as Eliot suggests in *Middlemarch*, is the "telescopic watch" that fails to register the subtle motivations of folks like Mrs. Cadwallader, description is the microscope (55).

In *The Antinomies of Realism*, Fredric Jameson argues that realism emerges from a dialectical tension between "pure storytelling," on the one hand, and the "impulses of scenic elaboration, description, and above all affective investment," on the other (11). Prioritizing the latter of Jameson's two antinomies, *Impressions* grounds realism in the affectively charged, descriptive practice that grounds the character sketch genre. Amanpal Garcha has shown how Eliot and other Victorian authors incorporated elements of their early-career sketches into the fabric of their novels in the form of "descriptive, imagistic writing" that bleeds into "philosophical meditation" (229). Eliot began her literary career with the sketch form in *Scenes of Clerical Life* (1857, 1858), each "scene" of which centers on a single character.[15] In returning to the sketch form at the end of her literary career, Eliot can be seen to reflect upon and to theorize the practice of

---

14. *Vorticellae* also appear in Lewes's *Sea-side Studies* (56) as well as in his essay "Only a Pond!" (597)—as Henry, "George Eliot" (47–51), and Wormald (501, 516–17) discuss in greater detail.

15. The three tales included in *Scenes of Clerical Life* are "The Sad Fortunes of the Rev. Amos Barton," "Mr. Gilfil's Love Story," and "Janet's Repentance."

character description foundational not only to her fiction but to realism more broadly. "I always thought I was deficient in dramatic power, both of construction and dialogue, but I felt that I should be at my ease in the descriptive parts of a novel," Eliot wrote in 1857 in a diary entry entitled "How I Came to Write Fiction" (*Journals* 289). In *Impressions*, such "descriptive parts" take center stage, as she turns away from narrative to embrace what Garcha calls the "discursive plotlessness" of the sketch form (Garcha 225).[16]

To Sketch a Species

While Eliot is hard to type, she would not be alone in turning to the character sketch at the end of the nineteenth century. In the decade following the publication of *Impressions*, this "old" mode of character depiction would return to trouble the transition from plot-driven narrative to the experiments with perspective and sense perception undertaken in aestheticism. In works such as Vernon Lee's *Baldwin: Being Dialogues on Views and Aspirations* (1886) and Walter Pater's *Imaginary Portraits* (1887), aestheticist writers subordinated plot to lengthy, impressionistic descriptions of the effect of the physical world on the body.[17] In tension with individualized and psychologized notions of character also developing at this time, the turn-of-the-century character sketch located character on the surfaces of bodies, clothes, and other observable things.

The late Victorian character sketch tends to focus on the material effect of character on the writing process itself, drawing attention not only to the objecthood of the narrator but to the objecthood of the author of the literary work. In *Human Documents: Character-Sketches of Representative Men*

---

16. One of Eliot's most iconic philosophical musings occurs in the seventh chapter of *Adam Bede*, entitled "In Which the Story Pauses a Little." This passage also consists in an extended reflection on the practice of characterization. Often read as a manifesto for realism, the passage calls for more "squat figures, ill-shapen nostrils, and dingy complexions" in fiction, invoking the tradition of Dutch painting as exemplary in its representation of everyday people (195). On the descriptive impulse of seventeenth-century Dutch art, see Svetlana Alpers, who argues that within this painterly tradition "attention to the surface of the world described is achieved at the expense of the representation of narrative action" (xxi).

17. Pater's conclusion to *Studies in the History of the Renaissance* (1873) is an important touchstone here, tied to, as his notion of "impressions" is, the "weaving and unweaving of ourselves" (119). As Morgan points out, although "Pater and Eliot are often conceived as espousing antithetical models of subjectivity... [,] Pater's vision of a social world that includes physical matter is better understood as a transposition of Eliot's networks and webs" (170).

and Women of the Time (1895), Arthur Alfred Lynch proposes that "man's intellectual work is determined in great measure by his physical constitution and his emotional quality," giving examples such as "Byron's lame foot" and "Carlyle's dyspepsia" (v). Such writers would follow *Impressions* in situating character squarely in the body, a move that—like Eliot's own "dyspeptic" narrator's attempt to write the "natural history" of his "inward self"—works through the fraught relation between materiality and writing (89).

By the time Eliot turned to the descriptive genre of the character sketch at the end of the nineteenth century, the heyday of the Theophrastan sketch had long since passed. The ancient Theophrastus's *Characters* had been made famous by a 1592 Latin translation by Isaac Casaubon—a name familiar to Eliot readers, to be sure—which inspired a surge of imitations throughout the seventeenth century.[18] Undoubtedly, the most popular was Jean de La Bruyère's *Les Caractères de Théophraste traduits du grec avec Les Caractères ou les moeurs de ce siècle* (1688), which went through eight editions in six years and to which *Impressions* directly refers.[19]

Scholars of the novel have long suggested that the character sketch's "flat" portraits of ethical and social types were replaced by the "round," individualized characters of the novel.[20] In *The Economy of Character* (1998), however, Deidre Lynch reframes this history, directing our attention to a different set of terms. In Lynch's history, as character stretched further across the axis of plot, it cleaved from the surface and materiality of the body, becoming an "inner" as opposed to an "outer" quality. It was not until the late eighteenth century, she contends, that the expanded market for printed matter facilitated new strategies for distinguishing public from private personas, and character came to be understood as something deep and hidden. According to Lynch, the novel was "founded on the promise that it was this type of writing that tendered the deepest, truest knowledge of character" (28). But the production of characters with

18. According to Haight, Eliot was familiar with Isaac Casaubon and "knew his fine edition of Theophrastus's *Caractères*" (448). In *Middlemarch*, when Casaubon becomes ill, the town doctor prescribes him with two novels with clear connections to the Theophrastan tradition by the eighteenth-century writer Tobias Smollett: *The Adventures of Roderick Random* (1748) and *The Expedition of Humphry Clinker* (1771) (269).

19. La Bruyère's text was first translated into English in 1698 under the title *The Characters or the Manner of the Age*. Shaftesbury's *Characteristics of Men, Manners, Opinions, Times* (1711) is also an important referent here.

20. According to Forster, "round" characters are three-dimensional, develop and change, and are original and individual, while "flat" characters are two-dimensional, remain the same, and are mere types (67). I discuss Forster's distinction at greater length in the coda to this book.

private interiors was not always the aim of fiction, nor would it necessarily continue to be, even in the hands of novelists like Eliot.

Impressions marks a unique moment in character's historical dialogue with depth and surfaces. Here, in 1879, character seems almost anachronistically apparent; rather than a hidden or buried kernel of personality or moral fiber, it is a surface phenomenon produced through a dialogue between outward observations and inward beliefs. The *Impressions* chapter "So Young!" highlights the role that circumstances have in the production of a character named Ganymede, an aging dandy who continues to believe himself "girlishly handsome," despite having grown older and less attractive (101).[21] Ganymede's self-delusion occurs when "outward confirmations" of his youth uttered during his boyhood come to form the basis of his "habitual inward persuasion" (103). And yet, while these outer forces are indeed internalized, Ganymede is more than the passive product of his circumstances; rather, his character is generated through a dialectic between inside and outside that compounds to ensure the stability of his self-image: "Being strongly mirrored for himself in the remark of others," Theophrastus explains, "[Ganymede] was getting to see his real characteristics as a dramatic part, a type to which his doings were always in correspondence" (100).

Notice that, instead of typing Ganymede by interpreting his behaviors as a sign of some unchanging characterological essence, Theophrastus suggests that he performs his identity *in reference to* a type. Ganymede, importantly, is not an invert—he just believes it a "disturbing inversion of the natural order that any one very near to him should have been younger than he" (103).[22] And yet, while Eliot does not suggest that types are prefigured or inherent, the concept of the type plays an important role in *Impressions*. While interested in descriptive detail, the text calls for a typological systematicity in the description of character, complicating the suggestion of some scholars that her realism eschews typological thinking for a particularism in which every character appears individual and unique.[23] In its investment in the natural-historical notion of the type, *Impressions* recalls the aims of eighteenth-century sketch writers, who "described not men, but manners, not an individual but a species" (Fielding 189), more than those of nineteenth-century authors, many of whom saw themselves as

---

21. In Greek mythology, Ganymede is the most beautiful of mortals. He is abducted and granted eternal youth by Zeus.

22. It is uncertain whether the word *inversion* would have carried any queer connotation in 1879. The German sexological term *konträre Sexualempfindung* (from which the English word *inversion* is derived) had been in parlance since 1870.

23. This is implied, for instance, by Armstrong (127–28), and J. H. Miller (*Form* 84).

producing "original, discriminated, and individual person[s]" (Scott 514). Indeed, the book's title, *Impressions of Theophrastus Such*, puts it in conversation with this older, typological model of characterization by echoing the original Theophrastus's ancient sketches, each of which begins with the formula "Such a type who…" (Henry, "Introduction" xviii).[24]

In the previous chapter, we saw how, *pace* Gallagher, *Middlemarch*'s characters are indeed not always "category defiers," instantiations of types that nonetheless always deviate from the type they are supposed to exemplify ("George" 64). As I argued there, Eliot's 1871-72 novel negotiates between the particular and the general to develop a theory of how character, as the impersonal material substrate of subjectivity, develops in relation to its milieu. In dialogue with the contemporary philosopher of science Isabelle Stengers, I presented this practice as an instance of *mesoanalysis*, a literary-descriptive mode that proceeds *par le milieu* (meaning "through the middle" or "through the environment") to investigate how character emerges through physical interactions. In *Impressions*, the meso looks slightly different, elaborated as it is through the intermediary category of the type. I say that the type is intermediary because when we speak of a "type," we usually speak of a type *of* something (in this case, a type of *person*). The type is neither too specific nor too general; rather, it is a kind of middle ground, a category to which some but not all belong. Not only is type that which intercedes between the very particular to the very general, types also link the part to the whole—not in the sense that everyone who belongs to a given type is exactly the same as every other person of that type, but in the sense that one *shares qualities with those of one's type* (and, indeed, that one can grow to share qualities with them, especially when one inhabits the same milieu).

Presenting her characters as instances of types of people that are recognizable to readers through extreme or excessive behaviors that define those types (e.g., "A Too Deferential Man," "The Too Ready Writer"), in *Impressions*, Eliot navigates the tension between the specific and the general, the individual and the group, in order to theorize the specifying and pluralizing role of "circumstance" in character formation. One of the philosophical questions that *Impressions* sets out to answer is to what extent a given quality or behavior is "accidental" to a person (a philosophical concept that can be traced back to Aristotle). Each sketch in *Characters* begins with a description of an abstract characterological quality (complaisance, arrogance, superstition, irony) and then moves on to describe a particular man exemplifying that quality. Likewise, Eliot's sketches often start with a

---

24. Fortenbaugh translates the original Greek "Toioutos tis, hoios" to "someone such as to…" (17).

meditation on a generally observable behavior, situation, or emotion, and after a paragraph or so, turn then to a human instantiation of the phenomenon she is describing. Exploring the specifying, pluralizing "such" of the ancient Theophrastus's refrain "Such a type who...," Eliot's sketches investigate the mesological link between a specific person's actions and the "type" of person who performs those actions.

The sketch of Touchwood, an incendiary type whose name refers to wood that easily catches fire, begins with the question "What is temper?" (56). This sketch, however, quickly moves to consider the role temper plays in our understanding of character itself (something the historical Theophrastus's sketches do *not* do). Why is temper thought to be accidental to a person's character while other characteristics are thought to be essential parts of personality? Too often, Eliot's narrator remarks,

> we hear a man declared to have a bad temper and yet glorified as the possessor of every high quality. When he errs or in any way commits himself, his temper is accused, not his character.... If he kicks small animals, swears violently at a servant who mistakes orders, or is grossly rude to his wife, it is remarked apologetically that these things mean nothing—they are all temper. (56)

In questioning the distinction between acts and identity, Theophrastus thus can be seen to preempt the critique of "the dualism of Character and Circumstance" that the ethologist A. F. Shand leveled against contemporary thinking about character ("Character" 210). As we saw in the introduction to this book, Shand advocated against regarding circumstances "as something external to Character and acting upon it from the outside," calling for the formation of an ethology that would follow novelists in emphasizing the "dynamical" relation between character and milieu (210).

In his 1914 study *The Foundations of Character*, Shand proposed that character had its basis in complex systems of sentiments that form over time, crystallizing into behavioral tendencies. And he turned to literature as a model for understanding these affective systems. We do not know which specific works Shand had in mind when he argued that the scientist, like the novelist, should "conceive of the problem as essentially dynamical" (1). In its suggestion that character dynamically forms in relation to circumstances, as well as its attention to the affective basis of character, Eliot's *Impressions* would seem like a good candidate. Indeed, as we will see in the next section, Eliot's fiction directly informed the theory of character formulated by another of England's foremost scientists of character, the physiological psychologist and aesthetic theorist James Sully.

The Natural History of Human Life

Eliot's own experience of human finitude interrupted her composition of *Impressions*. In November 1878—nine days after Eliot's manuscript was sent to the publisher—Lewes died, putting an end to their twenty-four years together. Halting editorial work on *Impressions* until the following year, Eliot set out instead to complete Lewes's five-volume magnum opus, *Problems of Life and Mind*, the last two volumes of which remained unfinished. When *Impressions* was finally published, it included a separate prefatory notice explaining the delay in publication, with reference to the "domestic affliction of the Author," a slip of paper that directs the reader to consider Eliot's and Lewes's corporeality (quoted in Henry, "Introduction" xxxvn5).

While finishing Lewes's treatise in psychology, Eliot enlisted the help of their close friend James Sully, who shared with Eliot and Lewes a fascination with the effects of reading on the body—and with the question of character in literature. Sully's 1874 essay collection *Sensation and Intuition: Studies in Psychology and Aesthetics* (owned and read multiple times by both Eliot and Lewes) stood at the forefront of research about the physiological effects of reading.[25] For Sully, the literary text was a unique interface in the back-and-forth between inner experiences and external stimulations that constituted consciousness.

Character was central to Sully's literary-theoretical inquiry into the physiological effects of reading. In his research he asked how it was that literature, though the medium of language, was able to reproduce the sensory experience of human objecthood in its reader's mind. To return to Lewes's distinction discussed earlier, Sully asked how it was that the novelist could employ "the Logic of Signs" to activate "the Logic of Feeling."

In developing his literary theory of character, Sully would look not only to his colleague Lewes's research in physiological psychology, but also to Eliot's fiction, wherein he discovered a model for comprehending the relationship between feelings and words. In his 1881 essay "George Eliot's Art," published in the science journal *Mind*, Sully celebrated Eliot's ability to track her characters from "their remote beginnings in early life, when impressions are most powerful and enduring and habit takes its shape for life," and showing "how they have come to be" through "the intricate play of circumstance" (385). He said that Eliot's novels offer "large scientific insight into character and life" (378). But how? While it is "a tolerably easy

25. Lewes's diary reports that the couple read *Sensation and Intuition* on July 12, 1874, and many times thereafter (Shuttleworth 230n17).

matter" to represent in literature such things as thought and speech, Sully writes in his essay "The Representation of Character in Art" that the fiction writer uses words "to suggest to the reader's mind… an intricate series of visual and other impressions, such as those conveyed by the person's figure, dress and outward carriage, by the varying cadences of his voice, and so on" (*Sensation* 285). When properly executed, that is, literature uses "the descriptive word" to itself create "impressions," generating memories of previous experiences and their "corresponding sensations." Through the activation of dormant feelings already present in the observer, description directs readers to "partake in the vivid interest of present reality" (285–86).

As both Sully and Lewes stressed in their thinking about language, the "sensuous medium" of words does more than generate imaginary thought-worlds (Sully, *Sensation* 284). Rather, as Sully argues, "the *representation* of human character in fiction appears sufficiently real to awaken just the same species of feelings which would be excited by the *presentation* of a similar type of character in real life" (288). When successful, that is, the author not only translates the Logic of Feeling into the Logic of Signs in her construction of literary characters; she also uses the Logic of Signs to *trigger* the Logic of Feeling in the reader. In other words, the successful novelist activates, through their descriptions, a person's memories of the physical world in order to generate feeling through language.

Some twenty years earlier, in her essay "The Natural History of German Life" (1856), Eliot made an argument similar to Sully's about the potential of literary description to shuttle one back to the world from which one's impressions first emerged. "It is an interesting branch of psychological observation," she writes, "to note the images that are habitually associated with abstract or collective terms—what may be called the picture-writing of the mind, which it carries on concurrently with the more subtle symbolism of language." The degree of fixity of the image associated with a given word, Eliot goes on to hypothesize, might be "a tolerably fair test of the amount of concrete knowledge and experience which a given word represents in the minds of two persons who use it with equal familiarity" (107). The vividness of the images conjured in one's mind speaks to the wealth of experience one has had with the thing described, and the words of a successful description create impressions that recall the world from which they arose. For Eliot, as for Sully, the affective power of the literary text does not induce fantasy; on the contrary, it pulls one back to the textures, densities, and layers of the physical world. As Eliot's Theophrastus puts it, "a fine imagination… is always based on a keen vision, a keen consciousness of what *is*"; it is an "energy constantly fed by susceptibility to the veriest minutiae of experience" (109–10).

Recent scholarship on Eliot has focused on how the burgeoning mind and brain sciences of the period influenced her representation of the embodied and adaptive mind.[26] While later psychologists would increasingly localize character in the human brain, the science of natural history that forms the focus of her 1856 essay and 1879 sketches would continue to view character as more dispersed—that is, as the collection of physical qualities and behaviors that render any organism or species distinct.[27]

We saw in the previous chapter how Eliot borrowed vocabulary from the field of physics to represent the "diffusive" quality of character. Natural history seems to have offered her a similarly rich framework for detaching the notion of character from the individual mind. Scholars who founded the study of Eliot's connections to science have suggested that Eliot turned away from her early interest in the "static science of natural history" and toward a more logical and experimental model of scientific practice—one that stressed that the deepest truths are initially invisible and can be discovered only with the imagination or reason (Shuttleworth 22).[28]

In contrast to this work, in which *Impressions* receives little if any attention, I contend that Eliot maintained a profound interest in the observational sciences until the end of her career. Her forays into English tide pools in the 1850s to collect polyps and anemones with Lewes for his *Sea-side Studies* (1856, 1858) were just the beginning of a lifelong fascination with the sensuous modes of collection and arrangement that ground natural-historical work.

Much is lost in approaching Eliot's work as a symptom of a large-scale shift in modern science away from the descriptive and inductive practice of natural history and toward the more argumentative and deductive model of modern biology. As historians of science have demonstrated, narratives of the "emergence" of experimental biology or the Darwinian "revolution" overlook not only the long history of morphological and evolutionary thought (Secord; Desmond), but also the continued import of observational sciences like natural history to nineteenth-century culture

---

26. See especially M. Davis, *George*.

27. Many psychologists of the period also resisted this gradual localization. Lewes and Sully, for instance, emphasized the role of the spinal cord and the nervous system in mediating sensations productive of character; in his ethology, Shand would focus on the role of the sentiments, a concept that was equal parts corporeal and mental. On character in Victorian psychology broadly, see M. Davis, "Psychology."

28. Dolin has argued that in Eliot's later novels we see the presence of "what scientists called 'hypothetico-deductive' modes, the discovery of what is unknown, and even to the microscope, unknowable, by presenting a hypothesis which can be tested and verified" ("George" 194).

(Nyhart; Ritvo). Natural historians have not only continued to practice into the twenty-first century, they have also retained the respect of the scientific community, which has relied heavily on their systematic documentation.

As Lynn Nyhart has argued in the context of Germany, while modern experimental zoology excluded some of natural history as unscientific, it incorporated major aspects of it into its theory and practice. Although many nineteenth-century zoologists advocated a strictly morphological perspective focused on anatomical form and development, others argued for a zoology that would incorporate natural history's emphasis on systemics, the study of relations between species and their organization in nature. Thus, nineteenth-century biologists like the life history scientist Karl Theodor Ernst von Siebold insisted on an observation-based practice that would retain natural history's attentiveness to the network of relations in which organisms participate, including their behaviors, habits, and other readily observable traits. Like the animal ethologists who followed him (discussed at greater length in chapter 5 in relation to Schreiner), Siebold wondered about the tendency of his contemporaries to look only at morphology in their studies of animals: "But where is the observation of the way of life of these animals, why does one learn so little of the activities of those very animals whose [anatomical] organization is known with the utmost precision?" (quoted in Nyhart 432).

In "The Natural History of German Life," Eliot echoes the life history scientist's emphasis on observable traits, activities, and ecological relations over morphological structures. Responding to the work of the German sociologist Wilhelm Riehl, she argues for a literary-sociological practice she calls "the Natural History of social bodies," a practice that would depict human interaction through "gradually amassed observations" (131, 127). In this early formulation of her realist aesthetic, Eliot maintains that knowledge of a people derives from the sensory experience required to produce a detailed description rather than from conceptual familiarity with ideals and abstract categories. Not unlike her anthropologist contemporaries, Eliot insists that to understand how a people lives, one needs the experiential knowledge of the naturalist as much as the theoretical knowledge of the physicist, chemist, or physiologist. "Just as the most thorough acquaintance with physics, or chemistry, or general physiology will not enable you at once to establish the balance of life in your private vivarium," she suggests, so too one cannot know or describe a people only by theorizing; one must observe and converse with them in person (130–31).

Anticipating Shand's investment in induction, rather than deduction, as the basis for a science of character, Eliot invokes Riehl's observation-based methodology as a springboard for the formulation of a theory of realist literature. Like Riehl, whose "vivid pictures" of German people rely on empirical as well as conceptual knowledge (134), she advocates a detailed and engaged yet unromantic mode of literary description that would account for the diversity of the human species. Beginning with the particular and moving to the general, the inductive mode Eliot champions in her essay is a link between the practice of literary characterization and the practice of natural history—both sciences of character that toggle between the micro and the macro, the individual and the type, to impose order on the chaos of the world.

Eliot's comments here thus speak to a culture of natural-historical writing more central to the Victorian period than is sometimes recognized in literary studies. Amy King has shown how the techniques of close observation developed by natural history resound in the Victorian novel's attention to detail, its long descriptive passages, and its fascination with nonhuman things.[29] If Darwin's theory of evolution "provided 'plots,'" King writes with reference to Gillian Beer's classic study *Darwin's Plots* (1983), then "natural history continued to model—far beyond its professional demise—descriptive techniques, detail, and interest in describing the small scale and the local that became essential to the realist novel in Britain" ("Reorienting" 158).

Whereas other novels worked to proliferate descriptive detail, however, *Impressions* looks back to the desire of natural-historical writing to disentangle words from things, to let organisms stand naked in their physical being. More than this, in situating the human as an object of natural-historical inquiry, Eliot's final work decenters and dehierarchizes the human within the *scala naturae*. It positions the human humbly, as many pioneering naturalists, such as George-Louis Leclerc, Comte de Buffon, had, "in the class of the animals, which he resembles in everything material" (Buffon, quoted in Sloan 112).[30] It does so, I have been arguing, in and through the concept of character, which, as the dynamic material substrate of subjectivity, conditions the perception of both human and nonhuman life forms.

After the Human

As *Impressions* implies, science and literature might benefit equally from the power of what Sully called "the descriptive word" to highlight charac-

---

29. On the particular in Victorian natural history, see Merrill (esp. 64).

30. On the emergence of a "natural history" of humanity in the late seventeenth and early eighteenth centuries, see Sloan, who argues that in the hands of Linnaeus and Buffon, "human beings for the first time were arranged, as a taxonomic group, with the rest of organic nature" (118).

teristics held in common by seemingly disparate forms of life. Why study the human in isolation, and how? Why—if we share our being with so many other creatures—should our perspective on the human be solely a human one? For Eliot, the human being is not the most important knower or observer, pitted against the unknowing physical being of nonhuman objects of inquiry (with the Logic of Signs always superior to the Logic of Feeling). Rather, all perceptive beings lie on a single ontological plane. One might experience oneself as a center, but the surface is infinite.

To close this chapter, I will unpack one more moment in the literary critique of human-centered ontologies Eliot offers in *Impressions*, one that positions literature as a kind of nonhuman extension of the human body: "a delicate acoustic or optical instrument," as she put it in 1855, "bringing home to our coarser senses what would otherwise be unperceived by us" ("Rev. of 'Westward Ho!'" 289). In *Impressions*, every character's blind spot consists in an overestimation of their own perceptive abilities: the belief that they see more or better than other creatures. Pushing this argument about the limit of human knowledge to its extreme, the chapter "Shadows of the Coming Race" tells the story of mechanical automata that "transcend and finally supersede" the human because of their ability to communicate without the "fussy accompaniment of consciousness" (138, 140). These inorganic posthumans evolve out of tools intended to enhance human perception, "micrometers and thermopiles and tasimeters which deal physically with the invisible, the impalpable, and the unimaginable," such as "a microphone which detects the cadence of the fly's foot on the ceiling" (138). Undermining the suggestion that consciousness renders human beings superior to other beings, Eliot playfully imagines in "Shadows" an alternative hierarchy of being in which consciousness is a burden rather than a boon.

Structured as a Platonic dialogue between Theophrastus and his friend Trost, the chapter speculates about a future race of creatures that would "carry on the most elaborate processes as mutely and painlessly as we are now told that the minerals are metamorphosing themselves continually in the dark laboratory of the earth's crust" (142). The rise of these "steely organisms," Theophrastus explains to the incredulous Trost, would eventually enable "banishing from the earth's atmosphere screaming consciousnesses which, in our comparatively clumsy race, make an intolerable noise and fuss to each other about every petty ant-like performance" (138, 139). In this posthuman, postlinguistic world, "changes as delicate and complicated as those of human language" are carried out by "beings who will be blind and deaf as the inmost rock.... [T]here may be, let us say, mute orations, mute rhapsodies, mute discussions, and no consciousness there even to enjoy the silence" (142).

"Shadows" might be interpreted as a reaction to the "conscious automaton" debates of the 1870s among T. H. Huxley, Herbert Spencer, William James, and John Elliott Cairnes.[31] John Fuerst has read this chapter as a prescient vision of the digital computer, as an imagining of the kinds of symbolic logic that would produce the first forays into artificial-intelligence research (45). Most relevant to my purposes, however, is the radical thought that "Shadows" makes possible through its dalliance with science fiction: Theophrastus's musings confront us with the possibility of a world in which consciousness is not the precondition for reality, a world in which communication is nothing like human language but instead involves metamorphic, material processes unburdened by "the futile cargo of a consciousness" (141). In ancient Greek, I noted earlier, *kharaktēr* (χαρακτήρ) refers to the tool for writing as well as the impression made in wax writing tablets. Theophrastus's words enact this double impression: he writes, and a world hitherto unimaginable is impressed upon our senses, for words, ironically, in their materiality can lead us to imagine a world without words as its medium.

Although Eliot's work is typically aligned with the humanism of an earlier generation of German theorists, elements of the anti-anthropocentric thinking emergent in Friedrich Nietzsche's philosophy can be found in *Impressions*.[32] In 1873, five years before Eliot started writing *Impressions*, Nietzsche began his essay "On Truth and Lies in a Non-moral Sense" (published posthumously in 1896) with a fable in which "clever beasts" who invented "knowing" perish after just a short time on earth, taking their consciousnesses with them (114). This fable, Nietzsche writes, is intended to demonstrate "how shadowy and transient, how aimless and arbitrary the human intellect looks within nature" (114).

The same could be said of the fable presented in "Shadows." Nietzsche's conscious beasts take their form of consciousness to be the highest and best. However, "if we could communicate with the gnat," Nietzsche writes, "we would learn that he likewise flies through the air with the same solemnity, that he feels the flying center of the universe within himself" (114). Eliot's story likewise draws attention to egoism as a condition of embodied perception, human or otherwise. Taking "the humble mollusc" as an example, at a different point in *Impressions*, Theophrastus points out that although one might imagine such an insignificant creature "to have a

---

31. On the conscious automaton debates, see Offer. The Victorian novelist Samuel Butler read the chapter, less convincingly, as a plagiarized section of his novel *Erewhon* (Henkin 97).

32. A. Miller has likewise drawn productive parallels between Eliot's project in *Impressions* and that of Nietzsche ("Bruising, Laceration").

sense of his own exceeding softness and low place in the scale of being," in reality he is "inwardly objecting to every other grade of solid rather than to himself" (41). As both Eliot and Nietzsche demonstrate through powerful analogy, if every being overestimates its role in the *scala naturae*, there may be no reason to think of human beings as the highest or most intelligent creatures—or even to think of human language as the most efficient or best mode of communication. Rather, as Nietzsche argues in his essay, language is merely an agreed-on set of norms that erases the differences and particularities of the sensible world.

In the published version of *Impressions*, the dark and dystopian chapter "Shadows" is followed by a more optimistic one, "The Modern Hep! Hep! Hep!," which explores the role of the nation in a global human society.[33] As the page proofs demonstrate, however, Eliot initially intended "Shadows" to be the final chapter, but it was inexplicably moved to the penultimate position just before publication.[34] Nancy Henry has suggested that Eliot may have backed away from the radical implications of ending with "Shadows" ("Introduction" xxxiv).[35] The possibility of this alternative ending of *Impressions* motivates the conclusion to this chapter, which explores whether in "Shadows," Theophrastus transforms into a kind of expansive, hybrid entity that can peek outside the human perspective and experience the "nonhuman independence" he longed for in the first chapter. Andrew H. Miller has argued, "Present then from the start, Theophrastus's anxiety that he is not human dilates into full-blown skepticism at the moment of molting itself, the point of his conversion into a new self" ("Bruising, Laceration" 307). Indeed, when Theophrastus is pressed to defend his theory about the end of humanity at the hands of a robotic species, there arises the possibility of such a conversion not only into a new self but into a new species. As he explains to Trost:

> [I]t is less easy to you than to me to imagine our race transcended and superseded, since the more energy a being is possessed of, the harder it must be for him to conceive his own death. But I, from the point of view of

---

33. Of all the essays in *Impressions*, "The Modern Hep! Hep! Hep!" has received the most critical attention. Newton examines the problematic reception of this chapter, which often is separated from the book and read as a straightforward expression of Eliot's views on the Jewish question.

34. In the final page proofs at the Harry Ransom Center at the University of Texas, Austin, "Shadows" is the last chapter, and no comments from Eliot or the editor indicate the impending switch.

35. As Henry points out, while "Shadows" leaves Theophrastus in "temporary fragmentation," "'The Modern Hep' reconstitutes Theophrastus fully within a community" ("Introduction" xxxiv).

a reflective carp, can easily imagine myself and my congeners dispensed with in the frame of things and giving way not only to a superior but a vastly different kind of Entity. (140)

In nineteenth-century England, *carp* might have been read as a reference not only to the fish but also to the combining form used in botanical discourse to denote the fruit and seed pods of plants: as in *hemicarp*, a half-fruit unit, or *mericarp*, a one-seeded unit.[36] The terms *carpos* (fruit) and *pericarpion* (seed), moreover, were coined by none other than Theophrastus of Eresus, in an effort to develop a special botanical terminology (Singer 178). What is more, the word *carp* is reminiscent of Theophrastus's interest in the negative, the base, and the minor, since *to carp* can, of course, mean to talk too much or to complain. This pejorative sense is connected to the otherwise neutral definition of *carp* as "discourse" or "the power of speech" itself, which was more common between the twelfth and seventeenth centuries. Theophrastus: fish, word, fruit-bearing plant; carp capable of imagining humanity's extinction. Whereas the all-too-human Trost cannot conceive of the end of his species, his interlocutor, this ghost of a dead philosopher and literary entity, can imagine it and can imagine embodying it.

"I try," Eliot wrote to a friend in 1870, "to delight in the sunshine that will be when I shall never see it any more. And I think it is possible for this sort of impersonal life to attain great intensity, possible for us to gain much more independence, than is usually believed, of the small bundle of facts that make our own personality" ("To Mrs. Robert Lytton" 107).[37] By the end of *Impressions*, Theophrastus seems to have gained such independence, to have unwoven his personality to the extent that he begins to feel such intensity, an affective intensity not unlike the nonhuman roar on the other side of silence. His text appears to have achieved, if only momentarily, the state which Daniel Deronda longs for when, in a "half-involuntary identification of himself with the objects he was looking at," he attempts to "shift his centre till his own personality would be no less outside than the landscape" (*Deronda* 160). Fascinated by similar remarks across Eliot's oeuvre, George Levine has read the author's frustration with the limits of perception in terms of nineteenth-century epistemological narratives of objectivity in which the body is seen as an impediment to knowledge, and

36. *OED Online*, Oxford University Press, s.v. "carp," accessed October 11, 2011. In *Middlemarch*, Casaubon's scholarly rival is likewise named Carp, and Carp's associates are Pike and Tench.

37. This is probably a reference to David Hume's theory of the self as a "bundle or collection of different perceptions" (188).

revelation must thus occur in the "negation of embodiment" (*Dying* 69). To situate Eliot's anxiety about selfhood in this scientific-epistemological frame, however, risks obscuring the affective aims of her literary project as it seeks to render tactile a reality beyond the human. Her frustration with the limits of human perception, I have been arguing, abides not in the desire to transcend or obliterate the bounded materiality of the human observer, but rather to more fully inhabit that objecthood—to identify oneself with the "the objects [one is] looking at."

In the literary-turned-philosophical realism of *Impressions*, we find a curiously sensational Eliot, intent on imagining what reality might feel like if one could crack through one's all-too-human vantage—if, through the "sensuous medium" of words, one might unravel one's "personality" into mere impressions and sensorial states, moving through the Logic of Signs to inhabit more fully the Logic of Feelings. For Lewes, as for many nineteenth-century philosophers, this latter, material semiotic, was thought to be inherently inferior to linguistic communication: according to the aesthetic theorist Charles Blanc, for instance, where "intelligent beings have a language represented by articulate sounds," unintelligent beings such as nonhuman animals and vegetables "express themselves by cries or forms, contour or carriage" (4). (Lowest in Blanc's hierarchy are minerals, which "have only the language of color" [4]—the focus of my next chapter.)

Across her literary corpus, Eliot expresses a deep curiosity about the operations of latter, nonlinguistic semiotic—the language in which character is written. "If we had a keen vision and feeling of all ordinary human life, it would be like hearing the grass grow and the squirrel's heart beat, and we should die of that roar which lies on the other side of silence. As it is, the quickest of us walk about well wadded with stupidity" (*Middlemarch* 182). This well-known passage is typically interpreted as a call for the extension of our sympathies to all members of the human species. Such an extension is said to have the impossible goal of achieving a kind of god's-eye view, an extra- or superhuman position from which one could comprehend the totality of human thought and feeling. The reading of *Impressions* undertaken in the preceding pages, however, opens up another possible interpretation of this line: that to have "a keen vision and feeling of all ordinary human life" might actually require not *more* subjectivity—more consciousness, more sympathy, or more language—but rather less.

The Racialization of Surface in Hardy's *Sketch of Temperament* and Hereditary Science

[CHAPTER THREE]

It is not improbabilities of incident but improbabilities of character that matter.

THOMAS HARDY, January 2, 1886, *Life and Work*

In the previous chapter, we saw how in *Impressions of Theophrastus Such*, George Eliot distanced herself from the plot-driven genre that had made her famous, returning to the more ponderous, philosophical form with which she had begun her career as a fiction writer—the sketch. Two decades later, Thomas Hardy would likewise turn away from the novel genre, famously quitting fiction writing altogether and recommitting himself to his first literary love, poetry. Hardy's turn-of-the-century generic shift is not typically understood, as I have described that of Eliot, as an experiment in the formal and philosophical limits of realism. It is more commonly explained as a reaction to the public response to his novels, which scandalized readers with their sexual explicitness and relentless pessimism. "After the appearance of *Jude the Obscure* in 1895 and its intensely hostile reception," J. B. Bullen writes, Hardy "abandoned the writing of fiction" (*Thomas* 213). Similarly, Dennis Taylor narrates how in the aftermath of the *Jude* controversy, Hardy turned to poetry in the hopes of finding refuge from moralistic readers: "Hardy said he gave up novel-writing," Taylor explains, "because of the furor raised over the novel by the churchmen and Mrs. Grundys of the time" (363). As evidence of Hardy's growing frustration with the conservativism of his critics, Taylor cites the following lines from Hardy's diary, dated October 17, 1896: "Poetry. Perhaps I can express more fully in verse ideas and emotions which run counter to the inert crystallized opinion—hard as a rock—which the vast body of men have vested interests in supporting" (*Life* 302). These lines are frequently cited in scholarly accounts of Hardy's abandonment of the novel. They are typically interpreted to mean that Hardy traded in novels for poetry because he believed the opacity of poetic language would allow him to more obliquely question social norms and thus avoid the charges of impropriety often leveled against his fiction.¹

Consistently left out of such analyses, however, are the lines directly preceding Hardy's remarks about the potential of poetry to "counter to the inert crystallized opinion." These other lines, though little cited, suggest that Hardy's decision to stop writing fiction was motivated by more than the controversy surrounding the content of his novels. Directly before the above-cited passage on poetry sits a short note concerning the descriptive tactics of the Romantic-era poet George Crabbe, which reads: "A novel, good, microscopic touch in Crabbe. He gives surface without outline, describing his church by telling *the colour of the lichens*" (*Life* 302).

At first glance, the note on Crabbe would appear to have little to do with the ensuing reflection on the affordances of poetry. Upon closer examination, however, this comment seems to have inspired Hardy's remarks on the capacity of poetry to house "ideas and emotions which run counter to inert crystallized opinion." Just as Crabbe refrains from describing the intransigent outline of the church—attending instead to the colorful lichens that paper its surface—so, too, Hardy speculates, might poetry soften hard lines and enliven the inert. A former surgeon known for his detailed depictions of the English countryside, Crabbe stressed the significance of the specific and local to poetry's transformational power.² His poems, criticized by Romantic devotees of Imagination as overly detailed and uninspired, are characterized by a fidelity to empirical reality and commitment to factual accuracy.³ But if Crabbe's Romantic contemporaries did not appreciate his tendency to focus on "the painful realities of actual existence" (218)—as Crabbe once described the aim of his poetry—Hardy, it would seem, found much to admire in Crabbe's descriptive impulse,

---

1. Millgate, for example, interprets these lines to mean that poetry offered Hardy "not only greater possibilities of artistic fulfilment, but also, more mundanely, a technique for polemical indirection" (352). Likewise, literary critic Barbara Hardy writes in an analysis of this passage, "After *Jude*, he was forced to recognize that prose fiction was taken to be argumentative and dogmatic, in a way in which poems were not" (160).

2. Crabbe's most well-known poem, *The Village* (1783), was written in protest against Oliver Goldsmith's *The Deserted Village* (1770), which Crabbe thought overly idyllic and sentimental.

3. Crabbe's contemporary William Hazlitt, for example, dismissed his poems as "mere matters of fact," which, consisting of "merely literary description," "described merely what was there" (311). See McGann, "The Anachronism of George Crabbe," for more on the Romantic response to Crabbe's realist poetics.

which is said to manifest itself in a specific formal strategy: the giving of "surface without outline."[4]

Hardy's reflections in his 1896 diary entry on the aesthetic tension between "surface" and "outline" reframe the critical narrative of his decision to quit fiction writing from a story of the clash between the controversial content of his novels and Victorian social mores to the tale of an abiding formal commitment to cultivating a realism that, like Crabbe's "microscopic touch," highlights the capacity of people and things to attain character through encounters at the surface. Like all realisms, Hardy's was much more than a desire to transparently reflect reality. It manifested itself in a set of historically and culturally specific concerns and was deployed through a carefully crafted set of formal techniques. The aim of the artist should not be to copy reality, Hardy maintained; it was rather "to show more clearly the features that matter in those realities" (*Life* 239).[5] This chapter argues that Hardy's realism inheres in, among other things, a practice of description that attends carefully to qualities on the edges and exteriors of bodies and that, in so doing, emphasizes the capacity of bodies for slow, iterative change. Some of these qualities stick, becoming a part of the essence of the thing, and others slough off, lost forever, as character attains its shape in and through cycles of accumulation and subsidence, the accretive processes that in Hardy's fiction mark all bodies—whether flesh, paper, or stone.

Although a body might "make certain admissions by its outline," the narrator of *The Return of the Native* (1878) observes, "it fully confesses only in its changes" (52). With regard to character at least, the surface is the site of that change. Returning to a concept introduced earlier in this book, I approach what Hardy called "surface" and "outline" not as opposites but as two aspects of the aesthetic phenomenon that Eliot called "form"—two "features" of reality, in Hardy's parlance, that an artist might choose to emphasize in their representation of that reality. For Eliot, as we saw in chapter 1, form is defined by two principles: first, "by the intrinsic relations or composition of the object"; and second, "by the extrinsic action of other

---

4. As Crabbe wrote in his preface to *Tales* (1812), "Fiction itself, we know, and every work of fancy, must for a time have the effect of realities" (Crabbe, *Poetical Works* 218).

5. Hardy often distanced himself from realism, once going so far as to claim that "'realism' is not Art" because the goal of art should be "a disproportioning—(i.e., distorting, throwing out of proportion) of realities" (*Life* 239). If we do not understand realism as "copyism" (to borrow another of Hardy's terms), however, then there is still justification for describing Hardy as a realist insofar as he participates in and innovates on that literary tradition ("Science" 136). On Hardy's relationship to realism, see also Kornbluh, chap. 5; and Jaffe, chap. 4.

bodies upon it" ("Notes on Form" 234). To focus one's characterization on the outline of a body is to emphasize the first of these two principles (the presentation of a form as an internally determined, autonomous unit). If, as Eliot suggests, "fundamentally, form is unlikeness," outline configures this difference as a limit between inside and outside (232). To focus one's characterization on the surface of a body, on the other hand, is to configure difference in terms of a relational site or contact zone. Attention to surface thus emphasizes the second of Eliot's two formal principles, the representation of a form as externally determined and dependent. In his character descriptions, Hardy tends to prefer surface to outline; and Hardy's narrators express concern when characters are reduced to "forms without features," forms "without more character than that of being the limit of something else" (*Madding Crowd* 85).

To shift the narrative of Hardy's abandonment of the novel from questions concerning censorship and critical response toward questions regarding formal tension between surface and outline might initially seem like an unpromising avenue, one that risks minimizing the social and political concerns that drive Hardy's fiction. However, as we will see, in Hardy, surfaces are not neutral canvases but rather the site where time and space collide to produce historical and social meaning, as Elaine Scarry, in particular, has underlined. Across Hardy's novels, Scarry observes, "Man and world each act on the surface of the other; each alters the other's surface either by adding new layers to it or subtracting layers from it: an addition takes the form of a film or skin" ("Work" 92). These alterations, while they might appear merely aesthetic, are Hardy's way of theorizing the value-laden relation between a person's character and the activities that shape it.

Consider, as an example of Scarry's claim that in Hardy's fiction, "man alters the world only by consenting to be himself deeply altered," the character Diggory Venn of *Return of the Native*, a farmer whose red skin is the mark of his trade as a reddleman, a peddler of a red dye used to mark sheep ("Work" 96). Though Scarry doesn't treat him, the reddleman lends force to her claim that surfaces in Hardy index the encounter between a person and his milieu, which impresses itself upon him. "Ordinary in shape, but singular in colour, this being a lurid red," Venn's outline may be common, but his surface harbors the trace of his unique bodily experience, a labor that stains his skin, as well as that of those he encounters (Hardy, *Return* 7).

Through Venn, Hardy would seem almost to literalize Frederick Douglass's claim in *My Bondage and My Freedom* (1855), that "a man's character greatly takes its hue and shape from the form and color of things about him" (61). And like Douglass, whose narrative warns against the dangers of reading a person's "hue and shape" as signifying anything essential about their character, Hardy highlights how Venn's skin color is incorrectly interpreted by others to signify his inferiority. Venn's skin color is the direct product of his environment, an "accident of its situation," his work with reddle, which "stamps unmistakably, as with the mark of Cain, any person who has handled it half an hour" (*Return* 78, 76). Unlike that of Douglass, though, Venn's "stain" is temporary: "I should be as white as you if I were to give up the trade," he informs an onlooker (73). Socially, however, Venn's red skin marks him as an outsider whose very humanity is thrown into question as a result of his ambiguous racial status: "He might have been an Arab, or an automaton," remarks the character Damon Wildeve, upon observing Venn looking like a "red-standstone statue" (235).[6]

Despite being as English as the next inhabitant of Egdon Heath, Venn is ostracized because of his surface-level difference from the other characters: "ye bain't bad-looking in the groundwork," remarks one observer, "though the finish is queer" (30). Indeed, the precondition for Venn's entrance into the social world of the novel is a revelation of his white "groundwork" (30)—an act of "stain removal" (to borrow a phrase from the philosopher of race J. Reid Miller, whose work I will shortly turn to) that divorces Venn's body from the space and activity that had long marked it. Where Venn's red skin previously had marked him as "queer," after he quits his occupation and emerges "white" at the end of the novel, his normative humanity is reinstated: "What shall we have to frighten Thomasin's baby with, now that you have become a human being again?" Clym Yeobright, Thomasin Yeobright's cousin, asks Venn after announcing that Venn has finally "got white of his own accord" (*Return* 395, 394).

What I describe as Hardy's *aesthetics of surface* is epitomized in his suggestive characterization of Venn's red skin, a realist representational strategy that formally prioritizes the interactivity of surface over the autonomy of outline and, in drawing attention to the way that circumstances "color" bodies, subverts the racial logics that subtend English colonial ideology. Building on the previous chapter's concern with how character manifests itself in the body and its observable features, this chapter shows how Hardy puts pressure on these racial logics by implying that surfaces point not to deeper inner truths but rather to the layered histories that circumstantially produce them. Where the other characters of *Return of the Native* interpret Venn's red skin as a sign of a difference that must be erased as a precondition for his incorporation into their community, Hardy's descrip-

---

6. Batchelor has broadly argued that in history of Western art color is often presented "the property of some 'foreign' body—usually the feminine, the oriental, the primitive, the infantile, the vulgar, the queer or the pathological" (22–23).

tions present Venn's skin as the index of his dynamic, affective relation to his milieu—the erasure of which coincides with the erasure of his character. To return to terms discussed in chapter 2, we might say that Hardy echoes Eliot in presenting character as written in a material semiotic that follows a "Logic of Feelings" rather than a "Logic of Signs" (Lewes, *Problems* 3.2:227). And like Eliot too, he would turn to the character sketch genre at the end of his novelistic career to explore the workings of this material semiotic.

For Hardy did not actually turn his attention entirely to poetry following the composition of his diary entry on Crabbe's descriptive preference for surface over outline, as is often implied; nor did he stop writing fiction after the publication of *Jude the Obscure*, as is often presumed. Instead, Hardy returned to a work that, at least at first, would seem to directly reverse the strategy admired in Crabbe—the giving of "surface without outline." This work was *The Well-Beloved: A Sketch of Temperament* (1897), a novel that, in its reduction of its characters to bare and unchanging outlines, warns against the aesthetic suppression of character's dynamic, variable surfaces, which register bodily histories.

First serialized in 1892 under the title *The Pursuit of the Well-Beloved*, the novel was republished in volume form under its new title, *The Well-Beloved: A Sketch of Temperament* in 1897.[7] Perhaps because of new publishing constraints, or perhaps because Hardy's own ideas and goals for the novel had changed in the intervening years, the 1897 edition of *The Well-Beloved* "was by no means a 'reprinting' but a radical rewriting" that produced "a new novel," as Patricia Ingham has noted (xxxvii). *The Well-Beloved*'s indeterminate position in Hardy's corpus has meant that critics have felt authorized to overlook it when addressing his decision to stop writing fiction at the turn of the century. However, as the fulcrum between two distinct periods in Hardy's career—and a reflection upon the author's thirty years of experience writing fiction—*The Well-Beloved* is a crucial site for understanding Hardy's unique brand of realism and the genre he increasingly felt was inhospitable to it.

Where others dismiss the novel as "one of the oddest items in the Hardy canon," I show how this seemingly uncharacteristic work actually reveals a consistent theme across his corpus: an interest in exploring the

---

7. *The Pursuit of the Well-Beloved* was serialized simultaneously in the *Illustrated London News* and *Harper's Bazaar* from October to December 1892 and published in single-volume form in March 1897. *The Well-Beloved* thus bookends *Jude*, which was serialized from December 1894 to November 1895 and appeared in single-volume form in November 1895. All citations of the text in what follows refer to the 1897 edition unless otherwise noted.

ability of character to transform in response to local and specific contexts (P. Morton 200). While Hardy's frustration with the social conservatism of his critics was no doubt a motivating factor behind his decision to stop writing fiction, deeply intertwined with this social frustration was an abiding formal commitment: the cultivation of a realism adequate to the task of revealing how character emerges, spontaneously, through interactions at the surface.

Throughout this book, I have been arguing that the realist novel, particularly as it developed in the final three decades of the century, offers a theory of how character forms in response to circumstances. Hardy's 1897 novel is a key text in my literary-historical narrative insofar as it offers another compelling theory of what the ethologist A. F. Shand would later describe as the "dynamical" relationship between character and milieu (*Foundations* 1). Not only does *The Well-Beloved* theorize character's circumstantiality, however, it also draws out the ethical consequences of attempts to repress that circumstantiality by critiquing the eugenic discourses that informed the emerging science of heredity. In its narration of the genetic transmission of character across three generations of the same family, *The Well-Beloved* reveals how early theories of biological inheritance were historically intertwined with eugenicist attempts to preserve so-called English racial continuity by insulating (white) bodies from circumstantial influence. The next section explores how Hardy's novel critically engages the fascination with the fundamental sameness underlying differences between parent and child in the then nascent science of heredity, showing that, in racializing the surface of the Well-Beloved, Hardy draws attention to the unmarked whiteness of her ideal. Diving deeper into the racial history of hereditary science, the subsequent section sketches out the historical and conceptual connection between this late nineteenth-century science and the modern European racial paradigm that informed it—a paradigm in which skin color emerged as the most salient marker of racial difference. Finally, reading Hardy's novel in conversation with Darwin's thinking about generation, the final section of this chapter suggests that Hardy's novel offers an alternative theory for conceptualizing racial character by setting up an analogy between the accretive temporality of rock formation and the iterative process of biological inheritance that generates organisms always different from, and yet tied to, their progenitors. Through its descriptions of the white oolitic limestone that composes its setting—the Isle of Slingers, modeled after England's limestone Isle of Portland—as well as its iterative narrative structure, which introduces difference with every repetition, *The Well-Beloved* mobilizes Darwinian faith in the generation of difference against eugenic attempts to preserve and perpetuate the same.

The Color of Heredity

The Well-Beloved narrates the successive attempts of a neoclassical sculptor, Jocelyn Pierston, to capture in both art and life the woman who most perfectly embodies the Platonic form of a woman, whom he calls his "Well-Beloved." Chasing after her "ghostly outlines" as they manifest themselves in woman after woman—including three generations of women from a single family—Jocelyn forsakes the embodied particularity of the women he encounters in favor of the Well-Beloved's idealized form (324).

As time passes, Jocelyn's lovers become more and more physically identical, until eventually, the Well-Beloved only appears within a particular genetic line—that of the Caro family of his native Isle of Slingers. After the unexpected death of Jocelyn's childhood love and cousin, Avice Caro, the Well-Beloved is passed on, as if through the mechanism of heredity, to the daughter of Avice and another man, Ann Avice Caro—and then subsequently also to Avice's granddaughter, Avice Caro the third. While the women Jocelyn desires all seem to perfectly embody the Well-Beloved, the artist's hopes that each woman will manifest her ideal are repeatedly dashed, as differences in circumstance and upbringing produce frustratingly individualized results. The Well-Beloved always rematerializes with a difference.

In this section, I read *The Well-Beloved* in conversation with nineteenth-century theories of heredity to show how Hardy's novel brings its broader critique of idealisms to bear on the operation of whiteness as an unmarked ideal in scientific discourse of the period. The epigraph to the 1897 edition of the novel, "One shape of many names" (a phrase taken from Percy Bysshe Shelley's "The Revolt of Islam"), epitomizes a misogynist trope one finds in other Hardy novels, in which the particularities of individual women are eliminated in service to a disembodied ideal. Thus, Hardy's epigraph, as Ingham remarks in her introduction to the novel, "describes not only Jocelyn's behavior, but that of the narrators in Hardy's early novels who try to impose a single ideal of womanliness on all heroines" (xxi).[8] Through the figure of the Well-Beloved, however, Hardy can be seen to critique not only the ideal of the feminine but also the racial implications of the standardization of character across the host of social and cultural fields, especially new scientific theories that sought to explain how and

---

8. In *A Pair of Blue Eyes* (1873), for instance, Elfride Swancourt's suitor, the reviewer Henry Knight, explains his knack for writing about women by saying, "All I know about women, or men either, is a mass of generalities" (124).

why the characters of parents and children resemble one another by positing the existence of a biological unit transmitted across generations. Attention to the role of color in both Hardy's novel and hereditary discourse of the period reveals how the conceptualization of this new biological unit entailed positing a kind of neutral, value-free site of characterological inscription that was perceived to be always already white.

On February 19, 1889, Hardy jotted down an idea in his diary: "The story of a face which goes through three generations or more, would make a fine novel or poem of the passage of Time. The difference in personality to be ignored" (*Life* 226). Hardy, it turns out, would write both the novel and the poem. Published in 1917, his poem "Heredity" begins: "I am the family face; / Flesh perishes, I live on." The ghostly form that Hardy describes in his poem as "The eternal thing in man, / That heeds no call to die" finds its expression in narrative form in *The Well-Beloved*. While the individual women the Well-Beloved inhabits are born and perish, the Well-Beloved's transcendent form lives on eternally. Much more than a figure for the constancy of Jocelyn's love, as Bullen has observed, the Well-Beloved is a figure for a new biological constancy thought to structure the living world. Interpreting the Well-Beloved as "a metaphor for the building blocks of genetic inheritance," Bullen notes that as the Well-Beloved is passed on through three generations of women, she resembles the genetic substance the German biologist August Weismann called *Keimplasma* (or germ plasm) ("Hardy's" 82).

"How it is that such a single cell can reproduce the *tout ensemble* of the parent with all the faithfulness of a portrait?" Weismann asked in his lecture "The Continuity of the Germ Plasm as the Foundation of a Theory of Heredity" (1885) (*Essays* 1:165). His answer was that a colorless plastic substance is transmitted, unaltered, from parent to child, facilitating the perpetuation of biological sameness across generations.

Hardy read Weismann's collected *Essays upon Heredity* (translated into English in 1889) in late 1890 (J. H. Miller, *Fiction* 169).[9] But he also would have encountered related concepts through English scientists such as Charles Darwin, Francis Galton, and Herbert Spencer—all of whom had developed competing biological theories of inheritance, as we will see.[10]

9. On Hardy's engagement with theories of heredity in *Jude the Obscure*, see Steinlight, *Populating the Novel*, chap. 5.

10. The fundamental mechanism of heredity remained unclear until the early twentieth century. While Mendel had already published his now-famous essay "Studies on Plant Hybridization" in 1865, the essay would not achieve wide circulation until the early 1900s, when it was rediscovered by scientists who had arrived at similar conclusions.

While convincing, Bullen's observations about the genetic implications of Hardy's representation of the Well-Beloved underestimate the degree to which the novel is concerned with race. *The Well-Beloved*'s concern with the racialization of character is especially apparent in the 1897 version of the novel, which draws out the racial implications of Jocelyn's desire by inserting additional references to the Caros' pedigree. In one such addition, the narrator details the Caros' "Roman lineage, more or less grafted on the stock of the Slingers" (232). "What so natural as that the true star of his soul would be found nowhere but in one of the old island breed?" the narrator muses with regard to Jocelyn (232).[11] In aligning the Well-Beloved with the pale skin and light hair of the Caro women, as well as the white marble of Jocelyn's neoclassical sculptures, Hardy draws attention to the latent whiteness of Victorian ideals of femininity—a whiteness imperceptible to the artist Jocelyn, who believes in the neutrality of his ideal. But before we can go on to understand the important role color plays in this novel, we must understand the essential role of form.

As "the Idea, in Platonic phraseology—the essence and epitome of all that is desirable," the Well-Beloved is initially described as a disembodied form or essence (an *eidos*, to use Plato's term) that only ever imperfectly manifests itself in the bodies of real women (257). Representing this form in terms of outline, in the first half of the novel, she is presented as a colorless, lineated figure that manifests itself in women with skin, eyes, and hair of various shades. When asked the color of Mrs. Nichola Pine-Avon's eyes when the Well-Beloved is inhabiting her, Jocelyn responds, "Her eyes? I don't go much in for colour, being professionally sworn to form" (262). As becomes clear, Jocelyn understands form solely in terms of outline. His aesthetic-romantic vision echoes that of neoclassical artists who "emphasized outline over surface" in their drawings of ancient engravings—to borrow a phrase from Jonah Siegel in his account of late Victorian neoclassical art (192).[12]

---

11. Dolin has likewise highlighted the fantasy of racial purity at work in Angel Clare's fascination with Tess's "unsophistication" in *Tess of the d'Urbervilles*, remarking that "Tess and the other dairymaids must, in this fantasy, be virginally English: unspoiled stock of the true race" ("Melodrama" 339).

12. J. Thomas has observed that Jocelyn particularly resembles one neoclassical artist with whom Hardy corresponded during the 1880s, the sculptor Thomas Woolner, who was known for his white marble sculptures of women portraying feminine ideals and archetypes (217). By the time Hardy had composed *The Well-Beloved*, the neoclassicism of sculptors such as Woolner and draftsmen such as John Flaxman was beginning to give way to a new sculptural paradigm—what Hardy's close friend Edmund Gosse in 1894 termed *New Sculpture*. In the work of New Sculptors such as Frederick Leighton and Hamo Thornycraft, Gosse writes, one finds "something far more vital and nervous

In their line drawings and engravings, turn-of-the-century neoclassical artists sought to manifest what the art historian Robert Rosenblum has described as "a distilled immutable ideal, shed of sensuous qualities and fixed for eternity through the precision of drawn or engraved outlines" (186). But while Jocelyn, like many nineteenth-century neoclassical artists, believes his aesthetic ideal to be colorless, as the novel progresses, the Well-Beloved's outlines are revealed to have a repressed colored content: a fetishized white surface that, although it goes unremarked, is loaded with cultural value. This revelation occurs through a shift in the ontological metaphors Hardy uses to describe the Well-Beloved, which change about halfway through the novel as the Well-Beloved becomes associated with the Caro family's bloodline.

I borrow the term *ontological metaphor* here from George Lakoff and Mark Johnson, whose foundational study in the philosophy of science, *Metaphors We Live By*, shows how scientists turn to three key ontological metaphors—the container, the substance, and the object/entity—in order to conceptualize material entities (25). Within Lakoff and Johnson's framework, we might say that within the first half of the novel, the Well-Beloved is described as a container that can be filled with any aesthetic content: "Four times she masqueraded as a brunette, twice as a pale-haired creature, and two or three times under a complexion neither light nor dark," the narrator explains (203). After her manifestations in Laura, "the flaxen-haired edition," Marcia, a woman with "Juno's classical face and dark eyes," as well as other women of varying physical appearance, however, the Well-Beloved is substantialized, becoming forever associated with the pale-skinned, light-haired phenotype of Avice Caro and her offspring. The narrator explains the Well-Beloved's transformation from container to substance with an analogy from the plastic arts: "It was as if the Caros had found the clay but not the potter, where other families whose daughters might attract him had found the potter but not the clay" (251). While in the first half of the novel, the Well-Beloved stands in inverse relation to materiality, often appearing in "the absence of the corporeal matter" (202), in the second half, she becomes material—and only the Caros "possessed the materials for her making" (251).

The shift in ontological metaphors Hardy uses to describe the Well-Beloved echo a shift in the figural language of the life sciences of the period. As historians of science have shown, while during much of the nineteenth century (especially following the formulation of cell theory in the 1830s), the fundamental unit of life was conceived as a kind of bounded

---

than the soft following Flaxman dreamed of; a series of surfaces, varied and appropriate, all closely studied from nature" (140).

container, as the century came to a close, biologists called into question the structural emphasis of cell theorists who, in focusing their attention on the cell walls and nucleus, had treated the plasm in between as mere filler.[13] In my exploration of George Eliot's characterization of human figures in terms of an amorphous, plastic substance in chapter 1, I treated one of the most influential English expressions of the new "plasmic" conception of life, T. H. Huxley's 1868 lecture, "On the Physical Basis of Life." Huxley's lecture, published in the *Fortnightly Review* just a few months later, proposed that the physical basis of all living systems is a semifluid, colorless material, which he called *protoplasm*.[14] "More than a substratum for vital forces," as Robert Brain has observed, "protoplasm showed the way to a physiological theory of heredity" (40). In his lecture, Huxley draws on research undertaken on the European continent earlier in the century by botanists such as Hugo von Mohl and Carl Nägeli to argue that all bodies are revealed to be composed of tiny, heritable "colorless corpuscles" (138) circulating in the blood. Huxley writes:

> If a drop of blood be drawn by pricking one's finger and viewed with proper precautions and under a sufficiently high microscopic power, there will be seen, among the innumerable multitude of little, circular, discoidal bodies, or corpuscles, which float in it and give it its color, a comparatively small number of colorless corpuscles, of somewhat larger size and very irregular shape. If the drop of blood be kept at the temperature of the body, these colorless corpuscles will be seen to exhibit a marvelous activity, changing their forms with great rapidity, drawing in and thrusting out prolongations of their substance, and creeping about as if they were independent organisms. The substance which is thus active is a mass of protoplasm, and its activity differs in detail, rather than in principle, from that of the protoplasm of the nettle.[15] (138–39)

13. According to historian of biology Daniel Liu, "Whereas before the 1840s, nonliving formless materials were thought to become organized living forms by a process of separation or coagulation of a viscous fluid, after the 1840s formless and viscous fluids were thought to be themselves active, and capable of many of the basic phenomena of life" (893). My understanding of how the ontological metaphors are used to describe the fundamental unit of life shift is indebted to Liu's account.

14. The first recorded use of the word *protoplasm* was by the Czech anatomist Jan Purkyně in 1839. It was taken up again and popularized by the German botanist Hugo von Mohl (Liu 894).

15. In its suggestion that, viewed under a microscope, our bodies appear to be comprised of tiny, "colorless corpuscles," Huxley's protoplasmic theory of life retains some elements of Darwin's more particulate theory of inheritance, to be discussed in the following section (Geison 375). Darwin had written to Huxley three years prior to his

Early theorists of heredity often thus conceptualized the physical basis of life as a durational (uncolored) sameness underlying all (colored) difference. As Huxley argues, the apparent differences between all organisms fade away under the microscope. "What, truly," Huxley asks, "can seem to be more obviously different from one another in faculty, in form, and in substance, than the various kinds of living beings? What community of faculty can there be between the brightly-colored lichen, which so nearly resembles a mere mineral incrustation of the bare rock on which it grows, and the painter, to whom it is instinct with beauty, or the botanist, whom it feeds with knowledge?" (131). The answer is that underneath the surface of these "brightly-colored lichen," which themselves differ in shape, pigment, and many other apparent qualities from the human beings who paint and study them, lies a fundamental sameness: "a physical, as well as an ideal, unity" that "does pervade the whole living world" (133). For Huxley, as for many nineteenth-century European biologists, this "unity" would be located, among other places, in the matter of the body itself.

When I turned to Huxley in chapter 1, I did so to argue that Eliot's character descriptions in *Middlemarch* literalize the tendency of nineteenth-century scientists to conceive of character in terms of a dynamic plastic matter, capable of transformation through social and physical interactions. Here, I want to put pressure on the neutrality of this claim and the theories it draws upon by remarking that the desires to establish a universal, standardized conception of life often entailed positing a kind of neutral site of inscription that is always already white. The philosopher J. Reid Miller has argued that ethical theories that presume a fundamental, valueless ground upon which value is added or inscribed share the same structure as racial theories that explicitly or implicitly figure nonwhite bodies as "stained" and present white bodies as neutral or unmarked. "Does value by its very definition exhibit the structure of the stain as what 'colors' both the world and its inhabitants and thus, simultaneously, tarnishes, distorts, and hides those initial existents as they arise to consciousness as value-neutral?" Miller asks in *Stain Removal: Ethics and Race* (40). His critique of the notion of a valueless ground from within the philosophical field of ethics allows us to recognize how nineteenth-century representations of the fundamental substance of life tend to present this inheritable matter as a valueless ground upon which genetic information is inscribed. Just as, for Huxley (as for many other nineteenth-century European biologists), life itself was said to inhere in a colorless, plastic substance that underlies all apparent difference, as Eliot's description of Rosamond as "a white soft

---

lecture, providing him with a draft of his manuscript "The Hypothesis of Pangenesis," which outlined an early version of his theory of inheritance.

living substance" would indicate, such colorlessness was often figured in terms of whiteness (*Middlemarch* 324).[16]

To conceptualize this dynamic plastic matter, Hardy, as we saw before, turns to the figure of clay to signal a shift in the nature of the Well-Beloved from a raceless form to a racialized matter. In his lecture on "On the Physical Basis of Life," Huxley turns to this same figure when he makes the case that "protoplasm, simple or nucleated, is the formal basis of all life. It is the clay of the potter; which, bake it and paint it as he will, remains clay, separated by artifice, and not by nature, from the commonest brick or sundried clod" (142). Clay, of course, is not colorless (and neither were the ancient Greek and Roman sculptures that neoclassical artists so fetishized), but Huxley's metaphor dissociates it from color, which arrives by baling and painting, as he construct a new colorless and neutral biological universal: all life forms are united in a fundamental substance, which "paint it as [one] will, remains clay."

Quite different from that of Huxley, Hardy's clay metaphor reveals the substance of life itself to have a repressed, colored content. It does so by drawing attention to the whiteness of Jocelyn's aesthetic-romantic ideal—the Avices' "white teeth," "white neck" (248), and skin "white as the sheets" (279) are refracted in the "white blocks" (211) that Jocelyn carves into sculptures of white women—and by underlining how this whiteness makes women more sexually and socially desirable: "the exceeding fairness of [Nicola Pine-Avon's] neck and shoulders, which, though unwhitened artificially, were without a speck or blemish of the least degree" (222–23). Throughout the novel, references to women's use of "pearl-powder," a cosmetic used to artificially whiten skin, suggest that whiteness—far from a neutral and valueless ground—it itself is kind of paint, a marked surface with its own value (222). In coloring the supposedly neutral and empty form of the Well-Beloved, Hardy thus constructs an aesthetics of surface that draws attention to her latent racial content.

In associating the Well-Beloved with the white skin of the Caro women, as well as the white marble out of which Jocelyn's sculptures are fashioned, the novel demonstrates what art historians have long underlined: that neoclassical aesthetics historically affirmed cultural conceptions of whiteness as both neutral and ideal.[17] More than revealing the latent whiteness of Jocelyn's aesthetic-romantic ideal, however, the novel's color games

---

16. On how nineteenth-century discourses of whiteness intersected with those of plasticity and impressiblity in the American context, see Schuller.

17. On how the fascination with clean lines and white surfaces in neoclassicism affirmed cultural conceptions of whiteness as both neutral and ideal, see Painter (chap. 5); Nelson; Purdy; and Batchelor.

uncover the racial implications of the construction of the fundamental unit of heredity as a durational form (a form figured variously throughout the history of science as a container, a substance, and an object/entity) posited not only to explain but also, much more normatively, to facilitate the perpetuation of sameness across generations.

Ann Anlin Cheng has argued that "we cannot address the history of modern surfaces without also asking after the *other* history of skin, the violent, dysphoric one—the one about racialized nakedness inherited from the Enlightenment so necessary to Western constructions of humanity" (*Second* 11). What this chapter's attention to the racialization of surface in *The Well-Beloved* shows is that the ideology of the human to which Cheng refers functions not only by burying racial difference so deep within the flesh that it can never be overcome, but also by *epidermalizing* difference such that its ephemerality is made to stand in contrast to a durational whiteness that is presented as the world's ground.

Hardy's novel allows us to see how the science of heredity—in its conception of how sameness and difference are relayed across biological time though the biological unit later called the *gene*—relied upon an understanding of whiteness as foundational and durable, with color appearing as additive and ephemeral. Attending to the ways in which Jocelyn's desire for the Well-Beloved is biologized throughout the novel shows how Hardy's novel troubles racial epistemologies that approached bodily surfaces, particularly the skin, as signifying deeper social and biological differences.

On the Whiteness of the Ground

One of the most striking aesthetic features of the setting of Hardy's novel, the Isle of Slingers, is that it is an island of monolithic whiteness. Upon returning home to the isle from London at the novel's start, Jocelyn is struck by "the unity of the whole island as a solid and single block of limestone four miles long.... All now stood dazzlingly unique and white against the tinted sea" (179). The white "unity" of the limestone isle is then aligned with the whiteness of the island natives, who, isolated from the mainland, are the product of centuries of inbreeding. As the narrator explains, the Caros, like many other island families, are "the outcome of the immemorial island customs of intermarriage and of prenuptial union, under which conditions the type of feature was almost uniform from parent to child through generations: so that, till quite latterly, to have seen one native man and woman was to have seen the whole population of that isolated rock, so nearly cut off from the mainland" (278).

In focusing on the discourse of otherness at work in Hardy's description of the "strange beliefs and singular customs" of the inhabitants of the

Isle of Slingers in *The Well-Beloved*, critics of the novel have overlooked the possibility that the isle might represent less of an otherworldly or "othered" place of fantasy than England itself, where a growing racial consciousness was working to align Englishness with whiteness (171). One exception is Angelique Richardson, who has observed that Hardy's isle is "a microcosmic figuring of an imperial head-quarters"; "a bastion of nationality," she points out, "it is home to a breed which has worked continually to resist contamination from the mainland" ("'Some Science'" 326).[18] In line with Richardson, I read Jocelyn's desire for the Caro women as a commentary on the discourses of racial purity in nineteenth-century race science, which would become only more pronounced in English culture as the century turned. Consider here the argument made by the English race scientist Robert Reid Rentoul, who in one of his many diatribes against miscegenation in his 1906 book *Race Culture; or Race Suicide?* attributes degeneracy to the crossing of racial lines in reproduction. After arguing that "heredity is the great cause" of all racial difference, Rentoul makes the case for the preservation of racial groups through selective breeding:

> The inter-marriage of British with foreigners should not be encouraged. A few of us know the terrible monstrosities produced by the intermarriage of the white man and black, the white man with the redskin, the white man with the native Hindu, or the white man with the Chinese. From the standpoint of race culture it is difficult to understand the action of those who advocate the naturalization of foreigners. (5)

Rentoul's comments signal his participation in a modern racial paradigm in which skin color is held to be the most obvious and important marker of racial difference. In Rentoul's framework, "white," "black," and "red" are skin colors, each of which is taken to signify a biologically distinct race. Moreover, his suggestion that the biological distinctions among these racial groups might be maintained through controlled breeding speaks to his proficiency in the nascent science of heredity, a science that posited phenotypical differences such as skin color were not the product of climate or other environmental factors but rather an *internal* biological unit inherited across generations. Two conceptually and historically intertwined paradigms are thus at work in Rentoul's eugenic proposition: a racial paradigm in which skin color emerges as the key signifier of racial difference; and a hereditary paradigm in which a biological unit buried deep within the body is thought to be the key determinant of that dif-

---

18. Richardson examines the role of eugenics in late Victorian culture more extensively in her book *Love and Eugenics in the Late Nineteenth Century*.

ference. I elaborate, in greatly truncated terms, the histories of these two intertwined paradigms in what follows. The following detour through the history of science is important if we are to comprehend the significance of *The Well-Beloved*'s whitened aesthetic, which troubles such racial epistemologies in which the body's surface had become the site of difference, and the body's inner core, the site of sameness.

Historians have shown how the notion that skin color was the central marker of racial difference has a relatively short history—one that can be traced to the late seventeenth and early eighteenth centuries in Europe.[19] In *The Moment of Racial Sight*, Irene Tucker builds on these histories to argue that the dermatological conception of race arose in part due to the decline of the humoral model of medicine, in which a body's physical features were understood to be products of that body's immediate environment. As the eighteenth century progressed, this model was gradually supplanted by an anatomical model of the body in which such traits are stabilized within the body as part of the standardization of medical practice. The earlier humoral model, Tucker observes, conceived of the body as highly sensitive and affectable to outside forces, and phenotypical differences were often thought to be the product of a person's immediate surroundings. Skin played an important role in this model: an absorptive membrane, it was the site through which a body's relationship to its environment was facilitated. As Tucker puts it:

> Skin functioned as the porous boundary between forces within a given humoral body and the environmental forces outside it, which meant that skin color was understood to be affected by things like the amount of sunlight in a given locale and was expected to change as an individual's environment changed. Skin color was just one register among many of human variety; temperament was likewise understood to be the effect of the interaction of bodily humors and climatic forces. So although bodies were essentially particular and changeable, they tended to manifest similarities to other bodies that shared their environment. ("Before" 147)

Tucker argues that the shift from this temperamental conception of human difference to that of race as a biologized essence visible on the skin

19. According to Benthien, "As early as the seventeenth century, visually differentiated skin color becomes the primary characteristic by which ethnic differences is defined" (11). Tucker locates this shift later, claiming that "in the final quarter of the eighteenth century, skin suddenly came to be privileged as the primary sign of racial difference" ("Before" 145). On the role of skin color as a racial signifier in the nineteenth and twentieth centuries, see Stepan. On the historical and cultural function skin and skin color more broadly, see Connor; and Jablonski.

occurred not out of a fascination with the apparent differences between groups of humans but rather out of an attempt to comprehend their fundamental sameness. As she proposes, "we begin to notice and to care deeply about the color of other people's skin at the moment in history we understand our bodies to be... fundamentally like other people's bodies" (*Moment* 13). Within the anatomical model, which radically standardized the body by proposing that all bodies are essentially the same, skin becomes especially significant for its capacity to bring forth the effects of prior causes—problems that are understood to originate inside of bodies and thus cannot be directly observed. As an "immediately visible sign," that is, the skin would become central to the emergence of modern medicine (*Moment* 17).

In this new paradigm, "skin went from being the porous boundary connecting bodies and environments to a boundary that concealed the defining likeness of one body with every other" ("Before" 146). *The Moment of Racial Sight* narrates how in the modern racial paradigm—a paradigm, in Tucker's view, not opposed to but rather contiguous with the theory dominant in critical theory today in which skin color operates as an arbitrary sign—skin color comes to take on its significatory nature as a superficial, semiotic covering that papers over a fundamental sameness.

Part of the upshot of Tucker's argument is that the liberal notion of race as mere surface differentiation is an extension rather than an overturning of the racial paradigm that emerged across the late eighteenth and early nineteenth centuries—a paradigm believed to be more essentialist than that insisting that skin color is an arbitrary sign. Fanon has shown that the production of "racial epidermal schema" coincides with the construction of the surfaces of bodies (especially Black skin) as sites of signification whose color collects together disparate experiences, histories, and behaviors under a single sign (84). And Hortense Spillers has powerfully demonstrated how the "undecipherable markings" on the beaten body of the enslaved African are overwritten in the rise of skin color as technology for grouping and interpreting bodies, a technology that not only erases corporeal singularity, but also overwrites their surfaces with legible "hieroglyphics"—a "Logic of Signs," to return to Lewes' concept, that suppresses and erases a "Logic of Feelings" (67).[20] Reading Tucker alongside these foundational Black studies scholars allows us to see how racialized subjects are not only materialized as "flesh" (through the institution of chattel slavery and other biopolitical technologies that reduce Black sub-

---

20. In her foundational essay, "Mama's Baby, Papa's Maybe: An American Grammar Book" Spillers suggests that a "seared, divided, ripped-apartness" characterizes the enslaved African, who is fungible and nonindividuated "flesh" (67).

jects to fungible matter) but also *dematerialized* as supplements whose arbitrary and ephemeral difference—a difference often said today to subsist "merely on the surface"—is necessary to the perpetuation of whiteness as the world's ontological ground.[21]

Through the figure of the Well-Beloved, Hardy's novel critically engages the racial paradigm I have been elucidating, in which surface-level differences are seen to paper over a fundamental sameness coded as an all-encompassing and universalizing whiteness. It does so by parodying Jocelyn's subordination of the variability and ephemerality of surface to structural integrity of outline in his aesthetic-romantic quest. Notice how Well-Beloved appears in women perceived by Jocelyn to be "essentially the same person" due to their physical likeness (237). "On the surface," the women whom the Well-Beloved inhabits all differ from one another; however, "shining out" underneath their variable surfaces is always "that more real, more interpenetrating being whom he knew so well" (243). Hardy racializes the Well-Beloved, I have been suggesting, by "coloring in" her "ghostly outlines," cultivating an aesthetics of surface that draws attention to the latent whiteness of Jocelyn's supposedly neutral ideal. These outlines are yet further colored in their figuration as the white limestone of which the isle is composed, a figuration through which she becomes the site of the island women's fundamental sameness to one another, a sameness that is the biological ground of the island world.

While the original Avice is initially said to have "a ground-quality absent from her rivals" (232), this "ground-quality" is then generalized to include other island women when it is suggested that Jocelyn "could not love long a kimberlin—a woman other than of the island race, for her lack of this groundwork of character" (232). Daniel Wright has remarked upon the frequency with which Hardy uses the word "groundwork" throughout his novels, noting that the word is often suggestive of a blank canvas or

21. In making this argument, I build upon Fanon's foundational thinking about the epidermalization of race in *Black Skin, White Masks* in order to trace an intertwined but slightly different logic, by which nonwhite skin color emerges as a mark of a difference that is temporary and thus eliminable. My thinking here aligns with that of Cheng, who asks "what happens when we consider ornamental forms and fungible surfaces, rather than organic flesh, as foundational to race making" (*Ornamentalism* 4). Cheng's analysis of how Asiatic femininity is ornamentalized as what she calls a "portable supraflesh" pushes critical race theorists to distinguish between the ways that black, yellow, and other racialized subjects are positioned in relation to the flesh (6). I am more interested here in charting the logic of surface differentiation that arose in the eighteenth and nineteenth centuries in Europe to simultaneously unify and distinguish between racialized bodies—a legacy that persists today in the discourse of multiculturalism. On the discourse of multiculturalism in relation to anti-Blackness specifically, see Sexton.

white primer upon which difference can be seen to erupt. Wright reads the "overwhelming whiteness" of Hardy's "groundwork" as an "assertion of power," noting that "Hardy's movements in and around the blankness of the groundwork... [are] perhaps more easily available to the white novelist than to the novelist of color" ("Thomas" 1031). *Pace* Wright, I suggest that Hardy's explicit racialization of this "groundwork" in *The Well-Beloved* indicates an awareness of the racial implications of his novel's whitened aesthetics—an aesthetics of surface in which whiteness is invoked "precisely to debunk the idea of its inertness or its indifference," as Wright himself observes (1029).

Such an awareness is signaled not only through the novel's racialization of the Avices' "groundwork" through its alignment with the white ground of the isle, but also through their surname, Caro, which is itself, etymologically speaking, suggestive of a white biological substance. According to Lewis and Short's popular Latin dictionary from 1879, the name has its roots in the Latin *caro*, meaning "flesh" or "pulp," specifically in relation to the interior of a fruit or "the inner white part of the wood of trees."[22] Its Greek equivalent is *kréas* (κρέας), meaning "meat," "flesh," or "body"; and its Germanic root is *Kern*, meaning "kernel," "germ," "core," "marrow," or "essence."[23] The white, inner, core-like quality of the name Caro—as well as its German root, *Kern*—is also reminiscent of Weismann's *Keimplasma* (whose root *Keim* means "seed," "nucleus," or "germ"), the "nuclear substance" said to exist in the core of every cell (Weismann, *Essays* 2:346). Building on cell theory, Weismann suggested that germ plasm is able to be passed on unchanged throughout generations, in part because of its location in the nucleus of the cell. Its interior location meant that it was insulated from the body's more porous membranes and thus could not be altered by somatic experience. When pushed to explain how organisms indeed attain new characters in response to local and specific interactions throughout their lives, Weismann posited the existence a second, altogether autonomous substance, *Somatoplasm* (or soma plasm). Where germ plasm was unchangeable and durable, Weismann posited, soma

---

22. Ethan Allen Andrews, *A Latin Dictionary Founded on Andrews' Edition of Freund's Latin Dictionary: Revised, Enlarged, and in Great Part Rewritten by Charlton T. Lewis and Charles Short* (Oxford: Clarendon, 1879), s.v. "caro."

23. Andrews, *Latin Dictionary*, s.v. "caro." Hardy claimed that "'Caro' (like all other surnames) is an imitation of a local name... this particular modification having been adopted because of its resemblance to the Italian for 'dear'" (*Life* 304). A hostile reviewer in 1897, however, noted that "*Caro, carnis* [flesh] is the noun with the declension of which Mr. Hardy is perpetually and everlastingly preoccupied in his new book" (quoted in Ingham 340n3).

plasma was transformable and perishable.[24] This latter substance, imprinted through experience, could not be inherited. The "enclosed" nature of the germ system meant that the sensory experiences would have no effect whatsoever on the organism's genetic makeup—a boundary known to this day as the *Weismann barrier*.[25]

Building on the work of historians of race and racial science, I have been tracking the emergence of two conceptually intertwined movements: the transformation of skin from an impressible surface into a site for the signification of a difference papering over a fundamental sameness, and the conceptualization of the fundamental unit of heredity as a plastic, colorless substance or entity thought to facilitate the transmission of sameness across generations. As the historians of science Staffan Müller-Wille and Hans-Jörg Rheinberger have demonstrated, moreover, these two movements are not only conceptually but historically intertwined. Both enacted a severing of the body from its milieu, a severing that occurred as scientists sought to distinguish between biologically inherent and environmentally variable traits.

As Müller-Wille and Rheinberger show, the science of heredity arose when the forces of globalization and colonialism pushed scientists to account for the surprising stability of certain traits in the face of bodily mobility. They write:

> Knowledge of heredity started to unfold where people, objects, and relationship among them were set into motion.... Mobilizing plants and animals, for instance, was a precondition for being able to distinguish between inherited and environmentally induced traits in organisms. Only when organisms were actually removed from their natural and traditional agricultural habitats could environmental differences manifest themselves in trait differences, and only then could heritable traits manifest their steadiness against a background of environmental change. (16–17)

A desire to maintain regularity and consistency in the face of variation drove early attempts to understand the mechanisms through which traits are

24. As McNabb notes in his history of evolutionary anthropology in Victorian England, "For Weismann the germ plasm carried the unchanging code for each generation, which was faithfully copied from parent to offspring. It could not be affected by anything happening in the body. Variation within the reproductive germ plasm occurred very occasionally by what we today would call random copying errors" (189–90).

25. According to von Sydow, "Weismann has to be regarded as the founder of what was later called the *central dogma of molecular biology*: no information could be passed from the phenotype to the gentotype, from any cell molecules to the DNA" (120).

passed on from generation to generation: "Only when these [environmental] ties were dissolved in favor of a variety of relationships between forms and modes of transmission," Müller-Wille and Rheinberger write, "did a need arise for a complex metaphor like heredity to be applied in order to account for the proliferating phenomena of change and stability" (18).

What Müller-Wille and Rheinberger describe as the "obsession of the scientific mind with regularity at the expense of contingency and complexity" would be pushed to its extreme by eugenic scientists such as Galton who sought to control the development of the English "race" (16). Although unaware of Weismann's work until the 1890s, Galton had come to a similar conclusion about the closed nature of the "germ system"—a conclusion that, as the historian of genetics Ruth Cowan has shown, was informed by his eugenic convictions.[26] Like Weismann's germ plasm substance, Galton's "stirp" (from the Latin *stirpes*, meaning "root"), was said to persist entirely unchanged through reproduction, but only some of its characters were expressed in each generation. Because, for Galton, "heritable gemmules could not be associated with the somatic tissues and by extension that any alterations they sustained (acquired characteristics) would not be transmitted to progeny," an organism's physical and mental character could be manipulated entirely through reproduction (Gillham 185).

Galton's eugenic convictions are already apparent in his first published essay on the topic of heredity, "Hereditary Talent and Character" (1865), which emphasizes the manipulable quality of character: "It would seem as though the physical character of future generations was almost as plastic as clay, under the control of the breeder's will," Galton writes. "It is my desire to show, more pointedly than—so far as I am aware—has been attempted before, that mental qualities are equally under control" ("Hereditary" 1:157). Turning, as Hardy and Huxley had before him, to clay as a metaphor for the malleability of life, Galton proposes that the fundamental stuff of character is plastic. On its face, this claim might appear similar to what I attributed to Eliot in chapter 1. Quite unlike Eliot, however, whose descriptions of characters in terms of soft matter in her novel *Middlemarch* are formulated to show how contingent, unwilled circumstances and encounters determine character, Galton's vision of plasticity

26. Cowan explains the logic behind Galton's rejection of acquired characters as follows: "If acquired characters could be inherited the eugenic program for social reform would become meaningless, why encourage people to limit the number of their children or choose better marriage partners (a difficult process) when the human race could be improved through sanitary reform or educational reform (an easier process) and these 'acquired' improvements could be transmitted to the next generation?" (409).

has no room for environmental contingency. Rather, as he underlines, the character of the species is entirely "under the control" of the breeder.

Where Galton hoped to excise outside influence from the picture—to uncover the unchanging laws of character so as to manipulate them—his cousin Charles Darwin maintained that characterological variations arise, at least in part, as a result of unpredictable external causes. It is thus worth pausing here to note, via the example of Darwin's theory of pangenesis, that not all theorists of heredity sought to excise environmental contingency from the picture. As Darwin underlined in *The Origin of Species*, the transformation of species "depends on many complex contingencies," including "the slowly changing physical conditions of the country, and more especially on the nature of the other inhabitants" (306). His interest in environmental contingency predisposed him to accept the inheritance of acquired characteristics. Where Galton's stirp, like Weismann's germ plasm, was thought to persist across generations unchanged, only imperfectly represented by each child, what Darwin called "gemmules could be altered by the impact of the environment and habit" (Holterhoff 662). The theory of pangenesis held that microscopic units are expelled from cells and transmitted to offspring through the blood, a theory Darwin constructed to account for the spontaneous generation of variations over time.

An exchange between Galton and Darwin in December 1875 in which they discuss their competing theories of inheritance is telling for what I take to be the fundamental difference between their respective approaches to character—the former enclosed and insulated, the latter relational and hybridized.[27] In a letter composed on December 18, 1875, Darwin suggests that the difference between their approaches largely concerns where gemmules are located. Darwin proposes that Galton's belief that germ cells are contained entirely within the reproductive system cannot fully account for how the characteristics of organisms blend to produce hybrids. Darwin objects to Galton's view, wondering that if gemmules are so isolated, how is it that they spontaneously mix to produce entities that are thoroughly "intermediate in character" (Darwin to Francis Galton, December 18, 1875, quoted in Pearson, *Life* 189). He introduces the following thought experiment about the generation of a hybrid from two different plants:

27. Historians of science emphasized the extent to which Galton's reasoning in this letter anticipates the Mendelian ratios (Olby 636). Darwin's theory of pangenesis, on the other hand, would, as Geison explains, "be rapidly swept out of court by more satisfying explanations (in particular Weismann's theory of the continuity of the germ plasm)," dismissed as a "mysterious and inexplicable failures of genius" (379).

If 2 plants are crossed, it often or rather generally happens that every part of [the] stem, leaf—even the hairs—and flowers of the hybrid are intermediate in character; and this hybrid will produce by buds millions on millions of other buds all exactly reproducing the intermediate character. I cannot doubt that every unit of the hybrid is hybridized and sends forth hybridized gemmules. Here we have nothing to do with the reproductive organs. (189)

Throughout his letter Darwin emphasizes the hybrid nature not only of the organisms, but of the gemmules themselves ("every unit of the hybrid is hybridized and sends forth hybridized gemmules"). His suggestion is that for the two plants to be so thoroughly "intermediate in character," all of their cells, not merely their reproductive cells, would have to mix.

In his response, composed the following day, Galton downplays the opposition between their two theories. However, his approach to the matter reveals a deep ideological difference between the two thinkers: "Let us deal with a single quality, for clearness of explanation," Galton wrote, his reductionism already indicating a methodological difference (Pearson, *Life*, 189). Returning to Darwin's example, Galton asks Darwin to imagine two organisms, one white and one black, which combine to produce a gray organism, and he sketches the diagram shown in Figure 3.

On the top row are a white form and a black form whose germs are shown to be white and black, respectively. The second row of the diagram models the gray organism that would result if the two reproduced. This gray form is then modeled at two scales: (1) at the microlevel of the germ, and (2) on the macrolevel of groupings of such germs. The diagram thus

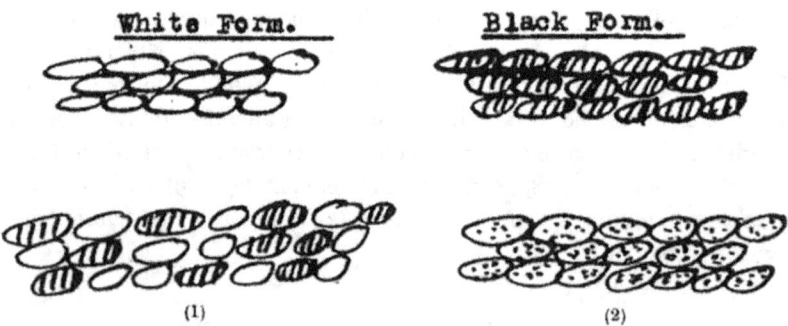

3. Francis Galton, Diagram of White, Black, and Hybrid Grey Forms. Galton's letter to Charles Darwin (December 18, 1875). From Karl Pearson, *The Life, Letters and Labours of Francis Galton*, vol. 2 (Cambridge: Cambridge University Press, 1924), 189.

illustrates Galton's view that the child of a black parent and a white parent will appear gray not because it possesses "hybridized gemmules," as Darwin suggests, but rather because it possesses a combination of black and white gemmules inherited from its two parents.

Galton suggests that the binarism of his black-and-white diagram is simply "for clearness of explanation," but I read this image as indexing the epistemology of racial difference that I have been tracking—one in which whiteness is the neutral ground and pigment is figured as an addition or supplement, a stain on the surface of the ground. Notice first how the white forms in Galton's diagram are prioritized both temporally and spatially: white forms combine with black forms, their purity maligned in the second row with lines and dots. In contrast to Darwin, moreover, who insists on hybridity at every scale, down to the level of "hybridized gemmules," Galton's diagram insists on a categorical difference between white and black gemmules, which combine to produce the appearance of grayness. Jennifer DeVere Brody has written that "the desire to see white as 'white' and black as 'black' drives the division of the world according to absolute correspondences between colors, characters, and categories" (12). What Brody describes as "English culture's preoccupation with... miscegenated figures" that threaten the division between "white" and "black" is nowhere more apparent than in Galton's diagram, which retains whiteness and blackness as absolute values (the former foundational and the latter additional) in its theory of mixing (4).[28]

As the case of Galton demonstrates, the debates around the fundamental mechanism of heredity that emerged at the turn of the century, in particular those concerning whether such a unit is affectable by the environment, were shot through with the same anxieties about contamination and infection—anxieties that informed more explicit racial thinking such as that of Rentoul discussed earlier. The notion put forth by both Galton and Weismann, that the genetic material of the organism can be altered only through reproduction, never via physical encounters and experiences, thus was not only analogically but homologically intertwined with a desire to protect and insulate whiteness (aligned variously with the English, Europeans, and other populations) from contaminating outside contact—a

---

28. A similar racial logic can be seen to inform the nineteenth-century racial categories of *mulatto* (a person who is half Black), *quadroon* (a person who is one-quarter Black), *sextaroon* (a person who is one-sixteenth Black), and so on—categories that explain the race of a person using a complex arithmetic in which the fundamental elements are black and white units whose fundamental and binary difference is never called into question.

desire that had informed the science of heredity since its inception, both in its vision of color as supplementary and in its fascination with continuity at the level of the genes.

Late nineteenth-century narratives of what the Victorian historian Edward Augustus Freeman called the "unbroken national being" of the English people aspired to erase colonial and other encounters that led to "mixing," as well as to falsely paint the picture of an originary (white) being who could be tainted in the first place (22).[29] Hardy's representation of Jocelyn's sculptural obsession with protecting and molding the character of the Avices does not just contest the ethics behind this eugenic desire to protect and mold the character of the English race; like Darwin, he also calls into question that project's *very scientific viability*, asking to what extent it is even possible to excise environmental contingency and hybridity from the picture. His novel thus forms an exemplary instance of what this book calls the *science of character*: through attention to the role of circumstance in the formation of character, his novel develops an ethological account of the contingent encounters that make people who they are.

In his proposal for an imagined science of character, Mill proposed that if the laws of character were uncovered, they would affirm "tendencies, not facts" (*System* 870). Mill's suggestion that his "ulterior science," despite being attentive to the causal mechanisms at work in the production of character, could never be predictive accords with the sense Hardy had about his literary practice. In his narratives about specific fictional people who enter specific situations, he does not explain how character necessarily or universally forms (indeed, his literary project—much more than that of Eliot—is critical of claims to universality); rather, they describe how character forms *here* or *there*, holding character open to the unforeseen and the unexpressed registered in Mill's description of his science as "ulterior." But where Mill understood the circumstantiality of character to be an obstacle to the elucidation of its principles, Hardy uses literary character both to critique and to better *theorize* heredity in his novel, intervening in the discussions about the nature of the germ system that took place between Weismann, Galton, and Darwin.

In a discussion of Hardy's thinking about heredity in *Jude the Obscure*, Emily Steinlight observes that Weismann's "biological model, applied to the scale of a single life, slows down evolutionary processes so radically that biographical time looks almost static," rendering it "harder to rec-

---

29. On fantasies of racial continuity, see Baucom, *Out of Place*; and Peppis. Both discuss Edward Freeman's racialist justification of England's parliamentary system of government in his *The Growth of the English Constitution* (1872).

oncile with the novelistic concept of character and with the logic of plot" (*Populating* 183). Indeed, even across the scale of the generation, *The Well-Beloved* demonstrates that change is difficult to manifest. But while Jocelyn expects that each Caro woman will be a direct copy of the original Avice, given their shared "groundwork of character," his expectations that each generation will act and look the same as the last are repeatedly frustrated when differences are introduced at every interval. While Jocelyn treats these differences as subsisting merely on the surface, the novel deploys both character and plot to insist that these differences are substantial. Using narrative repetitions to explore what I call the *accretive* quality of character, *The Well-Beloved* draws attention to the tendency of character to accumulate new qualities in response to its environment. It thus proposes an alternative model of character to that of Weismann and Galton, in which the body is divided into a stable and standard interior and a changing and variable exterior. In what I describe as Hardy's accretive theory of character—a theory already apparent in earlier works such as *The Return of the Native*—physical qualities such as skin color are presented not as the effect of an interior cause but rather as the trace of an externalized activity, an event, encounter, or experience. Such an approach is consistent with Darwin's thinking about character in *The Origin of Species*, which emphasizes the extent to which bodies are both imprint and are imprinted by their environments.

Accretions of Character

Among the changes Hardy made to the 1897 edition of *The Well-Beloved* was a new subtitle, *A Sketch of Temperament*, a phrase that announces the novel's concern with character as well as with the sketch form that, as we have already seen, had recently reemerged as an alternative to popular, plot-driven fiction.[30] Like Eliot's *Impressions of Theophrastus Such*, which invokes the genre of the character sketch in order to reflect on the role of description in realism, Hardy's "sketch" constitutes a similarly reflexive moment in the history of realist characterization. Where *Impressions*, as we saw earlier, turns away from plot toward description, however, Hardy's final novel embraces what Frederic Jameson, in his *Antinomies of Realism*, calls "pure storytelling" over and against the "impulses of scenic elaboration, description," and "affective investment" (11).

Rehearsing with stunning conventionality the plots that had come to dominate Victorian fiction—the bildungsroman and the marriage plot,

---

30. On the resurgence of the sketch form in the late nineteenth century in "avant-garde plotless works," see Garcha (224).

in particular—*The Well-Beloved* emerges as a formal protest against what Hardy, at the end of the nineteenth century, felt the novel had become: a mechanical, plot-driven form, no longer able to register what he called the "spontaneity" of character. In August 1893, Hardy wrote a letter to the Parisian newspaper *L'Ermitage* that stated: "I consider a social system based on individual spontaneity to promise better for happiness than a curbed and uniform one under which all temperaments are bound to shape themselves to a single pattern of living" (*Life* 274). Hardy's letters, essays, and diary entries of the period suggest that the novel genre had become for him one such "curbed and uniform" system. In a contribution to a forum on contemporary fiction in the *New Review* published in 1890, he lamented that the publishing industry—specifically the magazine serial and the library system—prevented novelists from revealing the "spontaneity" of character through its institution of a rigid set of socially acceptable plots ("Candour" 18). As Hardy complains there, the contemporary novelist must either "whip and scourge [his] characters into doing something contrary to their natures [in order] to produce the spurious effect of their being in harmony with social forms and ordinances, or, by leaving them alone to act as they will, he must bring down the thunders of respectability upon his head" ("Candour" 18–19).

In this section, I read the figure of the Well-Beloved as the vehicle of Hardy's critique of the fate of character in the Victorian novel, whose "variety," as Gillian Beer has argued, "is oppressed by the needs which generate plot" (*Darwin's* 223). Hardy once explained his decision to quit writing novels with the suggestion that the genre was "gradually losing artistic form, with a beginning, middle, and end" (*Life* 309). Rather than resisting such narrative disintegration, however, *The Well-Beloved* seems actively to embrace it. The figure of the Well-Beloved is the locus of the novel's experimentation with narrative cyclicity: each time a particular woman fails to embody her ideal fully, the marriage plot is restarted and Jocelyn's quest begins again. The measured, progressive tempo of Jocelyn's Bildung narrative is highlighted in the novel's three parts: "A Young Man of Twenty," "A Young Man of Forty," and "A Young Man of Sixty." The feminine cyclicity of the Avices, on the other hand, motors Jocelyn's character development; each iteration serves as the new object of desire in his quest—Avice Caro I, Avice Caro II, Avice Caro III. "I see—I see now," Avice II exclaims in the 1892 edition of the novel, as if aware of her narrative instrumentalization, "I am—only one—in a long, long row!" (15).[31]

---

31. Avice's utterance is a repetition of a line from *Tess of the d'Urbervilles* in which Tess, refusing Angel Clare's history lessons, expresses her frustration with the repetitious nature of history: "Because what's the use of learning that I am one of a long row

Through its iterative narrative structure, in which repetition underscores the temporal and material difference of narrative events from events past, as well as its descriptions, which proceed additively, revealing what appear at first as bare outlines to be composed of layers, *The Well-Beloved* reveals the accretive quality of character—the capacity of human and nonhuman things to acquire qualities in response to local and specific pressures, producing beings slightly different from generation to generation, as well as from moment to moment. *The Well-Beloved* thus stresses the aesthetic and political dangers of stripping character of its "spontaneity"—the tendency of character to respond, unpredictably and contingently, to circumstances.

Returning home one day, for example, Jocelyn "guessed he should find his prospective wife and mother-in-law awaiting him with tea," but Avice III, absorbed in a book, ignores him. Confused and disappointed, Jocelyn feels his desire for her wane as "the white and cadaverous countenances of his studies, casts, and other lumber peered meditatively at him" (309). Thus, while to Jocelyn, the Avices all appear to be "essentially the same person" (239), the novel repeatedly undermines Jocelyn's perspective by insisting upon the differences of personality and appearance that characterize each generation.

In its insistence that variations always spontaneously erupt across the interval of a generation, *The Well-Beloved* can be seen to reflect Darwin's thinking about speciation in *The Origin of Species*. In chapter 10 of *Origin*, entitled "On the Geological Succession of Organic Beings," Darwin states, "I believe in no fixed law of development causing all the inhabitants of a country to change abruptly, or simultaneously, or to an equal degree" (308). Modification occurs, rather, as "slight differences accumulated during many successive generations" are "selected"—that is, when variations provide advantages to survival in a particular environment (31). While such changes are too protracted to be observed in real time, they can be observed in the strata of the earth's crust, which preserve evidence of species past in the form of fossils. But the geological record, Darwin is quick to point out, is far from a direct or perfect transcript of speciation. This is because—like the process of natural selection itself—

---

only—finding out that there is set down in some old book somebody just like me, and to know that I shall only act her part" (126). Like Tess, the women of *The Well-Beloved* are destined to act the part of all women before them. On the role of repetition in *The Well-Beloved*, see J. H. Miller, who argues that the novel "functions as an interpretation of [Hardy's] earlier novels or even as their parody. By presenting a schematic and 'unrealistic' version of the pattern they share," he writes, "it brings out their latent meaning" (*Fiction* 151).

the sedimentary rock that composes it likewise materializes according to a slow, iterative temporality, itself introducing small differences at every interval (308–12).

Periods of subsidence, in which sediment accumulates in shallow pools, allow fossils to solidify. Periods of land rise cause organic remains to be crushed or washed away. Cycles of accumulation and dissipation, subsidence and uplift, ensure that the geological record is uneven and gap filled: "As the accumulation of enduring formations, rich in fossils, depends on great masses of sediment being deposited on subsiding areas," Darwin explains, "our formations have been almost necessarily accumulated at wide and irregularly intermittent intervals of time; consequently the amount of organic change exhibited by the fossils embedded in consecutive formations is not equal. Each formation, on this view, does not mark a new and complete act of creation, but only an occasional scene, taken almost at hazard, in a slowly changing drama" (309).

Such a "slowly changing drama" is reenacted through the plot of *The Well-Beloved*, which likewise draws parallels between the accretive temporality of limestone (itself composed of skeletal fragments) and the iterative processes of biological inheritance that produce organisms always slightly different from, and yet tied to, their progenitors. What we might call Darwin's "fossil analogy"—his analogy between the iterative process of species modification and the iterative process of rock formation that, however unevenly, preserves evidence of the former within its layers—is likewise at work in Hardy's novel, which undermines Jocelyn's obsession with the perpetuation of the same by revealing character's tendency to change over time, both on the level of the individual and on the level of the family.

One might extend Darwin's analogy here to make the point that those who understand evolution to entail the gradual revelation of a pregiven form (what "preformationists" believed occurred on the level of the embryo, and which some later "recapitulationists" believed was mirrored at the level of phylogenic development) confuse the process of *fossilization* with that of *excavation*. Where the subtractive practice of excavation reveals a form preserved from the past, speciation, Darwin repeatedly emphasizes throughout *Origin*, is an "accumulative action" (45). In this reading, Hardy's protagonist—a sculptor who scrapes away layer upon layer of stone in the hopes of revealing the ideal form of a woman—appears as a kind of preformationist, misguided in his inability to come to grips with the accretive temporality of character. For Jocelyn, "succeeding generations of women are seldom marked by cumulative progress" (24). But where Jocelyn treats Avice Caro, her daughter, and her granddaughter as three versions of the same unchanging form, the novel in its own form affirms Darwin's claim that modification "depends on many complex contingencies" (306).

We saw in the previous section how, in contrast to his cousin Francis Galton, Darwin emphasized not only the fundamental hybridity of all organisms, down to the level of their gemmules, but also the capacity of all organisms to inherit characteristics acquired through somatic experience. The notion of "temperament" invoked in the 1897 title of Hardy's novel suggests a related understanding of character as a mixture or composition affected in large part by the environment. In the 1897 preface to the novel, Hardy highlights the extent to which his characters are intended to be perceived as products of their surroundings, noting that just as "certain soft-wooded plants which cannot bear the silent inland frosts... thrive by the sea in the roughest of weather," the white limestone isle "is a spot apt to generate a type of personage like the character imperfectly sketched in these pages" (173). In describing the Isle of Slingers as "a spot apt to generate" a protagonist such as Jocelyn, and later describing the Avices as derived from "some mysterious ingredient sucked from the isle," Hardy does not only introduce the analogy I have been tracing between the character of the isle to the character of its inhabitants (232). He also implies that one's character does not consist in some kind of transcendent *eidos*, but rather emerges, spontaneously, in response to one's surroundings.

In stressing the intimate connection between character and milieu, Hardy does not nostalgically call for a return to the humoral model of the body or, more disturbingly, the climatological understanding of race. Instead, he invokes the notion of "temperament" in order to envision a more corporeal yet relational alternative to the abstraction of "race" as a category for conceptualizing characterological difference, turning instead to locality as the instigator of such differences. This turn toward locality has less to do with physical geography (much less the geography of a nation-state such as England) than what, following Darwin, we might think of as the *geological* way that character forms successively in response to circumstances—that is, social and physical encounters that lend a person or people their unique quality. In this model, the body is not divided into an inside and an outside—the former the site of sameness and the latter the site of difference—but rather is composed of infinite strata, each of which the product of an interaction that has been absorbed into that body's being. Here, "race" is not a transcendental signified, the genotypical referent of a phenotypical trait such as skin color or a particular nose shape, but rather the accumulation of local and specific encounters into a multilayered form that takes on characteristic shapes and colors.

Such a geological model of character formation is inscribed in the rock of which the setting of the novel, the Isle of Slingers, is composed. Within

4. Stan Celestian, Oolite (2018). Photograph © Stan Celestian.

the oolitic limestone of the Isle of Slingers we discover another model of what I have been calling *human objecthood*, the extent to which the character of the human takes form according to laws of character that also govern those of "a rock or a tree," to return to James Sully's words. When Jocelyn returns to the isle from London at the novel's start and is struck by "the unity of the whole island as a solid and single block of limestone four miles long," he observes that "all now stood dazzlingly unique and white against the tinted sea, and the sun flashed on infinitely stratified walls of oolite" (179). Although the isle appears to be a single unified structure, upon closer inspection, that structure is composed of infinite layers composed of oolite—white rock that is itself composed of many layers. Oolitic limestone, or egg stone, is made of small, egg-shaped *ooids* that form in shallow pools when organic detritus such as bone fragments roll around in muddy micrite, causing calcite to accrete on the ooid's surface (Figure 4).[32] While the mechanism through which oolite forms is still unclear

---

32. In *The Ethics of the Dust*, Ruskin describes a process through which oolite is formed as follows: "The soft white sediments of the sea draw themselves, in process of time, into smooth knots of sphered symmetry, burdened and strained under increase of pressure, they pass into a nascent marble; scorched by fervent heat, they brighten and blanch into the snowy rock of Paros and Carrara" (358). The whiteness of the oolite in Ruskin's vision is contrasted with the "dark drift of the inland river" (358).

today, researchers speculate that bacterial film on the surfaces of the ooids contributes to the accretion of the inorganic chemical precipitate.

From the oolitic limestone of the Isle of Slingers emerges a model of character formation distinct from that of hereditary scientists such as Galton and Weismann, for whom the genetic structure of an organism was seen as insulated from the body's somatic surfaces. As a point of contrast, recall here Galton's "white forms," which appear gray when mixing with gemmules from "black forms," becoming stained through the introduction of black gemmules into their reproductive system. Recall also Huxley's "colorless corpuscles," the site of the sameness of all bodies—bodies whose interiors are the same but that differ on the surface, like the brightly colored lichen that grow on rocks. The ooids that compose the Isle of Slingers bear a certain visual similarity to these spherical white figures. However, where Galton's white forms and Huxley's colorless corpuscles are characterized by a clear division between inside and outside, substance and surface—the inner substance of the body persisting throughout time unchanged, and its surface either remaining unstained or becoming stained—oolite takes shape through a different, accretive logic through which encounters at the surface introduce small differences that are absorbed and preserved in each layer (Figure 5). In the accretion of layers,

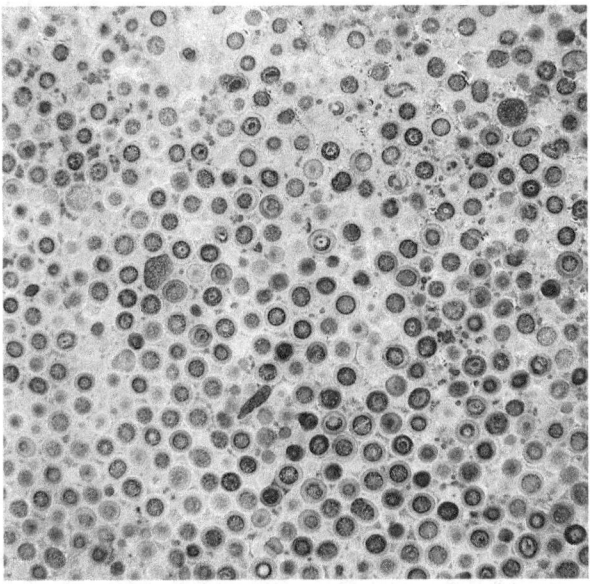

5. Grover Schrayer, Cross-section of Oolitic Limestone (2009). Photograph by © Grover Schrayer.

surface becomes substance. And no substance, it is worth underlining, is ever without surface.

In *Specters of the Atlantic*, Ian Baucom describes such an accretive temporality when he writes of the history of colonization, "Time does not pass, it accumulates, and as it accumulates it deposits an ever greater freight of material within the cargo holds of a present" (325). The "sedimentary poetics of duration" that Baucom observes at work in certain twentieth-century Caribbean writers highlights the persistence of the past in the present, as well as the way the past is altered and reframed in the current moment (325).[33] How might such a conception of history inform our understanding of character, and specifically English character, which, I have been arguing, Hardy's novel is concerned with in and through its figure of the Well-Beloved?

In 1874, John Morley, a British statesman and critic of imperialism, suggested that a conception of history as geologically layered might transform the notion of human character, writing that "character is considered less with reference to its absolute qualities than as an interesting scene with scattered rudiments, survivals and inherited predispositions" (24). Like Morley, who spatializes character into "an interesting scene" onto which the rudiments of the past emerge to color the present, Hardy projects the history of the island inhabitants onto the stratified rock of their isle, implying that although even England itself may appear from afar as "a solid and single block... dazzlingly unique and white," its layers are "infinitely stratified" (179). His descriptions of the accretion, mining, and sculpting processes that the limestone rock of the isle undergoes indicate the protracted material history of the island people. The rock itself is historically central to the livelihood of the inhabitants, in that the Pierston and Caro families having long worked in the quarrying business and the houses are "built of solid stone" (171). But more than a site of local labor, the rock preserves within its layers the racial and colonial history of the isle, as Hardy's descriptions of its material composition make clear.

I read these layers not merely as a ledger to be unearthed by archeologists or interpreted by historians, nor merely as remnants or remainders of a time past, but as the history of English character materialized.[34] As the historian Antoinette Burton has underlined, the notion—unfortunately

---

33. In my article "Durations of Presents Past," I suggest that the spatiotemporal logics of accretion and surface modulation as theorized by Ruskin can help to illuminate debates about the persistence of the past into the present in contemporary critical theory.

34. Walters has uncovered a similar meditation on "the evolution of the nation's profoundly composite being" in Dinah Mulock Craik's 1850 novel *Olive* (339).

still prevalent in the field of Victorian studies—that England ever was a racially or culturally homogenous nation is itself a fantasy, a fantasy of inside/outside, home/away that "was itself a technology of imperial rule" (28). In response to Burton, Elaine Freedgood has argued that England's layered history is repressed in the cultural production of England, and with it, the field of Victorian studies, as what she suggestively calls an "island of whiteness." As Freedgood points out, Britain "has several postcolonial histories that have been variously internalized: the defeat of the Roman Empire by invaders; the assimilation of Anglo-Saxon 'settlers' as natives; the long throwing off of the 'Norman Yoke'; and then the British empire, modeled on Rome, but aware of the various causes of the decline of that empire" ("Islands" 299).

For Freedgood, Hardy's novels are one place where this colonial history is made legible, for his novels not only refer to it but also index its many layers through their temporal-spatial schema. In Hardy's work, she writes, "historical periods seem to exist in a kind of sedimentation in characters and landscapes in which time moves at varying speeds, so that the colonized past of England is remembered in various names, places, and festivals, even if it is consciously forgotten" (300). The documentation of the movements of bodies that produce the physiology and characterology of Victorian England stands at the heart of the "island of whiteness" of *The Well-Beloved*—an isle in which the geological record of the rock preserves in its fossils fragments of the racial and colonial history of England, "Norman, Anglian, Roman, Balearic-British" (*Well-Beloved* 232).

Baucom has shown how the emergence of Englishness as a racial category relied upon the construction of narratives of genetic continuity, hereditary lines said to be unbroken in the face of war and conquest. With the analogy the novel sets up between the ground of the isle—composed of white limestone—and the genetic makeup of the Avices, whose whiteness is maintained in their lack of contact with outsiders, *The Well-Beloved* works to demystify narratives of Englishness as what Baucom calls "an essential and continuous identity" (*Out of Place*, 16) by subverting the national fantasies of racial continuity that hereditary scientists such as Weismann perpetuated in their biological theories of "the continuity of the germplasm" (*Essays* 1:161).

Notice how, just like the oolite—a rock composed of white forms that appear as unified spheres, but when bisected, are revealed to be multilayered—the Avices' own idealized whiteness is revealed to be the product of a series of iterative practices that give off the appearance of a totalizing white unity. Upon encountering Avice I for the first time as an adult, Jocelyn notices that she has been transformed into a kind of neutral material to appeal to suitors such as him. This process has been achieved through the severing of the intimate link between the body and the environment—a severing that, as we saw in the last section, was crucial to the construction of a science of heredity and the modern racial paradigm from which that science took cues in its division of the body into surface and depth:

> He observed that every aim of those who had brought her up had been to get her away mentally as far as possible from her natural and individual life as an inhabitant of a peculiar island: to make her an exact copy of tens of thousands of other people, in whose circumstances there was nothing special, distinctive, or picturesque; to teach her to forget all the experiences of her ancestors; to drown the local ballads by songs purchased at the Budmouth fashionable music-sellers,' and the local vocabulary by a governess-tongue of no country at all. She lived in a house that would have been the fortune of an artist, and learnt to draw London suburban villas from printed copies. (*Well-Beloved* 186)

Janet Bownas has convincingly argued Hardy's novels often reveal the link "between the process of colonization taking place in distant lands during the nineteenth century and processes occurring at the same time within Britain" (4–5). Indeed, this passage might be read as exploring the production and exportation of Englishness in both England and its territories in its representation of the production of the Avices' whiteness, revealed to be the product of incredible labor.[35] Avice I is taught to forget her island ancestry, to rid herself of her accent, and to value the aesthetic of the metropolis over that of the island where she was raised. A concern with the homogenization of character drives these lines in which "printed copies" of the London suburbs carry more currency than actual and unique homes found in the countryside. And Avice I's character, too, has been globalized: "her natural and individual life as an inhabitant of a peculiar island" has been erased in an attempt to render her legible and desirable to the kimberlins (those from the mainland). In drawing attention to the effort to have the Avices conform to certain standards of white Englishness, the novel thus can be read as a performative critique of the imperial logic through which Englishness itself had become portable, while at the same time inseparable from bodies perceived to be white.

"It should not be possible," Gayatri Chakravorty Spivak once forcefully contended, "to read nineteenth-century British literature without

---

35. R. Young has argued, "It is significant that compulsory national education was introduced in Britain in the late nineteenth century, for its rationale shared much of the spirit of colonialism. The inferior races, at home and abroad, had to be civilized and acculturated into the ideological dynamics of the nation" (51).

remembering that imperialism, understood as England's social mission, was a crucial part of the cultural representation of England to the English" ("Three" 243). If, as postcolonial scholars such as Spivak have long demonstrated, the so-called domestic novel itself was as integrally shaped by the English colonial mission as the so-called imperial novel, then even if Hardy's novels do not explicitly engage imperial themes or settings, they can still be seen to engage "the axioms of imperialism" (243).[36]

I read *The Well-Beloved* as anti-imperial fiction that narrates how local cultures confront and resist the whitening of character under the empire, which strips bodies of their locality in the attempt to reveal a sameness that, it turns out, can never truly be revealed, but must be *produced*. Not only does Hardy draw attention to the unmarked quality of whiteness, he also implicitly highlights how the prerequisite for belonging to this category is not only white skin but also the appearance of having transcended characterological specificity as such. Such "whiteness," the novel shows through its central figure, the Well-Beloved, who *might* appear in anyone, anywhere (though she largely appears only in the pale-faced Avices), had seeped into the very structure of the Victorian novel, whose narrative reduction of "all temperaments... to a single pattern," Hardy helps us to see, is a symptom of its absorption of the "axioms of imperialism."

I pointed out in the introduction to this chapter that even before he began to compose *The Well-Beloved*, Hardy already felt that the novel had calcified into a mechanical and repetitive form that was no longer capable of registering what he called the "spontaneity" of character. In an 1890 essay in the *New Review*, referenced earlier, he made the case that every form of the novel—as a result of moralistic readers, but also as a result of economic markets and the publishing formats those markets support, such as the magazine serial and the three-volume format—distorts, rather than "reflects and reveals life" ("Candour" 17). A particular target of Hardy's essay is the marriage plot, with its "regulation finish that 'they were married and were happy ever after'" (17-18). Throughout the essay, Hardy presents character as a dynamic, material phenomenon whose natural "spontaneity" is suppressed in works that force characters to act according to preapproved scripts.

One possible reading of the formulaic structure of *The Well-Beloved* is that Hardy has furnished readers with the predicable, mechanical model of character he felt resulted from such prescribed narratives. "One of the reasons why I consented to the reprinting of such a bygone, wildly romantic fancy," Hardy wrote to his friend Edmund Gosse directly following the

---

36. On the false binary between the "domestic" and "imperial" novels, see also Bivona, *Desire*; Hall and Rose; and Stewart.

publication of the 1897 version of the novel, "was that it would please Mrs Grundy & her young Person & her respected husband by its absolutely 'harmless' quality" ("To Edmund Gosse, March 31, 1897," 157). Hardy's letters from this period suggest that he supposed *The Well-Beloved* to be the very model of novelistic convention, "a book which nobody could say anything against" ("To Lady Jeune, March 29, 1897," 156).[37] Such lines affirm Michael Ryan's thesis that with *The Well-Beloved*, Hardy gave "publishers exactly what they wanted in a somewhat exaggerated, and indeed, caricatured form" (187). They also lend force to my more specific claim: that in stripping character of its dynamical relation to milieu, Hardy's final novel can be seen to generate an inverted realism—a realism that self-consciously fails to "reflect and reveal life" in its formal subordination of surface to outline.

Its narrative formulaic and repetitive, its landscape nearly monochromatic, *The Well-Beloved* lacks the cross-hatched descriptive detail, contingent encounters, and narrative detours characteristic of Hardy's fiction. When descriptions do occur, Hardy's language calcifies into plain and generic adjectives that reduce characters and landscapes to their barest outlines. Consider the following description of two of Jocelyn's love objects, Avice I and Nichola Pine-Avon. The passage opens with Avice's characteristically white skin, the outline of which is thrown into relief by the black silhouette of Nichola from Jocelyn's vantage:

> Engaged in the study of her ear and the nape of her white neck, he suddenly became aware of the presence of a lady still further ahead in the aisle, whose attire, though of black materials in the quietest form, was of a cut which rather suggested London than this Ultima Thule. For the minute he forgot, in his curiosity, that Avice intervened. The lady turned her head somewhat, and, though she was veiled with unusual thickness for the season, he seemed to recognize Nichola Pine-Avon in the form. (248)

In this black-and-white scene, the two women described interact, aesthetically, in the field of Jocelyn's gaze. Notice that any individuating qual-

---

37. Like many of Hardy's novels, *The Well-Beloved* was met with a hostile reception from critics, inspiring at least one reviewer to accuse Hardy of sexual impropriety. This reviewer for *The World* seems to have especially infuriated Hardy, inspiring him to send letter after letter detailing his utter disbelief that his novel had anything to do with the body. "There is more fleshiness in *The Loves of the Triangles* than in this story—at least to me," he wrote to his editor that same year (*Life* 286). *The Loves of the Triangles*, by G. Canning and J. H. Frere, was a 1798 parody of Erasmus Darwin's *The Loves of the Plants* (1789) that imagines the erotic life of geometric figures like parabolas and ellipses.

ities are subtracted to reveal more abstract and lineated forms: where Avice is reduced to body parts such as "her ear and the nape of her white neck," Nichola is only recognized as part of a larger, ambiguous "form" that is either the black mass of her attire or the shadow of the Well-Beloved herself. The scene is evacuated of both color and movement. In this frame, the only thing that rises to the status of a motion is when Nichola is said to have "turned her head somewhat." Though Avice "intervenes," her intervention is purely spatial and static in nature, standing, as she is, in the foreground.

Passages such as these, in which characters are described in terms of their static and unchanging outlines, are striking, given the aesthetics of surface that, I have argued, characterizes much of Hardy's previous fiction. In *Return of the Native*, as we saw at the start of this chapter, Hardy focuses his descriptive attention on Diggory Venn's unique surface over and above his common outline, noting that Venn is "ordinary in shape, but singular in colour, this being a lurid red." Venn is, of course, "not red by birth." And yet his redness is as essential to his being as anything else, it being the dynamical sign of his character: "He was not temporarily overlaid with the colour: it permeated him" (7).

I noted earlier that the revelation of Venn's white "groundwork" at the end of the novel allows Venn to assimilate into the social world of the heath. Edward Said once defined imperialism as "an act of geographical violence" resulting in the native's "loss of locality to the outsider" (225). Such loss of locality is nowhere more apparent than in the ending of *Return of the Native*, in which Venn "got white of his own accord" in an act of stain removal that makes possible his marriage and integration into the community from which he had been ostracized: "Diggory Venn, no longer a reddleman, but exhibiting the strangely altered hues of an ordinary Christian countenance" (394).

It might be tempting to read Venn's racial conversion narrative as reproducing the epistemology of race that I have been describing throughout this chapter, in which color emerges as a phenotypical or second-order phenomenon whose ground is a standardized, uncolored sameness shared by all. In removing Venn's "stain," it might be argued, Hardy replicates the logic according to which all bodies harbor a fundamental sameness in their outlines despite their differing surfaces. Alicia Christoff has read the ending of *Return of the Native* as perpetuating, rather than critiquing, such "white mythologies," arguing that, in its "pseudo-racialization of its white British characters," the novel unconsciously narrates the "coming into being of 'whiteness' as a racial and ethno-nationalist designation that functions precisely by refusing to see the bodies and labor of people of color"

(110–11).[38] But I want to suggest another reading—one in which the coincidence of Venn's narrative whitening with the addition of a "regulation finish that 'they were married and were happy ever after'" is no accident, but a stain removal that is *made* to coincide with narrative convention (Hardy, "Candour" 17–18).[39] This is not to say that Hardy himself was necessarily conscious of the racial implications of this coincidence (though he may have been), but rather that the textual apparatus of the novel allows for a reading of it as performatively reinstating the racial logics it enacts.

As Hardy explains to readers in a footnote in the 1912 Wessex edition of the novel, "the original conception of the story did not design a marriage between Thomasin and Venn. He was to have retained his isolated and weird character to the last, and to have disappeared mysteriously from the heath, nobody knowing whither—Thomasin remaining a widow.... Readers can therefore choose between the endings, and those with an austere artistic code can assume the more consistent conclusion to be the true one" (408). The fact that this tacked-on marriage plot ending coincides with the erasure of Venn's "weird character," as Hardy refers to it, allows for a reading of book six of the novel as a critique not only of the narrative conventions to which Hardy increasingly felt forced to conform, but also specifically as the way those narrative conventions had become aligned with racial narratives of Englishness as a portable category that nonetheless retained whiteness as a precondition for real inclusion. Such a reading of Venn's white fate as a performative capitulation to the demands of publishers has implications for my reading of the fate of character in *The Well-Beloved*. If, in order to conform to novelistic convention, Venn must be stripped of his colored, reactive surfaces, which bear the mark of his unique history and place, then the only thing left for novelistic character—if it is to find a home in a published novel—is to become a bare outline.

Wright has suggested that when Hardy self-consciously strips landscapes and characters of their color, he seems to "wonder what happens when that inventory of realist details becomes obscured to the point of blankness, the fictional world deprived of all but its barest outlines" (1030).

38. Much of Christoff's argument in her chapter accords with my own here, including not only her attention to the racialization of Venn but also her reading of how "Thomasin's dual-coded sexual and racial purity are designated as a whiteness so white as to be transparent in a vision of normative female sexuality against which Eustacia's own—dark, unruly, restless, exotic—will be contrasted throughout the novel" (118).

39. Leslie Stephen's final decision to reject *The Return of the Native* from *Cornhill Magazine* was, according to Hardy, because "he feared that the relations between Eustacia, Wildeve, and Thomasin might develop into something 'dangerous' for a family magazine" (Hardy, quoted in Maitland 276).

Indeed, this chapter has discerned from within the "ghostly outlines" of the Well-Beloved the ashen remains of Hardy's faith in realism—a realism of character of which he had initially believed the novel capable, and a realism in which, by the time he began composing *The Well-Beloved* in 1892, he had palpably lost faith.

Following his full-scale revision of the novel in 1897, Hardy would commit himself entirely to poetry—a genre that in his biography he says he worked to infuse with the "principle of spontaneity, found in mouldings, tracery, and such-like—resulting in the 'unforeseen' (as it has been called)" (*Life* 324), and which in *Jude the Obscure* manifests itself on the "time-eaten" walls of "lichened colleges" (71).[40] Such attention to the lively surfaces of things—including not only ornamental architectural facades but also stratified rock formations and colored skin—is a key tenet of Hardy's realism, which approaches character as likewise "resulting in the 'unforeseen.'"

---

40. In *Jude the Obscure*, the work yard of a stone mason is described as "a little centre of regeneration. Here, with keen edges and smooth curves, were forms in the exact likeness of those he had seen abraded and time-eaten on the walls. These were the ideas in modern prose which the lichened colleges presented in old poetry" (71). Thank you to Cannon Schmitt for this reference.

Schopenhauer and the Determination of Women's Character

[CHAPTER FOUR]

There is in fact no social philosophy, however logical and far-seeing on other points, which does not lapse into incoherence as soon as it touches upon the subject of women.

MONA CAIRD, "Marriage," *Westminster Review* (1888)

In 1894, the English critic Arthur Waugh characterized the "new school of realism" that had emerged in recent years as "chirurgical," complaining that New Realist authors, in reducing the human to the body and its physical functions, had generated a model of character "whose analysis may be of value to science, but is absolutely foreign to art" (217). According to Waugh, whereas "the most characteristic literature of the time has been introspective," the newest trend in realistic fiction in England has been to turn away from the mind and toward a "discussion of the passions and sensations" (213). "It is in this development that the new school of realism has gone furthest," Waugh remarks, before coming to his point: that, in contrast to the old realism, which had cultivated a cerebral and objective approach to reality, the new realism suffers from a troubling "want of restraint" (213, 217). That "women-writers are chiefly to blame" for this new, unrestrained realism explains for Waugh not only its thematic concern with the body and its impulses, but also the lack of control exercised in its characterizations themselves, which, in allowing subjective feeling to distort objective perception, have become "passion's slave" (218, 210).

Alluding to Irish novelist Sarah Grand's New Woman novel *The Heavenly Twins* (published the previous year, in 1893), which had scandalized readers with graphic descriptions of pregnancy and venereal disease, Waugh asserts: "There is all the difference in the world between drawing life as we find it, sternly and relentlessly, surveying it all the while from outside with the calm, unflinching gaze of criticism, and on the other hand, yielding ourselves to the warmth and colour of its excesses, losing our judgment in the ecstasies of the joy of life, becoming in a word, effeminate" (210). Critiquing the New Realism on the very grounds on which it was founded—verisimilitude—Waugh concludes that the female realist is doomed to failure unless she "throws off the habit of her sex, and learns to rely upon her judgement, and not her senses" (210).

Waugh's comments reveal the extent to which English readers were concerned that realism had been feminized when women writers entered the literary marketplace *en masse* and began cultivating their own distinct brand of realist aesthetics. The New Realism that emerged in the hands of New Woman novelists at the turn of the century was founded on a claim to a new intimacy with physical reality—an intimacy that, as critics such as Waugh intimated, risked collapsing the distinction between art and life. With women holding the pen, the supposedly distanced and cerebral perspective of the "old" realism had given way to the subjective and all too immediate sensations of the "new."

Of course, many of the so-called old realists had also been women. And many of them, too, had centered the materiality of the body in their representation of human character. For George Eliot, as we saw in chapter 2, the achievement of a "keen vision and feeling of all ordinary human life" demanded a reattunement of the human sensorium such that that one might hear "the grass grow and the squirrel's heart beat" (*Middlemarch* 182). Eliot's framing of realism as a tool for enhanced sensory perception, although it might have gone unrecognized by Waugh, paved the way for a new generation of women and feminist realists to understand realism in terms of the expansion, rather than the retraction, of feeling.

In the prefaces to their novels and stories, New Realist authors claimed to paint reality with a candidness hitherto unseen: "These stories are simply what they profess to be—studies from life," wrote Grand in the preface to her 1894 collection, *Our Manifold Nature: Stories from Life* (7). She proclaimed that her "close studies from life in the new vein of realism," as they were advertised in *Book News Monthly* (335), contained "no fiction whatever," their events occurring "exactly as described" (Grand, *Our Manifold* 9). While some critics admired Grand's realistic "character-drawing" ("Inspired" 267), marveling at how "each character and incident" burst forth with "marvelous creative force" ("Reviews" 268), others worried that when art veered too close to reality, it lost its charm.

Grand's detailed descriptions of bodily experiences such as childbirth and infidelity one such critic complained, were "too realistic," leading him to conclude that "therefore her work is inartistic" ("Table Talk" 269). Grand, for her part, responded to such attacks by insisting that for art to be worthwhile, it must be "true to life" (8). Earlier realists, she retorted, had merely produced the "effect of life," their characters painted up like stage actors made to "look natural in the glare of the footlights" (8). Her work, by contrast, would move "beyond the mere semblance and grasp the reality of life" (8). For Grand, however, along with other New Woman writers at the turn of the century, this reality was not a deeper moral or spiritual truth, such as the freedom of the will or the power of intersubjective exchange; nor was it the depths of the human psyche, more multifaceted and complex than that of any other animal. Rather, as New Realism's critics were quick to discover, this reality was to be found nowhere but in the flesh.

This chapter reengages the question of the dynamic materiality of character that has been explored across the previous three chapters by examining the crises of the will engendered by the New Woman novel, a genre whose deterministic representation of character has long been a source of critical controversy. Where Victorian critics such as Waugh attacked the New Woman novel for cultivating a realism centered around the body and its impulses, more recent feminist critics have struggled with the genre's representations of its female characters, who often meet with death, poverty, or other narratively punitive ends. Searching the New Women novel for an empowering vision of female agency, twentieth- and twenty-first-century feminist scholars have often been disappointed to find—to quote the foundational New Woman author Olive Schreiner—"a striving and a striving and an ending in nothing" (*Story* 74).[1]

1. In their three-volume study of twentieth-century women's writing, *No Man's Land* (1988), Sandra Gilbert and Susan Gubar read Schreiner's "heroine's tortured decline into death" in *The Story of an African Farm* as the symptom of an inability to conceive of women's freedom: "even while Schreiner argues for female freedom," they write in their assessment of her "narrative difficulties," "she cannot seem to represent such freedom in the life of her heroine" (53). Gilbert and Gubar's frustration with the ending of *The Story of an African Farm* is representative of a strain of feminist criticism according to which the political failures of the New Woman novel are intimately bound to its realist aesthetics, which minimizes female agency in its focus on the present of women's oppression. Contrasting the political realism of the New Woman novel with the idealist vision of utopian feminist fiction, in *Women and Fiction: Feminism and the Novel 1880–1920* (1979), to give one other example, Patricia Stubbs laments the New Woman novel's failure "to see a collective solution to women's problems" (126). This scholarship speaks to a broader critique of realism in poststructuralism, one lineage of which can be traced to the work of the French feminist theorist Hélène Cixous. "Cixous' negative attitude toward literary realism," Ledger notes, "has been hugely influential, to the extent that those feminist critics who have concerned themselves with New Woman fiction by women have more and more often tended to valorize the more obviously modernist output of some turn-of-the-century women writers over and above the realist writing of the majority of New Woman novelists and essayists" (192–93). In the French feminist context, see also Schor, who advocates for a revaluation of nineteenth-century feminist works that cultivate an "unattainable but enabling" (10) idealism opposed to a realism that "paint[s] things as they are and not as they should be" (31).

Within feminist criticism, the failures of the New Woman novel are often attributed to its inability to transcend the essentialisms of Victorian gender ideology and recognize the socially constructed nature of identity: "Positioned among social purists, Social Darwinists, and eugenicists," Angelique Richardson writes, New Woman "writers were concerned less with examining the unstable, socially constructed nature of selfhood and the body, than with grounding both the body and sex roles in the flesh and blood of evolutionary narrative," an approach that, she argues, led them ultimately to "represent sex as fixed, and character as largely determined by heredity" ("Eugenization" 228). Whereas for Victorian critics, the New Woman novel's aesthetic flaws were said to stem from its authors' characteristically feminine inability to control their impulses, for contemporary scholars, the genre fails politically because it is unable to rise above the biologizing discourse of its time. While they may agree on little else, then, the New Woman novel's early detractors and its later feminist critics both posit a minimal theory of agency behind the genre's New Realist aesthetic, which is said to fail to rise to the level of (political) art in that it manifests the physical constraints on women's action, rather than envisioning a future in which those constraints are lifted and agency exercised.

But New Women writers did not so much overestimate the extent to which women's character was determined as they redefined determination itself as a complex and often contradictory category—a plurality of historical, environmental, and biological forces that collide to give rise to character. While some strains of nineteenth-century feminism might have been motivated by the Millian precept that "we have real power over the formation of our own character" (*Autobiography* 177), the feminist writers I analyze here cultivated a politics premised on the deterministic notion that woman is "foredoomed by every circumstance of her life" (Grand, *Heavenly* 277).[2]

In her work on mid-Victorian representations of the fallen woman, Amanda Anderson shows how within literary and political discourse of the period, the female sex was often presented "as lacking the autonomy and coherence of the normative masculine subject" (*Tainted* 198). In contrast to men, who were presented as the intellectual agents of their own *Bildung* narratives, women, epitomized in Anderson's reading by the figure of the

---

2. As an example of the former, consider the Victorian feminist Josephine Butler, who in her calls for domestic reform advocated for broader education and extension of practices of self-cultivation though "the diffusion of home influence and character among the masses" (J. E. G. Butler xxx). On the appropriation of "the liberal values of individual autonomy and equal rights" by Victorian feminists more broadly, see Shanley (4).

fallen woman, appear "distortedly, as the mere effect of systemic forces—environmental, economic, sexual, and aesthetic" (1). Anderson's critique of this bifurcation of male and female into agential subject and determined object, respectively, leads her to advocate the extension of the category of subjectivity to women, who have been mistaken as determined objects. I contend, however, that the political force of this late Victorian realist genre lies precisely in its refusal to affirm such an agential model of subjectivity. Resisting gendered distinctions between "man" and "woman" framed in terms of agential capacity or incapacity, New Woman novelists draw attention to the objecthood of all humans by highlighting the extent to which all character is shaped by forces beyond individual control. I thus read their politically charged realism as an attempt to short-circuit what Anderson describes as an "impasse in Victorian social thought, the tension between the scientific explanation of character and society and the commitment to ethical and political transformation" (199). They did so by refusing to oppose intention and impulse, treating such forces instead as different manifestations of the same affectively charged force: Will.

I invoke the term "Will" here not in the traditional sense (i.e., as a voluntary and conscious intentional act), but rather in the nonvoluntarist sense proposed by the Romantic-era German philosopher Arthur Schopenhauer, a touchstone for many New Woman novelists and the focal point of this chapter. In his magnum opus, *The World as Will and Representation* (1819, 1844), Schopenhauer constructed a metaphysical system based on Kant's distinction between phenomenon and noumenon, arguing that although the world might appear to be composed of distinct entities—subjects and objects held together in the framework of "Representation" (*Vorstellung*)—in reality, the world ultimately consists of only a single, unified force: "Will" (*Wille*).

Throughout the 1880s and 1890s, Schopenhauer's name would be referred to in works by New Woman authors such as Amy Levy, Mona Caird, George Gissing, George Moore, and Thomas Hardy.[3] Moreover, of the intimate collection of novelists and intellectuals in the Men and Women's Club coordinated by the mathematician Karl Pearson throughout the late 1880s, a great many were engaged with Schopenhauer's work: Pearson himself, Havelock Ellis, Annie Besant, Mona Caird, and the New Woman

3. References to Schopenhauer occur—to name just a few New Woman novels and related texts—in Gissing's *Workers in the Dawn* (1880) and *The Unclassed* (1884); Moore's *A Drama in Muslin* (1886), *Confessions of a Young Man* (1889 edition), *Mike Fletcher* (1889), and *Esther Waters* (1894); Grand's *The Beth Book* (1897); Lee's *Baldwin* (1886); Levy's "A Minor Poet" (1884), "Sokratics in the Strand" (1884), and "To E." (1886); and Caird's *Stones of Sacrifice* (1915) and *The Great Wave* (1931).

novelist par excellence, Olive Schreiner, whose *The Story of an African Farm* (1883) is considered one of the founding texts of the genre. In what follows, I turn to Schopenhauer's concept of the Will—an all-pervasive, metaphysical force driving all earthly activity—as a means of better elucidating the political stakes of a feminism that did not place great faith in the power of the individual to transcend or transform their circumstances and that instead cultivated an understanding of character itself *as a circumstance*—a fortuitous encounter of forces temporarily reconciled.

"I am more than ever convinced that persons are successively various persons according as each special strand in their characters brought uppermost by circumstances," Hardy wrote in his diary in December 1890, a year before he began to compose the first version of *The Well-Beloved* (*Life* 241). Where Hardy had by this time begun to lose faith in the novel as a literary form capable of revealing the circumstantiality of character, however, New Woman novelists would be more sanguine. Doubling down on the suggestion that character is determined by milieu—insisting on the lack of agency of the individual in the face of circumstances—they reinvigorated the realist novel by pursuing with increased fervor the ethological project abandoned by Hardy: to generate a narrative account of the material forces at work in character formation.

In what follows, I elucidate the challenges posed by the New Woman novel and the New Realist aesthetic it pioneered to masculinist ideologies of subjectivity and self-making, thus providing new grounds for reevaluating what too often gets dismissed as political incoherence, defeatism, or lack of ambition in these works.[4] Highlighting connections between Schopenhauer's metaphysical theory of the Will and the representation of agency, instinct, and desire, in New Woman fiction—specifically, Grand's *The Heavenly Twins* (1893), Gissing's *The Unclassed* (1884), and George Egerton's *Keynotes* (1893), as well as Olive Schreiner's posthumously published *From Man to Man; or Perhaps Only* (1926), explored in my next chapter—I read Schopenhauer's philosophy as contributing to early feminist theory in its destabilization of historically gendered binary oppositions between subject and object, mind and body, will and drive.

In *The World as Will and Representation*, Schopenhauer asked how bodies could be part of a physical world—their actions determined by natural law—and yet also be experienced by subjects as free. His answer is that

---

4. See also Showalter, who argues that the New Woman novelist Olive Schreiner is "sadly underambitious" in her narrative-making, claiming that "the labors of construction and plotting were beyond her" (*Literature* 203, 197). Working to correct this view, Burdett argued that it is crucial that within Schreiner's novels "modern" and "European" feminism "cannot be narratively realized" (31).

all bodies are driven by a single force that manifests itself differently, depending upon the perspective from which it is experienced. "Hitherto, the concept of *will* has been subsumed under the concept of *force*," Schopenhauer wrote, "I, on the other hand, do exactly the reverse, and intend every force in nature to be conceived as will" (WR 1:111). In privileging will over force, he cut through the debate about free will versus determinism that pervaded the nineteenth century. His philosophy is not predicated on an ontological opposition of subjects (who are free) and objects (which are determined). Rather, all beings can be experienced, epistemologically, as subjects or objects, free or determined, depending on one's position. From the outside, things appear as physical objects with static traits and qualities; from the inside, they are experienced as concatenations of force. Not only does Schopenhauer "subjectivize" nonhuman things; he "objectifies" the human by highlighting how a person's dynamic thoughts, behaviors, and gestures materialize into what he calls *Charakter* in the eyes of the beholder (WR 1:126).

Schopenhauer considered himself to be an idealist, believing as he did that the world as we experience it (the world as representation) is an illusion. As I show through my analysis of a series of articles published on Schopenhauer in the late Victorian periodical press, however, Schopenhauer's English readers not only often interpreted him as a philosophical *realist* (holding the belief that reality exists independent of human perception) but also as a *materialist* (holding the belief that all of reality consists in matter or physical processes).[5]

Read in conversation with English materialist scientists, especially Darwin, as we will see, Schopenhauer was embraced by New Woman writers in England, whose dynamic materialist approach to character in literature accorded with his approach to the matter in philosophy. Schopenhauer's theory of the Will, when filtered through nineteenth-century British materialist science (especially Darwinism), offered a platform that enabled women and feminist writers to develop a model of character that decentered human consciousness and intention. The impulsive aesthetics they cultivated placed a premium on the nonconscious and nonvolitional forces with which women's failed agency had long been aligned. Reading the New Woman novel alongside Schopenhauer's philosophy of Will, as well as Nietzsche's theory of the will to power, I demonstrate how Schopenhauer's British women readers expose contradictions in his work between his own ontology and his politics, reconfiguring his philosophy in

---

5. As an example of the former, consider one 1890 reviewer's comment that Schopenhauer's "realistic doctrine of the Will formed in many respects a wholesome counterpart to abstract idealism of Hegel" ("Schopenhauer in English" 671).

order to challenge masculinist models of agency, rationality, and volition. While the conception of agency at work in the New Woman novel might appear to be defeatist, New Woman novelists ultimately can be seen to rework Schopenhauer's philosophy to cultivate a non-subject-centered politics in which character is determined through interactions between impulsive, codetermining bodies.

An English Start

In *Donna Quixote*, a novel serialized in Mary Elizabeth Braddon's journal, *Belgravia*, in 1879, a group of women gather to discuss "theories about nature and the future world" (167). The host of the gathering, a self-identified "pessimist" named Claudia, turns to "the doctrine of Schopenhauer" in order to expound her theory "that everything on this earth was constructed for the worst" (166). As Claudia proposes to the room full of women listening attentively, life is but "a trial of strength for the great rescuing and reorganizing force which is to regenerate man," a category that is said to include women, too (166).[6] "And the regenerating force?" asks a newcomer, unsure to what exactly Claudia is referring: "Claudia looked around the room benignly; glanced up to the ceiling; partly closed her eyes; opened them again; and then, in the tone of one who breathes a prayer or speaks out some solemn and sacred oracle, uttered the word 'Woman'" (166).

In this scene, a sense of inevitability is invoked in order to situate women as "the regenerating force" of the world. In the moments leading up to this passage, the women of the club had debated the potential and pitfalls of the word *nature*, some advocating that the term be thrown out completely. Claudia, however, convinces the group to opt instead for a redefinition of the term to account for its dynamic, transformative power and the role of women therein. After pondering whether nature is a "force" or "movement," the group eventually agrees to define nature as a "tendency," a guiding principle open to reconfiguration (262).

The fictional women that gather in this proto–New Woman novel register the growing interest of women readers in Schopenhauer in Victorian England: while during the first half of the nineteenth century few English readers had heard his name, throughout the second half, Schopenhauer would rise to widespread popularity in England, to be read by philosophers, novelists, and scientists alike. Like Claudia, Schopenhauer's New Woman readers often aligned the metaphysical force he called "Will" with the

6. As one woman at the club remarked, "When we speak of men, of course we mean women also" (163).

force of the feminine. "They desire to have 'a still woman.'... They create by stoppage a volcano, and are amazed at its eruptiveness," wrote George Meredith in her 1885 novel *Diana of the Crossways* (59). In conversation with Schopenhauer, for whom the Will manifests itself in humans, among other things, as an uncontrollable sexual impulse that "blows away... human laws and scruples," New Woman writers would invoke a sexualized, feminine force disruptive of Victorian moral codes and traditions (WR 2:553).

However, before we explore in greater depth Schopenhauer's theory of the Will and its significance for the New Woman novel, a few words about the philosopher's European reception are necessary. Before the 1850s, Schopenhauer was almost entirely unknown not only in England but also in Germany, where he had experienced what he described as "passive resistance" by the "guild of professors of philosophy" (quoted in Cartwright, *Schopenhauer* 518). In 1853, however, an article by the critic John Oxenford that appeared in the English journal the *Westminster Review* changed everything for the German philosopher. "My philosophy has just this moment set foot in England," Schopenhauer wrote to his friend Ernst Otto Lindner excitedly, in an article "with me as its subject" ("To Ernst Lindner, April 27, 1853," 309; translation mine).[7] Entitled "Iconoclasm in German Philosophy," the article presented Schopenhauer to English readers as a radical pessimist and determinist, making waves for his attack on German idealism. "Few will be those of our English readers who are familiar with the name of Arthur Schopenhauer," Oxenford's article begins. "Fewer still," the piece continues, "will there be who are aware that the mysterious being owning that name has been working for something like forty years to subvert that whole system of German philosophy which has been raised by the university professors since the decease of Immanuel Kant" (388–89). Why, Oxenford asks, is this radical philosopher almost entirely unknown not only in England, but in Germany, too? According to Oxenford, Schopenhauer's obscurity can be explained only by his radical iconoclasm—his rejection of the central dogmas of contemporary philosophy.

In Germany, Oxenford explains, Schopenhauer is not even "a professor of philosophy, is not a philosopher by trade, has no academical chair, and there has been an understanding among all the university philosophers to put down any man who is not one of their craft" (390). Present-

---

7. Oxenford had actually published an earlier review of Schopenhauer's work in the *Westminster Review* in 1852. Published anonymously the previous year, Oxenford's initial article on Schopenhauer, entitled "Contemporary Literature of Germany" (1852), did not generate the same response as "Iconoclasm in German Philosophy." Schopenhauer himself became aware of the first article only upon discovering the second.

ing the philosopher as a pariah whose insights are being ignored merely because of his lack of pedigree, Oxenford's article in the *Westminster Review* appealed explicitly to nonacademics. Where professional philosophers confound even the most intelligent readers with their inscrutable prose, Oxenford suggests, Schopenhauer is a philosopher of the people, his metaphysical system accessible and transparent: "Schopenhauer gives you a comprehensible system clearly worded, and you may know, beyond the possibility of a doubt, what you are accepting, and what you are rejecting" (393).

After the publication of Oxenford's article, as Hayden White has observed, Schopenhauer "moved to the very centre of European intellectual life,... not so much among professional philosophers as among artists, writers, historians, and publicists" (237). Translated into German later that year by the wife of Schopenhauer's friend Lindner and published in Berlin's popular *Vossische Zeitung*, Oxenford's article was key to Schopenhauer's long-awaited success in his home country.[8] The 1870s then saw a surge of articles published that introduced Schopenhauer's work to readers in Germany, England, and France, with translations of his major works following in the 1880s and 1890s.[9]

As the century progressed, his work would strike a particular chord with women writers, who discovered an unlikely ally in the pessimist philosopher. "Pray read the article on Schopenhauer next—I think it one of the best," wrote Maryann Evans—the novelist later known as George Eliot—to her friend Sara Hennell the month that Oxenford's article appeared ("To Sara Sophia Hennell" 95). Eliot, working anonymously at the time as the editor of the *Westminster Review*, was partly responsible for the publication of the article.[10]

After Eliot, who spent the early part of her career as a translator of German philosophy, completing the first English translations of David Friedrich Strauss's *The Life of Jesus* (1846) and Ludwig von Feuerbach's *The Essence of Christianity* (1854), a host of British women writers continued to facilitate Schopenhauer's reception, producing some of the earliest translations of his works and critical studies of his philosophy.[11]

8. In scholarship on Schopenhauer's reception, the translation of Oxenford's review into German is often credited to Lindner himself. Lindner's wife was a British émigré with language skills that exceeded those of her husband (Cartwright, "Parerga and Paralipomena" 119).

9. The first English translation of *Die Welt als Wille und Vorstellung* (by R. B. Haldane and J. Kemp) appeared between 1883 and 1886 under the title *The World as Will and Idea*.

10. The publication dates listed are those of Eliot's English translations.

11. In 1889, Mrs. Karl Hillebrand (née Jessie Taylor, later known as Jessie Laussot) published the collection *Two Essays by Arthur Schopenhauer*, which provided the first

What drew these British women writers to Schopenhauer's philosophy? Close attention to some of the earliest essays and studies of his work in English suggests that Schopenhauer's metaphysics, as it was interpreted by English readers, made possible an entirely new mode of *theorizing*, a mode of thought that turned away from grand metaphysical abstractions such as being, becoming, and the absolute, toward issues of everyday experience such as the nature of sex, love, and feeling. While other philosophers had addressed corporeal experience in the abstract, Schopenhauer tackled it head-on in chapters such as "The Metaphysics of Sexual Love" ("Der Metaphysik der Geschlechtsliebe")—a piece for which he would become particularly well known in England, and which would become a particular touchstone for feminist writers and activists.

What especially seems to have appealed to British women readers, however, was Schopenhauer's commitment to understanding the dynamic nature of embodied experience. In possessing these two aspects—dynamically experienced interiority and materially manifest exteriority—he suggests, the human is no different than any other thing, he suggests. This is because *all of reality* in Schopenhauer's philosophy can be experienced from these two perspectives: that is, from the outside, things appear as individuated entities with static traits and qualities, but experienced from the inside, they are concatenations of force. We can observe the truth of this claim, Schopenhauer argues, through the experience of our own bodies—the single "object" to which we have inside access. The contemporary philosopher Julian Young explains Schopenhauer's line of reasoning in terms of the notion of a black box:

> On the objective view of things—and, here, it doesn't make any difference whether the things in question are rocks, daffodils, dogs, other human

---

English translations of *On the Fourfold Root of the Principle of Sufficient Reason* (1813) and *On the Will in Nature* (1836). Numbering over 400 pages, Laussot's *Two Essays* provided a substantial introduction to Schopenhauer's thought. Thomas Hardy bought the collection within the year, reading and annotating it extensively while writing *Tess of the d'Urbervilles* (1891). In 1897, another collection of essays translated by a woman appeared. Whereas Hillebrand's *Two Essays* had brought together two of the philosopher's most challenging works, Mrs. Rudolf Dircks's *Essays of Schopenhauer* was a much more accessible compilation. Featuring translations of eleven of Schopenhauer's shorter essays on such topics such as love, authorship, and art, Dircks's *Essays* brought Schopenhauer to a more general audience. See Brilmyer, "Schopenhauer and British Literary Feminism," for more on how the often anonymous and unpaid work of women intellectuals like Eliot led to Schopenhauer's success in both England and Germany, as they produced and facilitated some of the earliest translations of his works and critical studies of his philosophy.

bodies or my own body—we observe the body in question affected by a cause which produces as an effect a given piece of behaviour.... So we have an input and output mediated by, as it were, a black box which we cannot open.... This would be the end of the story were it not for the single dramatic exception of my own body. (65)

From the recognition that Will is the essence or underlying nature of our own bodies, that is, we can reason that Will is in fact the nature of all perceptual bodies. Importantly, for Schopenhauer, one does not *know* so much as *feel* this truth, for it is through feeling (*Gefühl*), not rationality, that one can access through the body the nonrepresentational and immaterial realm of Will—the thing in itself.

Placing a new premium on emotion as a form of thought, Schopenhauer's metaphysics can thus be seen to appreciate traditionally feminized forms of knowledge. His was an experiential mode of philosophy that prioritized—at least in method—intuition over logic and reason. At the same time, however, Schopenhauer often went out of his way to denigrate feminine experience. His vitriolic essay "On Women" argued that while men possess the ability to rise above the primal urgings of the Will through contemplative reflection, women—subjective, too sympathetic, and always stuck in the present—are not capable of abstracting themselves from the strivings of the Will. He added: "[T]hat which is present, intuitively perceptual, immediately real exercises over them a power against which abstract ideas, established maxims, fixed resolves, and generally a consideration for the past and future, the absent and distant, are seldom able to do very much" (617). Initially published in 1851 as part of *Parerga and Paralipomena* and circulated thereafter as a stand-alone piece in the English-language press, "On Women" thus argues for women's metaphysical inferiority to men on account of their inability to overcome their more immediate feelings and impulses. Women, Schopenhauer argues, "always see only what is nearest to them, cling to the present, take the appearance of things for reality, and prefer trivialities to the most important affairs. Thus it is the faculty of reason by virtue whereof man does not, like the animal, live merely in the present, and surveys and considers the past and future; and from all this spring his foresight, wariness, care, anxiety, and frequent uneasiness" (*Parerga* 616). Schopenhauer claimed that women, lacking in reason, share with nonhuman animals an inability to overcome the strivings of the Will. Men, on the other hand, are able to distance themselves from what is most present and immediate in order to control and suppress the Will, reaching a higher state of consciousness through self-denial.

Schopenhauer's deterministic account of female subjectivity was welcomed by many Victorian readers, who believed it to be a necessary corrective to the "pretensions" of the New Woman. Writing in agreement with Schopenhauer's depiction of woman "as emphatically 'a lesser man,'" one reader observed: "the 'new woman' would rave at this satire on her pretension; and yet it would do her good to read what Schopenhauer has to say with as much calmness as she can command" ("Essays of Schopenhauer" 337). And yet many of Schopenhauer's male readers were disappointed to discover that with his theory of the Will, the philosopher had ultimately called into question not only the agency of women, but that of all subjects. Indeed, the same critic who had encouraged women to accept Schopenhauer's assessment of their lack of agency "with as much calmness as she can command" would repudiate this determinism—in no calm terms himself—upon realizing that it applied to "man" more generally (335). Lamenting Schopenhauer's "misanthropic and predominantly gloomy view of the world and of human existence," the critic posits that Schopenhauer's deterministic vision "can be palatable to no high-hearted sentient being with any courage or buoyancy in his nature" (335).

While Schopenhauer no doubt believed that men are superior to women, this superiority was not founded upon their possession of "more" agency than women, but rather, their ability to diminish suffering by comprehending—through reason, contemplation, or art—the truth of their condition. While Schopenhauer's male readers often interpreted him as depriving human beings of autonomy and freedom, however, robbing them of their status as agential subjects, his female readers found much more to appreciate in his thought than his low estimation of women.

The Character of the Will

In an essay published in the inaugural issue of the journal *Mind* in 1876, the Scottish philosopher Robert Adamson, while approving of other aspects of Schopenhauer's philosophy, contends that Schopenhauer is "fundamentally erroneous" in his determinism (505). For Schopenhauer, Adamson remarks, "Man is an accumulation of a thousand wants; his life a struggle for existence; a constant succession of cravings, temporary gratifications, and renewed desires" (505). Further, such a "subordination of Intellect to Will [is] the crowning inconsistency of Schopenhauer's philosophy" (508). Contending that Schopenhauer's philosophy is flawed in its failure to account for the agency the human subject clearly has, Adamson concludes that "the fundamental conception of a mighty Will, pulsating through all existence, and throwing off infinite forms again to absorb them into its own nothingness has shown itself to be full of inconsistency and contradiction" (508).

Schopenhauer's "subordination of Intellect to Will," to employ Adamson's phrase, appears to have troubled English philosophers for a number of reasons. The most significant of these was that in emphasizing the extent to which the human action is determined, Schopenhauer disturbs hierarchies according to which human intellect and volition trump all other forces. In discussions of human agency, the historian of science Rick Rylance has noted, Victorian philosophers and scientists tended to institute "categorical differences between man and the rest of nature, between humans and animals, and between moral and spiritual life and the rest of existence." "The will," Rylance observes, "was the special arena of action for the first terms in all of these pairings" (195).

Let us return to the distinguishing role volition plays in William Carpenter's essay, "The Physiology of the Will" (1871), discussed briefly in the introduction to this book. Carpenter's essay identifies three modes of action, the automatic, the voluntary, and the volitional—the last of which is said to be unique to the human. While "in the lower tribes of animals, a large part of the ordinary movements of Locomotion are of the same *primary* automatic character... being executed in direct response to a stimulus," in human beings, voluntary and eventually also "volitional power is gradually acquired" over such "automatic activities" through the "controlling power of the Will" (192–94). While Carpenter acknowledges that humans also are often subject to forces beyond their control—physiological drives and impulses such as the heartbeat, which "cannot be altered either in force or frequency by a *volitional* effort"—he argues that man can direct and govern such forces (193).

At stake in Carpenter's discussions of the will is the question of character, specifically whether, as part of the physical world, "our characters are in the first instance formed *for* us," as they would be in the case of animals and things (199). He had argued that "in proportion as the Will acquires domination over the Automatic tendencies, our characters are shaped *by* ourselves" (199). To allow one's character to be determined by forces other than one's own will, Carpenter implies, would be equivalent to losing one's humanity. Those unable to govern and direct their bodies properly are no more than "ill-conditioned automata" (216). While Carpenter makes no mention of the soul, his essay retains the imagery of dualist philosophers for whom "the body is regarded as a machine," and the soul its operator (Descartes 38). For René Descartes, foundationally, an understanding of matter as inert and mechanistic informs his claim that soulless, nonhuman animals are merely automata.[12] Similarly, Carpenter

---

12. As Powell explains, "The view of man which emerges from Descartes' philosophical writings is that of an amalgam of two substances: one material, and the other

invokes the Platonic image of the horse as a figure for those automatic, bodily actions always trumped by the human will by comparing the human body to "a horse under the guidance and control of a skillful rider," a "well-trained steed" onto which man "impresses his mandates" (199).[13]

Ten years before Carpenter, in his influential treatise, "On Liberty" (1859), John Stuart Mill had likewise implied that to fail to exercise one's moral agency is to become an unthinking automaton: "A person whose desires and impulses are his own—are the expression of his nature, as it has been developed and modified by his own culture—is said to have a character. One whose desires and impulses are not his own, has no character, no more than a steam engine has character" (264). Implicit in both Carpenter's metaphor of the automaton and Mill's figure of the steam engine is the claim that in failing to fully govern the development of their characters, humans risk becoming less than human. In *A System of Logic*, as we have already seen, Mill called for the formation of a science of character premised on the claim that "the greatest portion of character" is determined not by individual will but rather by "circumstances" (859). If Mill truly believed that character is the product of circumstance, however, how did he eventually arrive at the conclusion articulated much later—"that we can, by employing the proper means, improve our character" (*William Hamilton* 466)?

One answer to this question can be found in Mill's *Autobiography* (1873), in which he narrates the intellectual journey he went through to realize that despite the fact that character is determined by circumstances, we still can exercise volitional control over its formation. In a key passage, Mill describes a challenging phase of his life, in which

> the doctrine of what is called Philosophical Necessity weighed on my existence like an incubus. I felt as if I was scientifically proved to be the helpless slave of antecedent circumstances; as if my character and that of all others had been formed for us by agencies beyond our control, and was wholly out of our own power. I often said to myself, what a relief it would

---

immaterial. Man has both body and mind. These two substances interact in some way that remained mysterious even for Descartes. The mind is a spiritual substance, which is immortal and the source of man's freedom. Man's body is a machine, although a very complicated one" (209). As a body without a soul, the animal in Descartes's philosophy is likewise reduced to pure mechanism.

13. In *The Principles of Mental Physiology* (1874), Carpenter would further elaborate his theory of the freedom of the will, arguing there that "the control which the Will can exert over the direction of our thoughts, and over the *motive force* exerted by our feelings... tends to render the *Ego a free agent*" (27).

be if I could disbelieve the doctrine of the formation of character by circumstances. (175-76)

But while Mill initially feels dejection upon the realization that character is "formed for us by agencies beyond our control," he experiences an epiphany that allows him to overcome the feeling of helplessness before the determinative force of circumstance: "I pondered on the subject till gradually I saw light through it: I saw that the word necessity as a name for the doctrine of cause and effect applied to human action, carries with it a misleading association; and that this association is the main cause of the depressing and paralysing influence which I had experienced" (177).

As Mill eventually comes to realize, "our will, by influencing some of our circumstances, can modify our future habits or capabilities of willing" (177). His way out of the problem of circumstance is to reassert—as Carpenter would after him—that human agency trumps any other force. Because humans can choose their circumstances, Mill reasons, they can transform their character (albeit indirectly) by placing themselves in situations that give rise to the qualities they want to acquire. While Mill admits, in other words, that character is shaped by circumstances, he argues that a person's "own desire to mold it in a particular way is one of those circumstances" (*System* 840).

In making his argument about the relationship between character and the will, Mill not only elides the fact that some subjects have greater power over their circumstances than others (his reference to the "helpless slave" is all too telling). He also fails to see what I take to be the lesson of Schopenhauer and his feminist interpreters: that one's will—and as such, one's character—is never entirely one's own. In contrast to both Mill and Carpenter, as Adamson had pointed out in his essay, Schopenhauer believed that man's "character, his noumenal Ego, is determined for him" (505). This was because, in contrast to those philosophers for whom the will is precisely what allows human subjects to suppress their baser impulses, Schopenhauer argued that man, woman, animal, plant—indeed, even nonliving things—are moved by the same dynamic force, a force simply *experienced* as volitional. One of the earliest essays on Schopenhauer in English would draw attention to this point by way of comparison to Spinoza: "Spinoza says of a falling stone, that if it were conscious it would ascribe its movement to spontaneous action. Schopenhauer adds that the stone in thinking so would be right. For the law of gravity to which it obeys, and the motive which points out to human will the object of its desire, are convertible terms" (Hueffer 789).

It is worth underlining here that, in arguing, as Schopenhauer indeed does, that "if a stone projected through the air had consciousness, it would imagine it was flying of its own will," Schopenhauer does not make the animist claim that stones and other nonhuman things *have* agency or consciousness (WR 1:126). Rather, his point is that *if* the stone had consciousness, it would feel *as if* it were flying of its own free will in the same way that human subjects feel *as if* they freely move through the world—when in fact, they do not. Spinoza had argued that those who believe man to be "determined by nothing besides himself" misunderstand humanity as something opposed to nature (161). A close reader of Spinoza, Schopenhauer likewise situates the human within the natural world, stressing the extent to which a person's character is determined through its relations.

Schopenhauer, as we have already seen, argued that where all subjects experience their own actions *subjectively* as will, others experience them *objectively*, as a collection of physical traits and qualities that lend them their specific character. What we call "character," however, is ultimately just the reification of something fundamentally dynamic—an "inner impulse" that subjectively appears to be free but objectively appears to be determined (WR 2:342). As Schopenhauer continues in the above-cited passage on Spinoza's rock:

> Spinoza has his eye on the necessity with which the stone flies, and he rightly wants to transfer this to the necessity of a person's particular act of will.... I consider the inner being that first imparts meaning and validity to all necessity (i.e., effect from cause) to be its presupposition. In the case of man, this is called character; in the case of a stone, it is called a quality; but it is the same in both. Where it is immediately known, it is called *will*, and in the stone it has the weakest, and in man the strongest, degree of visibility, of objectivity. (WR 1:126)

Character thus concerns the crystallization of subjectively experienced, intentions, actions, and impulses into objectively observable material bodies with shape, color, and extension—what I have called *human objecthood*.

Rather than creating a dichotomy between the self-propelled intentions of humans and the forces that determined the natures of nonhuman things, Schopenhauer speaks of degrees or grades (*Stufen*) of Will, which appear more or less "objectified," depending on the perspective from which that being is experienced. Employing terms originally formulated by Kant, he draws a distinction between what he calls "empirical" and "intelligible" character. Empirical character is everything a thing is perceived to *do*. As John E. Atwell explains, it is the "total complex of actions that, occurring in space and time, are caused by the motives to which the intelligible character or underlying quality of the agent in question is susceptible" (46). Intelligible character is what makes these actions possible; existing outside of space and time, it is that particular material body's individual will which transforms motives into actions. For Schopenhauer, the distinction between intelligible and empirical character applies to all bodies, composed as they are of forces that allow them to change in shape, form, and quality as they interact with other bodies. As Schopenhauer contends:

> The way in which the character [of a human being] discloses its qualities can be fully compared with the way in which every body in nature-without-knowledge reveals its qualities. Water remains water with the qualities inherent in it. But whether as a calm lake it reflects its banks, or dashes in foam over rocks, or by artificial means spouts into the air in a tall jet, all this depends on external causes; the one is as natural to it as the other. But it will always show one or the other according to the circumstances; it is equally ready for all, yet in every case it is true to its character, and always reveals that alone. So also will every human character reveal itself under all circumstances, but the phenomena proceeding from it will be in accordance with the circumstances. (WR 1:139)

All bodies, it might be said, have "characters" that are the sum total of their actions or effects. Where humans might *appear* to be the most intentional and free, in truth, their actions, like that of all other things, are determined. In his belief that human action is the manifestation of a larger, prehuman force, Schopenhauer declared himself, in no uncertain terms, a determinist: "Actions have been declared to be free," he wrote, "which they are not... every individual action follows with strict necessity from the effect of the motive on the character" (WR 1:115).

What was it that might have interested women readers in Schopenhauer's deterministic theory of Will at a moment when liberal political theorists such as Mill were arguing for women's rights on the basis that every human being has a unique and individual will and the right to cultivate it? As Amanda Anderson has pointed out, Mill's theory of character as a malleable and self-governed property, while supposedly universal, did not apply to everyone in practice: even in his 1869 essay "The Subjection of Women" (likely coauthored with his wife, Harriet Taylor Mill), which argued for an extension of freedom and equality to women, Mill ultimately cannot avoid "casting women as somehow more subject to external conditioning than men" (Anderson, *Tainted* 37). In her 1993 book, *Tainted Souls and Painted Faces: The Rhetoric of Fallenness in Victorian Culture*, Anderson argues that Victorian portrayals of prostitutes and other sexually compromised women as the victims of circumstance manifest a widespread cultural anxiety about the possible lack of agency of all subjects, a threat newly emergent in what she describes as "materialist approaches to character" that stressed the subject's lack of freedom in cultivating his or her identity (4). The overdetermined character of so-called fallen women, Anderson proposes, "should be understood principally in relation to a normative masculine identity seen to possess the capacity for autonomous action, enlightened rationality, and self-control" (13). This is because the distinction between a "coherent and self-regulated identity" and a ruined or irrational subjectivity was gendered such that women were thought to be "far more liable to the lapses of control that defined a character as 'lost' or 'ruined'" (36). Driven by forces beyond her control, the figure of the fallen woman, in Anderson's reading, displaces anxieties about the threat of a materialist paradigm in which character is predetermined and agency restricted.

Anderson's analysis of the gendered nature of the Victorian debates about character formation is helpful for understanding why Schopenhauer's critics so often supported his description of women's as impulsive by nature, but balked when such descriptions were universalized to explain subjectivity in general (34). But her assumption that materialist theories of character were by and large a tool for perpetuating and naturalizing the subordination women overlooks the extent to which such materialist theories were mobilized against the model of "normative masculine identity" that *Tainted Souls and Painted Faces* sets out to critique (13). Under the category of *materialist*, Anderson groups thinkers as diverse as phrenologists, physiognomists, Darwinists, Owenites, and others. What unites such thinkers in her view is their tendency to view human character as determined by outside forces: where evolutionists such as Darwin emphasized the power of environment over character formation, socialist thinkers such as Robert Owen stressed the influence of social circumstance.[14] These "atomistic and mechanistic models of agency," Anderson contends, were unfairly projected largely onto female subjectivity, causing the fallen woman to be "perceived, distortedly, as the mere effect of systemic forces—environmental, economic, sexual, and aesthetic" (198). While she provides valuable insight into how the binary opposition between free will and determinism was mobilized to immobilize women, in grouping all nineteenth-century materialisms into a single frame, Ander-

---

14. On the significance of the Owenite doctrine of character formation in Victorian socialist feminism, see B. Taylor, who shows how Owen's theory was invoked by nineteenth-century feminists to promote "the idea that sexual response was an emotional event beyond the control of the human will" (42).

son risks overlooking the extent to which dynamic materialist approaches to character troubled binary oppositions such as will versus drive, intention versus impulse.[15]

Recent work broadly trafficking under the moniker *new materialism* has provided the grounds for reassessing and distinguishing between the many materialisms at work in nineteenth-century England. One impetus of this book is to examine how the more recent critical turn toward new materialism in critical theory can restage the reading of Victorian literary and philosophical thinking about character and, as such, the dynamic material forces thought to shape human life. The contemporary philosopher Elizabeth Grosz, for example, has turned away from the philosophical categories of intention, self-knowledge, consciousness, and motivation in her work on the history of subjectivity, advocating for greater attention to the role of physical and even biological forces at work in subject formation. In much of her work, Grosz has leaned heavily on Darwin, especially his theories of natural and sexual selection as models for understanding how such a multiplicity of forces combine to produce what I refer to throughout this book as "character."

While Grosz's philosophy remains focused on the question of the subject, it is committed to showing that subjectivity is "structured not only by institutions and social networks but also by impersonal or pre-personal, subhuman, or inhuman forces, forces that may be construed as competing microagencies rather than as a conflict between singular, unified, self-knowing subjects or well-defined social groups" (*Time* 6). While Darwin had long been dismissed by feminists as essentializing and mechanistic in his approach to life, Grosz's rereading of his work shows how the Victorian biologist's attention to "the movements of difference, bifurcation, and becoming that characterize all forms of life" offers an important critique of both essentialism and teleology by affirming the centrality of chance and encounter to the formation of all living organisms (17).[16]

Grosz's reinterpretation of Darwin can help us to better understand and appreciate the stakes of New Woman novelists' investment in Schopenhauer: what New Woman novelists can be seen to excavate from Schopenhauer's work is a rethinking of material reality itself a dynamic site of transformation. As we saw in this book's introduction, Schopenhauer argued

---

15. Such binaries were already troubled in the mid-nineteenth century, as Gallagher has shown in her account of how liberal political economists mobilized Owen's determinism to constrict a new conception of liberty (*Industrial* 13).

16. See Brilmyer, "Darwinian Feminisms," for more on how Darwin was taken up by nineteenth-century English feminists in order to challenge static and binary notions of sex.

that although matter "exhibits itself as a body," "its whole essence consists in acting" (*WR* 2:302, 305). And moreover, as one of his most influential woman readers would notice, Schopenhauer had actually aligned this active essence with the force of the feminine.

In his essay "On Women," Schopenhauer suggested that the "passions" of women are the "expression" of "nature's will" itself, and as such, their subjectivity is more determined than men (*Parerga* 618). This curious alignment of women with the Will was not lost on the author of the first book-length study on Schopenhauer in English, Helen Zimmern—a German émigré who came with her family to England after the revolutions of 1848. Nietzsche once referred to Zimmern as the woman "who introduced Schopenhauer to the English" (Kaufmann xiii). She would go on to introduce Nietzsche to the English as well, producing the first English translations of *Beyond Good and Evil* (1907) and *Human, All Too Human* (1909).[17] As Zimmern points out in her widely read 1876 study, *Arthur Schopenhauer: His Life and Philosophy*, despite his misogyny, Schopenhauer cannot help but put woman at the center of his philosophy. "Schopenhauer," she wrote, "recognizing the strength of instinct and keenness of intuition of the female sex, sees in it a closer manifestation of the original cause of being" (228).[18] Identified as she is with the determinative force of the Will, that is, woman ironically stands at the heart of Schopenhauer's metaphysics.

Zimmern's interpretation of Schopenhauer's Will opened up new avenues for theorizing women's agency outside the framework of free will versus determinism that tended to accompany discussions of character formation in Victorian England. Kathleen Frederickson has shown that, in post-Darwinian England, the distinction between instinct and volition would become so blurred that "by the end of the nineteenth century, it becomes increasingly untenable to see instinct as dialectically opposed to reasoned self-conscious action" (3). Schopenhauer's New Woman readers used this blurriness to their advantage, framing women's instincts—and the sexual instinct generally—as what Frederickson, in the parlance of psychoanalytic theory, describes as an "exit route from a Symbolic order" (8). Whereas Schopenhauer himself had advocated the renunciation of the Will, New Woman writers turned his philosophy against itself by affirming the impulsive model of subjectivity that he had denigrated as effeminate.

17. The publication dates listed are those of Zimmern's English translations.

18. While Oxenford's article lit the flame that started Schopenhauer's career, Zimmern's study set the forest ablaze, as it met the hands of authors like Robert Browning (Leslie White 92), Olive Schreiner (Lefew-Blake 50), and countless other British intellectuals.

In so doing, they imagined creative (if not always politically viable) ways out of patriarchy.

"All your elaborately reasoned codes for controlling morals or man do not weigh a jot with us, against an impulse, an instinct," wrote the New Woman writer George Egerton (née Mary Chavelita Dunne Bright) in her pathbreaking collection of short stories from 1893, *Keynotes* (28). Credited with the first mention of Nietzsche in English literature, *Keynotes*, in its celebration of bodily instincts and impulses, cultivates a Nietzschean approach to the force Schopenhauer called Will.

Schopenhauer, as we have seen, advocated an ethics of resignation in response to the constant striving of the Will. Nietzsche, by contrast, advocated for its affirmation, calling for an *amor fati*, in which life is affirmed through the desire to live out one's destiny: "to *have* to combat one's instincts—that is the formula for *décadence*: as long as life is *ascending*, happiness and instinct are one," he wrote in *Twilight of the Idols* (1889) (45). As in *Twilight of the Idols*, in *Keynotes*, instincts and impulses are things to be affirmed rather than denied, aligned as they are with the force of the feminine—what the character Claudia from *Donna Quixote* had called "the great rescuing and reorganizing force of man."

In one story, "Now Spring Has Come," Egerton's narrator describes women as "half creatures," who "by force of circumstances" are the "results of a fight of centuries between physical suppression and natural impulse to fulfill our destiny" (41). Her claim that women's natural drives have been unfairly suppressed and their natures fundamentally transformed picks up on an argument that was widespread among feminists at the turn of the century: that, as historian Lucy Bland explains the argument, "'in a state of nature' women's sexuality would be stronger than men's, but as products of years of suppression by 'civilization,' women's instinct was checked while men's sexuality had been encouraged" (Bland 18). This primitivist line of argumentation, which drew upon emerging research in social anthropology, was especially widespread among participants in London's important Men and Women's Club, including the feminist activist Loetitia Sharpe and the New Woman writers Olive Schreiner and Mona Caird.[19]

In her 1888 article "Marriage," Caird controversially framed marriage as one such institution of female sexual suppression.[20] Pronouncing mar-

---

19. Caird was not an official member; however, she was associated with the group and attended its 1887 meeting on birth control.

20. That same year, the *Daily Telegraph* ran a column in reaction to Caird's piece entitled "Is Marriage a Failure?" which is said to have drawn some 27,000 letters in response (Ledger 22).

riage a "vexatious failure," she contended that through "a sort of compound interest" in which the "instincts created by this distorting process" become only more and more distorted, society produces "more and more solid ground for upholding the established system of restriction, and the ideas that accompany it" (188). A reader of Schopenhauer who would later refer to him in two of her novels, *The Stones of Sacrifice* (1915) and *The Great Wave* (1931), Caird emphasizes the extent to which so-called woman's nature itself is the product of the patriarchal circumstances under which women have been forced to live (186). To do so, she draws upon the work of the German anthropologist J. J. Bachofen, a popular figure among late nineteenth-century feminists and whose 1861 study *Mother Right* (*Das Mutterrecht*) had argued that the matriarchal period ended when male hunters raided neighboring settlements and women became their property through right of conquest, thus founding the institution of marriage. Following Bachofen, Caird suggests that upon the introduction of the marriage system in which women were denied their freedom, women were historically produced as weak and submissive.[21]

Like Egerton, Caird draws upon the primitivist discourse of *instinct*, a term that, Frederickson has shown, "numbered among the key tropes that produced the savage figure that allowed academic anthropology to come into being" (102). A less essentializing line of reasoning would be employed by Sarah Grand in her essay "The New Aspect of the Woman Question" (1894), often credited with coining the term *New Woman*. In the essay, Grand highlights the social and cultural forces that combine to determine women's character, railing against the hypocrisy of men who actively encourage women to develop characters such as submissiveness and irrationality and then demean women for their possession of these qualities. "Man deprived us of all proper education," Grand writes, "and then jeered at us because we had no knowledge. He narrowed our outline on life so that our view of it should be all distorted, and then declared that our mistaken impressions of it proved us to be senseless creatures. He cramped our minds so that there was no room for reason in them, and then made merry at our want of logic" (272).

Although Grand critiques the mechanisms through which women have been trained to be less rational and more emotional, she does not presume that the qualities that have come to be characteristic of women

21. Citing Pearson's work on Bachofen, Caird argues that like the dog that, denied his freedom and exercise, becomes "dull and spiritless... miserable and ill-looking," women have become resigned and powerless as a result of their oppression by men (188).

are negative as such. Nor does Grand, as Caird and Egerton do, fetishize a state of nature that might be returned to should the oppressive forces of determination that produce women's character be lifted. Instead—like Zimmern and Egerton before her—Grand questions the *systems of value* through which reason and autonomy are upheld as cultural ideals, drawing attention to the way that such ideals are produced through a repression and exclusion of so-called "feminine" characters. Rather than calling for women to take up the position of the male subject, Grand rejects the suggestion that "woman should ape man and desire to trade places with him" (270).

Rather than advocate the extension of the masculine ideals of agency and autonomy to women, many New Woman novelists cultivated a feminist determinism that highlighted the nonvolitional forces that are productive of character. The origins of this feminist determinism can be traced back to, among other sources, Eliot's suggestion in *Middlemarch* that the human subject is not distinct from but rather "*a part of* that involuntary, palpitating life" (689, emphasis mine). In her very first article for the *Westminster Review* in 1851, Eliot indicated her belief in the existence of a determinist universe, affirming the "undeviating law in the material and moral world" and the "invariability of sequence which is acknowledged to be the basis of physical science, but which is still perversely ignored in our social organization"—lines that paint her decision to name her character Dorothea's love interest "Will" in a more Schopenhauerian light ("Rev. of *The Progress*" 31).

In her 1870s writings, as we have seen in previous chapters, Eliot would allow more space for deviation, indeterminacy, and variability than this 1851 comment would indicate. At the same time, she would continue to emphasize that character forms largely *involuntarily* through physical interactions, suggesting that "there is no creature whose inward being is so strong that it is not greatly determined by what lies outside it" (*Middlemarch* 784-85).[22] The New Realism pioneered by New Woman novelists throughout the 1880s and 1890s is indebted to Eliot's representation of the involuntary forces that determine the character of humans and other living beings. And it was formulated, among other ways, through a certain creative reading of Schopenhauer undertaken by British women writers, which turns the philosopher's ideas against himself in order to affirm the impulsive model of subjectivity he had denigrated as effeminate.

22. Eliot explores the problem of determination in connection to gender most explicitly in her novel *The Mill on the Floss*. On the question of Eliot's determinism, see Levine, "Determinism"; and Beer, "Beyond Determinism."

Impulsive Aesthetics

In its anti-essentialist variations, the model of character formation that emerges in the New Woman novel can be seen to prefigure strains of twentieth- and twenty-first-century theories of subjectivation, in which a person's identity is understood as the product of larger, impersonal power structures. However, as the centrality of the terms *impulse* and *instinct* to much late Victorian feminist thinking about determination would indicate, these authors often emphasized the presocial, biological drives that operated in tandem with circumstances to determine character. Schopenhauer had argued that every being bears within it an "inner impulse... called its character," which "does not act entirely from within, like a spring, but... waits for an external circumstance necessarily required for this action" (*WR* 2:342). Like Freud after them—who likewise turned to Schopenhauer to emphasize the biological nature of the sex drive—New Woman writers followed Schopenhauer in understanding this "inner impulse" as sexual and the circumstances that activated it as corporeal.[23] Schopenhauer's sexualized theory of the Will, filtered through English materialist science, offered women and feminist writers an alternative way of thinking about action: through complex networks of determination and coconstituted desire, rather than through self-propelled intention. His thinking on sexuality thus offers a useful framework for understanding only the subject matter of the New Woman novel, but its impulsive aesthetic, which performs the lack of agency attributed to its authors in its descriptions of the body and the physical world.

In her pathbreaking 1990 study, *New Women, New Novels: Feminism and Early Modernism*, Ann Ardis brought the New Woman novel into a new

---

23. In the preface to the fourth edition of his *Three Essays on the Theory of Sexuality* in 1920, Freud writes, "For it is some time since Arthur Schopenhauer, the philosopher, showed mankind the extent to which their activities are determined by sexual impulses" (xviii). The New Woman writers I analyze here can be seen to pave the way not only for Freud's theories but also those of the sex-positive psychoanalytical thinkers that followed his lead, such as Wilhelm Reich and Herbert Marcuse. In his essay "The Impulsive Character" (1925), Reich called for the evolution of "a psychoanalytic theory of character" focused on "the role played by drives in the formation of specific character traits" (Reich 5, 7). Reich's affirmative approach to the drives would inspire Marcuse in *Eros and Civilization* (1955) to question Freud's theory that civilization is necessarily "based on the permanent subjugation of the human instincts" and to call for a world free from sexual repression (Marcuse 4). The conceptual and historical linkages between the science of character that this book discovers in turn-of-the-century literature, science, and philosophy and the development of psychoanalysis are, however, a story for another time.

critical focus by arguing that the debates surrounding realist aesthetics at the turn of the twentieth century had less to do with aesthetics than with "the question of where sexuality figures in the whole of human character" (50). What distinguished the realism of the New Woman novel from the realisms before it, Ardis proposes, was its alignment of "reality" with "sexuality" (34). Differentiating itself both from prior versions of English realism and from French naturalism, the New Realism set out to describe a new source of human motivation and decision-making: the sex drive.

One of the most widely translated and reprinted texts by Schopenhauer in *fin-de-siècle* England was a short section of volume 2 of *The World as Will and Representation* entitled "The Metaphysics of Sexual Love." First translated into English in 1886 (as part of volume 2 of Haldane and Kemp's *The World as Will and Idea*), the piece put forth the controversial thesis that what humans call "love" is nothing more than the unconscious motivations of the sex drive. Just as the world itself appears to be composed of individuated objects but is actually composed of a dynamic force, the human might appear to be a self-contained unit but is actually a "concrete sexual impulse [*konkreter Geschlechtstrieb*]" (WR 2:512–13). The sex drive, Schopenhauer postulated, is "the desire that constitutes even the very nature of man [*der Wunsch, welcher selbst das Wesen des Menschen ausmacht*]" (512–13). Arguing that individual human desires always bend to the more generalized power of the force he called *Wille zum Leben* (will-to-live), Schopenhauer's essay controversially reduces all romance to the desire to perpetuate the species. At the same time, the piece also makes space for nonreproductive sexuality, including homosexuality, arguing that same-sex desire can be accounted for as part of nature's overarching will.[24]

24. Schopenhauer's 1859 appendix to the chapter on same-sex love predates not only that of the groundbreaking *Sexual Inversion* (1897), by Havelock Ellis and John Addington Symonds, but also those of the German sexologists Karl Heinrich Ulrichs and Richard von Krafft-Ebing, making him one of the first modern philosophers to address the topic at any length. In Germany, Schopenhauer's early theorization of homosexuality would be taken up by early gay rights campaigners such as Oswald Oskar Hartmann, whose *Das Problem der Homosexualität im Lichte der Schopenhauer'schen Philosophie* was published in 1897 by Spohr, the largest publisher in the German homosexual rights movement and one of the first publishing houses worldwide to print gay-affirmative works. In England, "The Metaphysics of Sexual Love" placed Schopenhauer at the center of debates about sex and sexuality at the turn of the century, becoming a reference point for early sexology, as well as for the British-born occult movement, theosophy, whose feminist socialist vision was closely tied to nineteenth-century sexual reform movements (Dixon). The fact that the British often leaned on the more patent and progressive theories of sexuality developed by nineteenth-century German

While some were scandalized by the naturalistic portrait of love and affection offered in "The Metaphysics of Sexual Love," others found the piece innovative and exciting. The *Westminster Review* called it "undoubtedly one of the most striking and original of his writings" (Todhunter 376). *The Nation* heralded it as formulating "for the first time, the modern theory of instinct" ("Schopenhauer in English" 510). Following Haldane and Kemp's 1886 translation, the essay would be retranslated and reprinted multiple times before the century's end—most notably by Mrs. Rudolf Dircks in 1897. Dircks's translation crossed the paths of the modernists D. H. Lawrence and George Bernard Shaw, both of whom reflected Schopenhauer in their representation of sexuality.[25]

In focusing on "The Metaphysics of Sexual Love," early discussions of Schopenhauer in the late Victorian periodical press worked to both materialize and sexualize his philosophy of Will. Schopenhauer often critiqued materialist scientists and philosophers for grounding their theories in the solidity of matter, when, as he argued, reality is composed not of solid objects, but of the dynamic and ultimately immaterial force of Will. "Materia mendacium verax" (Matter is a lie and yet true), he once wrote, proposing that while matter falsely appears to us as stable and solid, its true being "consists in its acting" (*WR* 2:305). In his insistence that "every object as thing-in-itself is will, and as a phenomenon is matter" (*WR* 2:307), however, the philosopher Dale Jacquette has proposed that Schopenhauer is at least "partly materialist" (30). As Jacquette observes, not only did Schopenhauer frequently draw on scientific theory to make his arguments, he maintained that (a part of the world as representation) the human mind is seated in the brain and the brain's material processes. Likewise, the art historian Jonathan Crary has argued that "although Schopenhauer termed his own philosophy 'idealist' and conventional accounts have routinely identified him as a 'subjective idealist,' such labels misconstrue the heterogeneous texture of his thought. Never has an idealist been so immersed in the details of corporeality or alluded to such a large range of texts about human physiology" (76).[26]

---

philosophers and scientists is especially clear from the connection between German and British sexology, which developed and deepened over the course of the century.

25. On Lawrence's annotations of Dircks's translation, see Brunsdale. On the connection between what Shaw called the "Life Force" and Schopenhauer's notion of the Will, see Grene (56–57).

26. Crary positions Schopenhauer, alongside Goethe, as the harbinger of a new wave of nineteenth-century philosophers and scientists who would emphasize the materiality of the observer. Schopenhauer himself was aware of the potential of that his philosophy would be seen as materialist: "my view will appear to physical, too material," he wrote, "however metaphysical, indeed transcendent, it may be at bottom" (*WR* 2:533).

That the English were drawn to what I believe is best characterized as Schopenhauer's dynamic materialism is apparent from various articles that cite his contributions to scientific thought. In his 1876 article in the journal *Mind*, Adamson remarks that in Schopenhauer's philosophy, "the fundamental physical unity [of Will] seems to be in harmony with the most recent physical conceptions" (492). Indeed, as previously discussed, Oxenford's important article from 1853 already had remarked that for Schopenhauer, "the body is the will itself in its manifested form, and in order to explain this view... all sorts of aid are borrowed from physiological science" (404). Drawing a similar conclusion, another of the earliest essays on Schopenhauer in English, "Schopenhauer and Darwinism" (1871), goes to great lengths to stress the groundings of Schopenhauer's theory in recent materialist science (specifically evolutionary theory). Written by a friend of Schopenhauer's, a German-English translator from Leipzig named David Asher, the essay pitches Schopenhauer's theory of the sexual impulse as the metaphysical backdrop to the theory of evolution.[27] "What Schopenhauer called 'the *metaphysics* of sexual love,'" Asher writes, "he might, had he been acquainted with Darwin's theory, have designated by the opposite name," a physics, "for his own speculations are now proved to be well grounded, and to have a thoroughly *physical*, or quite natural basis" (329). Contending that "Schopenhauer taught inductively what Darwin has proved inductively," Asher reads Schopenhauer as a natural philosopher whose theory that an impersonal and nonintentional will drives human decision-making can be confirmed with modern science. Indeed, Schopenhauer—trained in medicine prior to switching to philosophy—strove to make his philosophical claims compatible with the latest scientific findings.

Asher, for his part, argues that Schopenhauer's naturalism is perhaps even more radical than that of Darwin: whereas Darwin "in his speculations seems purposely to stop short of man," as Asher points out, Schopenhauer is unafraid to count humans as one of many animals and things driven by the sexual impulse (329). Just like animals and plants, Schopenhauer suggests, humans are organic beings whose attraction is ruled by forces greater than any one individual.[28]

While Asher, writing in early 1871, was right to point out that Darwin had hitherto shied away from bringing the human into discussions of evo-

27. Asher was a German-English translator from Leipzig who became friends with Schopenhauer midcentury. In 1857, Schopenhauer recommended that Asher translate his works following the model of Oxenford, who had translated various passages and lines from *The World as Will* in his 1853 essay, "Iconoclasm in German Philosophy" ("To David Asher, October 22, 1857").

28. Contemporary philosophers, such as Magee (156), have likewise drawn parallels between Schopenhauer's philosophy of Will and Darwin's theory of natural selection.

lutionary theory, Darwin would do just that within a few weeks. In *The Descent of Man, and Selection in Relation to Sex* (1871)—the first edition of which appeared the same month as Asher's article—Darwin famously brought man into the evolutionary schema, developing a social Darwinism indebted to the work of Herbert Spencer and scientists of sexuality. In *The Descent of Man*, Darwin put forth his theory of sexual selection—a theory that complicated the focus on survival of the fittest in his earlier works by drawing attention to the mechanisms through which certain inutile, aesthetic characters are passed on from generation to generation. Across the animal kingdom, Darwin observes, provocative colors, patterns, and organs are selected—often by females—not because they contribute to the fitness of the organism or species, but rather because they are sexually desirable. Whereas traits that render the species more fit are perpetuated through the force of natural selection, others are perpetuated merely "depending on the will" of the organism—a will that is less driven toward fitness and survival than toward fleeting pleasure (245).[29] "Why certain bright colours should excite pleasure cannot, I presume, be explained any more than why certain flavours and scents are agreeable," Darwin wrote, "but habit has something to do with the result, for that which is at first unpleasant to our senses, ultimately becomes pleasant, and habits are inherited" (115).

Attributing those characterological differences said to be distinctive of sex and race to arbitrary, habitual decisions, Darwin thus dispelled the notion (peddled by social Darwinists of the period) that either race or sex bears any necessary relation to fitness or survival. In stark contrast to scientific thinkers for whom sex was understood only in teleological terms (i.e., as the effort to produce fit offspring and perpetuate the species), one might say that both Schopenhauer and Darwin granted a place for the nonteleological nature of sexuality. Per Schopenhauer's pithy phrase, "beings exhibit themselves not as drawn from the front, but as driven from behind" (*WR* 2:352).

Indeed, even Darwin himself would come to recognize the similarities between his thinking on sex and that of Schopenhauer. One of the changes he made to the second edition of *The Descent of Man* was to include a quotation from the philosopher, who—in the intervening years—had become notorious for his theory of the Will: "as the German philosopher Schopen-

---

29. Grosz has shown that in *The Descent*, the forces of natural and sexual selection are at times represented as dueling forces—one geared toward the perpetuation of the life of the species, and the other often putting life at risk in the quest for sensation (*Chaos* 29–33).

hauer remarks," Darwin would add following his discussion of sexual selection in the 1874 edition, "the final aim of all love intrigues, be they comic or tragic, is really of more importance than all other ends in human life. What it all turns upon is nothing less than the composition of the next generation.... It is not the weal or woe of any one individual, but that of the human race to come, which is here at stake" (653).

Although Darwin attributes this quotation to Schopenhauer, the passage is actually plucked straight from Asher's 1871 article "Schopenhauer and Darwinism," which Darwin may have read to comprehend the relationship between his thought and that of the increasingly popular German philosopher. Asher's gloss of Schopenhauer's metaphysics of sexual love in this quotation cited by Darwin no doubt emphasizes the reproductive quality of sex ("the composition of the next generation"). However, it also takes sex out of the hands of the individual and her intentions, attributing love and affection instead to impersonal forces. As Adamson put it in his article in *Mind*, for Schopenhauer, "Man is an accumulation of a thousand wants; his life a struggle for existence, a constant succession of cravings, temporary gratifications, and renewed desires" (505). For his part, however, Schopenhauer did not believe that the Will facilitates *only* the perpetuation of life (the "will-to-live" was rather one of its manifestations). Indeed, much like Darwin in his theory of sexual selection (which explained why certain traits deemed beautiful might be selected even when they put the species' life in danger), and later, Freud, Schopenhauer understood the sex drive to be pleasure-oriented rather than survival-oriented. As such, it was a drive that resulted in death as much as life. In "The Metaphysics of Sexual Love," Schopenhauer explains how this "passion exceeding every other in intensity... overcomes all obstacles with incredible force and persistence, so that for its satisfaction life is risked without hesitation; indeed, when that satisfaction is denied, life is given as the price" (*WR* 2:532).

Across the final decades of the nineteenth century, these feedback loops of sexual theorizing, compounding and reverberating across continents and time, facilitated in many quarters a growing awareness of the human as a material creature motivated, like any other animal, by impulse and drive. Schopenhauer's philosophy, I have been arguing, was central to these discussions in the English context, where readers downplayed his idealism as they drew connections between his sexualized theory of the Will and materialist science. In the German-speaking world, Schopenhauer's theory of the Will was a source of inspiration for Nietzsche's notion of the will to power, Freud's theory of the sex drive, Wilhelm Wundt's concept of the impulsive act, and Ludwig von Feuerbach's notion of sensuous being—all of which would reach England before the end of the nineteenth century. "Is there, in general, any other force," Eliot had translated Feuerbach as saying in 1854, "the opposite of intelligence, than the force of flesh and blood,—any other strength of nature than the strength of the fleshy impulses? And the strongest of the impulses of Nature, is it not the sexual feeling?" (Feuerbach 91). In the 1880s and 1890s, however, it was Schopenhauer, more than Feuerbach, to whom New Realist writers turned to represent the force had come to be accepted as a new, important, and involuntary source of human behavior—the sexual drive.

Consider here, as a brief example of Schopenhauer's significance for late Victorian representations of sexuality, Gissing's 1884 novel *The Unclassed*. Introduced to Schopenhauer by Eduard Bertz in 1880, Gissing would directly engage the philosopher's work in his novels *Workers in the Dawn* (1880) and *The Whirlpool* (1897), as well as in his 1882 essay, "The Hope of Pessimism" (Argyle 135). It is in *The Unclassed*, however, where Schopenhauer's philosophy is put to its most interesting and sexually progressive ends. In line with the work of Egerton, Grand, and Caird discussed in the previous section, *The Unclassed* transforms the abject figure of the all-too-embodied and impulsive woman at the heart of Schopenhauer's metaphysics into its own ideal, one that a new generation of women—and men—might learn from. Multiplying Schopenhauer's singular Will into a plurality of bodily impulses, sensations, and drives, the novel makes the case that the marital system, with its opposition between angels and whores, upstanding gentlemen and seducers, will always "weaken affections" rather than strengthen them, pulling women and men apart rather than bringing them together (171).

Gissing's novel turns on an opposition between two female characters, Maud Enderby and Ida Starr, and their contrasting relationships with their impulses. Maud is a middle-class Christian woman who has learned to control and repress her body: "oppressed with the consciousness of sin," she is said to regard "every most natural impulse…as a temptation to be resisted with all her strength" (149). Ida, on the other hand—a prostitute struggling to find her way out of the profession—follows her impulses. And she stirs them in others, too. Upon encountering Ida, the novel's protagonist, Osmond Waymark, "felt his pulses throb at the sound of her voice and the touch of her hand" (109). Maud, by contrast, "had never made his pulse quicken, as it had often done when he had approached Ida" (235).

While Gissing risks reproducing through Maud and Ida an oversimplified angel/whore dichotomy, the novel is designed to critique such an opposition. As *The Unclassed* implies, it is through the idealization of the "angel in the house" as she who must suppresses her impulses that the conception of the "fallen woman" as determined and impulse-driven is produced in the first place.[30] In a chapter entitled "The Will to Live" (named after Schopenhauer's concept), Waymark invokes the German philosopher to convince Maud that self-renunciation leads merely to the distortion of desire. Critical of Schopenhauer's proposed ethics of self-denial (aligned throughout the novel with Maud's dogmatic Christianity), however, Waymark proposes an alternative philosophical system in which the Will need not be denied, but instead can be affirmed.[31] But his doctrine of the affirmation of the Will is lost on Maud, whose Christian family has indoctrinated her with the philosophy, "Life is given to us that we may conquer ourselves" (251). As a result, Waymark's relationship to her is stultified: "When he wrote his last letter to her, it had proceeded more from a sense of obligation than any natural impulse" (154).

Through its engagement with Schopenhauer, Gissing's novel implies that it is in vain that one attempts to control one's impulses, which erupt to frustrate our more conscious intentions: attempting to convince himself of his duty to Maud, Waymark "tried not to think of Ida in any way, but this was beyond his power. Again and again she came before his mind" (235). The involuntary nature of Waymark's reaction to Ida underlines the extent to which man for Gissing, to return to Mill's phrase, is indeed driven by "desires and impulses" not properly "his own." However, whereas Mill implies that ownership of such involuntary forces would be possible through the redirection, control, and repression of such bodily forces, in *The Unclassed*,

30. What I take to be Gissing's critique of the dichotomy between chaste and fallen women in his novel reflects a surprisingly insightful line of argumentation undertaken by Schopenhauer in his otherwise misogynistic essay "On Women." Citing London's 80,000 prostitutes, the essay proposes that prostitution emerges, ironically, out of the worship of pure and respectable women (*Parerga* 623). Pointing to the limited options for lower-class women who fail to marry, Schopenhauer asks provocatively, "What, then, are they but women who have become the most fearful losers through the monogamous institution, actual human sacrifices on the altar of monogamy?" (623). As he goes on to remark, prostitutes are "a publicly recognized class or profession whose special purpose is to protect from being seduced those [so-called pure] women favoured by fortune and have found or hope to find husbands" (623).

31. Much more interesting than the Christian doctrines of original sin to which the ever-repentant Maud subscribes, Waymark suggests, is the myth of Prometheus, which begins with a similar notion of sin but ends, through Hercules, with the affirmative injunction that one "live whilst it is called to-day" (225). Echoing Nietzsche, for whom Prometheus was also an important figure, Waymark tells Maud, "the doctrine of philosophical necessity, the idea of Fate, is with me an instinct" (225). Bridgwater has likewise drawn parallels between Nietzsche's philosophy and *The Unclassed*. As Argyle points out, however, any claim for direct influence is untenable (218n61). Gissing was likely not so much directly influenced by Nietzsche as drawing similar conclusions in response to Schopenhauer's philosophy.

among other New Woman novels of the period, another economy of the will emerges. Although at first, Waymark is seen to "repress his impulses," he eventually accepts his lack of control over his body, allowing himself to be "swayed between forces he could not control" (157). Thus, the novel can be seen to ask what it would mean for all subjects—including men—to accept their determination by forces beyond their control.

Though he does not treat the New Realism at any length, Fredric Jameson has compellingly argued, "Each realism is also by definition new: and aims at conquering a whole new area of content for its representation. Each wishes to annex what has not yet been represented, and has not yet ever been named or found its voice" (*Singular* 122–23). Following Jameson, one might argue that New Realism that emerged in the hands of women and feminist novelists at the end of the nineteenth century distinguished itself from realisms before it by creating a representational space for new materialist understandings of the human. The New Realism's representational concern with the body and its forces was immediately recognized by critics such as Waugh who, as we saw at the start of this chapter, cited such characterizations as evidence that such realism had been feminized. And yet, as I have indicated, New Realist authors were accused by critics of a lack of restraint, not only for the content of their representations but, formally, for their inability to control their own impulses in the production of those representations.

One year after Waugh's complaint that women realists were failing to paint reality with appropriate reflexivity and restraint, the critic James Ashcroft Noble attacked the New Realism on similar grounds, contending that the representation of human life in the genre was skewed by an "erotomania" that "unnaturally isolates" one aspect of life over the rest (493). Like Waugh, who had dismissed the New Realism as "passion's slave" (210), Noble suggests in his 1895 essay "The Fiction of Sexuality" that the thematic focus on sexuality in literature in recent years had led to a crisis of representation. The implied thesis of these new novels—according to Noble, that "sexual passion provides the main-spring of [human] action"—is, he argues, "a flagrant violation of the obvious proportion of life" (493). "The new fiction of sexuality," he continues, "presents to us a series of pictures painted from reflections in convex mirrors, the colossal nose which dominates the face being represented by one colossal appetite which dominates life" (493). Recalling Stendhal's 1830 realist maxim—"the novel is a mirror being carried along a road"—Noble's suggestion that the New Realism novel overstates the centrality of sexuality to subjectivity in the same way that a bad painter might overemphasize a nose submits realist characterization to the test of proportion that founded novelistic character in the first place.

In *The Economy of Character*, Deidre Lynch argues that throughout the eighteenth century, the distinction between *character* and *caricature* became increasingly crucial as the novel "worked to validate and naturalize a concept of character as representational" (3). As the novel emerged as a genre, she suggests, excesses of caricature were gradually devalued in favor of an aesthetic style that carefully controlled the number of "strokes" necessary to render a character realistic. The fact that these debates—which Lynch tracks from the mid-eighteenth to the early nineteenth centuries—continued well into the 1890s signals the enduring nature of the question of what constitutes a "realistic" character. Where critics such as Noble and Waugh attacked the lack of proportion they saw at work in New Realist representations of character as driven by its authors' unbridled desire, New Realist authors, as we have seen, often insisted that their novels were truer to reality than the portraits of human relations that came before them, which had suppressed the body and its impulses.

A powerful example is Grand's *The Heavenly Twins*, one of the main targets of Waugh's critique. Particularly throughout the novel's fourth chapter, Grand cultivates an innovative style of characterization that strips characters of identifying features to highlight how character forms through impersonal corporeal interactions. Originally published as a separate work in 1899, Grand's chapter, "The Tenor and the Boy—an Interlude," breaks the larger narrative of the novel to document a brief, yet consequential interaction between two characters referred to throughout the chapter largely only by the names "the Tenor" and "the Boy." While the Tenor's real name is eventually (and inconsequently) revealed to be David Julian Vanetemple, Esq., the Boy's name is, at the chapter's end, much more dramatically revealed to be Angelica Hamilton-Wells. A young woman who has disguised herself as her twin brother, Angelica is said to have concocted this gender-bending plan to forge a relationship with a man outside the pressures of courtship and marriage. A queer, prototrans narrative, "The Tenor and the Boy" narrates not only how Angelica becomes an object of desire for the Tenor, but also how, through her transformation into the Boy, Angelica experiences, as she puts it, an "awakening in which I recognized myself" (457).

In her depiction of the Boy, Grand emphasizes not so much how the individual Angelica transitions into Boyhood, but the characterological change undergone by the Boy as a result of his encounter with the Tenor. As a result of their interaction, the Boy's "whole demeanour, but his very nature seemed to change" (405). These changes range from alterations in his appearance ("His features had sharpened a little, his skin was transparent to a fault" [412]), to changes in behavior ("every movement was natural and spontaneous, like the movements of a wild creature, and as agile" [437]).

Grand presents this transformation not so much as a willful act of self-creation, but a reaction formation in response to the enjoyably objectifying gaze of the Tenor. "It was delightful to look at myself—an ideal self from afar off with your eyes," says the Boy; "Mentally and morally, I was exactly what you thought me" (456). The Boy also enjoys objectifying the Tenor: "'It is curious,' he broke off, gazing at the Tenor critically, 'that Angelica should specially admire your chin. It is your mouth that appeals to me.... I should think you're the sort of fellow that women would like to kiss'" (412).

In addition to the novel's progressive representation of gender, which lends itself to both feminist and trans-affirmative readings, what is particularly innovative about the chapter is its formal strategy of characterization. Forgoing almost entirely the use of proper names, the chapter relies on descriptions of bodies and movements, as well as dialogue, to lend consistency and specificity to the characters of its characters. A dialogue between the Tenor and the Boy hints at the effect of this descriptive strategy: "I never thought of your having a name," remarks the Tenor, to which the Boy responds, "Do you mean to say you think me such a nonentity?" (402). "Just the opposite," the Tenor replies, "Your individuality is so strongly marked that you don't seem to require to be labelled like other people, By-the-bye, what is your name?" (402). Grand's strategy of characterization functions similarly. Not only is the intensity of the Tenor and the Boy's interaction presented as emerging in and through the impersonality of their relation, but Grand's detailed descriptions of her characters' bodies and movements seem almost to obviate their need for proper names—their "individuality" being "so strongly marked" in and through the depiction of their gestures, tics, and other characteristic qualities that "Angelica" and "David" are nothing more than symbolic distractions to comprehending the Logic of Feeling that governs their immanent interaction.

Indeed, as the chapter's conclusion seems to imply—dismissing the significance of its big reveal—even the signifier "Boy," while certainly a useful category for obtaining social privileges, is not a very helpful description of a person's character: "it was only a change of idea really, the Boy was a girl and that was all" (446). At least this is what the Tenor seems to think in a moment of ambiguous, free indirect discourse, before getting swept up again in the logic that understands as unequal "two people of like powers, passions, impulses, and purposes simply because one of them is a woman" (447). In its presentation of "boy" and "girl" as generic categories that nonetheless determine how readers experience and interpret character, "The Tenor and the Boy" reverses the hierarchy between what G. H. Lewes had called "the Logic of Feeling" and "the Logic of Signs" (Lewes, *Problems* 3.2:227). Whereas Lewes, as we saw in chapter 2, subordinates the more corporeal and affective logic, the Logic of Feeling, to the conceptual, significatory logic, the Logic of Signs (which only the human possesses), Grand follows Eliot and Hardy in wondering whether character is expressed more immediately and perhaps more truly through the latter, more material semiotic—a characterological semiotic that does not require the symbolic bifurcation of bodies into Boy and Girl (or Angelica and David, for that matter), but speaks instead through "powers, passions, impulses."

Through their engagement of Schopenhauer, New Woman novelists thus worked to destabilize the binary opposition between masculine and feminine, which, for so many nineteenth-century thinkers, was founded on the assumption of the male subject's ability to transcend his impulses and the female subject's enslavement to hers. In granting dynamic power to the material world that women have long been identified with, Schopenhauer's theory of the Will might be read as transforming entities traditionally considered to be passive objects—the nonhuman, the inanimate, the feminine—into active, agential subjects. Different than extending agency to nonsubjects, I have been arguing that Schopenhauer's philosophy forces a reckoning with those aspects of human existence that are material, unconscious, and unwilled—the object within the subject. My aim in revealing the surprising significance of Schopenhauer for feminist writing and politics thus has not been, as it is for other recent critics interested in Romantic natural philosophy, to uncover "the active powers issuing from nonsubjects" (Bennett ix). Rather, it has been to comprehend, through New Woman novelists and their philosophical and scientific interlocutors, the extent to which humans *experience* their actions as volitional because of the nature of embodiment.

What might a feminist politics look like that does not advocate the extension to women a masculine model of subjectivity—a model defined by the ideals of rationality, reflection, and self-control—but rather highlights the extent to which the character of all subjects, because they are also objects, are determined by forces beyond their control? To pose such a question is to begin to comprehend not only the subject matter of the New Woman novel, but its very aesthetic, which cultivated a realism lacking in restraint.

The Intimate Pulse of Reality; or, Schreiner's Ethological Realism

[CHAPTER FIVE]

We all enter the world little plastic beings, with so much natural force, perhaps, but for the rest—blank; the world tells us what we are to be, and shapes us by the ends it sets before us. To you, it says—Work; and to us it says—Seem!... And so the world makes men and women.

OLIVE SCHREINER, *The Story of an African Farm* (1883)

We saw in the previous chapter how, in conversation with Arthur Schopenhauer, New Woman authors emphasized the determinative role of "circumstances" in character formation. In a fashion consistent with this view, Olive Schreiner's character Lyndall argues that while all beings enter the world with "natural force," their plasticity means that the environment has a greater deal of say in who they become than does their biological sex. In its emphasis on the social constraints placed on women's lives, Schreiner's novel *The Story of an African Farm* paved the way for many of the writers discussed in chapter 4, whose novels and essays politically engaged with "the woman question" of the turn of the century. Published under the pseudonym Ralph Iron, the novel placed Schreiner at the very center of late Victorian intellectual culture, granting her entry to progressive clubs in London like the Men and Women's Club. Most significantly, it founded a new genre—the New Woman novel.

When Schreiner had boarded a ship to England from South Africa in 1881 at age twenty-six, however, she was carrying the manuscript of not one, but three such novels with her. *The Story of an African Farm* would render her a British literary sensation. "Who could have foreseen that the new, and in many respects the most distinctive note of the literature of the last decade of the nineteenth century, would be sounded by a little chit of a girl reared in the solemn stillness of the Karoo, in the solitude of the African Bush?" wrote the critic W. T. Stead of Schreiner's first published novel in 1894 (Stead 65). The other two novels Schreiner had with her, *Undine* and *Saints and Sinners*, she would never finish. Schreiner had hoped the latter novel—which she retitled twice, first as *From Man to Man*, and again, just before she died, as *Perhaps Only*—would become her magnum opus. Her letters reveal the importance of this novel for her thinking: "every word of it is truth to me," she wrote to her close friend, the English sexologist Havelock Ellis in 1886, "& more & more so as the book goes on." But writing became difficult as she faced problems with her health. "I don't quite know what's the matter with me," she continues, "I'm so much knocked down. Will my book ever ever ever be done?" ("To Havelock Ellis, May 14, 1886"). *From Man to Man* occupied Schreiner for almost fifty years, from the early 1870s until a few years before her death in 1920.[1] In 1926, six years after Schreiner's death, her husband, Samuel Cronwright-Schreiner, published the novel in its inchoate form under the title *From Man to Man; or Perhaps Only*.[2]

From Man to Man develops many themes also treated in Schreiner's more famous novel: the rich intellectual life of women, the suppression of female sexuality, and the colonial situation in South Africa. It tells the story of two sisters, Rebekah and Bertie, who grow up in the Eastern Province of the Cape Colony and who go on to experience the trials of modern womanhood in Cape Town and London, respectively. Where Rebekah, an avid writer and naturalist, becomes an isolated housewife after marrying her philandering cousin, Frank, her younger sister, Bertie, is socially ostracized after a sexual experience with her tutor and eventually turns to prostitution. As the title of the novel suggests, these two women are trafficked "from man to man" in a world in which they are denied social and political independence, and where they are valued not for their "work" (intellectual and otherwise) but for their ability to "seem," to return to Lyndall's phrasing.

But the title of Schreiner's novel has another, more positive valence. Its prepositional structure gestures toward Rebekah's metaphysical theory—outlined in a series of diary entries interpolated within the novel—that the universe is composed not of distinct entities but rather complex networks of relations. The seventh chapter of the novel, "Raindrops on the Avenue," offers a window into these writings and details their composition process. In her notebooks Rebekah weaves together insights from philosophy, biology, and physics to argue that a state of ontological interdependence characterizes not only all living beings, who live in ecosystems that sustain them, but the physical world more broadly, which is held together

---

1. Schreiner began sending out the manuscript, originally titled *Saints and Sinners*, to publishers in 1881, before *The Story of an African Farm* (van der Vlies 247). It would be rejected by both Chapman and Macmillan, however. Following its initial composition in the early 1870s, scholars have identified four major periods of revision: from 1884 to 1886; from mid-1888 to spring 1889; from 1901 to 1902; and from 1906 to 1907 (Stanley 95). On the early manuscript of *From Man to Man*, see Ravilious. On the changes Cronwright made to the manuscript prior to publication, see Driver, "On Producing."

2. Driver's pathbreaking 2015 edition, published by the University of Cape Town Press, stands to enable and inspire yet more scholarship on this important novel.

by "internetting lines of action and reaction which bind together all that we see and are conscious of" (180). This metaphysical theory then forms the basis of Rebekah's critique of social Darwinism and eugenics, which, in emphasizing principles of competition and segregation over those of cooperation and community, she argues, fundamentally misunderstand nature. My analysis of Schreiner's last published novel focuses on this astounding chapter—one of the most pointed critiques of biological racism and sexism of the period. I show how the novel mobilizes a range of nineteenth-century materialisms, including not only evolutionary science but also Karl Marx's social philosophy, Schopenhauer's (partly materialist) metaphysics, and field theory in physics to cultivate a dynamic materialist characterology concerned with the ethical responsibility of the human in an "internetted" world.

Composed across the entirety of the period *The Science of Character* covers, *From Man to Man* weaves together many of the threads that I have been developing throughout this book: the transformation of realism in the hands of late Victorian women and feminist novelists; the aspiration of these novelists to generate literary knowledge of character not through the appropriation of disembodied, scientific ideals of objectivity but through affectively charged, aesthetic means; and finally, the capacity of fiction to develop its own "weak theories" of character through its descriptions of fictional people. At the same time, the science of character Schreiner develops in *From Man to Man* differs from that cultivated in the other novels I have analyzed in a few key ways. First, insofar as Schreiner's novel defers its plot for more than eighty pages to present a series of logical arguments posed by the protagonist, the "theory" elaborated in *From Man to Man* is much stronger than those in the works discussed in my previous chapters. Following Eliot in guiding realism away from the plot-driven narrative, Schreiner's "Raindrops" chapter pushes the "weak-theoretical" impulse I have been tracking across the archive of late Victorian realism to a new extreme by inserting what is essentially a work of natural philosophy into the middle of a novel.

But while the section of the novel I will analyze largely takes the form of a philosophical essay, the *literary mode* that Schreiner employs to narrate the composition of this essay is as essential to the science of character it elaborates as its argument.[3] In describing not only Rebekah's thoughts and ideas but also the makeshift study she uses to compose her writings

---

3. There is certainly much to say with regard to the obstacles Victorian women faced to participate formally in the discourses of science and philosophy, which may explain why Schreiner decided to present these essays in the form of a character's writings within a novel.

and which is attached to her children's room, the limited set of books to which she has access in the Eastern Cape, as well as the aches and pains of her body during pregnancy, the novel employs strategies of realist worldbuilding to bring philosophy back to the body and the world out of which it arises—highlighting the entanglement of theory with praxis, as well as science with emotion.

What I call Schreiner's *ethological realism* is founded on the premise that the description of reality is never an ethically neutral act, entangled as it is always with normative theories about how the world could or should be. Advocating for the production of a realism committed to social change, *From Man to Man* insists on the importance of ethics in the construction of any literary, scientific, or philosophical account of how character comes to be. In so doing, the novel offers an important object lesson for what, in our contemporary theoretical vocabulary, concerns the possibility of separating "description" from "critique."

Proponents of critique have worried that the "descriptive turn" in recent literary studies risks affirming the status quo by operating "according to the common-sense, positivistic epistemology" that refuses the imaginative speculation and cultural critique necessary to political action (Hensley 63).[4] In *From Man to Man*, however, Schreiner refuses to oppose description and critique, cultivating a realism that describes "what is" that nonetheless criticizes social inequalities. Depicting the challenges women face to speak their own truths and develop their own ontologies, the novel does not present either speculation or cultural critique as a necessary condition for feminist or antiracist politics. In narrating Rebekah's attempt to produce more sound descriptions of reality than those of her scientific counterparts, *From Man to Man* instead affirms the claim of the contemporary feminist science studies scholar Donna Haraway that "feminists have to insist upon a better account of the world; it is not enough to show radical historical contingency and modes of construction for everything" ("Situated" 579).

Like Haraway, who advocates for a "feminist objectivity" founded upon a recognition of the embedded and embodied nature of the observer, Schreiner employs realist literary conventions not to produce a disembodied, omniscient view from nowhere but rather to generate what Haraway

---

4. On description as a literary method, see Love, "Close But" and "Close Reading." In response to Love, Hensley has advocated that "we part ways with empiricist observation" and cultivate a stance of "a care for individual cultural objects" that would nonetheless recognize "the historical damage that all documents of Victorian modernity necessarily mediate" (60). Schreiner likewise centers around care in her ethics; however, she does not oppose it with empirical observation.

calls "situated knowledge" (581). As Rebekah writes, her children often interrupt her, requiring care. While such interruptions disrupt her work, causing her to lose her train of thought, they also inspire her argument that self-extension, love, and care are more fundamental than the principle of competition and struggle that have dominated theories of the natural world, from those of Thomas Hobbes to Herbert Spencer. Depicting one woman's "common hunger after a knowledge of reality," *From Man to Man* simultaneously enacts and reflects upon the desire- and care-driven practice of description in which both Rebekah, as a scientific naturalist, and Schreiner, as a realist novelist, are engaged (141).

A second significant difference between the science of character that emerges in Schreiner's novel and those of other late Victorian realists concerns the role of human social formations. Much more than the other authors discussed in this book, Schreiner centers human action, thought, and responsibility in her ethological vision, affirming Marx's 1844 claim that "the establishment of *true materialism* and of *real science*" entails "making the social relationship of 'man to man' the basic principle of the theory" (*Economic* 44). Marx's *Economic and Philosophical Manuscripts of 1844* were not published until after Schreiner's death. Still, the resonance between the title of Schreiner's novel and Marx's call for a materialism that would center the relationship from "man to man" is telling. Like her socialist contemporaries (Schreiner was close friends with Karl Marx's daughter, Eleanor Marx, and moved in socialist circles), Schreiner asks what literature can do to change the world it describes.[5]

Throughout her writings, Rebekah makes the case that tremendous energy is lost through "the individual tendency to expend force" in competition when it could be used to improve the whole through collective action (*From Man* 218). Recognition of the interconnected nature of the human social body, she suggests, allows us to perceive the extent to which humanity as a whole suffers when one of its parts is oppressed. "What has humanity not lost by the suppression and subjection of the weaker sex by the muscularly strong sex alone?" she writes in her critique of gender-based oppression, "We have a Shakespeare; but what of the possible Shakespeares we might have had, who passed their life from youth upward brewing currant wine and making pastries for fat country squires to eat… stifled out without one line written, simply because, being of the weaker sex, life gave no room for action and grasp on life?" (219).

Those familiar with Virginia Woolf's extended essay on the loss of

---

5. On how Schreiner's role in the socialist movement, see Stanley; and Gill. Perhaps Schreiner's greatest contribution to socialist philosophy is her study of gender inequality in labor practices in *Woman and Labour* (1911).

talent, power, and art as a result of women's obstacles to education and employment, *A Room of One's Own* (1929)—published two years after Schreiner's novel—will recognize *From Man to Man* as, per my view, a source text for the essay, and specifically its speculations about Shakespeare's imaginary sister.⁶ "Women," Woolf argues, "have not had a dog's chance of writing poetry" without five-hundred a year and a room of their own (*Room* 106). Woolf's essay tells the story of Shakespeare's imaginary sister, who dies unknown as a result of obstacles to education and employment even though she is as talented as her brother; Schreiner's novel makes a similar point by showcasing a life and a body of natural philosophical writing relegated to a woman's diary. Like Woolf, who demonstrates the necessity of "room for action and grasp on life" for women's intellectual work, Schreiner emphasizes the material conditions for the production of knowledge. Rebekah's work is made possible by the existence of a small room of her own, "made by cutting off the end of the children's bedroom with a partition" (171), creating a makeshift study that, as at least one scholar has noted, "bears an uncanny likeness" to the room Woolf would describe two years later (Kortsch 42).

Before I go on to unpack the materialist-feminist politics elaborated in Schreiner's novel, however, a few words about the pitfalls of its vision are necessary. As Schreiner scholars have long remarked, despite her long history of antiracist activism, Schreiner remains a colonial writer.⁷ The limits of *From Man to Man*'s vision for gender equality emerge (as in her other novels) in its shallow representation of Black and mixed-race Afri-

---

6. Woolf was characteristically reserved in her praise of Schreiner, calling her feminist precursor a "rather distant and unfamiliar figure" and "one half of a great writer" (quoted in Pierpont 26). In a review of Cronwright's *The Letters of Olive Schreiner* (1924), however, she describes her as "the equal of our greatest novelists" and "too uncompromising a figure to be disposed of" (Pierpont 26). The idea that Woolf had been considering the conditions for Shakespeare's success prior to the publication of Schreiner's *From Man to Man* is clear from two published letters Woolf wrote to the *New Statesman* in October 1920. In the second letter, Woolf writes, "It seems to me that the conditions that make it possible for a Shakespeare to exist are that he shall have had predecessors in his art, shall make one of a group where art is freely discussed and practiced, and shall himself have the utmost of freedom and action and experience" (*Congenial* 125). Neither letter, however, discusses a female Shakespeare, leaving open the possibility that Woolf was inspired in this regard by Schreiner, or that both were participating in a larger conversation about the possibility of a female Shakespeare. (Thank you to Mia Carter for helping me to uncover these connections many years ago.)

7. On how Schreiner's perspective was conditioned by "the colonial scene and her own place, as a white woman, within it," see Burdett, "Thrown Together" (119). The most sustained treatment of how the complexities of Schreiner's colonial position inform her fiction remains McClintock.

can women, many of whom remain nameless and are defined only by their work as servants or "ayahs" (nursemaids).[8] While I acknowledge the novel's clear representational limits, however, in what follows, I focus on the novel's philosophical claims about the interdependence of sexism, racism, and imperialism—forces that, in Rebekah's relational metaphysics, are implicated together in matrices of power. The notion that Schreiner herself was entrenched in such matrices should not prevent us from appreciating her novel's challenge to scientific justifications of imperial rule—no small feat for a work composed during the height of England's colonial reign.

Unlike many nineteenth- and twentieth-century feminist activists, who simply presumed the whiteness of the category of "woman" that grounded their politics, in *From Man to Man* Schreiner generates a science of character attentive to the operation of race as a category that intersects and magnifies gender oppression, cultivating what scholars today might recognize as a form of intersectional feminist theory.[9] In 1908, Schreiner severed ties with the South African Women's Enfranchisement League (of which she was vice president) as a result of their decision to exclude the suffrage of Black Africans in their demand for women's right to vote (Burdett 175). That same year, she wrote a letter to her brother outlining the "centre points" of *From Man to Man*—which were still occupying her attention after thirty years. One of the main aims of the novel, she wrote, was to "open up the whole question of our relation to the... darker races, & the attitude which says 'they are here for *our* interest for our *pleasure*, & to hell with them when they aren't that!' If only I could live to finish that book" ("To William Schreiner, June 4, 1908").

Nineteenth- and twentieth-century scientific discourse in England

---

8. On Schreiner's dehumanization of nonwhite characters in *The Story of an African Farm*, see Kreilkamp; and Fong. Kreilkamp argues that although "Schreiner does sometimes dehumanize her native African characters in troubling ways," such dehumanization is complex in "pushing beyond a humanist and anthropocentric worldview," and that ultimately her "novel clearly defines those who are most racist as the novel's most ignorant and benighted" (153). Fong reads *African Farm* differently, through the framework of Indigenous studies to show how a "Khoisan-centered apparatus can reveal moments in which the Indigenous worlds that surround the novel's settler spaces become legible, however fleetingly" (423).

9. Kimberlé Crenshaw's "Demarginalizing the Intersection of Race and Sex" (1989) is understood to be the founding text of intersectional feminist theory. Many of Crenshaw's claims are prefigured in the work of the twentieth-century Black feminist collectives and thinkers such as the Combahee River Collective and bell hooks, as well as that of the nineteenth-century abolitionist and women's rights activist Sojourner Truth.

drew frequent parallels between women and so-called "savage races," both of which were understood as less developed than the modern European male—an evolutionary logic frequently employed to justify colonialism. Schreiner's novel addresses this comparison not—as many of her white feminist contemporaries did—by distancing the modern European woman from her primitive counterpart, but rather showing that the same logic that justifies the oppression of the non-European by the European motivates the oppression of women across cultures, and by critiquing that logic. Against those who would seek to facilitate the "characteristics of the to-be-preserved races," Schreiner's character Rebekah advocates for a flourishing of all racial and sexual characteristics, developing a science of character committed to recognizing the importance of variation and codependence in both biology and society (160).

In her analysis of care and aggression across the natural world, Rebekah can be seen to anticipate the principles of ethology as they would come to be articulated in the decades following the publication of *From Man to Man* in the field of zoology. "Only for a few years at the turn of the century did Millian ethology find favor," the historian John Durant observes in his history of ethological science; "instead the term was taken up by biologists... devoted to the study of animals in their natural habitats" (161). This latter ethology had emerged from the work of the nineteenth-century French naturalist Isidore Geoffroy Saint-Hilaire, who, independent of Mill, had used the term *éthologie* to found a new science of animal behavior.[10] Whereas natural historians and morphologists focused on physical characteristics of their specimens, documenting their shapes, colors, and sizes from labs and studies, ethologists ventured into the weeds to study animal affects, habits, and instincts. Their mantra was "*emotions* and *attitudes* are just as much *characters* as are *colours* and *structures*" (J. Huxley 528n65).[11] In 1902, the zoologist William Morton Wheeler defined ethology as "the study of animals with a view to elucidating their true character as expressed in their physical and psychical behavior toward their living and organic environment" (974). The aim of this "most intimate Biology," as another early practitioner Jan Verwey called it, was to comprehend the

---

10. No historical link has been identified between the unrealized human science of ethology that Mill proposed in 1843 and that which Geoffroy launched much more successfully in 1854. According to Jaynes, "it was in ignorance of this English meaning that Isidore Geoffroy Saint-Hilaire rather casually recreated ethology as part of a large classification of biology in a very interesting discussion of the life sciences in 1859" (602).

11. D. Morris notes that, although buried in a footnote, this phrase from the British ornithologist Julian Huxley's 1914 study, "The Courtship Habits of the Great Crested Grebe," "could well be taken as the basic creed for modern ethology" (7).

social and affective lives of animals by embedding oneself in their natural habitats (Verwey 2n43).¹²

I have argued throughout this book that what Mill in 1843 called *ethology*, although it would never be established as a science, would find its home in the realist novel, a genre much better suited to theorizing how character forms in relation to circumstances than the empirical and rational sciences. In *From Man to Man*, we can observe another site through which the realist novel picks up threads left dangling by science—in this case, the science of animal ethology, which would not be systematically formulated until after Schreiner's death. Its narrative centered on a naturalist protagonist who, through close observation of the living world around her, draws parallels between the behavior of animals and humans, Schreiner's novel reflects the concerns of twentieth-century animal ethologists with the important role of milieu in the formation and observation of character. And like these ethologists, who centered care in their observational practice, Schreiner draws attention to the ethics in ethology—the question of how the human can and should comport itself in relation to a world of which it is an intimate part.

Across the following three sections, I show how Schreiner reveals the ethical implications of arenas traditionally thought to be devoid of human value and meaning.¹³ The first section, "The Ethics of Nature," focuses on *From Man to Man*'s interventions into evolutionary science, specifically its challenge to the social Darwinist mantra "the survival of the fittest." Here, I demonstrate Schreiner's commitment to drawing out the

---

12. Toepfer highlights the central role of time and motion in ethological science, noting that early ethologists "emphasized the dynamism of behavior in contrast to the stasis of animal shapes and figures fixed in a blueprint" ("Ethologie" 462-31, translation mine). Geoffroy, for example, counted "as ethological characteristics only those traits that are temporary or last for a short time—above all, movements of the extremities" (464, translation mine). Likewise, twentieth-century ethologists such as Jakob von Uexküll and Adolf Portmann would center their analysis on what they called "Zeitgestalt" (time-form) of the organism (464).

13. J. R. Miller has critiqued the phrase "ethics of" on the grounds that it "implies the coming of some object into consciousness prior to and independent of an 'ethical' process to which it is subsequently subjected" (1). "On this understanding," he writes, "to engage in an 'ethics of' is to bring the question of value, as if for the first time, to phenomena definable without reference to value" (1). While I agree with the upshot of Miller's argument (which I examined at greater length in chapter 3), I employ the phrase "ethics of" to highlight how Schreiner reveals these supposedly neutral and valueless phenomena to be ethically fraught, affirming Miller's claim that "value is not preceded by an earlier mode of difference—most notably, a purely descriptive difference to which value then can be said to apply, attach, or otherwise adhere" (6).

ethical implications of theories of nature as based on competition versus cooperation, and situate her work within the longer history of care ethics from nineteenth-century feminism to twentieth-century animal ethology. The second section, "The Ethics of Description," shows how Schreiner's New Realist aesthetic turns upon the same principle that drives Rebekah's critique of individualist, competition-driven ontologies: her philosophy of relation. Realism, Schreiner suggests, is both possible and necessary because the relations among things are themselves meaningful—they do not need to be *made* meaningful through parables or moral lessons. Finally, "The Ethics of Force" shows how Rebekah engages field theory and Schopenhauer's metaphysics to make the case that the characters of physical entities are not only interrelated but also co-constitutive of one another, their boundaries and qualities arising through relations of force.

The Ethics of Nature

Demonstrating a fascination with the natural world from a young age, Schreiner's character Rebekah grows up finding in the behavior of animals and plants echoes of human life, and vice versa. As an adult, she develops these connections into a full-fledged natural philosophy, which she composes at night, sequestered in her makeshift study filled with microscopes and fossils. The chapter "Raindrops on the Avenue" reveals the impressive extent of Rebekah's research, providing a window into the intellectual life that this mother of five maintains despite her extensive domestic duties. In this section, I sketch out the contours of Rebekah's critique of ethical systems "concentrated on personal aim" (219). Against those who would overlook the principle of care in favor of the principle of competition in their theories of the natural world, Rebekah makes the case that nature, in its very essence, demands care for the other. Without care, she contends, life would not perpetuate itself.

Rebekah's argument stands as an important posthumanist moment in the tradition of feminist care ethics, which stretches from eighteenth-century women's rights activists such as Mary Wollstonecraft to the recent work of the feminist materialist theorist María Puig de la Bellacasa.[14] Like much care-focused feminism before and after her, Rebekah's ethics takes the mother-child relation as its inspiration and model. As we will see, however, her critique of the masculine ideals of autonomy and self-making emerges from her observations of all forms of parenting, including those of nonhuman animals, which thus enables her to ask, in the words of Puig de la Bellacasa, "What does caring mean when we go about thinking and

---

14. On the longer history of care-focused feminism, see Tong.

living interdependently with beings other than human, in 'more than human' worlds?" (13).

Rebekah's primary target in her essay is the notion that the natural world is motivated principally by force of competition and perpetuates only those traits geared toward survival—an argument consolidated in the nineteenth-century English scientist Herbert Spencer's notion of the *survival of the fittest*. Following the publication of the first volume of Spencer's *Principles of Biology* in 1864, the phrase "survival of the fittest" was invoked across England and its colonies to explain why the extinction of the so-called lower races at the hands of the supposedly advanced races was natural and inevitable. Much more than a descriptive theory, it justified the removal of indigenous peoples, inspired missionary efforts, justified free-market capitalism, and lent support to various forms of social Darwinism—as well as its offshoot, eugenics.

Given a copy of Spencer's *First Principles* (1864-67) in her youth, Schreiner initially found compelling the English biologist's description of human society as one great organism whose parts were consistently evolving but mutually interdependent. An 1884 letter recounts the profound effect of Spencer's thinking on her worldview: "He helped me to believe in a unity underlying all nature," she writes to Ellis ("To Havelock Ellis, April 8, 1884"). Daniel Rigney has noted how although Spencer believed that both competition and cooperation drive evolution, he ultimately "understated the evolutionary value of cooperation within and among species as a means of survival," allowing readers to interpret his notion of the survival of the fittest to "imply the moral superiority of the wealthy, the powerful, and those of Northern European ancestry over the poor, the powerless, and the colonized" (Rigney 27). For these reasons, Schreiner eventually backed away from Spencer's theories, informing Ellis that "he has nothing else to give me now" ("To Havelock Ellis, April 8, 1884").[15]

---

15. Although Darwin himself never advocated an active eugenics program, in *The Descent of Man*, he began to embrace some of the tenets of his social Darwinist followers, writing that "at some future period, not very distant as measured by centuries, the civilised races of man will almost certainly exterminate, and replace, the savage races throughout the world" (183). The larger context of this quotation, however, reveals that Darwin in no way supported such a process. As he goes on to argue, the force of evolution had introduced and would continue to introduce breaks between the "races"—including that between "civilised man" and the "anthropomorphous apes" from which man evolved. Such gaps, Darwin suggests, would only continue to widen as man becomes "more civilised... even than the Caucasian" (183). Reviewed in *Cape Monthly Magazine* in the year it was published, *The Descent* "exerted a significantly greater impact on the Cape's reading public than *The Origin of Species* (1859)" and was taken up by various local proponents of racial segregation (Dubow 97). Dubow has shown how

From Man to Man contains Schreiner's most extensive critique of social Darwinism, in particular the injunction of its eugenicist proponents to "forcibly suppress, cut off and destroy the less developed individuals and races, leaving only the highly developed to survive," as Rebekah summarizes it (196).[16] Drawing from her own experience as a mother, her extensive research into evolutionary theory, and her own work as an amateur naturalist in Cape Colony, Rebekah uses Spencer's arguments against him to contend that the forces of "love and expansion of the ego to others" are more fundamental to life than the forces of competition and self-preservation (209).

One sees this force at work in the mother-child relationship, which Rebekah dwells on for some time. But this basic ethical principle is not limited to mothers; it is rather "a much wider feeling for the weak, which makes possible much of the higher animal life about us" (210). Breaking down the assumption that care is an essentially feminine quality, she writes, "You may say that mother-love forms an exception in the rule of nature, which, for perfecting life, demands the destruction of the weak by the strong. But what of the protective care of the male, not only of his own young and his related females, but of all the most helpless of his group?" (210).

Countering those who would see competition as the reigning principle of nature, Rebekah draws attention to instances of care and creativity in the natural world. She gives the example of the meerkat, which will always save the younger, smaller, and more helpless when a hawk approaches, without fear for itself. It is, she insists, "this creative (and not the destructive) power" that is the fundamental principle of nature (214). "To attempt to explain and sum up life by considering" only the element of competition, she argues, is to act "like the man who should attempt to represent a great musical symphony by playing its lower notes alone, like a man who should try to reproduce a great composer's masterpiece by striking all the discords in it without any of the harmonies into which they resolve themselves and with reference to which alone they have any meaning" (213). Such harmonious moments of love and care for the other capture

---

"reappraisals of the underlying racial affinities between Boers and Britons were intended to assist in the goal of securing a future of a united 'white man's country'" in the early years of the twentieth century, a shift that "entailed a corresponding stress on the need for more systematic separation of whites and blacks" (177). Schreiner finished reading *The Descent* in April 1873, after which, according to her husband, she immediately "thought out and began to write" the book that would become *From Man to Man* (Cronwright-Schreiner 92).

16. Not all social Darwinists supported eugenics; some opposed the practice, contending that active intervention in the evolutionary process would only weaken the species.

our attention less than moments of conflict and competition; however, this only proves their universality in contrast to the exception of violence and self-love.

That Rebekah so often grounds her ethical arguments in observations of the natural world might seem counterintuitive from our contemporary perspective, given that feminist theory today unfolds largely in the idiom of cultural critique. However, as the historian of science Cynthia Eagle Russett reminds us, "only at the very end of the century did cultural interpretations begin to achieve respectability; prior to that time they were simply dismissed as unscientific" (13). Given the "enormous prestige of science and the universal acceptance of its authoritative status in matters of sex difference," she notes, nineteenth-century feminists often "tried to confront scientific anti-feminism on its own terms" (13).

While I agree with Russett's overarching thesis, I want to stress the extent to which Schreiner's novel goes out of its way to work with rather than against science. In rendering her protagonist a naturalist and feminist, Schreiner demonstrates her passionate belief in the power of scientific observation to ground social critique. Rather than countering the views of her social Darwinist contemporaries by arguing, for instance, that scientific theory operates in a realm entirely separate from the social—that while Darwin's theories apply to "nature," they in no way apply to "culture"—Rebekah advocates more empirically sound theories of nature in order to develop more informed theories of culture, and vice versa.

In so doing, she actually moves against the broader tendency of her historical moment—which, as the historian of science Lorraine Daston has shown, saw the emergence of an epistemological divide between the laws governing nonhuman nature from those governing human action. While many Enlightenment thinkers looked to nature for guidance in matters of ethics, the nineteenth century saw the birth of the view held by many scientists and philosophers today: that "Nature simply is," and "it takes a human act of imposition or projection to transmute that 'is' into an 'ought.'" (479–580). In the words of the contemporary science studies scholar Bruno Latour, we might say that the nineteenth century saw a wedge driven between "matters of fact" and "matters of concern" (114). Long before Latour (drawing on the work of Schreiner's contemporary, the English philosopher Alfred North Whitehead) would question "the bifurcation of nature" into these two separate realms, Schreiner suggested that there is no such thing as a theory of nature devoid of ethical implications (Whitehead 26).[17] The moment we begin to observe nature, she implies, is the

---

17. What Whitehead in *The Concept of Nature* (1920) calls "the bifurcation of nature" concerns the separation of nature into that which is mind-independent and that

moment we open up our thinking to the realm of ethics. For this reason, it matters which metaphors, which epistemological rubrics, and which concepts we use when we interpret and theorize nature.

Whereas atomistic and agonistic figures highlight the competitive aspects of the natural world, the organicist vocabulary Rebekah employs highlights interconnection and relation. Karl Marx often employed the metaphor of society as a single organism to emphasize the interdependence of what he called society's "base" and "superstructure." For Marx, society's base—its relations of production (e.g., working conditions and property relations)—determine its superstructure—its cultural and political relations (e.g., its institutions and rituals). At the same time, he suggests, society's culture and traditions also maintain and legitimate its modes of production. We do not know for sure whether Schreiner read Marx's *A Contribution to the Critique of Political Economy* (1859). However, the ideas and terminology invoked in her "Raindrops" chapter bear some striking similarities to those Marx employs in that work. Referring to the notion of the "superstructure" in her description of the "culture, freedom, and civic rights" of the ancient Greeks, for instance, Rebekah points out that only some members of Greek society enjoyed these privileges (153). She then ties the unevenness of the superstructure to the unevenness of the base, what she describes as the "rotten foundation stone" of slavery and women's domestic labor (153).

To view human society, as Rebekah does, as a "pulsating, always interacting whole," rather than a collection of unrelated parts, is to realize that what has emerged from the oppression of some for the benefit of others is not a natural order in which only the fittest survive; it is an unhealthy and unbalanced ecosystem in which only a small percentage flourish, at the cost of many (181). She says, "All the civilizations of the past, in Egypt, in Assyria, in Persia, in India, what had they been but the blossoming of a minute, abnormally situated, abnormally nourished class, unsupported by any vital connection with the classes beneath them or the nations around?" (191). Rebekah stresses that the growth of the whole is always limited when some are left behind: "Is it not a paradox covering a mighty

---

which is subjective. This bifurcation has reemerged under another guise in more recent work in speculative realism and object-oriented ontology demonstrating that ontological questions are devoid of ethical significance. According to Bryant, for example, "it is striking that debates surrounding [speculative realism and object-oriented ontology] have been focused on questions of the social and political… given that SR, in the hands of its original four founders, has been a rather apolitical set of philosophical concerns focused on questions of the being of the real" (15). Harman has more explicitly argued that metaphysics and politics live in separate realms and that "philosophy should not be the handmaid of anything else" (Harman).

truth that not one slave toils under the lash on an Indian plantation but the freedom of every other man on earth is limited by it?... That the full all-around human life is impossible to any individual while one man lives who does not share it?" (194).

The organic connection that Rebekah believes characterizes nature demands a kind of care for the other, so reliant are things upon one another. Of the "abnormally nourished classes," she continues, "what had they resembled but the long, thin, tender, feathery, green shoots which our small rose trees sometimes send out in spring, rising far into the air, but which we know long before the summer is over will have broken and fallen, not because they have grown to a height which no rose tree can ever attain, for ultimately the whole rose tree may be much higher than the shoot, but because they have shot out too far before their fellow-branches to make permanence possible" (191). In this metaphor, the shoots of the rose tree, while higher than that of the mass of the tree, must always break off because "having no support, wind and weather will sooner or later do their work and snap them off or wither them" (191). In Rebekah's organicist vision, all things are interconnected like organs in a body: to injure one part is to injure the whole. If, as she argues, we "nowhere find an isolated existence," we need to recognize the effects of our actions (181).

Ecocritical scholars over the past few decades have worried that in its focus on wholeness, sympathy, and symbiosis, ecological theory sometimes "produces integration at the expense of alterity and coherence at the expense of possibility" (Griffiths and Kreisel 5-6). Where some dismiss the "touchy-feely, ultimately authoritarian organicism upon which claims of interconnectedness are usually built" (Morton, "The Ecological" 23), others argue that philosophies of nature broadly engage in "a primitivist fantasy that hinges on the violent erasure of the social" and perpetuates the "settler-colonial logic of modern Western culture" (Rosenberg). In her foundational study of English colonial relations, *Imperial Leather: Race, Gender, and Sexuality in the Colonial Contest*, Anne McClintock critiques what she calls Schreiner's "pantheism" on such grounds, maintaining that Schreiner's faith in an underlying unity risks subsuming difference into the colonial fantasy of a single totality.[18] Whereas McClintock concludes that Schreiner's "mystical faith in 'the unity of all things'" ultimately reveals an "imperial faith that a singular universal meaning animates the world" (265, 281), the historian Joyce Avrech Berkman is more sympathetic. "Schreiner's organicism was decidedly antihierarchical,"

---

18. "Her pantheism," McClintock argues, "for all its emotional integrity, was very much a metaphysical abstraction. As an abstraction, it served to conceal, and thereby to ratify, the very real imbalances in social power around her" (267).

Berkman argues, adding, "she insisted that, just as the mind is not superior to the heart or body, healthy social intercourse rests upon equality of races, classes, and sexes" (75).

Certainly, organicist metaphors of wholeness and interconnection might just as easily be mobilized for or against actual equality, as aptly demonstrated, for instance, in the case of Schreiner's contemporary, the South African politician Jan Christian Smuts. Smuts was a military leader and two-time prime minister of the Union of South Africa, who used research in botany and human ecology to naturalize racial divisions and justify the oppression of Black Africans. Smuts's theory of *holism*—a term he coined—was invoked to legitimize some of the harshest race laws of the twentieth century, leading the Black American writer W. E. B. Du Bois to describe Smuts in 1925 as "the greatest protagonist of the white race" (402).[19] In his philosophical manifesto *Holism and Evolution* (1926), Smuts draws on many of the same fields of study as Schreiner's novel (published that same year), including evolutionary theory, ecology, and physics, as well as Whitehead's process philosophy, to argue for a holistic understanding of nature. Closer attention to the different kinds of holism Schreiner and Smuts professed, however, reveals some crucial differences between the two thinkers.[20]

Schreiner met Smuts in 1899 and became a vocal critic of his policies from that moment forward. Following her return to South Africa in 1920, the year after Smuts became prime minister, Schreiner publicly chastised him for his shortsightedness on the "native question"—what she described as "not only South Africa's great question, but the world's great question" ("To Jan Smuts, October 19, 1920"). Against Smuts, who had argued that different rights applied to different racial groups, Schreiner, writing with her husband, Samuel Cronwright-Schreiner, advocated for putting "the

19. In "The Negro Mind Reaches Out" (1925), Du Bois cites the following remarks on voting rights from Smuts's 1925 address at the Imperial Conference: "If there was to be equal manhood suffrage over the Union, the whites would be swamped by the blacks. A distinction could not be made between Indians and Africans. They would be impelled by the inevitable force of logic to go the whole hog, and the result would be that not only would the whites be swamped in Natal by the Indians but the whites would be swamped all over South Africa by the blacks and the whole position for which the whites had striven for two hundred years or more now would be given up. So far as South Africa was concerned, therefore, it was a question of impossibility. For white South Africa it was not a question of dignity but a question of existence" (Smuts, quoted in Du Bois 402).

20. On how Smuts's holism informed his politics, see Anker, who argues that Smuts's segregationist policies were not at odds with but rather "fully consistent with his holistic philosophy of science" (157).

Native... on an equality with the white man in the eye of the law" (109-10). A holistic approach to the social body, as the example of Smuts's and Schreiner's opposing politics demonstrates, might result in two entirely different ends: one hierarchical and segregationist, the other committed to equality. Where Smuts worshipped a totalizing homogeneity (his mantra was "The whole is more than the sum of its parts"), Schreiner resists subordinating the part to the whole, arguing that the whole "lives *in all its parts*" (144, emphasis mine). Like Marx, she suggests that the chance for revolution is immanent in every part of the totality.

It is Schreiner's concept of *relation*, I will go on to argue in drawing parallels to her philosophy with later anticolonial thinkers such as Édouard Glissant and Léopold Sédar Senghor, that ultimately prevents her from subsuming difference into the totality of the whole or, like Smuts, covertly elevating one part over others. Against those who see only certain characters as desirable for the human race, Rebekah advocates for the fundamental equality and right to flourishing of all people and traits (196). She tackles the rampant biological racism of her era directly and unflinchingly: "Is there really any superiority at all implied in degrees of pigmentation, and are the European races, except in their egoistic distortion of imagination, more desirable or highly developed than the Asiatic?" Rebekah asks (202). Her answer is a resounding "no," and she attacks any other such answer from various angles.

One of Rebekah's most powerful points is that all which appeared to be superior and "civilized" about western and northern Europe at that time was built on the backs of those they deemed "savage": "When we look around us on what we call our civilization," she writes, "how little is really ours alone and not drawn from the great stream of human labours and creation so largely non-European?" (203). Demonstrating the literal dependence of the European on the non-European other, Rebekah works to deconstruct the myth of the autonomous and sovereign European subject, key in perpetuating and sustaining the inequalities of colonial rule.[21] The feminist decolonial theorist Chandra Talpade Mohanty has observed how "in drawing racial, sexual, and class boundaries in terms of spatial, and symbolic distance and actually formulating these as integral to the maintenance of colonial rule, the British defined authority and legitimacy

---

21. This is a point that anticolonial thinkers have often made; cf. Fanon's reflections on the human sciences in *Black Skin, White Masks*, and Spivak's argument that the ideology of the evolved European subject is perpetuated today in the discourse of human rights, which "may carry within itself the agenda of a kind of social Darwinism—the fittest must shoulder the burden of righting the wrongs of the unfit" ("Righting" 524).

through difference rather than a commonality of rulers and 'natives'" (58–59). Rebekah's organicist conception of the social body is aimed at collapsing such distances and distinctions, positing that because all races, genders, and classes are linked, violence against the "other" consists in violence against oneself.

The philosophy of relation forwarded by Rebekah might here be fruitfully aligned with that of Glissant, the turn-of-the-twenty-first-century Caribbean philosopher and poet who shares with Schreiner a commitment to understanding relation as the motivating force of culture. In *Poetics of Relation* (1990), Glissant draws an initial distinction between relation and totality in order to point out the risk of subsuming all difference and movement into a static unity. As he writes, "The difference between Relation and totality lies in the fact that Relation is active within itself, whereas totality, already in its very concept, is in danger of immobility. Relation is open to totality, totality would be relation at rest.... Relation is movement" (171). However, Glissant goes on to argue, relation can be conceived as its own form of totality—an "open totality" (206), a "totality in evolution" (133).

Reading Schreiner through Glissant, we can see how, in emphasizing relation, Schreiner highlights the instability of the whole. Her totality is not static and unified, but "fundamentally mobile," to cite the Senegalese poet and politician Léopold Sédar Senghor (29). While their politics were no doubt geared toward different aims (Senghor was focused on raising Black consciousness across Africa and its diaspora, and Schreiner on inspiring white English, Boer, and Black Africans to join together in the fight against racial inequality), the figures they use to mobilize their constituencies—Senghor, that of the "living, throbbing unity" (29) and Schreiner, that of the "a great pulsating, always interacting whole"—resemble one another in their commitment to thinking of the social body "as an active system rather than a stable thing" (Griffiths and Kreisel 10).

The scholars of Victorian literature and science Devin Griffiths and Deanna K. Kreisel have coined the term "open ecology" to describe environmental models that, while they highlight interconnection and symbiosis, retain a sense of openness and difference.[22] Citing Darwin's description of the "tangled bank" in *The Origin of Species* and Eliot's figure of the

---

22. "If modern ecocriticism has sometimes been hobbled by a restrictively organic, harmonious conception of how ecologies work," Griffiths and Kriesel write in "Open Ecologies," their special issue of the journal *Victorian Literature and Culture*, "we wager that a return to Victorian interrogations of natural and social collectives can furnish more open, less integrated models for how assemblages operate" (1).

"web" in *Middlemarch* as examples of such open ecologies, they see the nineteenth century as a rich resource for "this more open, more mutable notion of ecology" (3).

The term *Oekologie* (ecology) was coined in 1866 by the German biologist Ernst Haeckel, who called for the founding of a "science of the economy, of the habits, external relations of organisms to each other" (Stauffer 140).[23] Throughout the nineteenth century, however, Haeckel's *Relationsphysiologie* (relational physiology) overlapped extensively with another biological science—that which Isidore Geoffroy Saint-Hilaire had called *éthologie* twelve years earlier (Haeckel 238). During the nineteenth century, the differences between these two new sciences were negligible, with Haeckel and other scientists using the terms interchangeably (Toepfer, "Ethologie" 461).[24] Both proposed to study organisms in their natural habitats, and both took animal behavior (rather than physiology or morphology) as the focus of their analysis. At the turn of the century, however, the two sciences would eventually develop distinct methodologies and foci: where ecology increasingly relied on quantitative methods to analyze the systemic connections between organisms and their ecosystems, ethology developed an observation-based methodology for studying in more qualitative terms how organisms and species formed characters in response to their physical environments and social networks.

In the decades following Schreiner's death in 1920, European ornithologists such as Oskar Heinroth, Jan Verwey, and Julian Huxley laid down the fundamental principles of the science of ethology as it would come to be practiced throughout the twentieth century.[25] What increasingly distin-

---

23. In formulating his "relational physiology," Haeckel built on Darwin's understanding of living organisms as "bound together by a web of complex relations" (*Origin* 75).

24. Jaynes points out that Haeckel's 1866 definition of ecology as "the science of the economy, of the habits, external relations of organisms to each other" closely mirrors the French zoologist Alfred Giard's account of ethology in 1875 as "the study of the customs of animals and their mutual relationships" (Giard, quoted in Jaynes 604). See Durant for more on how throughout the nineteenth century ethology "overlapped extensively with 'Oecology'... whose exact nature was a matter of debate" (161).

25. Heinroth's four-volume *Die Vögel Mitteleuropas* (1924–33) is widely thought to have established the fundamental principles and methodology of ethology, leading some to label him "the single most important figure in the history of early ethology" (Durant 163). In the United States, ethology would be established slightly earlier in the hands of biologists such as William Morton Wheeler and C. O. Whitman. Durant identifies three main phases in the formation of the field of ethology—a "formative" phase until around 1930; a "classical" phase between 1930 and 1950; and a "mature" phase after 1950 (159).

guished ethology from ecology, as Durant has shown, was the question of character—specifically, the theory of these ethologists that nonhuman animals had "'characters' which can be understood, often by direct analogy with human character, on the basis of prolonged and sympathetic observation" (164). In their observation-based studies of birds and other animals, twentieth-century ethologists embedded themselves in the natural habitats of animals to observe how animals formed social and affective bonds that affected the development of their character: "having brought an understanding of human character to bear on their work with birds" and other species, moreover, as Durant notes, "many of the early ethologists could not resist the temptation to apply the results back to man" (190).

In focusing on not only how organisms *ecologically* interact, but how these interactions generate *ethological* differences in character, Rebekah anticipates the ethologist's concern with how habitual behaviors develop through social interactions. And, like them, she applies the insights she derives from observations of the natural world to her analysis of the human. Ethologists showed how animal behaviors such as the baring of teeth or bowing in submission, while originally spontaneous expressions of affect, became naturalized as part of the instinctive communication systems of different species. Rebekah makes a similarly sociobiological argument about women's so-called instincts. Although many women appear weak, she argues, they have merely learned how to perform this weakness as a tool for survival in a world that has prevented them from developing more explicit forms of power: "Because the stronger sex has so perpetually attempted to crush the physically smaller, the individuals who attempted to resist force by force being at once wiped out," Rebekah writes, the female sex has "acquired almost as a secondary sexual characteristic, a subtleness and power of finesse to which it now flies almost as instinctively as a crab to the water when it sees danger approaching" (219).

Not only does *From Man to Man* anticipate these ethologists' concern with the formation of animal and human character through social relations, the novel also models their care-focused methodology. In twentieth-century animal ethology, as the contemporary philosopher Vinciane Despret has observed, "the experimenter, far from keeping himself in the background, involves himself: he involves his body, he involves his knowledge, his responsibility and his future. The practice of knowing has become a practice of caring" (130).[26] As an example of this care-based ethological

---

26. Despret belongs to a new generation of philosophical ethologists who have built upon the insights of animal behaviorists to offer a more robust account of animal intelligence, communication, and emotion. For an introduction to philosophical ethology, see Buchanan, Bussolini, and Churelew.

practice, Despret turns to the work of the ornithologist Konrad Lorenz, who would go on to win the Nobel Prize in Physiology and Medicine in 1973. Known for his work on "imprinting"—the tendency of young animals to attach themselves emotionally to the object they encounter most frequently in their youth—Lorenz analyzed the behaviors that lead young geese to attach to their caregivers. But more than simply *observing* that care, as Despret underscores, Lorenz often *involved himself* in that care, becoming the imprinted object for several young birds. "Lorenz uses his own body as a tool for knowing," Despret writes, "as a tool for asking questions, as a means to create a relation that provides new knowledge: how does a goose become attached to its mother? Lorenz takes the mother's place, and becomes all at once a variable of the experiment" (129).

Lorenz's research demonstrated that the gender and even the species of the "mother" are less important than biologists had previously assumed. He showed this, crucially, by becoming a mother himself—that is, by involving his own body and feelings in his scientific practice. In so doing, he can be seen to affirm not only Rebekah's theory that "motherlove" pervades the natural world, but also that the practice of mothering itself, far from an obstacle to the production of good science, is a potential source of insight.

Many twentieth-century ethologists were nature conservationists whose observations of animal life served as the basis for their political advocacy. Underscoring the *ethics* in ethology, they drew attention to the inseparability of "matters of fact" from "matters of concern." The practice of description was central to both their science and their politics. In his 1971 lecture "The Fashionable Fallacy of Dispensing with Description," Lorenz defended the descriptive method of ethologists by arguing that although quantitative methods are perceived by many scientists to eliminate subjective bias, it is only by acknowledging the subjectivity of the observer that one can produce a good description. In the section of his talk entitled "Ethical Concerns," Lorenz highlights the roles that both individual experiences and cultural assumptions play in scientific study: "For the European," he writes, "Arab music is a chaotic kind of moaning, because the European ear is not trained to perceive the lawfulness of the oriental whole-tone scale" (8). It is only by coming to understand a system from the inside and on its own terms, he goes on to argue, that an observer can understand its logic—as well as grasp its ethical consequences: "The man whose eye is not trained to perceive the harmony of nature," he writes, echoing Rebekah's focus on interconnection in nature, "is absolutely blind to it and does not feel the least compunction in 'developing' the last beautiful spots still left on our earth, bulldozing down trees, covering everything with concrete and building luxury hotels" (8).

Lorenz's lecture is positioned as an intervention in scientific practice. His impassioned defense of description as a method for understanding "really complicated systems," however, is helpful for understanding how realist novels such as *From Man to Man* produce knowledge of character through their descriptions of fictional beings in fictional worlds (5). While Schreiner might have presented Rebekah's arguments in the form of a scholarly monograph, in elaborating her sophisticated critique of social Darwinism through the writings of a fictional character, she highlights the role of the body in knowledge production. Rebekah's diaries feature not only "discussions on abstract questions" (139), but also "great plans for the life that was to be lived—countries to be visited—books to be written—scientific knowledge to be gained—all written with absolute confidence" (140). The type and frequency of these entries vary depending on what is going on in Rebekah's life: after her marriage, for example, "the entries dwindled. Months passed in which nothing was written. After a child had been born and it had been necessary to lie still for weeks,... there were only short scraps" (140). Like Lorenz, who turns to description in order to represent the affective lives of animals in a way that charts and graphs cannot, Schreiner uses realist description to show how the most abstract knowledge is generated through embodied, affective experience, affirming one of the fundamental theses of this book: that when realist fiction attends to the observable, the particular, and the contingent, it theorizes.

The Ethics of Description

In a 1912 letter to Ellis, Schreiner outlines her theory that a person's "diary works (I mean simple, spontaneous, straight forward records of what one sees, feels, & does & thinks)" constitute an excellent site for comprehending the central role of emotion in scientific observation. As an example of affectively charged writing she cites Darwin, whose notes on plants and animals in his diaries reveal that "nature impresses him with great cosmic feelings" ("To Havelock Ellis, June 30, 1912"). Praising Ellis's own ability to "throw a whole world into a short critical or descriptive sentence," Schreiner encourages him to document his perceptions more often—to write, as she puts it, "who *you* saw where you went & felt interest, what you felt about *your* food & *your* room: & how the pictures impressed you."

We saw in chapter 2 how George Eliot, in her last published work of fiction, *Impressions of Theophrastus Such*, developed a theory of knowledge as a sensitive encounter by invoking the semantic connection between *character* and *impression*. In her letter to Ellis, Schreiner likewise describes character as a kind of imprinting: "I do see the actual world about me so *intensely*[. T]he men & women I meet print themselves on me.... Character! character! character! is what cuts deep into me" ("To Havelock Ellis, June 30, 1912"). In addition to people, Schreiner notes that she observes with equal intensity "the changes in the sky the weather the scene: all nature is immensely important." Not only do "*material* things" imprint themselves on her, but, as she explains to Ellis, her characterizations of things and people in turn bear the mark of her unique character when she then transfers her feelings to the page. "The charm" of a person's diary, she suggests, "is that it is an expression of *their individuality*. A guide book has no charm because it expresses no individuality it is just a collection of facts" ("To Havelock Ellis, June 30, 1912").

Schreiner's representation of Rebekah's diary writings highlights the two meanings of the word *impression* alluded to in her letter to Ellis (and likewise explored by Eliot in *Impressions*): not only do Rebekah's writings bear the mark of her character, but the character of the world imprints itself on her, changing her character in and through her receptivity to it. Taking a break from her theorizing, Rebekah begins to draw human figures in her diary: "[S]he sank half back in the chair, still on her knees and, after a time, began slowly drawing with her outstretched hand the pictures of faces down one edge of the page she had written on. They came out slowly, one below the other, some with sharp features, some with dark beards and curls, some with blunt features, some grotesque and some beautiful" (186). Rebekah's literal "character sketches" in the margins of her essay reflect the descriptive impulse of Schreiner's novel itself, which interrupts the plot for over eighty pages to sketch Rebekah's character. Interspersing Rebekah's diary entries with detailed descriptions of her body, actions, and thoughts, *From Man to Man* uses description to simultaneously represent and theorize reality—performing the kind of weak theory I have argued characterizes late Victorian realism broadly.

From Man to Man, as we saw in the previous section, models the practices of care and description that would go on to define the twentieth-century science of animal ethology. My aim in this section is to show that the philosophy of relation formulated in Rebekah's diary entries serves as the basis of the novel's theory of realism—a theory not only articulated through Rebekah's words but also performed through Schreiner's description of her character. My thesis is that Rebekah's critique of individualist ontologies is intimately tied to the novel's New Realist aesthetic: it is only when one recognizes the interconnected nature of reality that realism, in Schreiner's ethological terms, become possible. Turn-of-the century critics of women-authored realist fiction worried that women's "passion for detail" distorted their ability to be neutral and objective (Courtney xxi). In his 1904 study, *The Feminine Note in Fiction*, for example, W. L. Courtney contends that the female-authored novel is too "strongly tinctured by the elements of her own personality," rendering it more like "the writing of personal diary" than a novel (xiii). In conversation with her realist predecessor George Eliot, as we will see, Schreiner uses Rebekah's diary entries as a space to theorize realism as a practice of peripatetic attention to worldly interaction and connection—one that accounts for the embeddedness of the human being in the reality it describes—thereby overturning the opposition between realism and embodied positionality that Courtney and other critics had posited when critiquing realist fiction by women for its lack of objectivity.

As I showed previously, Rebekah does not fault social Darwinism for grounding its claims about human society in observations of the natural world. Her critique turns rather upon the fact that the observations of social Darwinists are themselves flawed. In entirely overlooking principles of care and connectedness in favor of principles of competition and division, these scientists perpetuated a long history of oppression founded on a conception of reality, "a thing of shreds and patches and unconnected parts" (178).

This separatist ontology, Rebekah suggests—far from neutral or valueless—has ethical implications that it has carried with it since its inception. Historicizing this view of the universe, Rebekah suggests that it stems from a "Christian conception of the universe" in which God is understood to be the connective force of an otherwise disjointed world (179). In this ontology, the universe is understood to be a "heap of toys which a child gathers about it on the floor: doll, bugle, brick, book, having no subtle living connection with each other, being there only because the will of the child has brought them there" (179). In order to explain the connection between these parts, Christians postulate a "ruling individuality" that gives the disorderly and random order and purpose (179). A particular epistemology tends to accompany this ontology: "truth" here has nothing to do with attempting to discover the connection between the things themselves, but rather is defined as "knowledge of the will of the arbitrary ruling individual" (179).

But, to position the ruling individual as the fundamental source of all earthly value and meaning, Rebekah argues, is to forsake the actual interconnection of that is in motion around oneself. She rejects such hierarchies of value, fascinated as she is with relationships not only between humans and nonhuman things but also between nonhuman things themselves. As she points out, in the Christian view, "truth as it regards the shading of a feather on a bird's wing, the movement of a planet, the order of social growth, the structure of a human body, can be of no value" (179). Here, seekers of knowledge do not ask, "What is true?" but rather, "What will be the effect of such knowledge or such a statement?" (180).

It is for this reason, she explains, that Galileo's contention that the earth revolves around the sun needed to be suppressed by church authorities. Its effect on the beliefs of the world's rulers was too great. Rebekah criticizes the instrumentalization of knowledge in the Christian system, in which the only thing of import is "knowledge of certain facts for a definite purpose"—the purpose of producing meaning, always for man and through God (180).

Fortunately, another outlook has emerged in recent years, Rebekah tells us. Modern scientific thought is marked by a desire to know the intimate structure of reality, regardless of its purpose, use, or effects. In "this new intellectual conception of the nature of the Universe" we find a rekindled "desire for exact knowledge of reality, of things exactly as they were, first and before all things" (177). This is because of the principle of homology, which, central to the rise of modern materialist science, has allowed things to take on a value greater than themselves. "The prism I hold in my hand," Rebekah writes, "rightly understood, may throw light on the structure of the furthest sun; the fossil I dug out on the mountain side this morning, rightly studied, may throw light on the structure and meaning of the hand that unearths it (180). The physiologist, likewise, carefully examines a tiny drop of blood under a microscope, not because that particular drop is so special but because it might help to explain the organism of which it is a part. Here, "there is no small truth—all truth is great!" (181). Whereas in the Christian view, God is required in order to make sense of a disenchanted and disconnected world, in this new view, no outside organizing force is necessary, as things are understood to be always already in intimate relation: "For us once again," Rebekah writes, "the Universe has become one, a whole, and it lives in all its parts. Step by step advancing knowledge has shown us the internetting lines of action and reaction which bind together all that we see and are conscious of" (180).

Rebekah's view of reality as a web of relation opens up the door not only to new ontologies, but also new aesthetic practices. While an instrumentalized view of the world can only produce art with a "definite purpose," Schreiner suggests, a theory of the universe as being comprised fundamentally of "internetting lines of action and reaction" allows for the emergence of a representational paradigm in which each and every piece of reality merits description (180). In making this argument, Schreiner not only can be seen to build upon Eliot's claim that "the fragment of a life, however typical, is not the sample of an even web" (*Middlemarch* 779), but also her call in "The Natural History of German Life" for a literary-descriptive practice based on "gradually amassed observations" (127). Like Eliot, whose essay questions the value of idealized portraits of the English peasantry with a "moral end" (131), Rebekah advocates a turn away from morality-driven representations in art, toward practices of close attention: "Better the true picture of a beggar in his rags than the willfully false picture of a saint" (*From Man* 198). For Rebekah, the ultimate symbol of morality-driven art is the fig leaf, which covers the genitals of the ancient statues in the books she orders from England. For some, "the human nature falsely painted because it seemed undesirable to paint it as it is, the fig-leaf tied across the loin of the noblest statue, gives no pain and is still art." For Rebekah, however, "the perception of the willful suppression of truth [is] emotionally painful" (186). She longs to understand artworks "in [the] climates that produced them," rather than in a book that decontextualizes its art objects, separating them from the cultures that gave rise to them (187).

Buildings on Eliot's earlier attempts to account for the role of sensation in realism, Schreiner stresses the pleasure and eroticism at work both in writing and in experiencing the realist art object. Rebekah's writing is said to stem from "that curious hunger for exact knowledge of things as they are, of naked truth about things small or great, material and also psychic" (177). Likewise, the experience of close and detailed description affords a certain pleasure: "the representation of the smallest or slightest aspect of life, if we are conscious of truth in it," she argues, "satisfies an emotional need in us and becomes for us, so far at least, an object of satisfaction" (186). This emphasis on the pleasure of realistic art might seem at first to depart from the kind of realism Eliot envisioned. Amanda Anderson, for instance, has argued that the sympathetic realism that Eliot cultivates, while critical of some forms of detachment, ultimately institutes an "ideal of critical distance" (*Powers* 4). For George Levine, moreover, "Self-abnegation and the realist openness to the hard unaccommodating actual had gone together in her works" (*Dying* 171). Schreiner, however, draws out the important role of the affect, and, ultimately, the erotic at work in Eliot's realism, which I have framed in this book as being a project of sensory enhancement.

The figure of the "pulse," invoked consistently by both Eliot and Schreiner, and which is explored in the introduction to this book, is a favorite of both writers. In *From Man to Man*, Schreiner reconfigures what Neil Hertz calls "George Eliot's pulse" into a kind of life force, drawing together creatures human and nonhuman, material and immaterial. As Rebekah writes:

> Between spirit that beats within me and body through which it acts, between mind and matter, between man and beast and plant and earth, between life that has been the life it is, I am able to see nowhere a sharp line of severance, but a great, pulsating, always interacting whole. So that at

last it comes to be, that, when I hear my own heartbeat, I actually hear in it nothing but one throb in that life which has been and is—in which we live and move and have our being and are constantly sustained. (181)

Within this passage, one can hear an echo not only of the Bible ("For in him we live, and move, and have our being" [Acts 17:28]), but also of Eliot's *Middlemarch*, in which Dorothea, as discussed previously, upon feeling her own heartbeat, realizes that she too is "a part of that involuntary, palpitating life" and cannot "look out on it as a mere spectator" (741). As in Eliot, in Schreiner, the pulse is a mark of the physical intimacy between the observer and the world she observes.

Schreiner never met Eliot (Eliot died the year before Schreiner arrived in England); but, like many women, she seems to have felt a physical, if not erotic, connection to her through her writing.[27] After reading *Romola* for the first time, Schreiner observed, "George Eliot seems to live again in it, and one finds her grand old heart beating though it" ("To Isaline Philpot, March 1886"). Returning to the language of the heartbeat, Schreiner approaches reading as a form of embodied connection. In her letters, she expresses her desire to encounter Eliot physically, to greet her with the intimacy of a kiss: "I wish George Eliot was alive," she wrote in 1883, "I would like so to ask her to let me kiss her" ("To Philip Kent, May 12, 1883"). Similarly, in *From Man to Man*, Rebekah's relationship to the authors of the books she cherishes is shot through with desire: Her books "seemed to love her. Behind each was hidden the mind of some human creature which at some time had touched her own; they were all the intellectual intercourse she had ever known. Not one was there because it was a rare or old copy, or had an expensive binding; each one was there because at some time she had lived close to it and it had penetrated her" (175).

We might read Rebekah here similarly to the way that David Kurnick has read Eliot's Dorothea—as an "erotically impelled researcher" whose "pursuit of insight into the structure of reality" is informed by an immersive desire (597). In *Middlemarch*, Kurnick argues, reading is itself presented as a path to knowledge insofar as it allows observers to immerse themselves in the world they observe, rather than observing it from a critical distance. Schreiner seems to have picked up on Eliot's interest in literature as a space of affective possibility, and she borrows her figure of the pulse in order to signal that surge of feeling.

Through the character of Rebekah, we come to understand the realist

---

27. It is well known that Eliot had intimate, physical relationships with several of her female contemporaries, many of whom came to know her through her writings. The most intense of these was with Edith Simcox (Bodenheimer; Showalter, "Greening").

narrator not as a distanced and objective observer but rather as an intimately involved participant in the world, whose desire drives her descriptions. "The observer who studies and records behavior patterns of higher animals is up against a great difficulty," Lorenz observes in his early essay "Companionship in Bird Life" (1935), adding, "He himself is a subject, so like the object he is observing, he cannot be truly objective" (92). Lorenz goes on to argue, however, that the erasure of the scientist's personal experiences should not be the goal of all science. Indeed, sometimes ostensibly anthropomorphic concepts like falling in love or jealousy are in fact good descriptors for the feelings that animals are going through: "The most 'objective' observer cannot escape drawing analogies with his own psychological processes," Lorenz writes, adding, "language itself forces us to use terms borrowed from our own experience" (92).

In giving the reader access to Rebekah's thought processes as she composes her philosophy, Schreiner's "Raindrops" chapter might be read as *subjectivizing* the practices of observation and description foundational to scientific practice, highlighting, as Lorenz does, the linguistic and emotive practices that produce knowledge. In focusing on the physical aspects of Rebekah's character and the material condition of her writing process, however, the chapter does something else, as well: the novel inverts Lorenz's terms to show how the observing and describing subject is also an object—one upon which the world imprints itself. In his research on filial imprinting, Despret notes, Lorenz did not initially intend to be imprinted by the young geese he observed: The goose "surprises Lorenz by adopting him. Lorenz becomes ready to become a goose's mother and may therefore add to his scientific repertoire new questions about imprinting, new questions about attachment, new ways of collecting data, new competences and new ways of carrying out his scientific practice" (130). Put otherwise, it is in becoming the goose's object that Lorenz learns to become a better scientific subject—a better observer and a better describer.

In its attention not only to Rebekah's physical appearance but also to how the physical world she observes impresses itself upon her, Schreiner's novel highlights the objecthood of the human observer, encouraging a reflection on the realist narrator who observes Rebekah. In letters to her close friend, the mathematician Karl Pearson, Schreiner reveals her concern with the way that thought itself arises from corporeal vibrations of feeling.[28] In one such letter, she contests Pearson's view that "the senses of taste & touch seem to have no intellectual side," arguing that taste and

---

28. For more on "Schreiner's fundamental conviction that emotion or feeling cannot be kept separate, or expelled from, the sphere of intellect and reason," see Burdett, *Olive Schreiner* (90).

touch, among other senses, are *the very basis of* knowledge ("To Karl Pearson, July 3, 1886"). Echoing Eliot's argument in "Notes on Form in Art"— that touch is fundamental to the knowledge of form—Schreiner writes, "Touch, (the sense of pressure) most present in the hands & lips &c but more or less existing in… all tissues) is the root of almost all our intellectual knowledge." Where Pearson, as Schreiner understands him, believes that taste and touch can never "become aesthetic," Schreiner turns to both humans and nonhuman animals in order to counter his claim: "the cat," she points out, "uses her sense aesthetically when she rubs her face against velvet, & a dog when he comes & stands besides you & looks up into your face that you my touch him on the head" ("To Karl Pearson, July 3, 1886").

Schreiner works to cultivate this kind of corporeal knowledge through her third-person omniscient narrator, who mixes detailed and sensual descriptions of Rebekah's character with descriptions of her thought processes in a form of free indirect discourse, bringing together the descriptive and the theoretical into a form of weak theory. In so doing, she enacts the realist aesthetic that Rebekah calls for when she argues that, while the "true reproduction of a sunrise or a narrative that shows the working of a lofty spirit" are certainly "delightful," "art which reproduces the texture of a lady's dress or paints the picture of a small soul" produces more differentiated thought-emotions (198). Putting Rebekah's theory into practice in her description of her character, Schreiner tells the story of a "small" rather than a "lofty soul," describing her own character's dress, including the "ink-spot at the back of her little blue print skirt," among other details (186).

In this way, Schreiner's novel can also be seen to answer Eliot's call in the prelude to *Middlemarch* to tell the story of "Theresas" who never achieve the iconic status of their saintly namesake—women, Eliot writes, whose "loving heart-beats and sobs after an unattained goodness tremble off and are dispersed among hindrances, instead of centring in some long-recognizable deed" (4).[29] The ethics of description, as cultivated by both Eliot and Schreiner, highlights the ethical import of representing those whose effect on the world is not monumental but rather "diffusive," to return to Eliot's description of Dorothea in her novel's final lines (785). Such an ethics, as Schreiner's chapter makes clear, emerges from a conviction that the small, the slight, and the seemingly insignificant are important and worth describing. This aesthetic conviction, moreover, is tied

---

29. Compare here the call of *Adam Bede*'s narrator to turn from descriptions of "cloud-borne angels, from prophets, sibyls and heroic warriors, to an old woman bending over her flower-pot, or eating her solitary dinner" (195).

to an ontology, a belief that the universe is not a collection of static and unrelated parts, but rather "a pulsating, always interacting whole" (*From Man* 181).

The Ethics of Force

Referring to Immanuel Kant's metaphysical concept of the *Ding an sich* (thing in itself), in 1875, Eliot's longtime partner, the scientist and philosopher G. H. Lewes, posits a relational ontology similar to that of Rebekah when in the second book of *Problems of Life and Mind* he writes that "the search after *the thing in itself* is chimerical: the thing being a group of relations" (*Problems* 1.2:26–27). For Lewes, this search is not chimerical because there is no "reality" behind appearances; rather, he implies that it is Kant's concept that is misleading. This is because reality is not comprised of autonomous and self-contained "things" that exist "in themselves," but instead "relations." "Nothing exists in itself and for itself," Lewes writes; "everything in others and for others: *ex-ist-ens*—a standing out relation" (26–27). It is for this reason, he goes on to argue, highlighting the ethical implications of the relational ontology he posits, that "the highest form of existence is Altruism, or that moral and intellectual condition which is determined by the fullest consciousness—emotional and cognitive—of relations" (26–27).

Lewes's critique of the concept of the "thing in itself" and subsequent musings on ethics are helpful for comprehending Rebekah's line of argument in her diary. Like Lewes (whom Schreiner had most certainly read), Rebekah posits that the structure of reality is relational; and like him, too, she argues that it follows from this that "highest form of existence is Altruism." In what remains of this chapter, I show how Schreiner borrows insights from both philosophy and physics to put pressure on the *object* in *human objecthood*. She does so by modeling, through her character Rebekah, how to think in terms of (relational) forces rather than (individuated) *things*. In so doing, Schreiner joins other dynamic materialist thinkers of the nineteenth, twentieth, and twenty-first centuries in launching a critique of thing-based ontologies that fail to recognize that the character of human and nonhuman beings is generated through relations between components that do not preexist their relations.

Drawing on the field theory of Victorian physicists, Rebekah argues that seemingly discrete parts of the universe are not divided by a void but rather connected: "Between the furthest star and the planet earth we live on, between the most distant planet and the ground we tread on, between man, plant, bird, beast and clod of earth, everywhere the close internetted lines of interaction stretch; nowhere are we able to draw a sharp dividing line, nowhere find an isolated existence" (181). One of Schreiner's favorite words throughout the piece, the verb *to internet* (*inter-* [prefix] + *net* [v.]), captures the sense of active interconnectivity she understands as existing among all things. She takes this word from the field of physics, in which recent findings had shown that space itself is not an empty vacuum filled with solid bodies but is rather comprised of fields dynamically interacting with other fields.

The first recorded usage of the word *internet* appeared in 1883, in the physicist A. S. Herschel's letter to the editor in the journal *Nature*.[30] Herschel's letter was written in response to an essay by Charles Morris, entitled "The Matter of Space," published in *Nature* one month earlier. In his essay, Morris had contested the theory that space was either ether or a vacuum, proposing that space itself—like matter—was comprised of "minute particles, moving with intense speed" (349). His findings showed that "matter is present everywhere throughout the universe, as well in interstitial space as in the bodies of the spheres" (349). Writing in support of Morris's article, Herschel's letter recounts his awe at the "marvelous maze of internetted motions" that Morris so "correctly and truthfully described" (458). Schreiner's phrasing "internetting lines of action and reaction" echoes Herschel's "marvelous maze of internetted motions." Just like these physicists, Rebekah suggests that the so-called space between things is illusory; "nowhere are we able to draw a sharp dividing line, nowhere find an isolated existence." For Schreiner, as becomes clearer throughout the piece, matter consists in a kind of creative activity, bringing the "things" it comprises into relations that produce character.

"With increasing insistence," Michael Tondre has observed, nineteenth-century physicists "conceived the microcosmos in terms of shifting interrelations rather than of clear-cut monads" (21). Throughout the long period during which Schreiner composed *From Man to Man*, these physicists were stirring major controversy among religious thinkers. One of the most widely criticized expressions of the materialist position was the physicist John Tyndall's 1874 address to the British Association for the Advancement of Science at Belfast—large extracts of which were published in the South African newspaper the *Cape Monthly* in 1874, before Schreiner left for England, and the entirety of which would be published by Longmans, Green & Co the same year. Tyndall's Belfast address undermined Christian metaphysics by implying that no God was necessary to explain the dynamic motions of the universe. Narrating a history of scientific materialism that stretched from the ancient Greek atomists Epicurus and Democritus, through the Roman poet-scientist Lucretius, and finally to con-

---

30. *OED Online*, Oxford University Press, s.v. "internet," accessed October 11, 2011.

temporaneous scientists such as Darwin and Haeckel, Tyndall argued that after the long detour that was Christian theology, nineteenth-century physics and biology were poised to validate the insights of ancient Greek and Roman atomists.

Rebekah's essay, too, is predicated on a fundamental connection between Victorian and ancient thinkers, suggesting that Schreiner may have encountered Tyndall's speech either as she began to compose *From Man to Man* in the 1870s, or afterward, as it circulated in print. Like Tyndall, who begins his address by declaring that "an impulse inherent in primeval man" is "the spur of scientific action to-day" (1) before tracing this impulse to understand "natural phenomena" back to "the science of ancient Greece" (11), Rebekah begins her essay with the suggestion that an ancient curiosity about the natural world has reinfused scientific thinking in the present: "to find any true likeness to the modern feeling," she suggests, we need to "go back to the life and thought of classical days, especially to the life and thought of Greece in the fourth century before Christ" (*From Man* 177). And also like Tyndall, who argues that if we understand the "agent" of Nature not as a separate entity, but as the "active and mobile part of the material itself" ("Address" 25), then matter retains its activity and unpredictability without requiring belief in a primal mover, Rebekah argues against posting a "ruling individuality" that gives the disorderly and random order and purpose (*From Man* 25).

But while Rebekah's poetic account of the interconnected nature of all physical reality certainly reflects Tyndall's scientific portrait of "predetermined internal relations… independent of the experiences of the individual," subtle differences in her language suggest that, to her, Tyndall has not gone far enough in his speculations (52). In Tyndall's atomistic vision, the world is comprised of particles that "produce by their subsequent inter-action all the phenomena of the material world" (26). Rebekah, however, significantly avoids mention of words denoting discrete units such as "particles," "atoms," and "molecules," preferring instead a smoother vocabulary of "forces," "pulses," and "lines." This difference in vocabulary is striking given how closely Rebekah's writings echo other aspects of Tyndall's speech. Where Tyndall describes "molecules" that "remain unbroken and unworn" throughout history as "the foundation stones of the material universe" ("Address" 26), for example, Rebekah refers instead to "long unbroken lines of connection" between herself and life three million years ago (*From Man* 180).

In Tyndall's speech, what remains "unbroken" are molecules, as the analogy between molecules and "foundation stones" suggests. For Schreiner, however, what is durable are not such forms themselves, but rather the "lines of connection" between them. Where the physicist's atomic vision centers upon the random motions of *particles*, moreover, Schreiner's metaphysics, slightly differently, centers upon a "stretching out, uniting creative *force*" (213, emphasis mine).

Schreiner's aversion to the atomic theory of matter might be explained by her distaste for metaphysical theories that reduce the universe to "a thing of shreds and patches and unconnected parts" (179). While Schreiner directs her critique, as Tyndall did, at Christian metaphysics, which cannot think of relation without positing an extrinsic form of divine connectivity, her critique of theories of the universe as being comprised of "unconnected parts" might also be applied to the atomic theory that Tyndall touts. As Marx noted in his doctoral dissertation on ancient atomism, "atoms are their own singular objects [*ihr einziges Objekt*], and can relate only to themselves [*können sich nur auf sich beziehen*]" (*Differenz* 25, translation mine). Given Schreiner's investment in connection and relation, it is easy to understand why she might avoid the theory of matter as being comprised of discrete, self-sufficient, and indivisible units bouncing off one another in the void. Her version of materialism privileges forces over things, placing the novel in a lineage of dynamic materialist thought, according to which relationality can be understood through primacy of force.[31]

The critique of atomism as a mask for an incipient dynamism finds one of its earliest articulations in Schopenhauer's *The World as Will and Representation*. As discussed in the previous chapter, Schopenhauer argued there that although matter exhibits itself as a body, "its whole essence consists in acting" (*WR* 2:305). He arrived at this conclusion, the reader will remember, by reflecting on the experience of the body, the single "object" to which we have "inside access." His dual-aspect metaphysics turns on the notion that although we as humans experience ourselves subjectively as dynamic, introspective agents, others experience us "objectively" as physical bodies with qualities and character. In possessing these two aspects—a dynamically experienced interiority and a materially manifest exteriority—human beings, he maintains, are no different than any other physical thing. Indeed, all of reality, Schopenhauer proposes, can theoretically be experienced from these two perspectives. From the outside, things appear as individuated entities with static traits and qualities, but experienced from the inside, they are concatenations of force.

As the contemporary philosopher Julian Young explains, Schopenhauer

---

31. Deleuze once argued that one of Nietzsche's most important teachings consists in his insistence that "only force can be related to another force" (*Nietzsche* 6). As Deleuze argues, "atomism attempts to impart to matter an essential plurality and distance which in fact belong only to force" (6).

opposed "the view that the world's ultimate constituents are tiny chunks of matter in terms of whose behaviour everything else is to be explained" (59). Ridiculing attempts to render concrete and thinglike that which is inherently dynamic, Schopenhauer described atomism as a "revolting absurdity" (WR 2:305):

> Schopenhauer understands good science to hold that the ultimate constituents of matter are extensionless centers of pure 'causality,' in other words of force. The natural world is nothing but space filled with (as modern science calls them) force fields. These fields of force, as Schopenhauer puts it, 'objectify' themselves—are experienced by us—as perceptible bodies, yet outside of the human mind such bodies have no existence. When we say that a body is 'hard heavy, fluid, green, alkaline, organic and so on,' we are merely reporting the 'action or effect' of force fields on the human mind. (J. Young 59)

Even before field theorists such as Michael Faraday empirically showed that objects were not bounded, contained units but rather concatenations of force, Schopenhauer had argued that matter and force were two sides of the same coin. As he put it, "every object as thing-in-itself is will, and as a phenomenon is matter" (WR 2:307).

In his 1885 lecture "Matter and Soul," Schreiner's friend Karl Pearson turns to Schopenhauer to interrogate the theory that matter was comprised of discrete, solid bodies, arguing that the very perceptibility of matter depends on the forces that move it. As Pearson argues there, materialism need not render the world static and spiritless if we understand matter itself as a crystallization of force. Calling into question oppositions between spirit and matter, organic and inorganic, and ideal and material, Pearson attacks the "dogma," as he calls it, that "matter is something everywhere tangible, something hard, impenetrable" (23). Instead, he proposes, we might follow Schopenhauer in understanding that "the basis of the universe, the reality popularly termed matter, is *will*" (32). "The great fact of all physical experience," Pearson writes, is that "bodies are able to change each other's motions" (25). "Is there any other phenomenon of which we are conscious that at all resembles this apparently spontaneous change of motion?" he asks rhetorically, elaborating:

> There is one which bears considerable resemblance to it. I raise my hand, the change of motion appears to you spontaneous; the how of it might be explained by a series of nerve-excitements and muscular motions, but the why of it, the ultimate cause, you might possibly attribute to something you termed my will. The will is something which at least appears capable

of changing motion. But something moving is capable of changing the motion of something else. It is not a far step to suggest from analogy that the something moving, namely matter, may be will. (32)

Schopenhauer, as we have seen, had argued that forces that cause a rock to fall or a chemical reaction to occur are metaphysically identical to human will—the difference being merely that the former are experienced by the human from the outside and the latter from the inside. Closely following Schopenhauer's line of reasoning, Pearson argues that the force of motion makes the perception of matter as such possible. As he writes, "if everything in the universe were brought to rest, the universe would cease to be perceptible, or for all human purposes we may say it would cease to be" (25). His central claim is, like that of Schopenhauer, that "matter and force are two entities always occurring together, by means of which we can explain the whole working of the universe" (24).

Pearson and Schreiner were at their closest at the time Pearson gave his talk "Matter and Soul" in December 1885.[32] Letters between the two show that Pearson had invited Schreiner to attend the lecture, sending her a ticket. She did not attend, however, explaining herself with the excuse, "my mind was in such a wild maze I shouldn't have gained much" ("To Karl Pearson, August 7, 1886"). But she did read the published version the following year and found it quite exciting. As she wrote Pearson in August 1886, just a few months before their friendship would begin to suffer from the social pressures of the Club, "I think 'Matter & Soul' the most *perfect* thing you have written, the thing I read with small internal grunts of approval, 'that's right! That's just as it ought to be!' sort of feeling" ("To Karl Pearson, August 7, 1886"). The following year, Schreiner would leave London after a "blow-up" in which various members of the club accused her of being "in love" with Pearson (Dampier 47). Even in the years following her break with Pearson in late 1886, his work, as well as Schopenhauer's, remained on her mind as she worked to revise *From Man to Man* between 1888 and 1889.[33]

32. Pearson and Schreiner were close until 1886, when their friendship suffered a break after members of the club informed Pearson that Schreiner was in love with him, which she always denied. They continued to correspond intermittently until 1889, and she wrote him once in 1890 to congratulate him on his marriage to Maria Sharpe, another member of the club.

33. In 1888, Schreiner wrote to Ellis concerning Pearson, Schopenhauer, and her troubles composing *From Man to Man*. Before moving on to discuss Schopenhauer and the negative effects of celibacy on writing, she defended Pearson's *The Ethic of Freethought* (1888)—the collection of essays in which "Matter and Soul" would be

Schreiner began reading Schopenhauer as early as March 1885, nine months before Pearson would give his lecture on the philosopher, raising the possibility that Schreiner had introduced Pearson to Schopenhauer, and not vice versa. "I have been looking at that life of Schopenhauer today," she wrote to Ellis in March 1885, referencing Helen Zimmern's influential 1876 study, *Arthur Schopenhauer: His Life and Philosophy*:

> If I had ever read him, or even knew before I came to England that such a man existed, one would say I had copied whole ideas in the *African Farm* and *From Man to Man* from him.... There's something so beautiful in coming on one's very own most inmost thoughts in another. In one way it's one of the greatest pleasures one has. That Life by Miss Zimmern is very well written.... The women's rights women are going mad, it seems to me. The latest idea is to set up a women's parliament to legislate for women and children! ("To Havelock Ellis, March 2, 1885"; ellipses in original)

Schreiner's quick change of topic—from her identification with Schopenhauer to a frustration with the separatist leanings of the women's rights movement—might at first seem like a non sequitur. But I read this ellipsis less as a trailing off and more as a synapse fire, a bridge linking metaphysics to ethics that one often crosses while reading Schreiner's fiction. For her, literature was a place where philosophical questions about the structure of the universe play out in specific bodies, voices, and actions. Her novels move seamlessly from high philosophical issues to everyday life, from metaphysics to ethics and back again, affirming the contemporary feminist science studies scholar and physicist Karen Barad's claim that "questions of ethics and of justice are always already threaded through the very fabric of the world" ("Interview" 69).

In her 2007 book *Meeting the Universe Halfway: Quantum Physics and the Entanglement of Matter and Meaning*, Barad turns to twentieth-century Danish physicist Niels Bohr's experiments on wave-particle duality to argue that individual entities are the product of what she calls "intra-actions" that "produce determinate boundaries and properties" (138). Bohr's famous double-slit experiment showed that whether a beam of light manifests itself as a particle or a wave when it moves through an apparatus with two slits depends on how the light beam is measured. His conclusion was notably different from that of his contemporary, the German physicist Werner Heisenberg, whose *uncertainty principle* maintained that the

---

reprinted—calling it a "very brave thing" to have published ("To Havelock Ellis, January 27, 1888").

reason the light beam's wavelike behavior changes to that of a particle is because the observer himself disturbs the phenomenon he measures. The problem for Bohr was not uncertainty, but rather indeterminacy: whether the light manifests itself as a particle or a wave depends upon the apparatus, not the observer. "In a stunning reversal of his intellectual forefather's schema," Barad writes, "Bohr rejects the atomistic metaphysics that takes 'things' as ontologically basic entities," instead positing that "relata do not preexist relations" (*Meeting* 138, 140).[34]

While Barad, whose unique blend of deconstructive philosophy and quantum theory reacts against the linguistic turn of the century, remains distant from Schreiner historically, her commitment to theorizing relationality in conversation with findings in physics renders her a fellow traveler in the quest to draw together disparate strands of knowledge—specifically physics, philosophy, and feminist theory—together with the aim of constructing a relational ontology she terms "agential realism" (*Meeting* 26). For Barad, matter is not a thing, but rather an *acting*. And yet, she argues, there are no "agents," given that "relata" (i.e., individual things or objects) do not ontologically "preexist" their "relations" (140)—that which connects or brings them together. Barad notes that she tries "to stay away from using the term 'agent,' or even 'actant,' because these terms work against the relational ontology" she elaborates. This is because, as she explains, "agency for me is not something that someone or something has to varying degrees, since I am trying to displace the very notion of independently existing individuals" ("Interview" 54).

Barad's theory that "relata do not preexist relations" recalls many of the dynamic materialist moments that I have touched on throughout this chapter: Schopenhauer's critique of atomism and his nonvolitional concept of Will; Lewes's critique of "the search after *the thing in itself*," based in the view that entities that exist are not *things* but rather *relations*; and the arguments of animal ethologists, who, like the Millian ethologists before them, said that character forms in *dynamical* relation to its milieu. All these arguments are refracted in the prism of *From Man to Man*, in which relationality is taken to be the fundamental principle not only of ontology, but also ethics and aesthetics. Because matter is taken to be a dynamic activity that produces individuated objects with perceptible qualities in and through relations, every tiny part of the world is significant for its potential to affect everything else. What I have described as Schreiner's ethological realism is founded on this principle: truth itself is to be found not in autonomous things, but in the linkages between them—and, as such, ethical

---

34. Barad's argument here reflects that of Haraway, who likewise argues that "beings do not pre-exist their relatings" (*Companion* 6).

questions concerning how beings should relate to one another are woven into the very fabric of the world.

One can witness this ethological principle at play in Schreiner's earlier novel, *The Story of an African Farm*. In her preface to the second edition, Schreiner contrasts her own narrative method with what she calls the "stage method" of other novelists (xxxix). In the stage method, characters act with "an immutable certainty," according to which "each one will reappear and act his part" (xxxix). "But there is another method," Schreiner continues, "the method of the life we all lead. Here, nothing can be prophesied. There is a strange coming and going of feet. Men appear, act and re-act upon each other, and pass away" (xxxix). Announcing a turn away from conventional narrative, Schreiner's preface can be seen to articulate what Jed Esty has described as *African Farm*'s departure from the "the linear or teleological time of the bildungsroman" (422). Indeed, attention to *From Man to Man*'s more philosophical moments suggests that Schreiner incorporates elements of the sketch form and the diary genre in order to disrupt the forward-moving temporality of plot. In addition to commenting on the nonlinearity of its narrative structure, however, the preface to *African Farm* notably also gestures toward a new understanding of character. That is, within her novel, Schreiner implies, one finds not singular and stable individuals (each of whom "acts" their "part") but rather relational, fleeting figures (who not only act but also *re*-act, before diffusing into the ether).

This new understanding of character—as produced through "internetting lines of action and reaction," in the words of Rebekah in *From Man to Man*—has been heralded by scholars as a modernist notion. Tracing Schreiner's influence on Virginia Woolf and other English modernists, Jade Munslow Ong, for instance, has read the preface to *African Farm* as a "modernist manifesto" that "eschew[s] conventions of nineteenth-century realism" (14). Indeed, Schreiner's focus in her preface on the minute and nonlinear motions that lend incoherent shape to "the life that we all lead" bears some similarity to Woolf's description of falling particles creating a diffraction pattern on the mind, in her essay "Modern Fiction" (1919, 1925).[35] "Let us record the atoms as they fall upon the mind in the order in which they fall," wrote Woolf; "let us trace the pattern, however disconnected and incoherent in appearance, which each sight or incident scores upon the consciousness" (161). But while Schreiner's novels certainly "anticipate a number of modernist fictional techniques," as Esty

---

35. Woolf's essay was first published unsigned in 1919, under the title "Modern Novels" in the *Times Literary Supplement*. In 1925, it was republished under the title "Modern Fiction" in *The Common Reader*—this time with her name appended.

also observes, their aesthetic innovations are powerfully illuminated just as sharply through the lens of New Realism, which, as I hope this and the previous chapter have shown, cultivate a dynamic materialist model of character that departs from the more agential and developmental model found in the bildungsroman as much as the modernist fiction produced in its wake (407).[36]

What is to be gained, however, in pausing before aligning Schreiner's representational techniques with those of modernists such as Woolf? Although Schreiner's preface might certainly be read as the novelist's biographers Ruth First and Ann Scott have read it—as "positively advocating a method in a way that anticipates Virginia Woolf" (whose discussion of Shakespeare's imaginary sister, we saw earlier, may have taken cues from Schreiner's novel)—her work remains distinct from that of psychological modernists focused on the representation of "consciousness" (First and Scott 92). While Schreiner's descriptions of Rebekah's essays and their composition process in *From Man to Man* certainly represent subjective thought and emotion, they are less invested in "atoms" falling "upon the mind" than they are in the physical "lines of action and reaction" (*From Man* 180) that animate the "coming and going of feet" (*African Farm* xxxix). Schreiner's realism, I hope to have shown, is less psychological than it is *ethological* in its concern with the objecthood of the observer and the relations that give rise to that observer.

Already in 1997, the feminist literary scholar Sally Ledger observed with a certain skepticism the tendency to view New Woman fiction as "a form of early modernist writing" (180). While Ledger welcomes this tendency insofar as it brings into "focus a body of work which has been badly neglected" (180–81), she underscores that the New Woman novel "owed a huge debt to literary realism," an aesthetic that "offered a vehicle for feminist expression which is almost unparalleled in literary history" (194).

This and the previous chapter have built on the foundational work of Ledger and other feminist scholars to elucidate a genre too often lost "between the literary grand narratives of Victorian realism and high modernism" (Ledger 181). Not only were Schreiner and other New Woman novelists *indebted* to realism, however; they entirely reconfigured it. Not only did they "appropriate an avowedly masculine aesthetic to feminist ends

---

36. Esty helpfully frames *African Farm*'s aesthetic innovations not only in terms of modernism but also in terms of naturalism, arguing that it is in that novel that "we can begin to grasp the shifts—from realism to naturalism, from self-made protagonists to environmental victims, from regional to global maps of uneven development, and from apparent class mobility to racialized class stasis—that took place as the Victorian bildungsroman was reorganized in the world of fin de siècle imperialism" (410).

when they affiliated themselves with the 'new realist' school" (Ledger 180). They created that school. They did so by demanding better and more accurate methods for describing reality, modes of attention that sought to do justice to the dynamic materiality of the character of the world—as well as that of the human being doing the describing.

Spontaneous Generations of Character between Realism and Modernism

[CODA]

Somewhere between 1924 and 1927, character theory changed. Four years after Olive Schreiner's death, Virginia Woolf gave a lecture on character at Girton College, Cambridge University, entitled "Mr. Bennett and Mrs. Brown" (1924). One year after *From Man to Man* finally appeared in print, E. M. Forster delivered a series of lectures on novelistic form, also at Cambridge (Trinity College), which was published later that year under the title *Aspects of the Novel* (1927). Among other influential concepts, Forster's lectures introduced the terminological distinction, still widely cited in character theory today, between "flat" and "round" characters. The distinction can be summed up as follows: flat characters are two-dimensional types that remain the same throughout the course of the story; round characters are three-dimensional, particularized individuals who develop and change as they encounter differing circumstances. In the terms of Woolf's lecture, we might say that round characters simply *seem more real*. And "it is only if the characters are real that the novel has any chance of surviving," Woolf reminded the women of Girton College in the spring of 1924. "Otherwise, die it must. But, I ask myself, what is reality? And who are the judges of reality?" (10).

Forster's answer, delivered to the men of Trinity College in the spring of 1927, is relatively straightforward: "When a character in a book is real," the author "will give us the feeling that though the character has not been explained, it is explicable" (63). By this, Forster meant that a character seems real when we have a sense that something is being held back about them—something that is *possible* to know, but that we do not. This is because, for Foster, the key ontological difference between "those two allied species, *homo sapiens* and *homo fictus*" is their differing limits of knowability (55). In both fiction and reality, the limit of this knowability is, for Forster, the body—both the vehicle of and obstacle to knowledge of a person.

In the real world, he explains, a person's interior life being foreclosed to us: "We know each other approximately, by external signs" (47). In fiction, on the other hand, "if the novelist wishes; their inner as well as their outer life can be exposed" (47). The construction of a realistic character thus requires the subtle negotiation of the boundary between inside and outside in order to produce for the reader a sense of the "secret life, which each of us leads privately and to which (in his characters) the novelist has access" (83). "And by the secret life," Forster clarifies, "we mean the life for which there is no external evidence" (83).[1]

Forster's distaste for excessive "external evidence" with regard to the representation of character is shared by Woolf in "Mr. Bennett and Mrs. Brown." In their obsession with "buttons and wrinkles" (10), "ribbons and warts" (10), "decoration and upholstery" (16), Edwardian novelists such as Arnold Bennett, Woolf demurs, have "laid an enormous stress upon the fabric of things" (18). "For Woolf there is a need to go beyond the register of appearances," Peter Brooks has noted, reading her lecture as a reaction against the "descriptive imperative" realist novel (18-19).[2] Where Woolf remains somewhat cryptic in her lecture about what exactly the writer should focus on, if not on such appearances, Forster is more direct: the deftness with which a novelist represents a character's interiority, he maintains, is a distinct marker of success. "The speciality of the novel," he writes, "is that the writer can talk about his characters as well as through them or can arrange for us to listen when they talk to themselves. He has access to self-communings, and from that level he can descend even deeper and peer into the subconscious" (84).

What Forster calls "depth" is a key aspect of roundness, but it is not the only one. Other aspects of round characters are "complexity" (72), "incalculability" (78), "definiteness" (113), and "vitality" (71). It is depth, however—along with, to a lesser extent, definiteness—that has been emphasized by literary historians after Forster, who trace the historical move-

1. D. A. Miller makes an extremely similar argument in *The Novel and the Police* when he claims that "the hermeneutic problem put to characters [is] the discrepancy between inside and outside (such that the former can never be counted on to represent the latter, which it is rather constituted to disguise)" (206). In arguing that "the Novel is the genre of 'secret singularity,'" *The Novel and the Police* echoes to a great degree *Aspects of the Novel*, in which novelistic character is said to be constructed through the production of a "secret life, which each of us leads privately"—the important difference being that what Forster appreciates about the novel is for Miller the lynchpin of its disciplinary apparatus (208).

2. In her work on the function of description in the fiction of Woolf and other modernist writers, Zhang complicates this reading by stressing "the hyperrealism of modernist aesthetics, the insistence of hewing more closely to the likeness of life" (149).

ment of character from inside to outside, surface to depth, and type to individual across the eighteenth and nineteenth centuries in Europe as the novel rose to prominence. For Ian Watt in *The Rise of the Novel* (1957), famously, what distinguishes novelistic characters from earlier iterations is a "subjective and inward direction" that offers access to "private feelings" (177). Relatedly, for Nancy Armstrong in *How Novels Think* (2005), the construction of a "human subject with the restlessness to grow" is achieved in the novel genre through "transforming the body from an indicator of rank to the container of a unique subjectivity" (4). Even Deidre Lynch, whose *The Economy of Character* (1998) questions the inevitability of the narrative of the novel's "historical rendezvous with psychological depth" (124), maintains that early novelists distinguished themselves from their predecessors by presenting the "truths of character" as "matters of inner meaning" (13).[3] Tracing the complex and shifting tensions between public and private, general and particular, body and mind, all of these scholars complicate elements of Forster's literary framework and history. At the same time, they all implicitly affirm his underlying literary-historical thesis—that at some point, the "flatness" of earlier modes of characterization was replaced by the "roundness" of novelistic character.

However, there are a few issues with this story—both the original and its many retellings. For one thing, Forster's story is itself a retelling, its central argument and terms borrowed from a Victorian critic to whom I will turn shortly. For another, with each version the story changes slightly. Close attention to these alterations to the literary history of character reveals, among other things, the aesthetic concerns of those critics doing the telling. In this coda, I jump backward and forward in literary history to examine what novel critics believed to be the precondition for a realist character in the two historical moments that bookend this study: 1870–1872 and 1924–1927. My aim is not so much to poke holes in the history of novelistic character as it has traditionally been told (though a few holes may, incidentally, be poked), but rather to explain why the story I have been telling in *The Science of Character* has thus far remained untold. It has remained untold as a result of certain terminological elisions that have al-

---

3. For all of the previously cited authors, the novels of Jane Austen are a special turning point in the narrative of characterological roundness, albeit for slightly different reasons. For Forster, Austen's characters "are more highly organized. They function all round" (75). For Watt, Austen produces a "psychological closeness to the subjective world of the characters" (302). For Armstrong, Austen's novels achieve a "delicate synthesis of individual self-expression and social subjection" (54). And for Lynch, "Austen handles point of view so that listening in on the self-communing language of depth that endows a heroine with an inner life consistently involves hearing in the background the murmurs of the crowd" (210).

lowed the story of character's "inward turn" to reign supreme, even in accounts designed to critique this narrative.

What I take to be the most significant terminological elision—that between depth and vitality—appears to have been introduced in the first few decades of the twentieth century when Forster, Woolf, and other novelist-critics, reflecting on the formal innovations and historical achievements of the genre, *renarrated* the history of novelistic character, subtly positioning themselves as that story's dénouement. I will argue that, particularly as the notion of *roundness* has been understood by historians of the novel after Forster to be synonymous with *depth*, the formal distinction between flat and round actually obscures the innovations of turn-of-the-century realist authors who did not place great faith in the production of interiority, and in so doing, aspired to produce characters that pulsated with life rather than sounded with depth.

Throughout the previous five chapters, we have seen how the long-recognized hallmarks of nineteenth-century realist character—interiority, individuality, and the capacity for intellectual and moral growth (all aspects of Forster's roundness)—would be replaced in the late Victorian period with a more materialist set of ideals, among them: plasticity, impressibility, spontaneity, impulsivity, and relationality. This coda adds to the list another quality: vitality, a concept that to some extent sutures together and (if we are not careful) risks subsuming the rest. We must be careful because although each of the qualities I list above has, at some moment or another, been thought to define life as such, the authors of interest to me here call into question the ontological exceptionality of life in their attempt to create lively and spontaneous characters out of the stuff of words.

Before we get to the question of life and its emergence, however, we must go back to depth because it is this term that holds the key to understanding how that character theory changed between 1924 and 1927. I noted earlier that what Forster calls "roundness" is defined by referring to a host of other qualities, including but not limited to depth. Flat characters, by contrast, are said to be "simple" (71), "unalterable" (69), "easily recognized" (68), and are said to produce "repetitive pleasure" (75). As an example of a flat character, Forster cites Mrs. Micawber from Dickens's novel *David Copperfield*: "the really flat character can be expressed in one sentence such as 'I never will desert Mr. Micawber.' There is Mrs. Micawber—she says she won't desert Mr. Micawber, she doesn't, and there she is" (67). Indeed, a good many of Forster's examples of flat characters are taken from Dickens, whose "people are nearly all flat" (71). And yet, as Forster will go on to argue, although Dickens makes frequent use of "types and caricatures, people whom we recognize the instant they re-enter," he is still "very clever at transmitting force" (72). Through a unique "conjuring trick," Dickens is often able to produce the *appearance* of roundness. "Nearly every one can be summed up in a sentence," Forster concludes, "and yet there is this wonderful feeling of human depth. Probably the immense vitality of Dickens causes his characters to vibrate a little, so that they borrow his life and appear to lead one of their own" (71). In so doing, Dickens is able to "trick the reader into a sense of depth" (72).

In making his argument about the fake depth of Dickens's characters, Forster borrows heavily from a writer from a previous generation: the Victorian literary critic and scientist G. H. Lewes. Fifty-five years earlier, in an 1872 article entitled "Dickens in Relation to Criticism," Lewes had made a suspiciously similar argument about Dickens: that although memorable and distinctive, his characters lack, in his words, "the distinctive peculiarity of organic action, that of fluctuating spontaneity" (148–49).[4]

Although Forster does not acknowledge Lewes's influence (his name is not mentioned throughout *Aspects*), the similarities between their arguments are striking. Forster suggests that Dickens creates "types and caricatures, people whom we recognize the instant they re-enter" (71), while Lewes says that Dickens's characters are "types" furnished with "some well-marked physical trait; some peculiarity of aspect, speech, or manner which everyone [recognizes] at once" (146). Forster claims that a round character "has the incalculability of life about it" (78); Lewes says that Dickens's characters "have nothing fluctuating and incalculable in them" (149). And like Forster, Lewes cites the Micawbers to make his point, noting that Mr. Micawber is "always presenting himself in the same situation, moved with the same springs, and uttering the same sounds, always confident on something turning up, always crushed and rebounding, always making punch—and his wife declaring she will never part with him, always referring to the talents of her family" (148).

Even Forster's clever explanation of why Dickens's characters, despite being essentially flat, still sometimes *seem* round seems to have been borrowed from Lewes. Echoing Forster's claim that Dickens is "very clever at transmitting force" (72), Lewes writes: "For though his weakness comes from excess in one direction, the *force* which is in excess must never be overlooked" (149, emphasis mine). As Lewes argues, although Dickens's characters are fundamentally mechanistic and entirely unlifelike, he still manages to produce the appearance of "spontaneity" by having his char-

---

4. In his analysis of Dickens, Lewes may himself have been influenced by Hippolyte Taine, who "claims that Dickens animates inanimate objects by projecting his 'ever-welling passion' onto them" in his 1856 review, "Charles Dickens: son talent et ses oeuvres," as Logan has noted ("Primitive" 37).

acters repeat their statement or action until they appear to be animated with the spark of life, thus producing the "hallucination" that they are "like reality" (149).

For all their similarities, however, there is at least one key difference between Lewes's and Forster's arguments. As we saw earlier, Forster concludes that despite his faults, Dickens is still able to produce "this wonderful feeling of human depth." In Lewes's analysis, however, while complexity, vitality, and incalculability are all key concepts, depth goes unmentioned. An analogy constructed by Lewes speaks to the conspicuous absence of that term. In order to illustrate his point, that Dickens's characters "want the distinctive peculiarity of organic action, that of fluctuating spontaneity," Lewes invites his reader to think of Dickens's characters like frogs whose brains have been removed in a scientific experiment: "Place one of these brainless frogs on his back," Lewes the physiologist writes, "and he will at once recover the sitting posture... tickle or prick him and he will push away the object, or take *one* hop out of the way; stroke his back, and he will utter *one* croak. All these things resemble the action of the unmutilated frog, but they differ in being *isolated* actions, and *always the same*: they are as uniform and calculable as the movements of a machine" (148–49). Their singular "aspect, speech, or manner" figured in the singular croak, the singular hop of the vivisected frogs. Dickens's characters, Lewes suggests, are more like machines than actual living beings. Policing the boundaries of realism through the concept of vitality rather than depth, Lewes implies that a truly realistic character is not necessarily deep, but *lively*.

Lewes's criticism of Dickens is an early literary-critical marker of the history of realist character this book has been tracing. In the final decades of the nineteenth century, as we have seen, English novelists began to conceive of character less in terms of the individual human personality or psychology and more in terms of a dynamic materiality untethered to human subjectivity. Witness the characterological distinction introduced by the fictional character Eva Clough in W. S. Holnut's 1895 New Woman novel, *Olympia's Journal*. Distinguishing between the "rigidly determined characters" of earlier novels and the "inconsistencies and marvelous surprises of human nature" of the new, Eva argues that because the novel "need not now-a-days depend on its plot" and "the tendency in literature and art is toward realism," new avenues for the representation of character have been opened (34–35). Expanding the notion of character to include not only "man, woman, and child," but also "cat or dog," Eva praises the ability of certain novelists to render salient an "inconceivable number of original impulses" (36). She says to her interlocutor, an aspiring novelist, "It is upon these complicated and often conflicting passions that the skillful novelist works, tearing off the mask which convention (and very properly so) obliges us to wear, and studying, meditating upon, and finally understanding what lies below" (36). Significantly, however, "what lies below" is figured by Eva not psychically, as the inner truth of a person's mind, but *physiologically*, as "impulses... so often twisted in and out of one another that they resemble nothing so much as (you will pardon me I am sure—I can think of no better simile) the entrails of animals one sees hanging up in a slaughterhouse" (36).

As the case of *Olympia's Journal* underscores, the formal distinction between flat and round characters constructed to account for earlier modes of novelistic character is of limited critical utility for comprehending how late Victorian authors distinguished their "New Realism" from realisms of old in centering their project on human objecthood, not human subjecthood. Like Lewes in his critique of Dickens (twenty-odd years earlier), Eva expresses frustration not with the lack of psychological depth, but with the lack of dynamic material force in earlier novelistic characters, describing them as "vapid posturing creatures without stamina or force, fit only for a waxwork show" (36).

Perhaps because of an emphasis on historical continuity—perhaps because the twentieth-century critics who established interiority as the high-water mark for novelistic character were laying the groundwork for their own characterological innovations—the literary science of character between 1870 and 1920 this book has been tracing has often been presented as a kind of gap or stopover between the ends of an inward-leaning realism and the beginnings of a more fully interiorized modernism. Is not the great literary-historical legacy of "roundness," as conceptualized by Forster in 1927, the "inward turn" of the novel that he, Woolf, and other European modernists are said to have initiated in their focus on interiority?

In their foundational volume *Modernism, 1890–1930*, Malcolm Bradbury and James McFarlane trace at the turn of the century the rise of an "introverted novel," a genre marked by the presence of characters that "seem to assert against their author the right to greater freedom, to profounder psychological depth" (Bradbury and Fletcher 397). Moreover, in their more recent intellectual history of the concept of modernism, Sean Latham and Gayle Rogers trace the shift "away from material reality and toward the expression of some inner truth or vision" in late nineteenth-century fiction, noting how modernist authors challenge "the established conventions of realism" by developing new literary modes such as "the almost entirely unpunctuated stream of consciousness in the novel" (11–12).

Historians of realism, when moving beyond the nineteenth century, likewise narrate the "inward turn of narrative" from the desire to "penetrate the appearances" of the city in Balzac (Brooks 22) to an "overriding concern with the workings of consciousness" in Woolf (18). In his classic study *Mimesis: The Representation of Reality in Western Literature*, Erich Auerbach famously closes his sweeping account of the long history of realism with Woolf's 1927 novel *To the Lighthouse*, showing how the "exterior events" of the nineteenth-century realist novel lose "their hegemony, [and] serve to release and interpret inner events" (538). More recently, in *Reading the Modern British and Irish Novel 1890–1930*, Daniel R. Schwarz tracks "the beginnings of the psychological novel" from "Thomas Hardy's last novel *Jude the Obscure*" (37) to Forster's "psychological nuances of character" in his 1924 novel *A Passage to India* (244). (We are not only back with Woolf and Forster, we are also again in 1924 and 1927.)

To what extent is the inward turn of these narratives of character colored by, or even directly attributable to, the novelist-critics with whom these literary histories inevitably end? What other ways might there be of the turn-of-the-century novel than that of "introversion"?[5]

Recent scholarship by Marta Figlerowicz and Megan Ward has shown how, subsumed under the historical narrative of the novel's inward turn, there is a host of other ways of representing character—many of which involved (and by no means required) the rejection of flatness. Whereas these scholars seek to reevaluate and recuperate "flatness," I take a different tack in what remains of this coda, pivoting away from Forster's terms entirely in order to excavate a different characterological binary, one used by many Victorians themselves: the vital versus the mechanistic. Long central to European natural-philosophical discourse, this much older, scientific binary would reemerge in both the 1870s and the 1920s to account for the shifting relationship between character and plot at times when new publication formats, experiments in narration and description, and the destabilization of the ontological distinction between life and nonlife opened up new possibilities for novelistic form. The concept of *depth* no doubt remains useful for understanding the innovations of many early novelists as well as many modernist writers. Setting it aside, however, will allow us to perceive a less familiar lineage of English fiction—one that stretches from the 1870s fiction of George Eliot, through the turn-of-the-century novels

---

5. From within modernist studies, Fredric Jameson has been a vocal critic of the narrative of the "inward turn," arguing that "ideologies of the modern have been misleading in their insistence on some 'inward turn' of the modern or on its increasing subjectivization of reality" (*Singular* 135). "At best," he observes in a fashion consistent with my argument here, "there stirs... an apocalyptic dissatisfaction with subjectivity itself" (135). Thomas Davis has recently elucidated an "outward turn" in late modernism that bears some resemblance to the earlier realist lineage I am tracking here in its focus on the "depthlessness of... characters' inner lives" (34).

of Hardy, Schreiner, and other New Woman novelists, and forward to the 1920s writings of the American author Gertrude Stein.

Around the same time that Forster was working to establish the criterion of depth as an ideal for novelistic character, Stein was cultivating an exteriorized, typological approach to characterization that emphasized the shared texture of character. "I love it that every one is of a kind of men and women," she writes in her 1925 novel *The Making of Americans*, "always I am looking and comparing and classifying of them, always I am seeing their repeating" (289). Stein continues: "Always more and more I love repeating, it may be irritating to hear from them but always more and more I love it of them. More and more I love it of them, the being in them, the mixing in them, the repeating in them, the deciding the kind of them everyone is who has human being" (289). Throughout *The Making of Americans*, Stein makes frequent use of repetition in order to generate what Ada Smailbegović has described as a "sense of *liveliness* within linguistic phenomena" (14). This "liveliness" is generated through the literary performance of what Stein calls *insistences*, repetitions of words and phrases slightly different from one another, pronounced with slightly different emphases.

In her 1934 lecture "Portraits and Repetition," delivered upon her return to the United States from France, Stein outlines the philosophical and aesthetic principles behind her use of repetition in fiction.[6] As she argues, life is distinct from nonlife in its inability to repeat itself. Where machines repeat themselves verbatim, Stein proposes, living organisms can only *insist*. To insist is to produce repetitions with a difference: "What makes life," she writes, "is that the insistence is different, no matter how often you tell the same story if there is anything alive in the telling the emphasis is different.... It is like a frog hopping he cannot ever hop exactly the same distance or the same way of hopping at every hop" (167).

As with Lewes more than sixty years earlier, in Stein's lecture, the frog crops up as a figure for theorizing life in terms of an incalculable spontaneity. Whereas for Lewes, however, the calculable and unspontaneous repetitions of the vivisected present evidence that life is absent in Dickens,

---

6. Stein's lecture "Portraits and Repetition" is concerned with explaining her method in the character-centered works she called "portraits," imagistic and largely nonnarrative sketches of fictional personalities. In theorizing the role of insistence in the production of character, however, the lecture can be seen to theorize a practice that Stein employs throughout her literary corpus, including *The Making of Americans*, in which insistence is likewise taken up as a technique.

Stein proposes an equal and opposite theory—that life emerges where repetitions without difference fail to occur—as the basis for a literary method. Stripped of its spontaneity, Lewes's frog was a vehicle for a critique of characters that were not real enough. Stein's frog, on the other hand (unscathed by the physiologists' scalpel), is a model for the production of real and lively characters. As if answering Lewes's call for a "fluctuating spontaneity" of character, Stein arrives at the same insight—that living beings never repeat themselves exactly—and uses it to spontaneously generate her characters.

What to make of these two sets of frogs, separated not only by sixty-odd years but by another, seemingly vaster conceptual distance—that between realism and modernism? Fredric Jameson has proposed that "the dynamic whereby modernist innovation cancels its pre-existing literary paradigms and representations extends back to its beginnings, in which it confronts and cancels this first of all literary paradigms which is realism itself" (*Singular* 122). As he goes on to observe, however, qualifying this statement, "the problem is that all consequential realisms themselves do exactly this, and that looked at more closely and replaced in its own specific context, each successive realism can also be said, in this sense, to have been a modernism in its own right" (122–23).

We have seen how throughout the 1920s, Forster and Woolf set the stage for their own characterological innovations by recasting the history of character as one in which the more externalized characters of earlier novelists would be canceled and replaced by those with more interiority. And we have also seen how in the late Victorian period, various New Realist novelists distinguished their realism from the realisms of old by heralding the replacement of the stiff characters of midcentury fiction with their more impulsive figures. Under Jameson's capacious rubric, both of these dynamics are "modernist"—but on entirely different terms. Whereas the first centers on depth (as opposed to flatness), the latter centers on vitality (as opposed to mechanicity).

To observe the subtle, if still overlapping, differences between these character dynamics allows us to view their history in a less linear and progressive fashion (a realism that gives way to a modernism) and instead as two conceptually distinguishable, if also historically intertwined, genealogies that track across the nineteenth and twentieth centuries. As an example of literary-historical blockages that occur when we fail to distinguish between them, consider Omri Moses's 2014 study *Out of Character: Modernism, Vitalism, Psychic Life*. There is much to admire in Moses's study, which argues that the concept of character would be reinvented and reconfigured by modernists rather than dissolved in the modernist notion of "impersonality." But because Moses follows Forster in lumping depth together with vitality, the transition between Victorian and modernist modes of characterization is presented as a radical break (5).

Out of Character opens with an "instructive contrast" between the "morally recalcitrant conception of people" that one discovers in the fiction of George Eliot and other Victorian novelists and the "fluid identifications, emotive capacities and ad hoc relations that allow subjects to adjust to their circumstances" that characterize the work of modernists such as Henry James, T. S. Eliot, and Stein (5–6). Because George Eliot is said to present character in terms of a "fixed quality that James, Stein, and T. S. Eliot do not accept or recognize" (13), these latter modernist authors are presented as "pushing against her methods of characterization" (6). But Eliot's own statements about character belie Moses's claim that where Eliot understood character as static and essential, these modernist authors approached character as dynamic and relational. Moses distinguishes modernists from their realist predecessors by arguing that they "imagined character as a process, not a substance, and gave singular attention to the manner in which that process unfolds" (6). Eliot's narrator in *Middlemarch*, however, as we recall from chapter 1, states that "character is a process and an unfolding" (140). Whereas Moses claims with regard to Eliot that "[c]haracters, in her terms, enjoy solidity" (7), Eliot's narrator contradicts this claim by insisting that "character is not cut in marble—it is not something solid and unalterable" (694). Finally, whereas Moses argues that Eliot's characters "endure in their own separate nature" (7), Eliot's narrator maintains that "there is no creature whose inward being is so strong that it is not greatly determined by what lies outside it" (784–85).

These misrecognitions arise out of an attempt to distinguish between Victorian and modernist modes of characterization along the lines that the former lodged character within the fixed matter of the body, and the latter in the dynamism of the mind. In chapter 1 of this book, however, we saw that Eliot breaks down such an opposition by insisting that character is both *dynamic* and *material*, insisting that because character is lodged within the body, it is indeed "something living and changing" (694). Descriptions such as that of Mr. Brooke as "a very good fellow, but pulpy; he will run into any mould, but he won't keep shape" (65), or Rosamond Vincy's persistence as what "enables a white soft living substance to make its way in spite of opposing rock" (324), as we saw, develop a vocabulary for the plasticity of character that emphasizes how character forms dynamically in response to circumstances.

Modernist authors such as Stein were not unique in their descriptions of "the fluid identifications, emotive capacities, and ad hoc reactions that allow subjects to adjust to their circumstances" (Moses 5). Observe, for instance, the affinities between Eliot and Stein's styles of characterization that become perceptible when we focus on their representation of the materiality of character rather than of psychic life. Like Eliot, who describes her characters in terms of plastic matter throughout *Middlemarch*, Stein describes her characters in *The Making of Americans* as if they were composed of a "mediumly fluid solid fructifying reacting substance" that enters different qualitative states (345). Similar to Eliot, whose characters undergo state changes from liquid to solid and back again, Stein taxonomizes her characters according to their physical composition and relative states of rigidity, describing "some with a lump hard at the center liquid at the surface, some with the lump vegetable or wooden or metallic in them" (345). Smailbegović has suggested that Stein's materialist descriptors speak to her training in medicine and biology, which allowed her to explore how "the textural or the haptic properties of specific, microscopic tissues could produce the forms of activity and reactivity that could give rise to the character effects" (194).

More broadly, this materialist mode of description extends and elaborates on a realist literary tradition of conceptualizing character in dynamic material terms, a tradition that, as we have seen, emerged with unprecedented force in the late nineteenth century, and of which Stein might be considered a twentieth-century inheritor. Both Eliot and Stein are concerned to produce lively, though not necessarily deep, characters whose dynamic materiality is emphasized in their descriptions of their characters in terms of a viscous, shape-shifting substance that takes on new forms and qualities through interactions.

How are we to understand the characterological ideal of "vitality" (or, as Smailbegović calls it, "liveliness") to which both Stein and Eliot seem to aspire? The answer turns on the way in which the opposition between vitality and mechanism played out in what historians of science refer to as the *spontaneous generation controversy*.

The spontaneous generation controversy has a long and complicated history, extending from antiquity to present-day debates in physical chemistry about the nature and emergence of life.[7] Broadly speaking, it concerns whether life can be generated from nonliving matter. Whereas proponents held that under the right conditions, living things could be generated from nonliving materials, critics maintained that organisms could only be born of parents like themselves. One of the key issues that those engaged in the controversy set out to resolve was whether life is defined by some special vital force or is reducible to a set of mechanical principles. If organic

---

7. The most comprehensive account of the controversy remains Farley's *The Spontaneous Generation Controversy from Descartes to Oparin*.

beings can be generated through the simple rearrangement of inorganic material, some reasoned, then life is not particularly special. Thus, the controversy tapped into another age-old scientific debate—between vitalism and mechanism.

Historians of science have shown how vitalisms often arise when matter is perceived to be worryingly devoid of meaning, spirit, or purpose, erupting throughout history to infuse what is thought to be predictable and mechanistic, with an animating, teleological principle.[8] The irony is that in seeking to mend the tear between matter and meaning, vitalists often reinstate this very same binary by positing a hard-and-fast distinction between nonlife (which is explainable and calculable) and life (which is mysterious and unpredictable). Many critics of the spontaneous generation thesis reasoned along just these lines, most famously the vitalist scientist Louis Pasteur, who dealt the theory a serious blow in the 1860s when he showed that microorganisms populate the air. *Omne vivum ex vivo* (All life comes from life) was the motto touted by Pasteur and his followers in their attempt to prove that life was irreducible to mechanical principles.

A similar motto informs Lewes's essay on Dickens, which argues that, try as he might, Dickens is unable to spontaneously generate truly lively characters from his all-too-mechanical techniques. While he was no vitalist, Lewes reasons according to a similarly dualistic logic: there are characters that "mov[e] with the infinite fluctuations of organisms, incalculable yet intelligible," and there are those that "mov[e] like pieces of simple mechanism" ("Dickens" 146). Dickens's characters are of the latter sort: they might be life*like*, but their vitality is illusory. "It is the complexity of the organism which Dickens wholly fails to conceive," Lewes writes, underlining the mechanical quality of his characters. He adds, "His characters have nothing fluctuating and incalculable about them" ("Dickens" 149).[9]

---

8. Reill has shown that for eighteenth-century vitalists, "the basic failure of mechanism was its inability to account of the existence of living matter. Mechanists had posited a radical separation between mind and matter that only God's intervention could heal, either as the universal occasion for all phenomena or as the creator of a pre-established harmony between mind and matter" (7). Enlightenment vitalists sought to bridge such dualisms "by positing the existence in living matter of active or self-activiating forces, which had a teleological character" (7).

9. A similar concern with the nature of life crops up in Lewes's *Sea-side Studies*, which, as Kreilkamp notes, poses "subtle questions regarding residues of vitality, the possibility of 'spontaneous' movement and 'independent existence' without true life" (91–92). Writing about the movements of the tentacles of a medusa severed from its body, Lewes wonders there whether or not these tentacles should be considered alive. The conclusion at which he arrives in *Sea-side Studies* prefigures that made about

Perhaps the most disturbing implication of the theory of spontaneous generation, were it proven true, was that life was not the result of God's plan or some other natural order, but rather that it might emerge, randomly, through the spontaneous rearrangement of molecules. To the extent that Dickens does succeed in producing lifelike characters, Lewes suggests, in line with spontaneous generation skeptics, he does so entirely accidentally. Indeed, what appears to be especially disturbing from Lewes's point of view is not only Dickens's mechanistic characters but also the mechanistic activity through which they are produced. Invoking the philosophical distinction, discussed at greater length in chapter 2, between what in *The Problems of Life and Mind* he calls "the Logic of Feeling" (which both nonhuman animals and humans use to sense the world) and "the Logic of Signs" (which humans use to communicate), Lewes suggests that it is not only Dickens's characters but also Dickens himself who is less than human: "Dickens sees and feels, but the logic of feeling seems the only logic he can manage. Thought is strangely absent from his works.... Compared with that of Fielding or Thackaray, his was a merely *animal* intelligence" (151). Thus, Lewes concludes that Dickens, beyond any intention of his own, generates the sense of liveliness through his own unthinking repetitions.

Scholars of George Eliot have convincingly read Lewes's essay as an attempt to open up space for the mode of characterization that was being developed in *Middlemarch*. Rosemary Ashton, for example, has read Lewes's account of Dickens's style of characterization as a negative for appreciating that of Eliot's "psychological realism" (257). Likewise, drawing connections between Lewes's essay and Eliot's fiction, Richard Menke has argued that in conversation with Lewes, "Eliot was imaginatively appropriating laboratory techniques in her fiction in order to produce depth psychology" (619). In focusing on how, in contrast to the perceived flatness of Dickens's characters, those of Eliot's are palpably rounder, these scholars read Lewes's essay through a Forsterian lens (and understandably so, given how deeply this framework has been absorbed in studies of the novel). That is, despite the fact that Lewes laments the lack of "spontaneity" and "incalculability" of Dickens's characters, both Ashton and Menke take depth to be the implied antipode to mechanicity. It seems likely enough to me that Lewes's critique of Dickens is indeed positioned to pave the way for Eliot's fiction. In returning to *Middlemarch*, however, I want to highlight a subtle difference between Eliot's and Lewes's thinking about the distinction between mechanical and lively characters: whereas

---

Dickens's characters: namely, that "they are not alive, in spite of movements, apparently spontaneous" (*Sea-side* 58–59).

Lewes's essay, in opposing mechanicity to vitality, echoes scientific contemporaries such as Pasteur in instituting a hard-and-fast distinction between life and nonlife—implying as he does that the line between the two can never be traversed—*Middlemarch* looks forward to a moment in which that boundary would be troubled.

Indeed, the trouble was already brewing in 1870, when Eliot began to draft a fragment of a novel entitled "Miss Brooke." In September of that year, the English scientist T. H. Huxley gave a lecture called "Biogenesis and Abiogenesis" at the British Association for the Advancement of Science in Liverpool. A key turning point in the spontaneous generation controversy, Huxley's address identified a path to legitimacy for a theory that many other scientists of the period had been attempting to debunk. He put a finer point on the debate by distinguishing between two types of spontaneous generation: the first, which he called *biogenesis*, concerned the generation of living beings from organic or "pre-existing living matter"; the other, *abiogenesis*, concerned the theory that organisms could be generated from inorganic compounds (236).[10]

What Huxley called biogenesis had by and large been the focus of the spontaneous generation controversy of the eighteenth and early nineteenth centuries (think here of experiments with the generation of maggots from rotting meat or—more apt for my purposes—frogs from mud; think here also of *Frankenstein*, which refers to galvanic attempts to reanimate corpses with electricity). As the nineteenth century progressed, the possibility of biogenesis was seeming increasingly unlikely. On Pasteur's heels, the Irish scientist John Tyndall played an important role in the theory's demise by demonstrating that complete sterilization requires multiple boilings; what appeared to be spontaneous emergence of bacterial life in jars was due to improper sterilization, Tyndall showed, building on the work of his mentor, Pasteur.

The theory of abiogenesis, on the other hand, as Huxley indicated in his lecture, had not yet been ruled out entirely. Indeed, more than this, it was seeming increasingly likely. If, as Darwin and other nineteenth-century evolutionary thinkers had recently suggested, all life evolved from a common ancestor, where did this ancestor come from? At some point in our planet's history, it appeared, life arose—indeed, spontaneously generated—from inorganic matter.

Darwin had famously avoided the question of the origins of life in his published writings. In a private letter to the scientist Joseph Hooker in February 1871, a few months after Huxley's lecture, Darwin ventures the fol-

---

10. What Huxley calls *abiogenesis* is sometimes also referred to as *heterogenesis*.

lowing speculation: "But if (and oh! what a big if!) we could conceive in some warm little pond, with all sorts of ammonia and phosphoric salts, light, heat, electricity, &c., present, that a protein compound was chemically formed ready to undergo still more complex changes…" ("To Joseph Hooker" 168–69). What Darwin here phrases only in the conditional would not be articulated with any certainty until a half century later, when in 1924, the Soviet biochemist Aleksandr Oparin outlined what would become known as the *primordial soup theory* in a small pamphlet called *The Chemical Origins of Life*. Extrapolating from Darwin's theory of evolution to account for the chemical evolution of life, Oparin controversially argued that the "spontaneous generation" supposedly debunked by Pasteur in fact occurred—if just once—when inorganic molecular aggregates assimilating organic compounds from their environment gave rise to the first living organisms.[11]

I rehearse here this truncated history not so much to explain as to exploit the fact that the notion of spontaneous generation—specifically, the theory of abiogenesis—arose as a stunning logical possibility both in the early 1870s and then again in the mid-1920s. In both moments, as the historian John Farley observes, investigations into the historical origins of life led to "the realization that organic matter was not unique, and that vital processes did not involve autonomous vital forces" ("Spontaneous," 1972, 286). What Farley describes as the "breakdown in the division between the organic and inorganic worlds" is addressed in *Middlemarch*, among other ways, through the novel's invocation of the English scientist Robert Brown (286).

In chapter 1, we saw how Tertius Lydgate gives to Camden Farebrother "Robert Brown's new thing—'Microscopic Observations on the Pollen of Plants'"—the pamphlet in which Brown famously observed the "very unexpected fact of seeming vitality" under his microscope in things neither alive nor organic (R. Brown 470).[12] At the time, Brown's contemporaries were skeptical of his findings, believing that "vitality" was only a characteristic of living things. As he moved on from pollen grains to observe this

11. Oparin's pamphlet, originally published in Russian, would not receive international recognition until 1938, when an English translation was published by Macmillan. Independent of Oparin, the British-Indian scientist J. B. S. Haldane arrived at a similar conclusion about the origins of life in his 1929 article "The Origin of Life," leading scientists to dub the heterotrophic theory of the origin of life the "Oparin-Haldane theory."

12. Kreilkamp argues that "Eliot investigates similar questions regarding the definition or status of life and nonlife" in *Middlemarch* through her treatment of Raffles as well as nonhuman animals (92).

motion in inorganic materials, however, Brown proposed that the "seeming vitality" he observed under his microscope did not actually correlate with the presence of life but was actually an attribute of all matter. Against those who maintained that some mysterious vital principle animates organic matter, that is, he held that *all* matter (including but not limited to the matter of living beings) was to a greater or lesser extent in motion, held together by intermolecular forces that loosen and tighten as that matter enters different states and is formed and deformed. Brown's 1828 claim that matter is not inert but rather is composed of tiny moving particles, forever changed the course of physics, leading to the coinage of the term *Brownian motion*.

Chapter 1 introduced the philosophical concept of emergence as a means of explaining how Eliot theorizes the generation of character in realist fiction. Against poststructuralist notions of the "reality effect," I argued that Eliot's engagement of the concept of Brownian motion, as well as James Clerk Maxwell's theory of Saturn's rings (the foundation for his later-developed theory of kinetic motion), encourages the reader to think of fictional worlds not as discursively constructed illusions, but as realities of a different scale. Like the particles that compose Saturn's rings, which move in such an irregular way as to produce stability at another scale, letters and words are arranged on a page to produce stable characters for different readers across time and space. Our collective sense of a fictional character is no falser than our sense of Saturn's rings. In both cases, interactions between subjects and objects generate qualities that are intra-active in the sense discussed in chapter 5 through the work of Karen Barad.

Insofar as it asks how genuinely the novel property of "life" arises out of changes to the structure of materials that are nonliving, abiogenesis is an exemplary case of emergence. Indeed, it is treated so in almost all philosophical and scientific studies of the term.[13] Two years before Huxley's lecture in Liverpool for the British Association for the Advancement of Science, Tyndall was exploring the question of emergence in just this sense. Remarking on the "tendency on the part of matter to organize itself, to grow into shape, to assume definite forms in obedience to the definite action of force," he postulated that "incipient life in fact, manifests itself throughout the whole of what we call inorganic nature" ("Scientific" 58). Far from life being essentially different from nonlife, life could be produced through the reorganization of matter under the right conditions,

---

13. See, for example, Humphreys. For a recent take on the emergence of life from the context of physical chemistry, see Spitzer, Pielak, and Poolman, who explore how a "disordered (high entropy) proto-bacterial system can be re-organized into an evolving living state" (4).

Tyndall suggested, undercutting the vitalism of his mentor, Pasteur, with a dynamic materialism devoid of any special vital force.

Framed in relation to literature, Tyndall's proposition is a much more fantastical one—that is, whether, under the right set of writerly and readerly conditions, vitality might be generated through an arrangement of words. Indeed, the question of whether and how life can be seen to emerge from marks on a page stands at the heart of Eliot's and Stein's respective literary projects, which are characterized by a shared desire to use language to produce a kind of motion that flickers across the interstices between the organic and the inorganic. Stein's early experiments in automatic writing asked what repetitive, nonconscious practices might reveal about a person's character. Like Stein, whose 1898 scientific essay "Cultivated Motor Automatism; A Study of Character in Its Relation to Attention" (1898) tests the ability of subjects "to learn movements and write spontaneously" through mechanical activities divorced from consciousness, in *Middlemarch*, Eliot turned to the mechanistic and mindless as a means of producing narrative motion, thus questioning the categorical distinction that Lewes and some of his scientific contemporaries had maintained between the vital and the mechanistic (296-97).

In December 1871, while Lewes was writing his essay on Dickens's characters, Eliot was about halfway through *Middlemarch*, which had just begun to appear in *Blackwood's*. With books 2 and 3 drafted, Eliot was hard at work that December on book 4—a book that introduces a rather minor character recognizable by a single feature, his "frog face" (*Middlemarch* 308, 443).[14] Upon his introduction to the novel, Joshua Rigg is described as "a man perhaps about two or three and thirty, whose prominent eyes, thin-lipped, downward-curved mouth, and hair sleekly brushed away from a forehead that sank suddenly above the ridge of the eyebrows, certainly gave his face a batrachian unchangeableness of expression" (312). *Batrachia* are "one of... four orders of Reptiles, including frogs, toads, newts, salamanders, etc., which have no ribs, and a soft scaleless skin, and breathe by means of gills during the early part, or whole, of their existence."[15] The fact that Batrachia undergo such radical transformation throughout the course of their lives no doubt lends the phrase "batrachian unchangeable-

---

14. Nancy Henry independently made the same discovery, noting in her address at the 2019 George Eliot Bicentenary conference at Leicester University that "[j]ust as Lewes was criticizing Dickens's characters as frog-like, Eliot was portraying Rigg as a frog—a strange, Dickensian interloper plashing among the Middlemarchers without interiority" ("George," 2020, 49).

15. *OED Online*, Oxford University Press, s.v. "batrachia," accessed October 11, 2011.

ness of expression" some irony. In comparison with a healthy, living frog, Rigg, by contrast, is mechanistic and waxlike. Indeed, Rigg remains parodically static throughout his short tenure in *Middlemarch*.[16] In the moments leading up to the reading of Peter Featherstone's will, Rigg sits in "unaltered calm" amid a sea of "complexions changing subtly" and then is said to "experience... no surprise" when he is named Featherstone's sole executor (315–16).

Read in conversation with Lewes's essay on Dickens, Rigg appears not only as a static and expressionless *person*, but as an unspontaneous and mechanistic character. Recall here Lewes's argument that to the extent that Dickens succeeds in producing lifelike characters, he does so through a little trick: he furnishes them with "some well-marked physical trait which everyone recognize[s] at once"; he then has them repeat this action until they appear to be animated with the spark of life. Eliot does something similar with Rigg's single remarked-upon feature, his frog face, which is referred to eight times throughout the novel.[17] This feature lends him a singular yet recognizable quality, giving him the appearance of life without true "fluctuating spontaneity." At least one reader seems to have been taken by this Dickensian strategy: "The Frog-Faced gentleman becomes at once a thing of flesh and blood," wrote Eliot's editor, John Blackwood, in response to her draft of book 4 in March 1872, just a few weeks after Lewes published his essay on Dickens ("To Mrs. Lewes" 255).

From Lewes's perspective, Blackwood has been tricked into believing that Rigg is a lively and spontaneous character when he is in fact mechanistic. From Eliot's point of view, however, Rigg is a different kind of mechanism, one more spontaneous than he might first appear. For the author of this complex, multiplot novel, he is a tool—a rig, that is—introduced to create suspense and facilitate narrative progression. Spontaneously appearing at Featherstone's funeral to be named the sole executor of the deceased's fortune (plot twist!), Rigg dashes Fred Vincy's dreams of inheriting his uncle's property. Rigg, the narrator later reveals, is Featherstone's illegitimate child, the product of his affair with an unknown woman with "frog features" (387). "The result" of such chance encounters, we are told,

16. One might argue that Rigg is so stiff as to resemble that taxidermy figurine of "preserved frogs fighting a small-sword duel" in Dickens's *Our Mutual Friend* (1864–65), perceived through a shop window by the minor character Wegg (his name likewise spelled with a double *g*) (77). As Henry observes, moreover, "Joshua Rigg is both a 'low character' and a frog. He comes from a pool (Liverpool), and while he doesn't croak, he does 'chirp' with a vile, presumably Liverpudlian accent" ("George," 2020, 48).

17. Rigg has a "frog-face" (308, 443), is "frog-faced" (311, 387, 488), and his mother has "frog features" (387).

"is sometimes a frog-faced male, desirable, surely, to no order of intelligent beings. Especially when he is suddenly brought into evidence to frustrate other people's expectations—the very lowest aspect in which a social superfluity can present himself" (387). Rigg's status as an unplanned child is suggestive, especially when one considers that perhaps Eliot herself may not have planned for Rigg, but eventually found him narratively necessary.

I mentioned earlier that when Eliot was composing book 4 of her novel, *Middlemarch* had already begun to appear in *Blackwood's*. With one book published and two more drafted, at least half the novel remained unfinished. Like many novelists of the period, Eliot composed *Middlemarch*, at least in part, as it was being serialized, a process that committed her to certain plot lines without necessarily knowing where they might lead.[18] Given his absence in previous books, it is not hard to imagine that Rigg may have been "brought into evidence" in order to frustrate not only Fred Vincy's expectations, but those of the reader, whose predictions as to who will inherit Stone Court are denied and whose interest is buoyed by Rigg's spontaneous appearance.

After he has finished with his job, Rigg is promptly eliminated. After passing Featherstone's property on to Nicholas Bulstrode and putting him into contact with the problematic character of John Raffles, he then disappears entirely from the novel: "Farewell, Josh—and if forever!" Raffles yells upon his narrative exit (390).

As the nineteenth century came to an end and the novel no longer needed to "depend on its plot," as Eva Clough observed in 1895, rigs like Rigg became increasingly unnecessary. Eliot's treatment of Rigg in her 1871–72 novel as a cog in the machine that was the multiplot Victorian novel is an important marker of this transformation; for when *Middlemarch* does introduce mechanical characters such as Rigg, it does so with a heightened awareness of their plot function. Beings such as Rigg, Eliot's narrator implies, are—or at least *should be*—superfluous. (The words "superfluity" [387], "residuary" [293, 316], and "residue" [317] crop up repeatedly with reference to Rigg.)

Indeed, Eliot seems almost as ashamed of Rigg the character as Featherstone is of Rigg the person. It is with a degree of uneasiness, her narra-

---

18. *Middlemarch* was serialized according to a new format that appeared in smaller installments that were distributed more slowly. With more than the usual lag time between installments, Eliot had time to respond to readers' reactions to her novel and its narrative. Martin has addressed the long-held "illusion that Eliot was unaware of critical opinion because of Lewes' careful watch," showing that her letters indicate the extent to which she "valued and needed positive responses" (72–73).

tor remarks, that she must call "attention to the existence of low people by whose interference, however little we may like it, the course of the world is very much determined. It would be well, certainly," she muses, "if we could help to reduce their number, and something might perhaps be done by not lightly giving occasion to their existence" (387).

Alex Woloch has suggested that *Middlemarch* is unique in the way that it refuses to choose between what he calls "the one and the many." As the nineteenth century progresses, he argues, "the novel gets infused with an awareness of its potential to shift the narrative focus away from an established center, toward minor characters" (19). I am suggesting that the implications of this development are more sweeping: that, in positioning Rigg as the kind of character that is simultaneously undesirable and yet ineliminable according to the rules of the genre, Eliot does more than open the door to the cultivation of a fictional world unstructured by characterological hierarchy of the one versus the many; she also envisions the possibility of disarticulating character from plot.

Of her attempt in *The Making of Americans* to "write the life of every individual who could possibly live on this earth," Gertrude Stein writes that her experiment was one of the equalization of value—value not in the moralistic sense but rather in a sense derived from painting: "I made endless diagrams of every human being," she says in an interview from 1946, "watching people from windows and so on until I could put down every type of human being that could be on the earth. I wanted each one to have the same value" ("Transatlantic" 16). "After all," she continues, "to me one human being is as important as another human being" (9). One might read Stein here as taking up the challenge, posed by Eliot in her self-conscious treatment of Rigg, to liberate character from what Eliot once called "the vulgar coercion of conventional plot" and take up instead the iterative temporality of repetition ("Leaves" 599). To cultivate a "fluctuating spontaneity" of character, both authors will imply, ironically entails not a rounding but a *flattening* of character. By flattening I do not mean the production of more typological and unchanging figures (i.e., in Forster's sense of the term *flat*); I refer instead to the flattening *of the hierarchies between* characters that plot-driven narrative turns upon.

The question of value is, of course, not only structurally but also thematically central to *Middlemarch*, a novel that narrates the life of a woman who will find for herself "no epic life" and whose "heart-beats and sobs after an unattained goodness tremble off and are dispersed among hindrances, instead of centring in some long-recognizable deed" (3). Recall here the conclusion to the novel, in which Dorothea, in a certain nose-thumbing to the developmental, forward-moving temporality of the bildungsroman narrative, does not become a more fully formed subject but is essentially dissolved: her "nature... spent... in channels which had no great name on the earth. But the effect of her being on those around her," we are reminded in the final paragraph of the novel, "was incalculably diffusive" (785).

Dorothea's incalculability would at first seem to place her opposition to Rigg, whose actions, to return to Lewes's phrase, are "uniform and calculable as... a machine" (Lewes, "Dickens" 149). In Lewes's framework, whereas Rigg is mechanistic, Dorothea is vital. As Eliot's narrator makes clear, however, it is only because of the narrative attention afforded to Dorothea that she is made to appear livelier than Rigg—two characters whose difference is no more ontological than that between life and nonlife. The difference inheres rather than how the stuff of which they are made is arranged.

Consider here the infamous opening to chapter 29 of *Middlemarch*, which begins, "One morning, some weeks after her arrival at Lowick, Dorothea," before the narrator, questioning the novel's focus on its protagonist, interrupts the diegesis, "—but why always Dorothea?" (261). This passage goes on to offer a kind of moral lesson about how everyone has their own point of view. What I want to highlight, however, is how this much remarked-upon thematic concern of the novel with the minor and the ordinary is refracted in and through the narrator's extradeigetic reflections on the simultaneously arbitrary (it doesn't matter who) and yet necessary (it has to be someone) arbitration of life.[19] In highlighting the *structural* value of both Rigg's mechanicity and Dorothea's vitality, Eliot seems to suggest that the novel genre, insofar as it requires both plot devices and protagonists, *turns upon* a kind of imbalance between its characters.

Of course, were one working with some other genre, some other set of formal or material constraints, such an imbalance might not be required. During her lifetime, Eliot saw the invention of the zoetrope, which produced a sense of incredible liveliness through the repetition of images that differed only slightly from one another. Stein's lifetime would be marked by the invention of film. As both of these technologies demonstrated, motion does not arise from stark contrasts or binary oppositions; rather, it is a science of small differences. "I was doing what the cinema was doing," Stein writes in "Portraits and Repetition," adding, "I was making a con-

---

19. Figlerowicz's observations about the "necessary finitude of a novel and of its characters" as well as the way that some realist novels draw special "attention to the limitations of their characters as objects of other people's interest" are especially relevant to the ethical implications of the musings of Eliot's narrator here (4).

tinuous statement of what that person was until I had not many things but one thing" ("Portraits" 176).

In his chapter on the importance of story in *Aspects of the Novel*, Forster addresses what he takes to be Stein's attempt to "abolish time" in narrative (41). "Well, there is one novelist who has tried to abolish time," he writes, "and her failure is instructive: Gertrude Stein... She wants to abolish this whole aspect of the story, this sequence in chronology, and my heart goes out to her" (41). According to Forster, Stein "fails because as soon as fiction is completely delivered from time it cannot express anything at all" (41).

While Forster is right that Stein's works resist "sequence in chronology," his inability to imagine what a story outside of sequence might look like leads him to misread her literary project as an attempt to entirely "emancipate fiction from the tyranny from time" (41). Stein's reflections of the concept of the "generation" in "Portraits and Repetition" make clear that her project is not about the elimination but rather the reconfiguration of time. As the double meaning of the word *generation* reveals, living repetitions (insistences) never circle back to the same moment (a repetition that would indeed produce narrative stasis); rather, they introduce small differences that produce narrative *motion*. "That is what a generation does," Stein writes, "it shows that moving is existing" (165).

Stein's thinking about generation recalls Hardy's narrative method in *The Well-Beloved: A Sketch of Temperament*, which, as we have seen, uses plot repetition to generate characterological spontaneity. Where Hardy's protagonist expects that each "renewed copy" of the Well-Beloved will be the same, Avice Caro II and Avice Caro III do not behave the same as Avice Caro I (298). Indeed, differences in the circumstances of the production of their character mean that each generation behaves and looks slightly differently, though certain elements of their character remain the same.

Hardy's novel, I argued in chapter 3, mobilizes a Darwinian attentiveness to the eruption of variation across the interstice of the generation against the eugenic fascination with the perpetuation of the same via the insulation of bodies from their environments.[20] In form, the novel also parodies the genre he felt was draining character of its "spontaneity" through the reduction of its plot structures to only those approved by editors and librarians. "The magazine in particular and the circulat-

---

20. Moses observes that Stein likewise engages Darwin in her thinking about generation, writing that "Stein, like Darwin, starts from the presumption that tendencies to similarity always coincide with processes of divergent variation. Innovation occurs as a result of small departures from previously assumed behaviors that build over time and are the product, at least in part, of decisions carried out" (120).

ing library," Hardy had complained in 1890, in general do not foster the growth of the novel which "reflects and reveals life" ("Candour" 17). The problem with the magazine serial and lending library system, he argued, was its generation of a "self-consciousness engendered by interference with spontaneity" (18–19).

After revising his 1897 *Sketch of Temperament,* Hardy abandoned the novel entirely to focus on poetry, a genre more hospitable to the "principle of spontaneity" he had hoped to cultivate in fiction (*Life* 324). Before him, Eliot had likewise turned away from plot, producing a series of typological sketches populated not with an increased number of incalculable Dorotheas, but rather a surprising number of Riggs. *The Well-Beloved* ends with Avice III on the brink of divorce and with Jocelyn's new bride-to-be, Marcia, being wheeled off to their geriatric wedding, mechanically going through the motions of the marriage plot: "That's how people are," Marcia informs Jocelyn in the 1897 revision, "wanting to round off other people's histories in the best machine-made conventional manner" (334).

Before her editor intervened, Eliot had wanted *Impressions of Theophrastus Such* to end with a sketch featuring a species of machinic beings that were able to communicate automatically without "the futile cargo of a consciousness" (141). "What *was* Victorian realism?" these late realist works would seem to ask as they push it—formally and philosophically—to its bitter end.

In 1868, when *Middlemarch* was still a germ, Eliot wondered whether all forms were accidental eruptions for which the possession of a consciousness was not especially required. In both art and life, form is "not born begotten by thinking it out," she writes, but rather emerges always in "a spontaneous and unreflective way" (235). Perhaps this is how literature itself emerged: "the rhythmic shouts with the clash of metal accompanying the huntsman's or conqueror's course were probably the nucleus of the ballad epic... the more or less violent muscular movement and resonance of wood and metal" possibly "the rude beginnings of lyric poetry" (235). In any case, literary forms are not generated by thought and certainly are not the result of a person's intentions. They are rather the product of "emotion, by its tendency to repetition," taking shape as they do through the "rhythmic persistence" of beating hearts and the clanging of blunt instruments (235). Indeed, Eliot goes so far as to argue, forms seem to emerge "in proportion as diversifying thought is absent.... Just as the beautiful expanding curves of a bivalve shell are not first made for the reception of the unstable inhabitant, but grow and are limited by the simple rhythmic conditions of its growing life" (235).

No form can live forever, Eliot reminds us. "A form, once started, must by and by cease to be purely spontaneous" ("Notes" 235). "Living words fed with the blood of relevant meaning" eventually calcify and slough off, "starved into an ingenious pattern work" (235). Still, the shell endures, its intricate molding left to be marveled at or studied by observers—or, if the structure remains habitable, occupied by a new pulse.

Acknowledgments

This book was written between two continents over ten years and has benefited from the support of more friends and spaces than I can name here. From Berlin to Philadelphia, and many places in between, I have found stability in motion through this project, which has been transformed by so many.

The origins of this book can be traced to my time as a graduate student in Comparative Literature at the University of Texas at Austin, where I found the most incredible mentors in Ann Cvetkovich and Tracie Matysik; they made everything possible through their intellectual capaciousness, generosity, and precision. What a rich intellectual life I had in Austin I am reminded of every time I think of Emily C. Bloom, Stephanie Rosen, Dustin D. Stewart, Jaime deBlanc-Knowles, Anna and Sebastian Langdell, Chris Raymond, Hannah C. Wojciehowski, Kathleen Stewart, Carol H. Mackay, and Neville Hoad. And Samuel Baker has remained a constant source of support, always nudging me and my sentences in the right direction. The lion's share of this book was drafted while adjuncting at three different institutions on three different subway lines in New York City. To those who helped me to get fed—literally, intellectually, and emotionally—those years, especially to Ada Smailbegović, Ronak Parikh, Matt Kipilman, Erika Sackin, Anthony Volodkin, Matt Moss, Emanuela Bianchi, Elaine Freedgood, Amy M. King, Stefanos Geroulanos, and to Molasses Books and the Brooklyn Institute for Social Research, I am deeply indebted.

The seeds of many of the ideas formulated here were planted during my time as an undergraduate at the University of Scranton, where Timothy K. Casey, William Rowe, Jody DeRitter, and Rebecca S. Beal taught me how to think. I encountered Eliot for the first time with Valerie A. Dodd at the University of Oxford, who showed me how to read for the silences and the movements of the body. Later, much of my best thinking would be done and undone in Berlin, where worlds clot together: I would not be the person I am without Bobby Benedicto, Daniel Colucciello Barber, Elisa Pereira Martins, Sergio Rigoletto, and Constanze Haas. I was galvanized to continue to lead my double life thanks to postdoctoral fellowships at the ICI Berlin Institute for Cultural Inquiry, where the intellectual dynamism of Christoph Holzhey, Claudia Peppel, Manuele Gragnolati, and Zairong Xiang pushed me to break down yet more disciplinary boundaries, and at the Leibniz Center for Literary and Cultural Studies, where I have learned a great deal from Eva Geulen, Georg Toepfer, and Eva Axer. I cannot imagine landing in a more exciting intellectual environment than at the Department of English at the University of Pennsylvania. There, David Kazanjian, Ania Loomba, Suvir Kaul, Rahul Mukherjee, David L. Eng, Melissa Sanchez, Emily Steiner, Whitney Trettien, Michael Gamer, Rita Copeland, David Wallace, and Timothy Corrigan, among so many others, make not only work but also life great. At the University of Oregon, where I began my professorial journey, I would especially like to thank William Rossi, Tres Pyle, Tim Cohen, Mary Wood, and Michael Allan.

The arguments in the following pages have especially been sharpened by the insights of Deidre Lynch, David Kurnick, Cannon Schmitt, Andrew H. Miller, Chi-ming Yang, Paul Saint-Amour, Jed Esty, Emily Steinlight, Heather Love, and one anonymous reader. Scott C. Thompson, Muriel Bernardi, Kerry McAuliffe, Ryan Fong, Rob Mulry, and Jae Yoon provided backup at key moments, and Bud Bynack was instrumental to this book's completion. For their encouragement and feedback over the years, I am also deeply appreciative of Nancy Henry, Jonah Siegel, Leo Bersani, Summer J. Star, Nathan Brown, Jonathan Kramnick, Ben Parris, Anna Kornbluh, Daniel Hack, Nasser Mufti, Zachary Samalin, Amanpal Garcha, Allen MacDuffie, Colby and Sam Gordon, Jenn Wilson, Carolyn Williams, Joseph Bristow, Grace Lavery, Greta LaFleur, and George Levine. At the University of Chicago Press, I am grateful to Alan Thomas, Randy Petilos, and Georgia Cartmill, as well as to Thinking Literature series editors, Anahid Nersessian and Nan Z. Da, for their thoughtfulness in guiding this project to its final state.

Earlier versions of chapters 1 and 2 have previously appeared as an essay, "Plasticity, Form, and the Matter of Character in *Middlemarch*," in *Representations* (2015, 130:1), and the article "'The Natural History of my Inward Self': Sensing Character in George Eliot's *Impressions of Theophrastus Such*" in *PMLA* (2014, 129:1). Portions of chapter 4 were included in the book chapter, "Schopenhauer and British Literary Feminisms" in *The Palgrave Schopenhauer Handbook* (2017). My work has been supported at various stages by the Humboldt Foundation, the German Academic

Exchange Service (DAAD), the Trustees' Council of Penn Women Faculty, the Wolf Humanities Center, the National Endowment for the Humanities Summer Seminar "Oscar Wilde and His Circle," and the Max Planck Institute for the History of Science. Chapters of this book have greatly benefited from rigorous discussion at the Conjuncture Series organized by the Multimedia Institute in Zagreb, the Res-Vic Nineteenth-Century Studies Group at Rutgers University, the Nineteenth-Century British Literature Colloquium at Columbia University, the Victorian Colloquium at Princeton University, the Theory and Environment Working Group at Haverford College, the V21 first book group, and the English departments of La Salle, Villanova, Yale, and Oregon State Universities: thank you to the coordinators, graduate students, and faculty who made all of these discussions possible.

The intellectual energy and care that Filippo Trentin brings to every day is beyond measure. His effect on this book and on my being is truly incalculable. To him, and to my family, Carleen, George, and Gracen Brilmyer, I owe the most. This book is for you.

Bibliography

Ablow, Rachel, ed. *The Feeling of Reading: Affective Experience and Victorian Literature*. Ann Arbor: University of Michigan Press, 2010.
Adamson, Robert. "Schopenhauer's Philosophy." *Mind* 1 (1876): 491–509.
Ahmed, Sara. "Willful Parts: Problem Characters or the Problem of Character." *New Literary History* 42, no. 2 (2011): 231–53.
Alaimo, Stacy, and Susan Hekman, eds. *Material Feminisms*. Indiana University Press, 2008.
Alpers, Svetlana. *The Art of Describing: Dutch Art in the Seventeenth Century*. Chicago: University of Chicago Press, 1984.
Anderson, Amanda. *The Powers of Distance: Cosmopolitanism and the Cultivation of Detachment*. Princeton, NJ: Princeton University Press, 2001.
———. *Tainted Souls and Painted Faces: The Rhetoric of Fallenness in Victorian Culture*. Ithaca, NY: Cornell University Press, 1993.
———. *The Way We Argue Now: A Study in the Cultures of Theory*. Princeton, NJ: Princeton University Press, 2005.
Anderson, Amanda, Rita Felski, and Toril Moi. *Character: Three Inquiries in Literary Studies*. Chicago: University of Chicago Press, 2019.
Anker, Peder. *Imperial Ecology: Environmental Order in the British Empire, 1895–1945*. Cambridge, MA: Harvard University Press, 2001.
Aquinas, St. Thomas. *St Thomas Aquinas: Philosophical Texts*. Translated by Thomas Gilby. London: Oxford University Press, 1952.
Arata, Stephen. "Realism." In *The Cambridge Companion to the Fin de Siècle*, edited by Gail Marshall, 169–87. Cambridge: Cambridge University Press, 2007.
Ardis, Ann L. *New Women, New Novels: Feminism and Early Modernism*. New Brunswick, NJ: Rutgers University Press, 1990.
Argyle, Gisela. *Germany as Model and Monster: Allusions in English Fiction, 1830s–1930s*. Montreal: McGill-Queen's University Press, 2002.
Armstrong, Isobel. "*Middlemarch*: A Note on George Eliot's 'Wisdom.'" In *Critical Essays on George Eliot*, edited by Barbara Nathan Hardy, 116–32. Abingdon, UK: Routledge, 1970.

Armstrong, Nancy. *Desire and Domestic Fiction: A Political History of the Novel*. Oxford: Oxford University Press, 1987.

———. *How Novels Think: The Limits of Individualism from 1719-1900*. New York: Columbia University Press, 2006.

Arnold, Matthew. *The Works of Matthew Arnold*. 15 vols. Edited by George William Erskine Russell and Thomas Burnett Smart. London: Macmillan, 1903.

Asher, David. "Schopenhauer and Darwinism." *Journal of Anthropology* 1, no. 3, (1871): 312–32.

Ashton, Rosemary. *G.H. Lewes: A Life*. Oxford: Oxford University Press, 1991.

"Atoms." *All the Year Round* 15, no. 360, (March 17, 1866): 235–38.

Atwell, John. *Schopenhauer on the Character of the World*. Berkeley: University of California Press, 1995.

Auerbach, Erich. *Mimesis: The Representation of Reality in Western Literature—Fiftieth-Anniversary Edition*. Translated by Willard R. Trask. Princeton, NJ: Princeton University Press, 2003.

Auyoung, Elaine. *When Fiction Feels Real: Representation and the Reading Mind*. New York: Oxford University Press, 2018.

Bagehot, Walter. *Physics and Politics; or, Thoughts on the Application of the Principles of "Natural Selection" and "Inheritance" to Political Society*. London: Kegen Paul, Trench, Trübner, 1891.

Baguley, David. *Naturalist Fiction: The Entropic Vision*. Cambridge: Cambridge University Press, 1990.

Bain, Alexander. *On the Study of Character: Including an Estimate of Phrenology*. London: Parker, Son, and Bourn, 1861.

Bakhtin, Mikhail. "The Bildungsroman and Its Significance in the History of Realism: Toward a Historical Typology of the Novel." In *Speech Genres and Other Late Essays*, edited by Caryl Emerson and Michael Holquist, 10–59. Austin: University of Texas Press, 1981.

Bal, Mieke. *Narratology: Introduction to the Theory of Narrative*. Edited by Christine van Boheemen. Toronto: University of Toronto Press, 2009.

Baltussen, Han. *Theophrastus against the Presocratics and Plato: Peripatetic Dialectic in the De Sensibus*. Leiden, Neth.: Brill Academic Publishers, 2000.

Barad, Karen. "Interview with Karen Barad." In *New Materialism: Interviews & Cartographies*, edited by Rick Dolphijn and Iris van der Tuin, 48–70. Ann Arbor, MI: Open Humanities Press, 2012.

———. *Meeting the Universe Halfway: Quantum Physics and the Entanglement of Matter and Meaning*. Durham, NC: Duke University Press, 2007.

———. "Posthumanist Performativity: Toward an Understanding of How Matter Comes to Matter." *Signs* 28, no. 3, (2003): 801–31.

Barthes, Roland. "The Reality Effect." In *French Literary Theory Today*, translated by Tzvetan Todorov, 11–16. Cambridge: Cambridge University Press, 1982.

Batchelor, David. *Chromophobia*. London: Reaktion, 2000.

Baucom, Ian. *Out of Place: Englishness, Empire, and the Locations of Identity*. Princeton, NJ: Princeton University Press, 1999.

———. *Specters of the Atlantic: Finance Capital, Slavery, and the Philosophy of History*. Durham, NC: Duke University Press, 2005.

Beasley, Edward. *The Victorian Reinvention of Race: New Racisms and the Problem of Grouping in the Human Sciences*. New York: Routledge, 2010.
Beer, Gillian. "Beyond Determinism: George Eliot and Virginia Woolf: Gillian Beer." In *Women Writing and Writing about Women*, edited by Mary Jacobus, 80–99. Abindon, UK: Routledge, 2012.
———. *Darwin's Plots: Evolutionary Narrative in Darwin, George Eliot and Nineteenth-Century Fiction*. New York: Cambridge University Press, 2009.
———. *Open Fields: Science in Cultural Encounter*. Oxford: Clarendon, 1996.
Bender, John. *Ends of Enlightenment*. Stanford: Stanford University Press, 2012.
Bennett, Jane. *Vibrant Matter: A Political Ecology of Things*. Durham, NC: Duke University Press, 2009.
Benthien, Claudia. *Skin: On the Cultural Border between Self and World*. Translated by Thomas Dunlap. New York: Columbia University Press, 2004.
Berkman, Joyce Avrech. *The Healing Imagination of Olive Schreiner: Beyond South African Colonialism*. Amherst, MA: University of Massachusetts Press, 1993.
Best, Stephen, and Sharon Marcus. "Surface Reading: An Introduction." *Representations* 108, no. 1 (November 2009): 1–21.
Bianchi, Emanuela. *The Feminine Symptom: Aleatory Matter in the Aristotelian Cosmos*. New York: Fordham University Press, 2014.
Bivona, Daniel. *Desire and Contradiction: Imperial Visions and Domestic Debates in Victorian Literature*. Manchester: Manchester University Press, 1990.
Bivona, Daniel Edward. "The Emergence of Emergence: G. H. Lewes, *Middlemarch*, and Social Order." *Dickens Studies Annual* 50, no. 1 (2019): 66.
Bland, Lucy. *Banishing the Beast: Feminism, Sex and Morality*. London: Tauris Parke, 2002.
Blackwood, John. "To Mrs. Lewes, March 13, 1872." In *The George Eliot Letters, 1869–1873*, vol. 5, edited by Gordon Sherman Haight, 255–56. New Haven, CT: Yale University Press, 1955.
Blanc, Charles. *The Grammar of Painting and Engraving*. Translated by Kate Newell Doggett. New York: Hurd and Houghton, 1874.
Bodenheimer, Rosemarie. "Autobiography in Fragments: The Elusive Life of Edith Simcox." *Victorian Studies* 44, no. 3 (2002): 399–422.
Book News Monthly. Advertisement for *Our Manifold Nature: Stories from Life* by Sarah Grand, April 1894, 335.
Bownas, Jane L. *Thomas Hardy and Empire: The Representation of Imperial Themes in the Work of Thomas Hardy*. Surrey, UK: Ashgate, 2012.
Bradbury, Malcolm, and Brad Fletcher. "The Introverted Novel." In *Modernism, 1890–1930*, edited by Malcolm Bradbury and James Walter McFarlane, 394–415. London: Penguin, 1976.
Brain, Robert Michael. *The Pulse of Modernism: Physiological Aesthetics in Fin-de-Siècle Europe*. Seattle: University of Washington Press, 2016.
Bridgwater, Patrick. *Gissing and Germany*. London: Enitharmon, 1981.
Brilmyer, S. Pearl. "Darwinian Feminisms." In *Gender: Matter*, edited by Stacy Alaimo, 19–34. Macmillan Interdisciplinary Handbooks. Farmington Hills, MI: Macmillan Reference, 2016.
———. "Durations of Presents Past: Ruskin and the Accretive Quality of Time." *Victorian Studies* 59, no. 1 (2016): 94–97.

———. "Plasticity, Form, and the Matter of Character in *Middlemarch*." *Representations* 130, no. 1 (May 2015): 60–83.

———. "Schopenhauer and British Literary Feminism." In *The Palgrave Schopenhauer Handbook*, edited by Sandra Shapshay, 397–424. Bloomington, IN: Palgrave Macmillan, 2017.

Brilmyer, S. Pearl, and Filippo Trentin. "Toward an Inessential Theory of Form: Ruskin, Warburg, Focillon." *Criticism* 61, no. 4 (2019): 481–508.

Brody, Jennifer DeVere. *Impossible Purities: Blackness, Femininity, and Victorian Culture*. Durham, NC: Duke University Press, 1998.

Brody, Selma B. "Physics in *Middlemarch*: Gas Molecules and Ethereal Atoms." *Modern Philology* 85, no. 1 (1987): 42–53.

Brooks, Peter. *Realist Vision*. New Haven, CT: Yale University Press, 2008.

Brown, Bill. *Other Things*. Chicago: University of Chicago Press, 2016.

Brown, Robert. "A Brief Account of Microscopical Observations... on the Particles Contained in the Pollen of Plants; and on the General Existence of Active Molecules in Organic and Inorganic Bodies." In *The Miscellaneous Botanical Works of Robert Brown*, 463–86. London: R. Hardwicke, 1866.

Brunsdale, Mitzi M. "The Effect of Mrs. Rudolf Dircks' Translation of Schopenhauer's 'The Metaphysics of Love' on D. H. Lawrence's Early Fiction." *Rocky Mountain Review of Language and Literature* 32, no. 2 (1978): 120–29.

Brush, Pippa. "Metaphors of Inscription: Discipline, Plasticity and the Rhetoric of Choice." *Feminist Review* 58, no. 1 (1998): 22–43.

Brush, Stephen G. "A History of Random Processes: I. Brownian Movement from Brown to Perrin." *Archive for History of Exact Sciences* 5, no. 1 (1968): 1–36.

Bryant, Levi. "Politics and Speculative Realism." *Speculations: A Journal of Speculative Realism* 4 (June 2013): 15–21.

Buchanan, Brett, Jeffrey Bussolini, and Matthew Churelew. "General Introduction: Philosophical Ethology." *Angelaki* 19, no. 3 (2014): 1–3.

Bullen, J. B. "Hardy's *The Well-Beloved*, Sex, and Theories of Germ Plasm." In *A Spacious Vision: Essays on Hardy*, edited by Phillip Mallett and R. P. Draper, 79–88. New Mill, UK: Patten, 1994.

———. *Thomas Hardy: The World of His Novels*. London: Frances Lincoln, 2013.

Burdett, Carolyn. *Olive Schreiner and the Progress of Feminism: Evolution, Gender, Empire*. New York: Palgrave Macmillan, 2001.

———. "Thrown Together: Olive Schreiner, Writing and Politics." In *Critical Feminism: Argument in the Disciplines*, edited by Kate Campbell, 107–21. Philadelphia: Open University Press.

Burton, Antoinette. *Empire in Question: Reading, Writing, and Teaching British Imperialism*. Durham, NC: Duke University Press, 2011.

Butler, Josephine Elizabeth Grey. *Woman's Work and Woman's Culture: A Series of Essays*. Cambridge, UK: Macmillan, 1869.

Butler, Judith. *Gender Trouble: Feminism and the Subversion of Identity*. New York: Routledge, 2006.

Caird, Alice Mona. *The Stones of Sacrifice*. London: Simpkin, Marshall, 1915.

Caird, Mona. "Marriage." *Westminster Review* 130, no. 1 (1888): 186–201.

———. *The Great Wave*. London: Wishart, 1931.

Canguilhem, Georges. "The Living and Its Milieu." Translated by John Savage. *Grey Room*, no. 3 (2001): 7–32.

Carlisle, Clare. "George Eliot's Spinoza: An Introduction." In *Spinoza's Ethics*, 1–60. Princeton, NJ: Princeton University Press, 2020.

Carpenter, William. "The Physiology of the Will." *Contemporary Review*, no. 17 (1871): 192–217.

Carpenter, William Benjamin. *Principles of Mental Physiology: With Their Applications to the Training and Discipline of the Mind, and the Study of Its Morbid Conditions*. Cambridge: Cambridge University Press, 1874.

Cartwright, David E. "Parerga and Paralipomena." In *Historical Dictionary of Schopenhauer's Philosophy*, 118–22. Lanham, MD: Scarecrow Press, 2005.

——. *Schopenhauer: A Biography*. Cambridge: Cambridge University Press, 2010.

Cheng, Anne Anlin. *Ornamentalism*. New York: Oxford University Press, 2019.

——. *Second Skin: Josephine Baker and the Modern Surface*. New York: Oxford University Press, 2013.

Cipolla, Cyd, Kristina Gupta, David A. Rubin, and Angela Willey, eds. *Queer Feminist Science Studies: A Reader*. Seattle: University of Washington Press, 2017.

Claggett, Shalyn. "Putting Character First: The Narrative Construction of Innate Identity in Phrenological Texts." *Victorians Institute Journal*, no. 39 (2011): 103–26.

Clifford, William Kingdon. "On Some of the Conditions of Mental Development." In *Lectures and Essays*, vol. 1. Cambridge: Cambridge University Press, 2011.

Cole, Eve Browning. "Theophrastus and Aristotle on Animal Intelligence." In *Theophrastus: His Psychological, Doxographical, and Scientific Writings*, edited by William W. Fortenbaugh and Dimitri Gutas, 44–62. Piscataway, NJ: Transaction Publishers, 1992.

Coleman, Piers. "Emergence and Reductionism." In *Routledge Handbook of Emergence*, edited by Sophie Gibb, Robin Findlay Hendry, and Tom Lancaster, 298–314. Abingdon, UK: Routledge, 2019.

Coleridge, Samuel Taylor. "Shakespeare's Judgment Equal to His Genius." In *The Collected Works of Samuel Taylor Coleridge*, vol. 5, edited by H. J. Jackson and George Whalley, 469–71. Princeton, NJ: Princeton University Press, 1987.

Collini, Stefan. *Public Moralists: Political Thought and Intellectual Life in Britain, 1850–1930*. Oxford: Oxford University Press, 1993.

Collins, K. K. "GH Lewes Revised: George Eliot and the Moral Sense." *Victorian Studies* 21, no. 4 (1978): 463–92.

——. "Questions of Method: Some Unpublished Late Essays." *Nineteenth-Century Fiction* 35, no. 3 (1980): 385–405.

Connor, Steven. *The Book of Skin*. London: Reaktion Books, 2009.

Coole, Diana, and Samantha Frost. *New Materialisms: Ontology, Agency, and Politics*. Durham, NC: Duke University Press, 2010.

Coombs, David Sweeney. *Reading with the Senses in Victorian Literature and Science*. Charlottesville, VA: University of Virginia Press, 2019.

Coriale, Danielle. "When Zoophytes Speak: Polyps and Naturalist Fantasy in the Age of Liberalism." *Nineteenth-Century Contexts* 34, no. 1 (2012): 19–36.

Courtney, William Leonard. *The Feminine Note in Fiction*. London: Chapman & Hall, 1904.

Cowan, Ruth Schwartz. "Francis Galton's Contribution to Genetics." *Journal of the History of Biology* 5, no. 2 (1972): 389–412.
Crabbe, George. *The Poetical Works of George Crabbe*. Edited by A. J. Carlyle and R. M. Carlyle. London: Oxford University Press, 1908.
Crary, Jonathan. *Techniques of the Observer: On Vision and Modernity in the Nineteenth Century*. Cambridge, MA: MIT Press, 1990.
Christoff, Alicia Mireles. *Novel Relations: Victorian Fiction and British Psychoanalysis*. Princeton, NJ: Princeton University Press, 2019.
Crenshaw, Kimberlé. "Demarginalizing the Intersection of Race and Sex: A Black Feminist Critique of Antidiscrimination Doctrine, Feminist Theory and Antiracist Politics." *University of Chicago Legal Forum* 140 (1989): 139–67.
Cronwright-Schreiner, Samuel C. *The Life of Olive Schreiner*. London: T. Fisher Unwin, 1924.
Damerow, Peter, Gideon Freudenthal, Peter McLaughlin, and Jürgen Renn. *Exploring the Limits of Preclassical Mechanics: A Study of Conceptual Development in Early Modern Science*. New York: Springer, 2011.
Dames, Nicholas. *The Physiology of the Novel: Reading, Neural Science, and the Form of Victorian Fiction*. New York: Oxford University Press, 2007.
Dampier, Helen. "Re-Readings of Olive Schreiner's Letters to Karl Pearson: Against Closure." In *Olive Schreiner and Company: Letters and Drinking in the External World*, edited by Liz Stanley, 47–71. Edinburgh: University of Edinburgh Press, 2011.
Darwin, Charles. *The Descent of Man and Selection in Relation to Sex*. Edited by James Moore and Adrian Desmond. London: Penguin, 2004.
———. *The Origin of Species*. New York: Bantam, 1999.
———. "To Joseph Hooker, February 1 [1871]." The Darwin Correspondence Project. 2020. www.darwinproject.ac.uk.
Daston, Lorraine, and Peter Galison. *Objectivity*. New York: Zone, 2010.
Davis, Michael. *George Eliot and Nineteenth-Century Psychology: Exploring the Unmapped Country*. Abingdon, UK: Ashgate, 2006.
———. "Psychology and the Idea of Character." In *The Oxford History of the Novel in English: Volume 3: The Nineteenth-Century Novel, 1820–1880*, edited by John Kucich and Jenny Bourne Taylor, 492–508. New York: Oxford University Press, 2011.
Davis, Thomas S. *The Extinct Scene: Late Modernism and Everyday Life*. New York: Columbia University Press, 2015.
Deleuze, Gilles. *Nietzsche and Philosophy*. London: Continuum, 2006.
———. *Spinoza: Practical Philosophy*. San Francisco: City Lights Books, 1988.
Descartes, René. *Discourse on Method and Meditations*. Translated by Elizabeth Sanderson Haldane and G. R. T. Ross. Mineola, NY: Dover, 2003.
Desmond, Adrian. *The Politics of Evolution: Morphology, Medicine, and Reform in Radical London*. Chicago: University of Chicago Press, 1992.
Despret, Vinciane. "The Body We Care For: Figures of Anthropo-Zoo-Genesis." *Body and Society* 10, no. 2/3 (2004): 111–34.
Dickens, Charles. *Our Mutual Friend*. Edited by Michael Cotsell. New York: Oxford University Press, 2009.
Dixon, Joy. "Sexology and the Occult: Sexuality and Subjectivity in Theosophy's New Age." *Journal of the History of Sexuality* 7, no. 3 (1997): 409–33.

Dodd, Valerie A. *George Eliot: An Intellectual Life*. Houndmills, UK: Palgrave Macmillan, 1990.

Dolin, Tim. "George Eliot and Victorian Science." In *George Eliot*, 190-215. New York: Oxford University Press, 2005.

———. "Melodrama, Vision, and Modernity: *Tess of the d'Urbervilles*." In *A Companion to Thomas Hardy*, edited by Keith Wilson, 21-35. New York: John Wiley & Sons, 2012.

Dolphijn, Rick, and Iris van der Tuin. *New Materialism: Interviews & Cartographies*. Ann Arbor, MI: Open Humanities Press, an imprint of MPublishing, 2012.

Dowling, Linda C. *Language and Decadence in the Victorian Fin de Siècle*. Princeton, NJ: Princeton University Press, 2014.

Douglass, Frederick. *My Bondage and My Freedom*. Edited by John David Smith. New York: Penguin Classics, 2003.

Driver, Dorothy. "On Producing a New Edition of from *Man to Man, Or perhaps Only*." *English in Africa*, 42, no. 1 (2015): 27-58.

Du Bois, W. E. B. "The Negro Mind Reaches Out." In *The New Negro*, edited by Alain Locke, 385-414. New York: Simon and Schuster, 1997. First published in 1925 by Albert & Charles Boni.

Dubow, Saul. *A Commonwealth of Knowledge: Science, Sensibility, and White South Africa 1820-2000*. New York: Oxford University Press, 2006.

Duncan, Ian. *Human Forms: The Novel in the Age of Evolution*. Princeton, NJ: Princeton University Press, 2019.

Durant, John R. "Innate Character in Animals and Man: A Perspective on the Origins of Ethology." In *Biology, Medicine and Society 1840-1940*, edited by Charles Webster, 157-92. Cambridge: Cambridge University Press, 1981.

Dworkin, Andrea. "Against the Male Flood: Censorship, Pornography, and Equality." In *Oxford Readings in Feminism: Feminism and Pornography*, vol. 8, edited by Drucilla Cornell, 19-44. New York: Oxford University Press, 2000.

Eagleton, Terry. *Criticism and Ideology: A Study in Marxist Literary Theory*. London: Verso, 2006.

Egerton, George. *Keynotes*. London: Virago, 1995.

Eliot, George. *Adam Bede*. London: Penguin, 1980.

———. *Daniel Deronda*. Edited by Graham Handley. Oxford: Oxford University Press, 2009.

———. *George Eliot's* Middlemarch *Notebooks: A Transcription*. Edited by John Clark Pratt and Victor A. Neufelt. Berkeley: University of California Press, 1979.

———. *Impressions of Theophrastus Such*. Edited by Nancy Henry. Iowa City: University of Iowa Press, 1996.

———. "Leaves from a Notebook." In *George Eliot's Works*, vol. 12, 585-607. New York: Thomas Nelson and Sons, 1906.

———. *Middlemarch*. Edited by David Carroll and Felicia Bonaparte. New York: Oxford University Press, 2008.

———. "Notes on Form in Art." In *Selected Essays, Poems, and Other Writings*, edited by A. S. Byatt and Nicholas Warren, 231-40. London: Penguin, 1990.

———. "Rev. of *The Progress of the Intellect* by R. W. Mackay." In *Selected Essays, Poems, and Other Writings*, edited by A. S. Byatt and Nicholas Warren, 268-85. London: Penguin, 1990.

———. "Rev. of 'Westward Ho!' by Charles Kingsley." *Westminster Review* 64 (1855): 288–307.

———. To Maria Lewis, June 21, 1841. *The George Eliot Letters*, vol. 1, *1852–1858*, edited by Gordon Sherman Haight, 97–98. New Haven, CT: Yale University Press, 1954.

———. To Mrs. Robert Lytton, July 8, 1870. *The George Eliot Letters*, vol. 5, *1869–1873*, edited by Gordon Sherman Haight, 106–7. New Haven, CT: Yale University Press, 1955.

———. To Sara Sophia Hennell, April 4, 1853. *The George Eliot Letters*, vol. 2, *1852–1858*, edited by Gordon Sherman Haight, 95–96. New Haven, CT: Yale University Press, 1954.

———. *The Journals of George Eliot*. Edited by Margaret Harris and Judith Johnson. Cambridge: Cambridge University Press, 2000.

———. *The Lifted Veil and Brother Jacob*. Edited by Helen Small. New York: Oxford University Press, 2009.

———. "The Natural History of German Life." In *Selected Essays, Poems, and Other Writings*, edited by A. S. Byatt and Nicholas Warren, 107–39. London: Penguin, 1990.

Ellis, Havelock, and John Addington Symonds. *Das konträre Geschlechtsgefühl*. Leipzig: G. H. Wigand's Verlag, 1896.

———. *Sexual Inversion*. Edited by Ivan Crozier. New York: Palgrave Macmillan, 2007.

"The Essays of Schopenhauer, The Expounder of Pessimism." *Self Culture* 6 (October 1897): 335–37.

Esty, Jed. *Unseasonable Youth: Modernism, Colonialism, and the Fiction of Development*. New York: Oxford University Press, 2013.

Fanon, Frantz. *Black Skin, White Masks*. Translated by Charles Lam Markmann. London: Pluto Press, 2008.

Faraday, Michael. *The Forces of Matter*. London: Richard Griffin, 1860.

Farina, Jonathan. "Character." *Victorian Literature and Culture* 46, no. 3/4 (2018): 609–12.

Farley, John. "The Spontaneous Generation Controversy (1859–1880): British and German Reactions to the Problem of Abiogenesis." *Journal of the History of Biology* 5, no. 2 (1972): 285–319.

———. *The Spontaneous Generation Controversy from Descartes to Oparin*. Baltimore: Johns Hopkins University Press, 1977.

Feuerbach, Ludwig von. *The Essence of Christianity*. Translated by George Eliot. Buffalo, NY: Prometheus Books, 1989.

Fielding, Henry. *Joseph Andrews*. Edited by Martin C. Battestin. Middletown, CT: Wesleyan University Press, 1967.

Figlerowicz, Marta. *Flat Protagonists: A Theory of Novel Character*. New York: Oxford University Press, 2016.

First, Ruth, and Ann Scott. *Olive Schreiner: A Biography*. New Brunswick, NJ: Rutgers University Press, 1990.

Fisher, Philip. "The Failure of Habit." In *Uses of Literature*, edited by Monroe Engel, 3–18. Cambridge, MA: Harvard University Press, 1973.

Fleissner, Jennifer L. *Women, Compulsion, Modernity: The Moment of American Naturalism*. Chicago: University of Chicago Press, 2004.

Fong, Ryan D. "The Stories outside the African Farm: Indigeneity, Orality, and Unsettling the Victorian." *Victorian Studies* 62, no. 3 (2020): 421–32.
Foote, Janet Voth. "Gissing and Schopenhauer: A Study of Literary Influence." PhD diss., Indiana University, 1967.
Forster, E. M. *Aspects of the Novel*. Harcourt, 1956.
Fortenbaugh, William W. "Theophrastus, the Characters and Rhetoric." In *Peripatetic Rhetoric after Aristotle*, edited by David C. Mirhady and William W. Fortenbaugh, 15–35. New Brunswick, NJ: Transaction, 1994.
Frederickson, Kathleen. *The Ploy of Instinct: Victorian Sciences of Nature and Sexuality in Liberal Governance*. New York: Fordham University Press, 2014.
Freedgood, Elaine. *The Ideas in Things: Fugitive Meaning in the Victorian Novel*. Chicago: University of Chicago Press, 2010.
———. "Islands of Whiteness." *Victorian Studies* 54, no. 2 (2012): 298–304.
———. *Worlds Enough: The Invention of Realism in the Victorian Novel*. Princeton, NJ: Princeton University Press, 2019.
Freedgood, Elaine, and Cannon Schmitt. "Denotatively, Technically, Literally." *Representations* 125, no. 1 (2014): 1–14.
Freeman, Edward Augustus. *The Growth of the English Constitution from the Earliest Times*. London: Macmillan, 1872.
Freitas-Branco, João Maria de. "Gegenstand." In *Historisch-kritisches Wörterbuch des Marxismus*, vol. 5, edited by Wolfgang Fritz Haug, 36–43. Hamburg: Argument Verlag, 2001.
Freud, Sigmund. *Three Essays on the Theory of Sexuality*. Translated by James Strachey. London: Hogarth, 1962.
Frow, John. *Character and Person*. New York: Oxford University Press, 2016.
Fuerst, John. "Concepts of Physiology, Reproduction, and Evolution of Machines in Samuel Butler's 'Erewhon' and George Eliot's 'Impressions of Theophrastus Such.'" *Samuel Butler Newsletter* 4, no. 2 (1981): 31–53.
Furst, Lilian R., and Peter N. Skrine. *Naturalism*. London: Methuen, 1971.
Gallagher, Catherine. "George Eliot: Immanent Victorian." *Representations*, no. 90 (2005): 61–74.
———. *The Industrial Reformation of English Fiction: Social Discourse and Narrative Form, 1832–1867*. Chicago: University of Chicago Press, 1988.
———. *Nobody's Story: The Vanishing Acts of Women Writers in the Marketplace, 1670–1920*. Berkeley: University of California Press, 1994.
———. "The Rise of Fictionality." In *The Novel*, vol. 1, edited by Franco Moretti, 336–63. Princeton, NJ: Princeton University Press, 2006.
———, ed. "Special Issue on Counterfactuals." *Representations* 98, no. 1 (May 2007): 51–52.
———. *Telling It Like It Wasn't: The Counterfactual Imagination in History and Fiction*. Chicago: University of Chicago Press, 2018.
Gallagher, Catherine, Paul K. Saint-Amour, and Mark Maslan, eds. "Forum: Counterfactual Realities." *Representations* 98, no. 1 (May 2007): 51–52.
Galton, Francis. "Hereditary Talent and Character, Part I." *MacMillan's Magazine* 12 (1865): 157–66.
———. "Hereditary Talent and Character, Part II." *MacMillan's Magazine* 12 (1865): 318–27.

Garcha, Amanpal. *From Sketch to Novel: The Development of Victorian Fiction.* New York: Cambridge University Press, 2009.
Garratt, Peter. *Victorian Empiricism: Self, Knowledge, and Reality in Ruskin, Bain, Lewes, Spencer, and George Eliot.* Madison, NJ: Fairleigh Dickinson University Press, 2010.
Gaskell, Elizabeth. *Ruth.* Edited by Tim Dolin. New York: Oxford University Press, 2011.
Gatens, Moira. "Compelling Fictions: Spinoza and George Eliot on Imagination and Belief." *European Journal of Philosophy* 20, no. 1 (2012): 74-90.
Geison, Gerald L. "The Protoplasmic Theory of Life and the Vitalist-Mechanist Debate." *Isis* 60, no. 3 (1969): 273-92.
Gilbert, Sandra, and Susan Gubar. *No Man's Land: The Place of the Woman Writer in the Twentieth Century.* New Haven, CT: Yale University Press, 1994.
Gill, Clare. "Reading the 'Religion of Socialism': Olive Schreiner, the Labour Church and the Construction of Left-Wing Reading Communities in the 1890s." In *The History of Reading*, vol. 2, edited by Katie Halsey and W. R. Owens, 48-63. Basingstoke, UK: Palgrave Macmillan, 2011.
Gillham, Nicholas Wright. *A Life of Sir Francis Galton: From African Exploration to the Birth of Eugenics.* New York: Oxford University Press, 2001.
Gissing, George. *The Unclassed.* London: Chapman & Hall, 1884.
———. *Workers in the Dawn.* Brighton, UK: Harvester Press, 1985.
Glissant, Édouard. *Poetics of Relation.* Ann Arbor: University of Michigan Press, 1997.
Goodlad, Lauren M. E. *Victorian Literature and the Victorian State: Character and Governance in a Liberal Society.* Baltimore: Johns Hopkins University Press, 2003.
Gosse, Edmund. "The New Sculpture, 1879-1894." *The Art Journal* 56 (1894): 138-42.
Grand, Sarah. *The Beth Book.* Edited by Jenny Bourne Taylor. Brighton, UK: Victorian Secrets, 2013.
———. *The Heavenly Twins.* Ann Arbor: University of Michigan Press, 1992.
———. *Ideala: A Study from Life.* Kansas City, MO: Valancourt, 2008.
———. "The New Aspect of the Woman Question." *North American Review* 158, no. 448 (1894): 270-76.
———. *Our Manifold Nature: Stories from Life.* London: William Heinemann, 1894.
Greiner, Rae. *Sympathetic Realism in Nineteenth-Century British Fiction.* Baltimore: Johns Hopkins University Press, 2012.
Grene, Nicholas. *Bernard Shaw: A Critical View.* London: Macmillan, 1984.
Griffin, Cristina Richieri. "George Eliot's Feuerbach: Senses, Sympathy, Omniscience, and Secularism." *ELH* 84, no. 2 (2017): 475-502.
Griffiths, Devin. *The Age of Analogy: Science and Literature between the Darwins.* Baltimore: Johns Hopkins University Press, 2016.
Griffiths, Devin, and Deanna K. Kreisel. "Introduction: Open Ecologies." *Victorian Literature and Culture* 48, no. 1 (2020): 1-28.
Grosz, Elizabeth. *Chaos, Territory, Art: Deleuze and the Framing of the Earth.* Columbia University Press, 2008.
———. *Time Travels: Feminism, Nature, Power.* Durham, NC: Duke University Press, 2005.
———. *Volatile Bodies: Toward a Corporeal Feminism.* Bloomington: Indiana University Press, 1994.

Grove, William Robert. *The Correlation of Physical Forces*. London: Longmans, Green, 1874.
Hadley, Elaine. *Living Liberalism: Practical Citizenship in Mid-Victorian Britain*. Chicago: University of Chicago Press, 2010.
Haeckel, Ernst. "Generelle Morphologie der Organismen." In *Generelle Morphologie der Organismen*, vol. 1. Berlin: De Gruyter, 1866.
Haight, Gordon Sherman. *George Eliot: A Biography*. Oxford: Oxford University Press, 1968.
Haldane, J. B. S. "The Origin of Life." *Rationalist Annual* 148 (1929): 3–10.
Hall, Catherine, and Sonya O. Rose, eds. *At Home with the Empire: Metropolitan Culture and the Imperial World*. New York: Cambridge University Press, 2007.
Hamilton, Kristie. *America's Sketchbook: Cultural Life of a 19th-Century Literary Genre*. Athens: Ohio University Press, 1998.
Haraway, Donna. *The Companion Species Manifesto: Dogs, People, and Significant Otherness*. Edited by Matthew Begelke. Chicago: Prickly Paradigm, 2003.
———. "Promises of Monsters: A Regenerative Politics for Inappropriate/d Others." In *Cultural Studies*, edited by Lawrence Grossberg, Cary Nelson, and Paula Treichler, 295-337. New York: Routledge, 1992.
———. "Situated Knowledges: The Science Question in Feminism and the Privilege of Partial Perspective." *Feminist Studies* 14, no. 3 (1988): 575–99.
———. *When Species Meet*. Minneapolis: University of Minnesota Press, 2007.
Hardy, Barbara. *Thomas Hardy: Imagining Imagination in Hardy's Poetry and Fiction*. London: Athlone Press, 2001.
Hardy, Thomas. "Candour in English Fiction." *New Review* (January 1890): 15–21.
———. *Far from the Madding Crowd*. Edited by Suzanne B. Falck-Yi and Linda M. Shires. New York: Oxford University Press, 2008.
———. "Heredity." In *Thomas Hardy: The Complete Poems*, edited by James Gibson, 434. Basingstoke, UK: Palgrave Macmillan, 2001.
———. *Jude the Obscure*. Edited by Ralph Pite. New York: Norton, 2016.
———. *The Life and Work of Thomas Hardy*. Edited by Michael Millgate. Athens: University of Georgia Press, 1985.
———. *A Pair of Blue Eyes*. Edited by Alan Manford. Oxford: Oxford University Press, 2009.
———. *The Pursuit of the Well-Beloved and The Well-Beloved*. Edited by Patricia Ingham. London: Penguin, 1998.
———. *The Return of the Native*. Edited by Alexander Theroux. New York: Modern Library, 2001.
———. "The Science of Fiction." In *The Nineteenth-Century Novel: A Critical Reader*, edited by Stephen Regan, 100–4. Abingdon, UK: Routledge, 2001.
———. *Tess of the d'Urbervilles*. Edited by Tim Dolin. New York: Penguin, 1998.
———. To Edmund Gosse, March 31, 1897. In *The Collected Letters of Thomas Hardy*, vol. 2, edited by Richard Little Purdy and Michael Millgate, 55–56. Oxford: Oxford University Press, 1980.
———. To Lady Jeune, March 29, 1897. *The Collected Letters of Thomas Hardy*, vol. 2, edited by Richard Little Purdy and Michael Millgate, 156. Oxford: Oxford University Press, 1980.

Harman, Graham. "Marginalia on Radical Thinking: An Interview with Graham Harman." *The (Dis)Loyal Opposition to Modernity*. http://skepoet.wordpress.com/2012/06/01/marginalia-on-radical-thinking-an-interview-with-graham-harman/.

Hartley, Lucy. "Constructing the Common Type: Physiognomic Norms and the Notion of 'Civic Usefulness' from Lavater to Galton." In *Histories of the Normal and the Abnormal: Social and Cultural Histories of Norms and Normativity*, edited by Waltraud Ernst, 101–21. Abingdon, UK: Routledge, 2006.

———. *Physiognomy and the Meaning of Expression in Nineteenth-Century Culture*. Cambridge: Cambridge University Press, 2005.

Harvey, W. J. "The Intellectual Background of the Novel: Casaubon and Lydgate." In *Middlemarch: Critical Approaches to the Novel*, edited by Barbara Nathan Hardy, 25–37. London: Athlone Press, 1967.

Hazlitt, William. *The Spirit of the Age; Or, Contemporary Portraits*. London: G. Bell & Sons, 1886.

Hegel, G. W. F. *Phenomenology of Spirit*. Translated by A. V. Miller. Oxford: Oxford University Press, 1977.

Heilmann, Ann. *New Woman Strategies: Sarah Grand, Olive Schreiner, Mona Caird*. New York: Manchester University Press, 2004.

Henkin, Leo Justin. *Darwinism in the English Novel, 1860–1910: The Impact of Evolution on Victorian Fiction*. New York: Russell & Russell, 1963.

Henry, Alvin J. *Black Queer Flesh: Rejecting Subjectivity in the African American Novel*. Minneapolis: University of Minnesota Press, 2021.

Henry, Nancy. "George Eliot, George Henry Lewes, and Comparative Anatomy." In *George Eliot and Europe*, edited by John Rignall, 44–63. N.p.: Scolar Press, 1997.

———. "George Eliot's Humans and Animals." *George Eliot Review* 51 (2020): 41–54.

———. Introduction to *Impressions of Theophrastus Such* by George Eliot, vii–xxxvii. Edited by Nancy Henry. Iowa City: University of Iowa Press, 1996.

Hensley, Nathan K. "Curatorial Reading and Endless War." *Victorian Studies* 56, no. 1 (2013): 59–86.

Herbert, Christopher. *Victorian Relativity*. Chicago: University of Chicago Press, 2001.

Herschel, A. S. "Reply to 'The Matter of Space' by Charles Morris." *Nature* 27, no. 698 (1883): 458–60.

Hertz, Neil. *George Eliot's Pulse*. Stanford: Stanford University Press, 2003.

Holnut, W. S. *Olympia's Journal*. London: G. Bell and Sons, 1895.

Holterhoff, Kate. "The History and Reception of Charles Darwin's Hypothesis of Pangenesis." *Journal of the History of Biology* 47, no. 4 (2014): 661–95.

Houwink, Roelof. *Elasticity, Plasticity and Structure of Matter*. Edited by H. K. de Decker and Roelof Houwink. Cambridge: Cambridge University Press, 1971.

Hueffer, Francis. "Arthur Schopenhauer." *Fortnightly Review* 26 (1876): 773–92.

Hughes, J. Donald. "Theophrastus as Ecologist." *Environmental Review* 9, no. 4 (1985): 297–306.

Hume, David. *A Treatise of Human Nature*. Oxford: Clarendon, 1978.

Humphreys, Paul. *Emergence*. New York: Oxford University Press, 2019.

Huxley, Julian S. "The Courtship Habits of the Great Crested Grebe (Podiceps Cristatus): With an Addition to the Theory of Sexual Selection." *Proceedings of the Zoological Society of London* 84, no. 3 (1914): 491–562.

Huxley, Thomas Henry. "Biogenesis and Abiogenesis." In *Collected Essays*, vol. 8, *Discourses: Biological and Geological*, 229–71. New York: Cambridge University Press, 2011.
———. "On the Physical Basis of Life." In *Collected Essays*, vol. 1, 130–65. New York: Cambridge University Press, 2011.
———. "Science and Culture." In *Collected Essays*, vol. 3, *Science and Education*, 134–59. New York: Cambridge University Press, 2011.
Ingham, Patricia. Introduction to *The Pursuit of the Well-Beloved and The Well-Beloved* by Thomas Hardy, xvii–xxxiii. London: Penguin Classics, 1998.
"Inspired by Ibsen?" *Literary World*, March 1894, 266–67.
Jablonski, Nina G. *Skin: A Natural History*. Berkeley: University of California Press, 2013.
Jackson, Zakiyyah Iman. *Becoming Human: Matter and Meaning in an Antiblack World*. New York: NYU Press, 2020.
Jacquette, Dale. *The Philosophy of Schopenhauer*. Montreal: McGill-Queen's University Press, 2005.
Jaffe, Audrey. *Vanishing Points: Dickens, Narrative, and the Subject of Omniscience*. Berkeley: University of California Press, 1991.
———. *The Victorian Novel Dreams of the Real: Conventions and Ideology*. New York: Oxford University Press, 2016.
James, William. *The Principles of Psychology*. New York: Dover, 1950.
Jameson, Fredric. *The Antinomies of Realism*. London: Verso, 2013.
———. *A Singular Modernity: Essay on the Ontology of the Present*. London: Verso, 2013.
Jaynes, Julian. "The Historical Origins of 'Ethology' and 'Comparative Psychology.'" *Animal Behaviour* 17, no. 4 (1969): 601–6.
Jenkins, Alice. "George Eliot, Geometry, and Gender." In *Literature and Science*, edited by Sharon Ruston, 72–90. Cambridge: D. S. Brewer, 2008.
Kant, Immanuel. *Lectures on Ethics*. Translated by Louis Infield. New York: Harper & Row, 1963.
Kaufmann, Walter. "Translator's Preface." In *Beyond Good and Evil: Prelude to a Philosophy of the Future*, ix–xviii. New York: Vintage, 1989.
King, Amy M. *The Divine in the Commonplace*. New York: Cambridge University Press, 2019.
———. "Reorienting the Scientific Frontier: Victorian Tide Pools and Literary Realism." *Victorian Studies* 47, no. 2 (2005): 153–63.
Kornbluh, Anna. *The Order of Forms: Realism, Formalism, and Social Space*. Chicago: University of Chicago Press, 2019.
Korsgaard, Christine Marion. *Self-Constitution: Agency, Identity, and Integrity*. New York: Oxford University Press, 2009.
Kortsch, Christine Bayles. *Dress Culture in Late Victorian Women's Fiction: Literacy, Textiles, and Activism*. Ashgate, 2009.
Kreilkamp, Ivan. *Minor Creatures: Persons, Animals, and the Victorian Novel*. Chicago: University of Chicago Press, 2018.
Kunin, Aaron. *Character as Form*. London: Bloomsbury, 2019.
Kurnick, David. "An Erotics of Detachment: *Middlemarch* and Novel-Reading as Critical Practice." *ELH* 74, no. 3 (2007): 583–608.

Lakoff, George, and Mark Johnson. *Metaphors We Live By*. Chicago: University of Chicago Press, 2003.
Laplace, Pierre-Simon. *Traité de Mécanique Céleste*. De l'imprimerie de Crapelet, Chez J. B. M. Duprat libraire pour les Mathématiques, et à Berlin chez F. T. de la Garde, 1799.
Latham, Sean, and Gayle Rogers. *Modernism: Evolution of an Idea*. Bloomsbury Academic, 2015.
Latour, Bruno. *Reassembling the Social: An Introduction to Actor-Network-Theory*. New York: Oxford University Press, 2005.
Lauster, Martina. *Sketches of the Nineteenth Century: European Journalism and Its Physiologies, 1830–50*. Basingstoke, UK: Palgrave Macmillan, 2007.
Law, Jules. *The Social Life of Fluids: Blood, Milk, and Water in the Victorian Novel*. Ithaca, NY: Cornell University Press, 2010.
Leary, David E. "The Fate and Influence of John Stuart Mill's Proposed Science of Ethology." *Journal of the History of Ideas* 43, no. 1 (1982): 153–62.
Ledger, Sally. *The New Woman: Fiction and Feminism at the Fin de Siècle*. Manchester: Manchester University Press, 1997.
Lee, Vernon. *Baldwin: Being Dialogues on Views and Aspirations*. London: T. Fisher Unwin, 1886.
Lefew-Blake, Penelope. *Schopenhauer, Women's Literature, and the Legacy of Pessimism in the Novels of George Eliot, Olive Schreiner, Virginia Woolf, and Doris Lessing*. Lewiston, NY: Edwin Mellen, 2001.
Levine, George. "Determinism and Responsibility in the Works of George Eliot." *PMLA* 77, no. 3 (1962): 268–79.
———. *Dying to Know: Scientific Epistemology and Narrative in Victorian England*. Chicago: University of Chicago Press, 2002.
———. "George Eliot's Hypothesis of Reality." *Nineteenth-Century Fiction* 35, no. 1 (1980): 1–28.
———. *The Realistic Imagination: English Fiction from Frankenstein to Lady Chatterley*. Chicago: University of Chicago Press, 1983.
Levy, Amy. "A Minor Poet." In *A Minor Poet and Other Verses*, 1–14. London: T. Fisher Unwin, 1884.
———. *Sokratics in the Strand*. Edited by Linda Eve Wetherall. Saint Paul, MN: University of St. Thomas Press, 2017.
———. "To E." In *A London Plane-Tree, and Other Verses*, 92–93. London: T. Fisher Unwin, 1889.
Lewes, George Henry. *Comte's Philosophy of the Sciences*. London: Henry G. Bohun, 1853.
———. "Dickens in Relation to Criticism." *Fortnightly Review* 17, no. 62 (1872): 141–54.
———. "Only a Pond!" *Blackwood Edinburgh Magazine* 85 (1859): 581–97.
———. *Problems of Life and Mind*. 5 vols. London: Trübner, 1874–79.
———. *Sea-side Studies at Ilfracombe, Tenby, and the Scilly Isles, and Jersey*. Edinburgh: Blackwood & Sons, 1858.
———. *Studies in Animal Life*. New York: Harper, 1860.
Liu, Daniel. "The Cell and Protoplasm as Container, Object, and Substance, 1835–1861." *Journal of the History of Biology* 50, no. 4 (2017): 889–925.
Logan, Peter Melville. *Nerves and Narratives: A Cultural History of Hysteria in 19th-Century British Prose*. Berkeley: University of California Press, 1997.

———. "Primitive Criticism and the Novel: G. H. Lewes and Hippolyte Taine on Dickens." *Victorian Literature and Culture* 46, no. 1 (2018): 125–42.
Lorenz, Konrad. "Companionship in Bird Life: Fellow Members of the Species as Releasers of Social Behavior." In *Instinctive Behavior*, translated by Claire H. Schiller, 83–128. New York: International Universities Press, 1948.
Lorenz, Konrad Z. "The Fashionable Fallacy of Dispensing with Description." *Naturwissenschaften* 60, no. 1 (January 1973): 1–9.
Love, Heather. "Close but Not Deep: Literary Ethics and the Descriptive Turn." *New Literary History* 41, no. 2 (2010): 371–91.
———. "Close Reading and Thin Description." *Public Culture* 25, no. 3 (2013): 401–34.
———. "The Temptations: Donna Haraway, Feminist Objectivity, and the Problem of Critique." In *Critique and Postcritique*, edited by Elizabeth Anker and Rita Felski, 50–72. Durham, NC: Duke University Press.
Lukács, György. *History and Class Consciousness: Studies in Marxist Dialectics*. Translated by Rodney Livingstone. Cambridge, MA: MIT Press, 1972.
———. "Narrate or Describe?" In *Writer and Critic: and Other Essays*, edited and translated by Arthur Kahn, Merlin, 1970, 110–48.
Lynch, Arthur. *Human Documents: Character-Sketches of Representative Men and Women of the Time*. London: Bertram Dobell, 1896.
Lynch, Deidre. *The Economy of Character: Novels, Market Culture, and the Business of Inner Meaning*. Chicago: University of Chicago Press, 1998.
Magee, Bryan. *The Philosophy of Schopenhauer*. New York: Oxford University Press, 1997.
Maitland, Frederic William, ed. *The Life and Letters of Leslie Stephen*. New York: Cambridge University Press, 2012.
Malabou, Catherine. "Addiction and Grace: Preface to Félix Ravaisson's *Of Habit*." In *Of Habit*, translated by Clare Carlisle and Mark Sinclair, viii–xx. London: Continuum, 2008.
———. *Plasticity at the Dusk of Writing: Dialectic, Destruction, Deconstruction*. Translated by Carolyn Shread. New York: Columbia University Press, 2009.
———. *What Should We Do with Our Brain?* Translated by Sebastian Rand. New York: Fordham University Press, 2008.
Marcuse, Herbert. *Eros and Civilization: A Philosophical Inquiry into Freud*. Boston: Beacon, 1974.
Marquard, Odo. "Das Fiktive als ens Realissimum." In *Funktionen des Fiktiven*, edited by Wolfgang Iser and Dieter Henrich, 489–95. Paderborn, Germany: Wilhelm Fink Verlag, 1983.
Martin, Carol A. "Revising *Middlemarch*." *Victorian Periodicals Review* 25, no. 2 (1992): 72–78.
Martin, Emily. *Flexible Bodies: Tracking Immunity in American Culture from the Days of Polio to the Age of AIDS*. Boston: Beacon, 1994.
Marx, Karl. *Differenz der Demokritischen und Epikureischen Naturphilosophie*. N.p.: Hofenberg, 1968.
———. *The Economic and Philosophic Manuscripts of 1844*. Translated by Martin Milligan. Moscow: Progress Publishers, 1974.
Maxwell, James Clerk. *The Scientific Papers of James Clerk Maxwell*. New York: Cambridge University Press, 2011.

McCarthy, Justin. *Donna Quixote*. London: Chatto & Windus, 1892.

McClintock, Anne. *Imperial Leather: Race, Gender, and Sexuality in the Colonial Contest*. Routledge, 1995.

McGann, Jerome J. "The Anachronism of George Crabbe." *ELH* 48, no. 3 (1981): 555–72.

McLaughlin, Brian. "The Rise and Fall of British Emergentism." In *Emergence or Reduction? Essays on the Prospects of Nonreductive Physicalism*, edited by Anskar Beckermann, 49–93. Berlin: De Gruyter, 1997.

McMillan, Uri. *Embodied Avatars: Genealogies of Black Feminist Art and Performance*. New York: NYU Press, 2015.

McNabb, John. *Dissent with Modification: Human Origins, Palaeolithic Archaeology and Evolutionary Anthropology in Britain 1859–1901*. Oxford: Archaeopress Archaeology, 2012.

Menke, Richard. "Fiction as Vivisection: G. H. Lewes and George Eliot." *ELH* 67, no. 2 (2000): 617–53.

Menon, Madhavi. *Indifference to Difference: On Queer Universalism*. Minneapolis: University of Minnesota Press, 2015.

Meredith, George. *Diana of the Crossways*. Detroit: Wayne State University Press, 2001.

Merrill, Lynn L. *The Romance of Victorian Natural History*. New York: Oxford University Press, 1989.

Mershon, Ella. "Ruskin's Dust." *Victorian Studies* 58, no. 3 (2016): 464–92.

Mill, John Stuart. *Autobiography*. In *The Collected Works of John Stuart Mill*, vol. 1, edited by John M. Robson and Jack Stillinger. Toronto: University of Toronto Press, 1981.

———. *An Examination of Sir William Hamilton's Philosophy and of the Principle Philosophical Questions Discussed in His Writings*. Vol. 9 of *The Collected Works of John Stuart Mill*, edited by John M. Robson and Jack Stillinger. Toronto: University of Toronto Press, 1979.

———. "On Liberty." In *The Collected Works of John Stuart Mill*, vol. 18, edited by John M. Robson and Jack Stillinger, 213–310. Toronto: University of Toronto Press, 1981.

———. "The Subjection of Women." In *The Collected Works of John Stuart Mill*, vol. 21, edited by John M. Robson and Jack Stillinger, 259–340. Toronto: University of Toronto Press, 1981.

———. *A System of Logic Ratiocinative and Inductive: Being a Connected View of the Principles of Evidence, and the Methods of Scientific Investigation*. Vol. 8 of *The Collected Works of John Stuart Mill*, edited by John M. Robson and Jack Stillinger. 1979. Reprint, Toronto: University of Toronto Press, 1981.

Miller, Andrew H. "Bruising, Laceration, and Lifelong Maiming; Or, How We Encourage Research." *ELH* 70, no. 1 (2003): 301–18.

———. *On Not Being Someone Else: Tales of Our Unled Lives*. Cambridge, MA: Harvard University Press, 2020.

Miller, D. A. *The Novel and the Police*. Berkeley: University of California Press, 1988.

Miller, J. Hillis. *Fiction and Repetition: Seven English Novels*. Cambridge, MA: Harvard University Press, 1985.

———. *The Form of Victorian Fiction: Thackeray, Dickens, Trollope, George Eliot, Meredith, and Hardy*. Notre Dame, IN: University of Notre Dame Press, 1970.
Miller, J. Reid. *Stain Removal: Ethics and Race*. New York: Oxford University Press, 2016.
Miller, Jane Eldridge. *Rebel Women: Feminism, Modernism and the Edwardian Novel*. Chicago: University of Chicago Press, 1994.
Millett, Paul. *Theophrastus and His World*. Cambridge: Cambridge University Press, 2007.
Millgate, Michael. *Thomas Hardy: A Biography Revisited*. New York: Oxford University Press, 2004.
Mohanty, Chandra Talpade. *Feminism without Borders: Decolonizing Theory, Practicing Solidarity*. Durham, NC: Duke University Press, 2003.
Moore, George. *Confessions of a Young Man*. London: Swan Sonnenschein, 1889.
———. *A Drama in Muslin: A Realistic Novel*. London: Vizetelly, 1886.
———. *Esther Waters*. Edited by David Skilton. Oxford: Oxford University Press, 1983.
———. *Mike Fletcher*. New York: Garland Publishing, 1977.
Morgan, Benjamin. *The Outward Mind: Materialist Aesthetics in Victorian Science and Literature*. Chicago: University of Chicago Press, 2017.
Morley, John. *On Compromise*. London: Chapman & Hall, 1874.
Morris, Charles. "The Matter of Space." *Nature* 27, no. 697 (1883): 349–51.
Morris, Desmond. "Foreword." In *The Courtship Habits of the Great Crested Grebe (Podiceps Cristatus): With an Addition to the Theory of Sexual Selection by Julian Huxley*, 6–14. London: Jonathan Cape, 1968.
Morton, Peter. *Vital Science: Biology and the Literary Imagination 1860–1900*. London: Unwin Hyman, 1984.
Morton, Timothy. *The Ecological Thought*. Cambridge, MA: Harvard University Press, 2012.
———. *Realist Magic: Objects, Ontology, Causality*. Ann Arbor, MI: Open Humanities Press, and imprint of MPublishing, 2013.
Moses, Omri. *Out of Character: Modernism, Vitalism, Psychic Life*. Stanford: Stanford University Press, 2014.
Müller-Wille, Staffan, and Hans-Jörg Rheinberger. "Heredity—the Formation of an Epistemic Space." In *Heredity Produced: At the Crossroads of Biology, Politics, and Culture, 1500–1870*, 3–34. Cambridge, MA: MIT Press, 2007.
Nancy, Jean-Luc. "Introduction." In *Who Comes after the Subject?* edited by Eduardo Cadava, Peter Connor, and Jean-Luc Nancy, 1–8. New York: Routledge, 1991.
Nature. Unsigned review of *Elementary Introduction to Physiological Science* (London: Jarrold and Sons, 1869). March 10, 1870.
Nelson, Charmaine A. *The Color of Stone: Sculpting the Black Female Subject in Nineteenth-Century America*. Minneapolis: University of Minnesota Press, 2007.
Newby, Diana. "Touching Life: Vitalism and the Victorian Novel." PhD diss. (in progress), Columbia University.
Newton, K. M. "George Eliot and Racism: How Should One Read 'The Modern Hep! Hep! Hep!'?" *Modern Language Review* 103, no. 3 (2008): 654–65.
Nichols, Shaun. *The Architecture of the Imagination: New Essays on Pretence, Possibility, and Fiction*. New York: Oxford University Press, 2006.

Nietzsche, Friedrich. "On Truth and Lies in a Non-moral Sense." In *The Nietzsche Reader*, edited by Keith Ansell-Pearson and Duncan Large, 114–23. Malden, MA: Wiley-Blackwell, 2006.

———. *The Twilight of the Idols and the Anti-Christ: Or, How to Philosophize with a Hammer*. Edited by Michael Tanner, translated by R. J. Hollingdale. London: Penguin, 1990.

Noble, James Ashcroft. "The Fiction of Sexuality." *Contemporary Review* 67, (1895): 490–98.

Nussbaum, Martha C. "Objectification." *Philosophy & Public Affairs* 24, no. 4 (1995): 249–91.

Nussbaum, Martha Craven. *Cultivating Humanity: A Classical Defense of Reform in Liberal Education*. Cambridge, MA: Harvard University Press, 1998.

———. *Subversion and Sympathy: Gender, Law, and the British Novel*. New York: Oxford University Press, 2013.

Nyhart, Lynn K. "Natural History and the 'New' Biology." In *Cultures of Natural History*, edited by N. Jardine, J. A. Secord, and E. C. Spary, 426–43. Cambridge: Cambridge University Press, 1996.

Offer, John. "Free Agent or 'Conscious Automaton'? Contrasting Interpretations of the Individual in Spencer's Writing on Social and Moral Life." *Sociological Review* 51, no. 1 (2003): 1–19.

Olby, R. C. "Francis Galton's Derivation of Mendelian Ratios in 1875." *Heredity* 20 (1965): 636–38.

Ong, Jade Munslow. *Olive Schreiner and African Modernism: Allegory, Empire and Postcolonial Writing*. New York: Routledge, 2017.

Oparin, Aleksandr Ivanovich. *The Chemical Origin of Life*. Springfield, IL: C. C. Thomas, 1964.

Oxenford, John. "Iconoclasm in German Philosophy." *Westminster Review* 59, (1853): 388–407.

Painter, Nell Irvin. *The History of White People*. New York: W. W. Norton, 2011.

Palmer, Alan. "Social Minds in Fiction and Criticism." *Style* 45, no. 2 (2011): 196–240.

———. *Social Minds in the Novel*. Columbus: Ohio State University Press, 2010.

Parrinder, Patrick. *Shadows of the Future: H. G. Wells, Science Fiction and Prophecy*. Liverpool: Liverpool University Press, 1995.

Parrinder, Patrick, and Andrzej Gasiorek, eds. *The Oxford History of the Novel in English: Volume 4: The Reinvention of the British and Irish Novel 1880-1940*. Oxford: Oxford University Press, 2011.

Pater, Walter. *Studies in the History of the Renaissance*. Edited by Matthew Beaumont. Oxford: Oxford University Press, 2010.

Pearl, Sharrona. *About Faces: Physiognomy in Nineteenth-Century Britain*. Cambridge, MA: Harvard University Press, 2010.

Pearson, Karl. *The Life, Letters and Labours of Francis Galton*. Cambridge: Cambridge University Press, 1914.

———. "Matter and Soul." In *The Ethic of Freethought and Other Addresses and Essays*, 21–44. London: Adam and Charles Black, 1901.

Peppis, Paul. "Thinking Race in the Avant Guerre: Typological Negotiations in Ford and Stein." *Yale Journal of Criticism* 10, no. 2 (1997): 371–95.

Philmus, Robert M. *Visions and Re-Visions: (Re)constructing Science Fiction*. Liverpool: Liverpool University Press, 2005.
Pierpont, Claudia Roth. *Passionate Minds: Women Rewriting the World*. New York: Vintage, 2001.
Plietzsch, Birgit. *The Novels of Thomas Hardy as a Product of Nineteenth Century Social, Economic, and Cultural Change*. Berlin: Tenea Verlag, 2004.
Powell, Betty. "Descartes' Machines." *Proceedings of the Aristotelian Society* 71 (1970): 209–22.
Puckett, Kent. "Stupid Sensations: Henry James, Good Form, and Reading *Middlemarch* without a Brain." *Henry James Review* 28, no. 3 (2007): 292–98.
Puig de la Bellacasa, Maria. *Matters of Care: Speculative Ethics in More than Human Worlds*. Minneapolis: University of Minnesota Press, 2017.
Purdy, Daniel. "The Whiteness of Beauty: Weimar Neo-Classicism and the Sculptural Transcendence of Color." *Amsterdamer Beiträge zur neueren Germanistik* 56, no. 1 (2004): 83–99.
Ravilious, C. P. "'Saints and Sinners': An Unidentified Olive Schreiner Manuscript." *Journal of Commonwealth Literature* 12, no. 1 (1977): 1–11.
Reich, Wilhelm. "The Impulsive Character." Translated by Barbara Goldenberg Koopman. *Journal of Orgonomy* 4, no. 1 (1970): 5–18.
Reill, Peter Hanns. *Vitalizing Nature in the Enlightenment*. Berkeley: University of California Press, 2005.
Rentoul, Robert Reid. *Race Culture, Race Suicide? (A Plea for the Unborn)*. New York: Walter Scott Publishing Company, 1906.
"Reviews: 'The Heavenly Twins,' by Sarah Grand." *Shafts*, February 1893, 268.
Richardson, Angelique. "The Eugenization of Love: Sarah Grand and the Morality of Genealogy." *Victorian Studies* 42, no. 2 (1999): 227–55.
———. *Love and Eugenics in the Late Nineteenth Century: Rational Reproduction and the New Woman*. New York: Oxford University Press, 2003.
———. "'Some Science Underlies All Art': The Dramatization of Sexual Selection and Racial Biology in Thomas Hardy's *A Pair of Blue Eyes* and *The Well-Beloved*." *Journal of Victorian Culture* 3, no. 2 (1998): 302–38.
Rigney, Daniel. *The Metaphorical Society: An Invitation to Social Theory*. Lanham, MD: Rowman & Littlefield, 2001.
Ritvo, Harriet. *The Platypus and the Mermaid and Other Figments of the Classifying Imagination*. Cambridge, MA: Harvard University Press, 1997.
Rosenberg, Jordana. "The Molecularization of Sexuality: On Some Primitivisms of the Present." *Theory & Event* 17, no. 2 (2014): n.p.
Rosenblum, Robert. *Transformations in Late Eighteenth Century Art*. Princeton, NJ: Princeton University Press, 1970.
Rothfield, Lawrence. *Vital Signs: Medical Realism in Nineteenth-Century Fiction*. Princeton, NJ: Princeton University Press, 1994.
Ruskin, John. "The Ethics of the Dust." In *The Library Edition of the Works of John Ruskin*, vol. 18, edited by E. T. Cook and Alexander Wedderburn. New York: Longmans, Green, 1905.
Russett, Cynthia Eagle. *Sexual Science: The Victorian Construction of Womanhood*. Cambridge, MA: Harvard University Press, 1991.

Ryan, Michael. "One Name of Many Shapes: *The Well-Beloved*." In *Critical Approaches to the Fiction of Thomas Hardy*, edited by Dale Kramer, 172–92. London: Palgrave Macmillan, 1979.

Rylance, Rick. *Victorian Psychology and British Culture 1850–1880*. Oxford: Oxford University Press, 2000.

Said, Edward W. *Culture and Imperialism*. New York: Vintage, 1994.

Sangiacomo, Andrea. "The Ontology of Determination: From Descartes to Spinoza." *Science in Context* 28, no. 4 (2015): 515–43.

Scarry, Elaine. "Work and the Body in Hardy and Other Nineteenth-Century Novelists." *Representations*, no. 3 (July 1983): 90–123.

Schaffer, Talia. *The Forgotten Female Aesthetes: Literary Culture in Late-Victorian England*. Charlottesville: University of Virginia Press, 2000.

Schopenhauer, Arthur. *The Art of Literature; a Series of Essays*. Translated by T. Bailey Saunders. London: S. Sonnenschein, 1891.

———. *Essays of Schopenhauer*. Translated by Mrs. Rudolf Dircks, London: Walter Scott Publishing Company, 1880.

———. *Parerga and Paralipomena: Short Philosophical Essays*, vol. 2. Translated by E. F. J. Payne. Oxford: Clarendon, 2001.

———. To David Asher, October 22, 1857. In *Gesammelte Briefe*, edited by Arthur Hübscher, n.p. Bonn: Bouvier, 1978.

———. To Ernst Lindner, April 27, 1853. In *Gesammelte Briefe*, edited by Arthur Hübscher, n.p. Bonn: Bouvier, 1978.

———. *The World as Will and Representation*. 2 vols. Translated by E. F. J. Payne. New York: Dover, 1969.

"Schopenhauer in English." *The Nation*, no. 1094 (1886): 510–11.

Schor, Naomi. *Breaking the Chain: Women, Theory, and French Realist Fiction*. New York: Columbia University Press, 1985.

Schreiner, Olive. *From Man to Man; or Perhaps Only*. Edited by Dorothy Driver. Cape Town: University of Cape Town Press, 2015.

———. *The Story of an African Farm*. Edited by Joseph Bristow. Oxford: Oxford University Press, 1992.

———. To Havelock Ellis, April 8, 1884. The Olive Schreiner Letters Project. *The Olive Schreiner Letters Online*. 2012. https://www.oliveschreiner.org/.

———. To Havelock Ellis, December 18, 1887. The Olive Schreiner Letters Project. *The Olive Schreiner Letters Online*. 2012. https://www.oliveschreiner.org/.

———. To Havelock Ellis, January 27, 1888. The Olive Schreiner Letters Project. *The Olive Schreiner Letters Online*. 2012. https://www.oliveschreiner.org/.

———. To Havelock Ellis, March 2, 1885. The Olive Schreiner Letters Project. *The Olive Schreiner Letters Online*. 2012. https://www.oliveschreiner.org/.

———. To Havelock Ellis, May 14, 1886. The Olive Schreiner Letters Project. *The Olive Schreiner Letters Online*. 2012. https://www.oliveschreiner.org/.

———. To Havelock Ellis, June 30, 1912. The Olive Schreiner Letters Project. *The Olive Schreiner Letters Online*. 2012. https://www.oliveschreiner.org/.

———. To Isaline Philpot, March 1886. The Olive Schreiner Letters Project. *The Olive Schreiner Letters Online*. 2012. https://www.oliveschreiner.org/.

———. To Jan Smuts, October 19, 1920. The Olive Schreiner Letters Project. *The Olive Schreiner Letters Online*. 2012. https://www.oliveschreiner.org/.

———. To Karl Pearson, July 3, 1886. The Olive Schreiner Letters Project. *The Olive Schreiner Letters Online*. 2012. https://www.oliveschreiner.org/.

———. To Karl Pearson, August 7, 1886. The Olive Schreiner Letters Project. *The Olive Schreiner Letters Online*. 2012. https://www.oliveschreiner.org/.

———. To Philip Kent, May 12, 1883. The Olive Schreiner Letters Project. *The Olive Schreiner Letters Online*. 2012. https://www.oliveschreiner.org/.

———. To William Schreiner, June 4, 1908. The Olive Schreiner Letters Project. *The Olive Schreiner Letters Online*. 2012. https://www.oliveschreiner.org/.

———. *Woman and Labour*. Cambridge: Cambridge University Press, 2013.

Schreiner, Olive, and Samuel Cronwright-Schreiner. *The Political Situation*. London: T. Fisher Unwin, 1896.

Schuller, Kyla. *The Biopolitics of Feeling: Race, Sex, and Science in the Nineteenth Century*. Durham, NC: Duke University Press, 2017.

Schurig, Volker. "Der Ideengeschichtliche Ursprung des Wissenschaftsbegriffs 'Ethologie' in der Antike." *Philosophia Naturalis* 20, no. 4 (1983): 435–52.

Schwarz, Daniel R. *Reading the Modern British and Irish Novel 1890–1930*. Malden, MA: Wiley-Blackwell, 2004.

Scott, Sir Walter. *Lives of Eminent Novelists and Dramatists*. London: F. Warne, 1887.

Secord, James A. *Victorian Sensation: The Extraordinary Publication, Reception, and Secret Authorship of Vestiges of the Natural History of Creation*. Chicago: University of Chicago Press, 2001.

Sedgwick, Eve Kosofsky. "Paranoid Reading and Reparative Reading, or, You're So Paranoid, You Probably Think This Essay Is about You." In *Touching Feeling: Affect, Pedagogy, Performativity*, 123–51. Durham, NC: Duke University Press, 2003.

Seneca, Lucius Annaeus. *Ad Lucilium Epistulae Morales*, vol. 3. Translated by Richard Mott Gummere. London: W. Heinemann, 1917.

Senghor, Léopold Sédar. "Negritude: A Humanism of the Twentieth Century." In *Colonial Discourse and Post-Colonial Theory: A Reader*, edited by Patrick Williams and Laura Chrisman, 27–35. New York: Columbia University Press, 1994.

Sexton, Jared. *Amalgamation Schemes: Antiblackness and the Critique of Multiracialism*. Minneapolis: University of Minnesota Press, 2008.

Sha, Richard C. *The Visual and Verbal Sketch in British Romanticism*. Philadelphia: University of Pennsylvania Press, 1998.

Shand, Alexander F. "Character and the Emotions." *Mind* 5, no. 18 (1896): 203–26.

———. *The Foundations of Character: Being a Study of the Tendencies of the Emotions and Sentiments*. London: Macmillan, 1914.

Shanley, Mary Lyndon. *Feminism, Marriage, and the Law in Victorian England*. Princeton, NJ: Princeton University Press, 1993.

Sharp, Hasana. *Spinoza and the Politics of Renaturalization*. Chicago: University of Chicago Press, 2011.

Sharples, Robert. *Theophrastus of Eresus: Sources for His Life, Writings Thought, and Influence*. Boston: Brill, 1995.

Showalter, Elaine. "The Greening of Sister George." *Nineteenth-Century Fiction* 35, no. 3 (1980): 292–311.

———. *A Literature of Their Own: British Women Novelists from Brontë to Lessing*. Princeton, NJ: Princeton University Press, 1999.

Shuttleworth, Sally. *George Eliot and Nineteenth-Century Science: The Make-Believe of a Beginning*. New York: Cambridge University Press, 1984.

Siegel, Jonah. *Desire and Excess: The Nineteenth-Century Culture of Art*. Princeton, NJ: Princeton University Press, 2000.

Silver, Sean. "The Emergence of Texture." *Journal of the History of Ideas* 81, no. 2 (2020): 169–94.

Simondon, Gilbert. "The Genesis of the Individual." In *Incorporations*, edited by Jonathan Crary and Sanford Kwinter. Translated by Mark Cohen and Stanford Kwinter, 297–319. New York: Zone Books, 1992.

Singer, Charles. "Biology." In *The Legacy of Greece*, edited by R. W. Livingstone, 163–200. Oxford: Clarendon, 1921.

Sloan, Phillip. "The Gaze of Natural History." In *Inventing Human Science: Eighteenth-Century Domains*, edited by Christopher Fox, Roy Porter, and Robert Wokler, 112–51. Berkeley: University of California Press, 1995.

Smailbegović, Ada. "From Code to Shape: Material-Semiotic Imbrications in the 'Particle Zoo' of Molecular Poetics." *Differences* 29, no. 1 (2018): 134–72.

———. *Poetics of Liveliness: Molecules, Fibers, Tissues, Clouds*. New York: Columbia University Press, 2021.

Spencer, Herbert. *The Principles of Psychology*. London: Longman, Brown, Green and Longmans, 1855.

Spillers, Hortense J. "Mama's Baby, Papa's Maybe: An American Grammar Book." *Diacritics* 17, no. 2 (1987): 65–81.

Spinoza, Benedictus de. *Spinoza's Ethics*. Edited by Clare Carlisle, translated by George Eliot. Princeton, NJ: Princeton University Press, 2020.

Spitzer, Jan, Gary J. Pielak, and Bert Poolman. "Emergence of Life: Physical Chemistry Changes the Paradigm." *Biology Direct* 10, no. 1 (2015): n.p.

Spivak, Gayatri Chakravorty. "Righting Wrongs." *South Atlantic Quarterly* 103, no. 2 (2004): 523–81.

———. "Three Women's Texts and a Critique of Imperialism." *Critical Inquiry* 12, no. 1 (1985): 243–61.

Stanley, Liz. *Imperialism, Labour and the New Woman: Olive Schreiner's Social Theory*. Abingdon, UK: Routledge, 2002.

Star, Summer J. "Feeling Real in *Middlemarch*." *ELH* 80, no. 3 (2013): 839–69.

Stauffer, Robert C. "Haeckel, Darwin, and Ecology." *Quarterly Review of Biology* 32, no. 2 (1957): 138–44.

Stead, W. T. "The Novel of the Modern Woman." *Review of Reviews* 10 (July 1894): 64–74.

Stein, Gertrude. "Cultivated Motor Automatism; A Study of Character in Its Relation to Attention." *Psychological Review* 5, no. 3 (1898): 295–306.

———. *The Making of Americans: Being a History of a Family's Progress*. Normal, IN: Dalkey Archive Press, 1995.

———. "Portraits and Repetition." In *Lectures in America*, 165–206. New York: Random House, 1935.

———. "A Transatlantic Interview." In *A Primer for the Gradual Understanding of Gertrude Stein*, edited by Robert Bartlett Haas, 11–35. Los Angeles: Black Sparrow, 1975.

Steinlight, Emily. *Populating the Novel: Literary Form and the Politics of Surplus Life*. Ithaca, NY: Cornell University Press, 2018.
Stengers, Isabelle, Brian Massumi, and Erin Manning. "History through the Middle: Between Macro and Mesopolitics." *Inflexions: A Journal for Research Creation*, November 2008. http://www.inflexions.org/n3_History-through-the-Middle-Between-Macro-and-Mesopolitics-1.pdf.
Stepan, Nancy. *The Idea of Race in Science: Great Britain, 1800–1960*. Hamden, CT: Archon Books, 1982.
Stewart, Maaja A. *Domestic Realities and Imperial Fictions: Jane Austen's Novels in Eighteenth-Century Contexts*. Athens: University of Georgia Press, 1993.
Stocking, George W. *After Tylor: British Social Anthropology, 1888–1951*. Madison: University of Wisconsin Press, 1998.
———. *Victorian Anthropology*. New York: Free Press, 1991.
Strauss, David Friedrich. *The Life of Jesus*. London: Williams and Norgate, 1879.
Stubbs, Patricia. *Women and Fiction: Feminism and the Novel, 1880–1920*. London: Methuen, 1981.
Sully, James. "The Aesthetics of Human Character." *Fortnightly Review* 9 (April 1871): 505–20.
———. "George Eliot's Art." *Mind* 6, no. 23 (1881): 378–94.
———. *Pessimism: A History and a Criticism*. London: Henry S. King, 1877.
———. *Sensation and Intuition: Studies in Psychology and Aesthetics*. London: Henry S. King, 1874.
———. *Studies of Childhood*. New York: D. Appleton, 1895.
Sydow, Momme von. *From Darwinian Metaphysics towards Understanding the Evolution of Evolutionary Mechanisms: A Historical and Philosophical Analysis of Gene-Darwinism and Universal Darwinism*. Universitätsverlag Göttingen, 2012.
"Table Talk." *Literary World*, March 1894, 269–71.
Tambling, Jeremy. "*Middlemarch*, Realism and the Birth of the Clinic." *ELH* 57, no. 4 (1990): 939–60.
Taylor, Barbara. *Eve and the New Jerusalem: Socialism and Feminism in the Nineteenth Century*. Cambridge, MA: Harvard University Press, 1993.
Taylor, Dennis. "*Jude the Obscure* and English National Identity: The Religious Striations of Wessex." In *A Companion to Thomas Hardy*, edited by Keith Wilsonessor, 345–63. Malden, MA: Wiley-Blackwell, 2009.
Thomas, David Wayne. *Cultivating Victorians: Liberal Culture and the Aesthetic*. Philadelphia: University of Pennsylvania Press, 2004.
Thomas, Jane. "Thomas Hardy, Thomas Woolner and *The Well-Beloved*: An Aesthetic Debate." *Thomas Hardy Journal* 20, no. 3 (October 2004): 132–38.
Thompson, Scott. "Between Metaphysics and Physiology: Lewes's Facultative Action and Eliot's Realism of Failure." *George Eliot–George Henry Lewes Studies* 71, no. 2 (2019): 125–42.
Todhunter, Maurice. "Arthur Schopenhauer." *Westminster Review*, April 1895, 364–78.
Toepfer, Georg. "Ethologie." In *Historisches Wörterbuch der Biologie: Geschichte und Theorie der Biologischen Grundbegriffe*, vol. 2, 461–80. Stuttgart, Germany: J. B. Metzler, 2011.

———. "Wissenschaft." In *Wörter aus der Fremde: Begriffsgeschichte als Übersetzungsgeschichte*, edited by Georg Toepfer and Falko Schmieder, 299–308. Berlin: Kadmos, 2018.

Tomkins, Silvan. *Affect Imagery Consciousness*. New York: Springer, 2008.

Tondre, Michael. *The Physics of Possibility: Victorian Fiction, Science, and Gender*. Chartlottesville: University of Virginia Press, 2018.

Tong, Rosemarie. *Feminine and Feminist Ethics*. Belmont, CA: Wadsworth, 1993.

Tucker, Irene. "Before Racial Construction." In *Theory Aside*, edited by Jason Potts and Daniel Stout, 143–59. Durham, NC: Duke University Press, 2014.

———. *The Moment of Racial Sight: A History*. Chicago: University of Chicago Press, 2012.

Tyndall, John. *Address Delivered before the British Association Assembled at Belfast, with Additions*. London: Longmans, Green, 1883.

———. "Scientific Limit of the Imagination." In *Essays on the Use and Limit of the Imagination in Science*, 52–65. London: Longmans, Green, 1870.

van der Vlies, Andrew. "The Editorial Empire: The Fiction of 'Greater Britain,' and the Early Readers of Olive Schreiner's *The Story of an African Farm*." *Text* 15, (2003): 237–60.

Vermeule, Blakey. *Why Do We Care about Literary Characters?* Baltimore: Johns Hopkins University Press, 2009.

Verwey, Jan. "Die Paarungsbiologie des Fischreihers." *Zoologische Jahrbücher* 48, (1930): 1–120.

Vrettos, Athena. "Defining Habits: Dickens and the Psychology of Repetition." *Victorian Studies* 42, no. 3 (2000): 399–426.

Walters, Alisha R. "Affective Hybridities: Dinah Mulock Craik's Olive and British Heterogeneity." *Women's Writing* 20, no. 3 (2013): 325–43.

Walton, Kendall L. *Mimesis as Make-Believe: On the Foundations of the Representational Arts*. Cambridge, MA: Harvard University Press, 1990.

Ward, Megan. *Seeming Human: Artificial Intelligence and Victorian Realist Character*. Columbus: Ohio State University Press, 2018.

Watt, Ian. *The Rise of the Novel: Studies in Defoe, Richardson and Fielding*. Berkeley: University of California Press, 2001. First published 1957 by Chatto and Windus (London).

Waugh, Arthur. "Reticence in Literature." *The Yellow Book* 1 (April 1894): 201–19.

Weheliye, Alexander G. *Habeas Viscus: Racializing Assemblages, Biopolitics, and Black Feminist Theories of the Human*. Durham, NC: Duke University Press, 2014.

Weismann, August. *Essays upon Heredity and Kindred Biological Problems*. Edited by Edward B. Poulton, S. Schönland, and A. E. Shipley. 2 vols. Oxford: Clarendon, 1889.

Wheeler, William Morton. "'Natural History,' 'Œcology,' or 'Ethology'?" *Science* 15, no. 390 (June 1902): 971–76.

Whewell, William. *The Philosophy of the Inductive Sciences: Founded upon Their History*. London: J. W. Parker, 1840.

Whipple, Edwin Percy. *Character and Characteristic Men*. Ticknor and Fields, 1866.

White, Hayden. *Metahistory: The Historical Imagination in Nineteenth-Century Europe*. Baltimore: Johns Hopkins University Press, 1973.

White, Leslie. "Browning's Vitalist Beginnings." *Browning Institute Studies* 15 (1987): 91–103.
Whitehead, Alfred North. *The Concept of Nature*. Cambridge: Cambridge University Press, 1920.
Woloch, Alex. *The One vs. the Many: Minor Characters and the Space of the Protagonist in the Novel*. Princeton, NJ: Princeton University Press, 2003.
Woolf, Virginia. *Congenial Spirits: The Selected Letters of Virginia Woolf*. Mariner Books, 1991.
———. "Modern Fiction." In *The Essays of Virginia Woolf: 1925–1928*, vol. 4, edited by Andrew McNeillie, 157–65. New York: Harcourt Brace Jovanovich, 1986.
———. *Mr. Bennett and Mrs. Brown*. London: Hogarth Press, 1924.
———. *A Room of One's Own*. Edited by Mark Hussey. New York: Mariner Books, 2005.
Wormald, Mark. "Microscopy and Semiotic in *Middlemarch*." *Nineteenth-Century Literature* 50, no. 4, (1996): 501–24.
Wright, Daniel. "George Eliot's Vagueness." *Victorian Studies* 56, no. 4 (2014): 625–48.
———. "Thomas Hardy's Groundwork." *PMLA* 134, no. 5 (2019): 1028–41.
Young, Julian. *Schopenhauer*. New York: Routledge, 2005.
Young, Kay. *Imagining Minds: The Neuro-Aesthetics of Austen, Eliot, and Hardy*. Columbus: Ohio State University Press, 2010.
Young, Robert. *Colonial Desire: Hybridity in Theory, Culture, and Race*. New York: Routledge, 1995.
Youngkin, Molly. *Feminist Realism at the Fin de Siècle: The Influence of the Late-Victorian Woman's Press on the Development of the Novel*. Columbus: Ohio State University Press, 2007.
Zhang, Dora. *Strange Likeness: Description and the Modernist Novel*. Chicago: University of Chicago Press, 2020.
Zimmern, Helen. *Arthur Schopenhauer: His Life and Philosophy*. London: Longmans, Green, 1876.
Zola, Émile. "The Experimental Novel." In *The Nineteenth-Century Novel: A Critical Reader*, edited by Stephen Regan, 104–17. Abingdon, UK: Routledge, 2001.
———. *Thérèse Raquin*. Oxford: Oxford University Press, 1867.

Index

Page numbers for illustrations are in italics, and for notes in the format 14n24. Titles of works are listed under the author's name.

abiogenesis, 234–35
accretion, 105, 109, 129, 131, 133–37
action, 161, 163–64, 168; interaction, 16–17, 18n29, 236
Adamson, Robert, 156–57, 171, 173
aesthetics: nonhuman experience of, 208; and pleasure, 205
affect, 14n24, 28, 53–54, 85, 92, 205–6. *See also* feeling
agency, 18–19; vs. circumstance, 158–59; critique of, 150–51, 167; limitations of, 149, 156; moral, 15–16, 157–58; nonhuman, 17; perceived failures of, 147; relational, 215–16; of women, 33–34, 146, 147–48. *See also* autonomy
Ahmed, Sara, 46
Anderson, Amanda, 147–48, 161–63, 205
animals, 244n21; behaviour, study of, 187–88; care, performed by, 191–92; character of, 199; ethology of, 198–200; frogs, 225, 228–29, 237–39; *Vorticellae* (single-cell organisms), 86–87
anthropocentrism, 99–100
appearance, 74, 127, 177, 221, 223–24; physical, 17, 37, 43, 62, 80, 113, 131. *See also* surfaces; whiteness
Ardis, Ann L., 168–69
Armstrong, Nancy, 221–22

Arnold, Matthew, 6
arrangement, 95
art, visual, 112–13, 204–5
Asher, David, 171, 173
Ashton, Rosemary, 233
atoms, 38n60, 60, 67, 68–69, 211–13
Atwell, John, 160–61
Auerbach, Erich, 227
Austen, Jane, 222n2
automata, 98–99, 157–58
autonomy, 45, 60, 84, 196–97; vs. circumstance, 15–16, 158–59. *See also* agency

Bachofen, J. J., 166
Bain, Alexander, 2n3
Bakhtin, Mikhail, 4, 4n5
Bal, Mieke, 9–10
Balzac, Honoré de, 226
Barad, Karen, 8, 48n7, 215–16, 236
Baucom, Ian, 136, 137
Beer, Gillian, 97, 130
behavior: human and nonhuman, 85–86, 187–88; and relationality, 199
Belgravia (journal), 151
Bender, John, 64–65, 66
Benthien, Claudia, 119n19
Berkman, Joyce Avrech, 194–95

Bertz, Eduard, 174
Bichat, Xavier, 57
bifurcation: of character, 16; gendered, 148, 179; of nature, 163, 192–93; subject/object, 148
bildungsroman, 4, 34, 129–30, 217, 218
binaries, 46, 227; destabilization of, 149, 162–63; gender, 163, 179; human-nonhuman, 157, 192–93; narratological, 83; racial, 126–27; vital-mechanistic, 38, 227–29, 232, 233–34, 237
biological science, 57–59, 85, 113–14; abiogenesis, 234–35; biogenesis, 234; cell theory, 58, 111, 114, 122–23; ethology in, 187–88, 198; primordial soup theory, 235; spontaneous generation controversy, 231–33, 235. *See also* hereditary science
blackness, 127
Blackwood, John, 238
Blanc, Charles, 102
Bland, Lucy, 165
blood, 114
body: as aesthetic object, 17; biological structures of, 57–59; blood, 114; boundaries of, 43; brain, 51; and circumstance, 2; description of, 140–41; feminized, 37; impressibility of, 80–81, 88–89, 133; knowledge, production through, 200–201; as machine, 157–58; materiality of, 16–17; and milieu, 123, 137–38; and mind, 157–58; mutability of, 105; New Realist engagement with, 144–45; as object, 20–21; and perception, 101–2; plasticity of, 51, 57–59; and reality, 144–46; sameness of, 120, 121, 141; social, 196–97; as states of matter, 43–44; surfaces of, 105–7, 120–21; and will, 20. *See also* embodiment; plasm; skin
Bohr, Niels, 215
Bownas, Janet, 138
Bradbury, Malcolm, 226
brain, 51
Bright, Mary. *See* Egerton, George

Brilmyer, S. Pearl, 64–65, 66, 136n33, 153n11, 163n16
Brody, Jennifer DeVere, 127
Brody, Selma B., 62n27
Brooks, Peter, 221
Brown, Bill, 24n39
Brown, Robert, 38, 48–49, 69–70, 235–36
Brownian motion, theory of, 69–70
Bryant, Levi, 192n17
Buffon, Comte de (Leclerc, George-Louis), 97
Bullen, J. B., 103, 111, 112
Burton, Antoinette, 136–37
Butler, Josephine, 147n2

Caird, Mona, 148, 165n19, 166n21
— *The Great Wave*, 148n3, 166
— "Marriage," 165–66
— *The Stones of Sacrifice*, 148n3, 166
Cairnes, John Elliott, 99
Canguilhem, Georges, 19n30
care, 183n4, 184, 188–92; ethics of, 189–90; ethology of, 199–200; and femininity, 191; in nature, 191–92, 194
caricature, 177, 223–24
Carpenter, William: "The Physiology of the Will," 19, 157–58; *The Principles of Mental Physiology*, 158n13
Casaubon, Isaac, 89
categorization, 71
causality, 66–67, 68
cell theory, 58, 111, 114, 122–23
chance, 233
change: of character, 51–53; formal, 55–56; through milieu, 106–7; possibilities of, 73–74, 105; of surfaces, 106. *See also* continuity
changes, in appearance, 177
character, 21; as aesthetic object, 11; bifurcation of, 16; commonality of, 37–38; constructed quality of, 10–11; definitions of, 14–15; empirical vs. intelligible, 160–61; flatness, 23–24, 89n20, 220, 222–24, 227, 240; heredity of, 17, 124–25; hierarchies of, 240–41; impressibility of, 76–77; inequalities

of, 240–41; "inward turn" of, 222–23; malleability of, 19–20; as material structure, 71–72; mutability of, 51–53; national, 15n25, 18; nonhuman, 6, 21, 199; perception, obstructed by, 81–82; physics of, 45–46, 55, 59; and realism, 5, 9–10, 177–78; roundness, 89, 220, 221–24, 223–24; science of development of (ethology), 1–3; as states of matter, 43–44; and subjectivity, 10, 12, 16; theorization of, 13; types, 12–13, 71, 79, 89n20, 90–92, 91; unrealized, 36; of women, 4n6. *See also* circumstance; depth; ethology; materialism, dynamic; milieu; relationality; volition

Cheng, Anne Anlin, 117, 121n21

Christianity, 203–4, 210–11, 232n8, 233

Christoff, Alicia Mireles, 141–42

circumstance, 2–3, 19n30, 74; vs. autonomy, 15–16, 158–59; and character, dualism of, 13–14, 35, 92; character as, 4–5, 149; overwhelming nature of, 33. *See also* milieu

circumstantiality, 39, 40–41, 58, 109, 128, 149, 166–67

civilization, 165, 168n23, 190n15, 193, 196–97

Cixous, Hélène, 146n1

classification, 71, 85, 95, 228

clay, 116

Clifford, William Kingdon, 77

Coleman, Piers, 67

Coleridge, Samuel Taylor, 56n17

collection, 95

colonialism, 136, 138, 185–86, 189–90, 194, 196–97

color, 113–17; vs. form, 113–14; lack of, 115–16, 140–41, 142–43; and sexuality, 172; skin, 106–8, 118–20, 121n21. *See also* whiteness

communication, 98–99, 100

competition, 163, 182, 184, 189–92, 203

complexity, 23, 221

consciousness, 25–26, 32, 98–99, 150

contagion, moral, 53–54

container (ontological metaphor), 113, 114

contingency, 3, 39

continuity: of character, 59, 90, 108, 132–33, 240; genetic, 122–25; historical, 226; racial, 109, 128, 137

Coombs, David Sweeney, 23, 24n37

cooperation, 182, 189, 190–91

Coriale, Danielle, 86

cosmology, 209–10

Courtney, W. L., 202–3

Cowan, Ruth, 124

Crabbe, George, 104–5

Craik, Dinah Mulock, 136n34

Crary, Jonathan, 28, 84, 170

Crenshaw, Kimberlé, 186n9

critical distance, 205, 206–7, 208

Cronwright-Schreiner, Samuel, 181, 190n15

Crookes, William, 16–17

crystallization, 62–63, 160, 213; metaphors of, 34, 73–74; of opinion, 103, 104

culture, 47, 205; and race, 118, 127, 139; relational, 192, 193, 197; of science, 6–7

Darwin, Charles, 111, 201, 242n20; on heredity, 114n15, 125–27; on milieu, 19n30, 162; on origins of life, 234–35; pangenesis theory, 125; plot, source of, 97; reinterpretation of, 163; and Schopenhauer, 171–73; and social Darwinism, 190n15; on speciation, 131–32
— *The Descent of Man*, 17–19, 172–73, 190n15
— *The Origin of Species*, 129, 131–33, 197, 198n23

Darwinism, 109; social, 32, 172, 182, 190, 203

Daston, Lorraine, 27, 192

Davis, Thomas S., 227n5

deduction, 12–13, 14, 96

definiteness, 60–61, 221, 236; lack of, 33, 44, 50–51, 71

degeneration, 118, 127

de la Rive, Arthur Auguste, 61

Deleuze, Gilles, 53–54, 55n14, 212n31

dematerialization, 121
depth: appearance of, 223-24; limitations of, 23; vs. mechanicity, 233; and roundness, 221-22; and surface, 90, 138; vs. vitality, 225, 227-28
Descartes, René, 157
description: and critique, 183-84; detail in, 97, 104-5, 205; ethics of, 189, 201-9; generic, 140-41; and human objecthood, 77-78; impressions, created by, 93-95; materialist, 231; nature of character, revealed by, 67-68; from observation, 79-80, 201-2, 204-5; problems of, 80-81; process of, 63-64; in realism, 87-88, 105; systems of, 85-86; of thought processes, 208. *See also* theory, weak
Despret, Vinciane, 199-200, 207
detail: in description, 97, 104-5, 205; as evidence, 221; and generalization, 71-73; in poetry, 104-5
determination, 18-19, 168
determinism, 147-48, 149-50, 156, 157, 161, 167
diary writing, 201-3, 217
Dickens, Charles, 223-25, 228-29, 232-34, 238
— *David Copperfield*, 223-24
— *Our Mutual Friend*, 238n16
difference, 17-19, 123-24, 129, 131, 196, 229; biological, 114-15; and form, 55-56; interdependence, challenged by, 194-95, 196; racial, 109, 115-17, 118-20
diffusion, 69-70, 208-9
Dircks, Mrs. Rudolf, 153n11, 170
disease, 53
disembodiment, 27
distance, critical, 205, 206-7, 208
diversity, 17-19
Dolin, Tim, 95n28, 112n11
Douglass, Frederick, 106-7
dualism, 157
Du Bois, W. E. B., 195
Dubow, Saul, 190n15
Duncan, Ian, 32, 33, 59n23
Durant, John R., 187, 198n25, 199

dynamic materialism, 16-17, 32-33, 218, 225-26, 230-31, 236-37; in Eliot, 46-47, 51-53; in Hardy, 139
dynamism, 16-17, 32-33, 107-8, 188n12

ecology and ecological theory, 194-95, 197-98
Egerton, George, *Keynotes*, 149, 165
Eliot, George, 5, 6, 167, 230; Feuerbach, influence of, 26n43; Feuerbach, translation of, 25, 174; form, concept of, 55-57, 105-6, 243-44; on Schopenhauer, 153; and Schreiner, 204-6; scientific reading of, 52, 61; sketch form, use of, 23, 76, 77-79, 90-92; Spinoza, translation of, 56
— *Adam Bede*, 88n16
— *Daniel Deronda*, 27, 80-81, 101
— "How I Came to Write Fiction," 88
— *Impressions of Theophrastus Such*, 23, 76-86, 89-92, 98-102, 201-2, 243; the body in, 80-81; narratology of, 83-85; the nonhuman in, 82-83, 98-102; publication of, 93, 100; "The Modern Hep! Hep! Hep!," 100-101; "Shadows of the Coming Race," 98-99, 100-101; "So Young!," 90; "Touchwood," 92
— *The Lifted Veil*, 75n1
— *Middlemarch*, 42-74; determinism in, 167; diffusion in, 69-70, 208-9; generalization vs. detail i, 71-72; interconnectivity in, 197-98; nonhuman entities in, 86-87; on origins of life, 235-36; plasticity in, 36-37, 45-49; publication history, 237, 239; reading in, 206; sensation in, 75-76; solidity/fluidity in, 60; structure in, 56-57; vitality in, 32, 233-34
— *Middlemarch*, characterization in: dynamic materialist, 46-47, 51-53; emergentist, 68-69; glutinous, 50-51; mesoscopic, 72-73; physics of, 45-46, 55, 59
— *Middlemarch*, characters in: Arthur Brooke, 50-51, 62; Nicholas Bulstrode, 53-54; Edward Casaubon, 56, 61-62,

89n18; Dorothea, 61–63, 69–70, 75, 206, 240–41; Tertius Lydgate, 49, 53–54, 56–58; Joshua Rigg, 237–40, 241; Walter Vincy, 50–51
— *The Mill on the Floss*, 167n22
— "The Natural History of German Life," 94, 96, 204
— "Notes on Form in Art," 55–56, 74
— *Romola*, 206
elitism, 193–94
Ellis, Henry Havelock, 169n24, 180–81, 189–90, 201
embodiment, 7, 21, 22; disembodiment, 27; of narrators, 83–84; negation of, 101–2; and reading, 206; Schopenhauer's philosophy of, 154–55; and thought, 207–8. *See also* body
emergentism, 45, 66–69, 236–37
emotion, 14n24, 28, 53–54, 85, 92, 205–6. *See also* feeling
Englishness, 118, 128, 136–39, 141–42
environment. *See* milieu
equality: of character, 240–41; racial, 196–97; social, 193–94. *See also* feminism
essentialism, 8n11, 80, 119–20, 147, 163, 168
Esty, Jed, 36n57, 217–18
ethics: and affect, 53–54; of care, 189–90; of description, 189, 201–9; and emotion, 53–54; of ethology, 200–201; of force, 189, 209–19; of literary representation, 23–24; of nature, 188–201
ethology, 54–55, 198–99; animal, 198–200; animals, 188; biological, 187–88; care-based, 199–200; ethics of, 200–201; intersectional, 186–87; J. S. Mill's theory of, 1–3, 13–14, 54–55, 187, 188; milieu in, 188, 216; of realism, 183, 184, 202–3, 216–17
eugenics, 15–16, 18, 109, 118–19, 124–28, 182
Evans, Mary Ann. *See* Eliot, George
evolution, theories of, 131–32, 171–72, 190–91
exteriority, 37, 90, 154–55

Fanon, Frantz, 26–27, 120, 121n21, 196n21
Faraday, Michael, 16, 60–61
Farina, Jonathan, 21
Farley, John, 235
feeling, 144–45, 154–55, 155–56, 233; Logic of (Lewes), 81, 93–94, 102, 108, 120, 178–79, 233–35. *See also* emotion
femininity: action, aligned with, 163–64; and care, 191; idealized, 110–11, 112; and materiality, 33–34; repression of, 167; value of, 167; whiteness of, 35, 112
feminism, 165–67, 179, 182–87; criticism by, 146–47; intersectional, 186–87; and natural sciences, 191–93; objectification, critique of, 25; and realism, 32–33, 144–46; scientific, 191–93; separatist, 215. *See also* New Woman novels
Feuerbach, Ludwig von, 25, 26n43, 173–74
fiction, 11–13; definitions of, 9; morality, challenges to, 103; philosophical discourse within, 182–83; structure of, 56–57, 139–40; teleology in, 4, 34, 129–30, 217, 218. *See also* metaphor; New Woman novels; novel, as genre; novel, New Woman; novel, realist; sketch form
field theory, 60–61, 189, 209–10
Figlerowicz, Marta, 23–24, 227, 241n19
figures (Haraway), 44
film, 241–42
First, Ruth, 218
Fisher, Philip, 52
fixity, 230
flatness, 23–24, 89n20, 220, 222–24, 227, 240
Fletcher, Brad, 226
fluids/fluidity, 51, 60, 61, 69–70, 72–73, 230
Fong, Ryan D., 186n8
force: of determination, 18–19; ethics of, 189, 209–19; human governance of, 157–58; interconnecting, 31–32; involuntary, 32; life, 114–16, 205–6, 231–37; and matter, 213–14; objects as concatenations of, 212–13; physical, 16; of Will (Schopenhauer), 148–49; women as, 151–52

form, 55–57, 105–6; vs. color, 113–14; emergence of, 243–44; ideal, 112–13; organic, 56n17; of solids, 61–62. *See also* novel, as genre; sketch form
formlessness, 33
Forster, E. M., 89n20, 229
— *Aspects of the Novel*, 220–25
— *A Passage to India*, 227
Frederickson, Kathleen, 164, 166
Freedgood, Elaine, 8n10, 52, 69, 137
Freeman, Edward Augustus, 128
Freud, Sigmund, 168, 173

Galison, Peter, 27
Gallagher, Catherine, 12–13, 14, 42, 71
Galton, Francis, 15–16, 17, 111, 124–28, *126*, 135
Garcha, Amanpal, 87, 88
Gaskell, Elizabeth, *Ruth*, 4
Geison, Gerald L., 58n22, 114n15, 125n27
gender, 30–31; bifurcation, 148, 179; binaries, 163, 179; and character formation, 162; essentialist models of, 147; inequalities, 182, 184–87; transitions, 178–79. *See also* femininity; masculinity
generalization: and detail, 71–73; by fiction, 13
Geoffroy Saint-Hilaire, Isidore, 2n2, 187, 198
geology, 109, 117, 131–35, *134*, *135*, 137, 204
geometry, 62–64, *64*
germ plasm (*Keimplasma*), 111, 122, 123n24–25
Giard, Alfred, 198n24
Gilbert, Sandra, 146n1
Gissing, George, 148
— *The Unclassed*, 148n3, 149, 174–76
— *Workers in the Dawn*, 148n3
Glissant, Édouard, 196, 197
gluten, 50–51
God, 203–4, 210–11, 232n8, 233
Gosse, Edmund, 139–40
grains, 50–51
Grand, Sarah, 30
— *The Beth Book*, 148n3
— *The Heavenly Twins*, 144–45, 149, 177–79

— *Ideala*, 34–35
— "The New Aspect of the Woman Question," 166–67
— *Our Manifold Nature*, 145–46
Greiner, Rae, 83
Griffin, Cristina Richieri, 83–84
Griffiths, Devin, 194, 197–98
Grosz, Elizabeth, 9, 48n7, 163, 172n29
ground, 107, 115–17, 121–22, 127, 129, 137, 141
Grove, William R., 16–17, 61n25
Gubar, Susan, 146n1

habit, 49–50, 52–53
Haeckel, Ernst, 198
Haldane, J. B. S., 235n11
Haldane, R. B., 169, 170
Haraway, Donna, 8–9, 28, 44, 183–84, 216n4
Hardy, Thomas, 18, 103–43, 148; dynamic materialism in, 139; human objecthood in, 134–35; novel genre, critique of, 129–30, 139–40; poetry, turn to, 103–4, 143, 243; as realist, 7n9, 105, 143; Schopenhauer, reading of, 149, 153n11; sketch form, use of, 103, 108, 129
— "Heredity," 111
— *Jude the Obscure*, 103, 108, 128–29, 143, 227
— *A Pair of Blue Eyes*, 110n8
— *The Return of the Native*, 105, 106–8, 129, 141–42
— "The Science of Fiction," 7–8, 13, 29–30
— *Tess of the d'Urbervilles*, 112n11
— *The Well-Beloved*, 35, 103–43, 242–43; accretion in, 131–32, 135–37; colonialism, critique of, 137–39; critical response to, 140n37; description in, 140–41; heredity in, 108–13; milieu in, 133–35; publication history, 108, 129, 139–40; whiteness in, 116–19, 121–22
Harman, Graham, 192n17
Hartmann, Oswald Oskar, 169n24
Hazlitt, William, 104n3
Hegel, G. W. F., 26
Heinroth, Oskar, 198

Heisenberg, Werner, 215–16
Henchman, Anna, 59n24
Henry, Nancy, 100, 237n14, 238n16
Hensley, Nathan K., 183
hereditary science, 109, 111, 114–19, 122–29, *126*
heredity, 109, 110–11, 117; of character, 17, 124–25
Herschel, A. S., 210
Hertz, Neil, 32
hierarchies: of character, 240–41; gendered, 165, 166, 182, 184–87; racial, 196–97; social, 193–94
Hillebrand, Mrs. Karl (formerly Jessie Taylor/Laussot), 153n11
histology, 57–59
holism, 193–96
Holnut, W. S., *Olympia's Journal*, 225–26
homogenization, 137–38
homosexuality, 169, 177–78
Houwink, Roelof, 60
human objecthood, 12, 20–23, 150, 209, 225–26; in Eliot, 45, 74, 78, 85, 101–2; in Hardy, 134–35; in Schopenhauer, 160, 212–13; in Schreiner, 207
humoral theory, 119
Humphreys, Paul, 68
Huxley, Julian S., 187, 198
Huxley, T. H., 6n8, 58, 99, 114–16, 135, 234
hybridity, 100, 125–27, *126*

idealism, 110, 170
identity: construction of, 147; dispersed, 69–70; national, 118, 128, 136–39, 141–42; unrealized, 36
ignorance, 62–63
imagination, 94
immorality, 53–54
imperialism, 137–39, 141, 185–86, 189–90, 194
impersonality, 6, 18, 101, 177–78, 229–30; in Eliot, 45, 72; of Will (Schopenhauer), 171
impressibility, 6, 129, 223; and accretion, 131, 133
impressions, 22, 77, 99, 207–8; linguistic, 81, 93–94

impulses, 52, 148, 158, 225–26; bodily, 28, 29, 31–32, 144, 146; sexual, 152, 168, 171–74, 175–76
impulsivity, 6, 19, 159–61, 168–79, 223; of women, 155, 157, 165, 174–76
incalculability, 221, 233, 240–41
inconsistency, 33, 35, 36, 69–70, 156, 225
indefiniteness, 33, 44, 50–51, 71
indeterminacy, 3, 167, 216
individuality, 12–13, 71, 73, 178–79, 184–85, 203
induction, 12–13, 14, 96–97
inequalities: of character, 240–41; colonial, 196–97; gendered, 182, 184–87; racial, 182, 186–87, 195–97; social, 193–94. *See also* feminism
Ingham, Patricia, 108, 110
insistence(s), 228–29, 242
instinct, 165, 166, 199
integrity, 53, 121
interaction, 16–17, 18n29, 236
interconnectivity, 56, 197, 200, 202–3, 209–11; of the body, 184; of force, 31–32; and relationality, 193–95
interdependence, 184–85, 193–96, 203–4; human-nonhuman, 189–90; ontological, 181–82; perception of, 200; social, 193–94
interiority, 37, 84, 154–55; and the body, 42–43, 89–90; and depth, 221–23, 226–27
internet (verb), 209–10
irregularity, 63–64, 236
iteration, 130–31, 139–40, 228–29, 240, 242–43

Jacquette, Dale, 170
James, William, 49–50, 52–53, 56, 99
Jameson, Fredric: on "inward turn," 227n5; on materiality, 9; on realism, 37, 87–88, 176, 229; on storytelling, 129
Jaynes, Julian, 187n10, 198n24
Jenkins, Alice, 60, 61, 62–63
Johnson, Mark, 113

Kant, Immanuel, 24, 25n40, 148, 209
Kemp, J., 169, 170

King, Amy M., 97
knowability, 220-21
knowledge: body, produced by, 200-201; intellectual, 81; of reality, 204-5; situated, 28, 183-84; through feeling, 81; totality of, 63, 102
Korsgaard, Christine Marion, 25n41
Krafft-Ebing, Richard von, 169n24
Kreilkamp, Ivan, 186n8, 232n9, 235n12
Kreisel, Deanna K., 194, 197-98
Kurnick, David, 206

La Bruyère, Jean de, 89
Lakoff, George, 113
Lamarck, Jean-Baptiste, 19n30
language: communication without, 98-99; critique of, 100; description through, 80-81; fluid possibilities of, 74; impressions of, 93-95; motion, production of, 237; in poetry, 103-5; status of, 102; writing, 99, 201-3, 217
Laplace, Pierre-Simon, 64n29
Latham, Sean, 226
Latour, Bruno, 192
Laussot, Jessie (formerly Taylor, later Mrs. Karl Hillebrand), 153n11
Law, Jules, 51
laws, characterological, 14-17
layers, 131-32, 133, 134-35, 137
Leclerc, George-Louis (Comte de Buffon), 97
Ledger, Sally, 146n1, 218-19
L'Ermitage (newspaper), 130
Levine, George, 27, 37, 82, 101-2, 205
Lewes, G. H., 57n21, 68, 95n27, 102; Logic of Feeling/Signs, 81, 93-94, 102, 108, 120, 178-79, 233-35
— "Dickens in Relation to Criticism," 224-25, 228-29, 232-34
— *Problems of Life and Mind*, 66-67, 81, 93, 209
— *Sea-side Studies*, 95, 232n9
— *Studies in Animal Life*, 87
liberalism, 14-15
life: boundaries of, 234; force, 114-16, 205-6, 231-37; generation of, 231-33; origins of, 234-37; theories of, 114-16

limestone, oolitic, 109, 117, 132, 133-35, *134, 135*
Lindner, Albertine, 153
literature: poetry, 29-30, 103-5, 143, 243; as science, 6-7, 29-30. *See also* fiction; metaphor; New Realism; New Woman novels; novel, as genre; novel, realist
Liu, Daniel, 114n13
liveliness, 6, 221, 223, 225-26, 241; vs. depth, 225, 227-28; inorganic, 235-36; vs. mechanicity, 38, 227-34, 237
Logic of Feeling/Signs (Lewes), 81, 93-94, 102, 108, 120, 178-79, 233-35
Lorenz, Konrad Z., 200-201, 207
Love, Heather, 23-24, 28n48, 77, 183n4
Lukács, Georg, 25
Lynch, Arthur Alfred, 88-89
Lynch, Deidre, 5, 10n18, 42, 89, 177, 222

machines, 98-99, 157-58
Malabou, Catherine, 47, 53, 56, 59
Marcuse, Herbert, 168n23
marginalization, 107, 118, 196-97
Marquard, Odo, 9
marriage, 165-66, 175n30
marriage plot, 129-30, 142, 243
Marx, Karl, 21n33, 25-26, 184, 193, 212
masculinity, 32n53, 147, 162, 167, 179, 218-19
materialism, 162-63, 210-12; and homology, 204; new, 163; ontological, 25; and relationality, 184; of Schopenhauer, 150, 170-71
materialism, dynamic, 16-17, 32-33, 218, 225-26, 230-31, 236-37; in Eliot, 46-47, 51-53; in Hardy, 139
materiality, 8-9, 16, 51-52; of the body, 57-59; character as structure of, 71-72; development of, 113; and femininity, 33-34; of narrators, 83-84; of the observer, 28; of racialized subjects, 120-21; and semiotic, inseparability of, 52; of writing, 99
matriarchy, 166
matter: active potential of, 47-49; fluids/fluidity, 51, 60, 61, 69-70, 72-73, 230; and force, 213-14; and habit for-

mation, 49–50; movement of, 69–70, 235–36; organic, 59; proteins, 50–51; relational, 216; rigidity, 45, 50–51, 72–73, 231; solids/solidity, 60–64, 64, 65, 69–73, 230; vs. Will, 170; and will, 20. *See also* particles

Maxwell, James Clerk, 64, 65, 65, 67–68, 69–70, 236

McCarthy, Justin, *Donna Quixote*, 151

McClintock, Anne, 194

McFarlane, James, 226

McLaughlin, Brian, 67

McNabb, John, 123n24

mechanicity, 225, 237–40, 243; vs. vitality, 38, 227–34, 237

Men and Women's Club, 148–49, 165, 214

Menke, Richard, 233

Meredith, George, 151–52

mesoanalysis, 38–39, 72–73, 91

metaphor: of crystallization, 34, 73–74; vs. figure, 44; ontological, 113, 114; organicist, 193

milieu, 13n23, 19n30, 109, 140; and the body, 123, 137–38; change through, 106–7; character's relation with, 72, 91–92, 107–9, 132–33, 140, 149; in ethology, 188, 216; in heredity, 124–28; in realism, 39. *See also* circumstance

Mill, Harriet Taylor, 161

Mill, John Stuart, 15, 56n18, 128; ethology, theory of, 1–3, 13–14, 54–55, 187, 188
— *Autobiography*, 158–59
— "Ethology, or the Science of Character," 1–3
— "On Liberty," 158
— "The Subjection of Women," 4n6, 161–62
— *A System of Logic*, 40–41, 53, 66–67, 158

Miller, Andrew H., 100

Miller, D. A., 24, 84, 222n2

Miller, J. Hillis, 111

Miller, J. Reid, 115, 188n13

Millgate, Michael, 104n1

Mind (journal), 93, 171, 173

modernism, 37, 217–19, 226–27, 229–30. *See also* Stein, Gertrude; Woolf, Virginia

Mohanty, Chandra Talpade, 196–97

Mohl, Hugo von, 58, 114

molecules, 60, 61–62, 211, 233

morality: agency of, 15–16, 157–58; failures of, 53–54, 86; fictional challenges to, 103

Morgan, Benjamin, 16–17, 23, 48

Morley, John, 136

Morris, Charles, 210

Morris, Desmond, 187n11

Morton, Peter, 108–9, 194

Moses, Omri, 229–30, 242n20

mothers/motherhood, 166, 189–90, 191, 200

motion: narrative, 237, 242; of particles, 69–70, 235–36. *See also* dynamism

Müller-Wille, Staffan, 123–24

mutability, 55–56, 105; of character, 51–53; formal, 55–56; of milieu, 106–7; of surfaces, 106. *See also* continuity

Nägeli, Carl, 58, 114

namelessness, 178–79

names/naming, 85, 110, 122, 177, 238n16, 242

Nancy, Jean-Luc, 12

narration, 83–85, 206–7, 217, 241; binaries in, 83; omniscient, 82, 83–84; relational, 217–18; storytelling, 29, 129. *See also* description

narrative structure: iterative, 130–31; motion in, 237, 242; non-linear, 217; and sequence, 242

Nation (journal), 170

nationality, English, 118, 128, 136–39, 141–42

natural history, 95–97

naturalism, 29–30, 218n36

natural sciences, 181–82, 183–84; abiogenesis, 234–35; biogenesis, 234; cell theory, 58, 111, 114, 122–23; and feminism, 191–93; primordial soup theory, 235; spontaneous generation controversy, 231–33, 235. *See also* hereditary science

nature: bifurcation of, 163, 192–93; care in, 191–92, 194; ethics of, 188–201

Newman, Francis, 63n28
New Realism, 7, 28, 29, 167, 202-3, 217-19; definitions of, 30-31, 36; sensation in, 144-46; and sexuality, 168-69, 176-77; women, representation in, 33-34
New Review (journal), 130, 139
New Woman novel, 30-34, 144-47, 151-56, 164-67; aesthetics of, 168-69; and modernism, 217-19; and realism, 218-19; and Schopenhauer, 148-49, 179. See also Caird, Mona; Egerton, George; Gissing, George; Grand, Sarah; Meredith, George; Schreiner, Olive
Nietzsche, Friedrich, 99-100, 164, 173, 212n31
— *Twilight of the Idols*, 165
Nikolaus, Jens, *Five Regular Solids*, 64
Noble, James Ashcroft, 176, 177
nonhuman entities, 77-78, 98-102; aesthetics of, 208; agency of, 17; behaviour of, 85-86, 187-88; character of, 6, 21; human, binaries of, 157, 192-93; human, interdependence with, 189-90; ontology of, 85-87, 98; perspective of, 82-83; semiosis of, 8-9; stones, 109, 117, 132, 133-35, *134*, *135*; subjectivity, 150. See also animals; object
nonvolition, 20-21, 150
novel, as genre, 4-6; bildungsroman, 4, 34, 129-30, 217, 218; character hierarchies, dependent on, 241; critique of, 129-30, 139-40; "inward turn" of, 226-28; philosophical discourse within, 182-83. See also modernism
novel, New Woman, 30-34, 144-47, 151-56, 164-67; aesthetics of, 168-69; and modernism, 217-19; and realism, 218-19; and Schopenhauer, 148-49, 179. See also Caird, Mona; Egerton, George; Gissing, George; Grand, Sarah; Meredith, George; Schreiner, Olive
novel, realist, 4-8, 4n6; character and milieu in, 13-14, 109, 140, 149; embodied, 29-30; moral challenges of, 103; and objectivity, 27; reality effect of, 64-68; and subject-object relationships, 21-22; by women, 144-46. See also New Realism
Nussbaum, Martha, 25n40, 71, 77
Nyhart, Lynn K., 96

object, 24-26; embodiment of, 21; forces, produced by, 61, 212-13; narrators as, 84; as ontological metaphor, 113; relational nature of, 216; subjects as, 25-27; thing in itself (*Ding an sich*), 20, 155, 170, 209, 213, 216
objecthood, human, 12, 20-23, 150, 209, 225-26; in Eliot, 45, 74, 78, 85, 101-2; in Hardy, 134-35; in Schopenhauer, 160, 212-13; in Schreiner, 207
objectification, 23-27, 24-25, 147-48, 178
objectivity, 27-28, 81-82, 84, 144-45, 192n17, 202-3
observation, 6n8, 22, 27-28, 78-79, 207; description from, 79-80, 201-2, 204-5; scientific, 95-97
omniscience, 82, 83-84, 183-84
Ong, Jade Munslow, 217
ontology, 26-27; and interdependence, 181-82; materialist, 25; metaphors of, 113-14; multiple, 69; nonhuman, 85-87, 98; object-oriented, 192n17; separatist, 203-4
Oparin, Aleksandr, 235
organicism, 193-95
others/othering, 107, 118, 196-97
outline, 104, 105-6, 112-13, 121, 140
Owen, Robert, 162
Oxenford, John, 152-53, 171

Palmer, Alan, 42n1
parenting, 189-90, 191, 200, 207
particles, 67, 217, 218; atoms, 38n60, 60, 68-69, 211-13; molecules, 60, 61-62, 211, 233; movement of, 69-70, 235-36; and waves, 215
Pasteur, Louis, 232, 234, 235
Pater, Walter, 88
patriarchy, 165, 166, 182, 184-87
Pearson, Karl, 148-49, 207-8, 213-15

perception, 7, 22–23; of interdependence, 200; limitations of, 81–82, 101–2; obstruction of, 81–82; of women, 62–63
permeability, 18, 119
personality. *See* character
pessimism, 151, 152
phrenology, 2, 80
physics: of character, 45–46, 55, 59; uncertainty principle, 215–16; wave-particle, 215–16. *See also* particles
physiognomy, 2, 17, 80
physiology, 93, 193, 204
plasm: germ plasm (*Keimplasma*), 111, 122, 123n24–25; protoplasm, 58, 114, 115–16; soma plasm (*Somatoplasm*), 122–23
plasticity, 6, 36–37, 43–60, 223, 230–31; active, 47–49; affective, 53–54; glutinous, 50–51; organic, 59; responsive, 49–50; and structure, 55–57; through heredity, 124–25; and will, 46–47
pleasure: aesthetic, 205; in color, 172; sexual, 17, 173; in storytelling, 29
plot, 97, 129–30, 139–40; character, disarticulated from, 240; deferral of, 182; devices, 238–39, 241–42; disrupted, 217; marriage, 129–30, 142, 243; punitive, of women protagonists, 146; refusal of, 36
poetry, 29–30, 103–5, 143, 243
posthumans, 98–102
power, 26–27
primitivism, 165, 166
primordial soup theory, 235
privacy, 10n18, 84, 89–90, 221–22
prostitution, 147–48, 161–62, 174–75
proteins, 50–51
protoplasm, 58, 114, 115–16
pseudoscience, 2, 17, 80
psychology, 1, 3, 14n24, 95; and character, 10, 79, 225; physiological, 93
Puig de la Bellacasa, María, 189–90
pulses/pulsing, 32–33, 205–6
purity, 18, 112, 118, 127, 142n38

race: ambiguous, 106–7; categorization of, 127n28, 195–96; Darwin's model of, 17–18; difference of, 109, 115–17, 118–20; and Englishness, 136–39; essentialist models of, 119–20; and intermarriage, 118; and subjectivity, 26–27, 120–21. *See also* whiteness
racism, 182, 185–87, 195–97
randomness, 233
rationality, 151, 155–56, 162, 166–67, 179
reading, 22–23, 24n37, 35n56, 206; physiological effects of, 93–94; scientific, 52, 61
realism: agential, 216; and character, 5, 9–10, 177–78; and circumstance, 39; description in, 87–88, 105; ethological, 183, 184, 202–3, 216–17; excessive, perceived as, 144–46; feminist, 32–33, 144–46; generalization in, 71; "inward turn" of, 226–27; and modernism, 229; perceived conclusion of, 37; philosophical, 150; in poetry, 103–5; poststructural critique of, 146n1; relationality of, 189; speculative, 192n17; through knowability, 220–21; by women, 202–3, 218–19. *See also* New Woman novels
Realism, New, 7, 28, 29, 167, 202–3, 217–19; definitions of, 30–31, 36; sensation in, 144–46; and sexuality, 168–69, 176–77; women, representation in, 33–34
reality: and the body, 144–46; emergentist accounts of, 66–69; and fiction, 7–8; knowledge of, 204–5; multiple, 69, 78; relationality of, 204–5, 209–10; scales of, 68–69, 236; without consciousness, 99
recognition, failures of, 62–63
regularity, 63–64, 64, 123–24
Reich, Wilhelm, 168n23
Reill, Peter, 232n8
relationality, 6, 16–17, 160, 223; affective, 53–54; agential, 215–16; and behavior, 199; difference, sustained by, 196; and interconnectivity, 193–95; and materialism, 184; of matter, 216; narrative, 217–18; physiological, 198; of realism, 189; of reality, 204–5, 209–10; and totality, 197

religion, 203–4, 210–11, 232n8, 233
Rentoul, Robert Reid, 118–19, 127
repetition, 130–31, 139–40, 228–29, 240, 242–43
representation: crisis of, 176; ethics of, 23–24
repression: of femininity, 167; of object, by subject, 26; of self, 27, 174–76
resemblance, 110–11, 113
Rheinberger, Hans-Jörg, 123–24
Richardson, Angelique, 118, 147
Riehl, Wilhelm, 96–97
rigidity, 45, 50–51, 72–73, 231
Rigney, Daniel, 189–90
Rogers, Gayle, 226
Rosenberg, Jordana, 194
Rosenblum, Robert, 113
roundness, 89, 220, 221–24, 223–24
Ruskin, John, 34–35, 134n32, 136n33
— *The Ethics of the Dust*, 34, 34n55
Russett, Cynthia Eagle, 192
Ryan, Michael, 140
Rylance, Rick, 19, 157

Said, Edward W., 141
sameness, 137–38, 141, 242n20; biological, 114–15; effacement of, 120, 121; genetic, 109, 110, 111, 113
Scarry, Elaine, 106
Schmitt, Cannon, 8n10, 143n40
Schopenhauer, Arthur, 18, 20–21, 28, 148–51, 163–64, 168n23, 189, 212–14; critique of, 156–57; and Darwin, 171–73; determinism, 149–50, 156, 159–60, 161; Eliot on, 153; Hardy's reading of, 149, 153n11; materialism of, 170–71; New Woman readership, 148–49, 151–52, 153–56, 164–67, 179; reception of, 152–53, 171; Schreiner's reading of, 214–15; and sexuality, 168–71; translation history, 152–54, 169, 170
— "On Women," 155–56, 175n30
— "The Metaphysics of Sexual Love," 169–70, 173
— *The World as Will and Representation*, 20–21, 148, 149–50, 153n9, 212–13
Schor, Naomi, 24–25

Schreiner, Olive, 30, 146, 165, 180–81; critical response to, 185n6; and Eliot, 204–6; evolution theory, reading of, 190–91; and modernism, 217–19; on observation, 201–2; and Schopenhauer, 214–15; Smuts, critique of, 195–96
— *From Man to Man: or Perhaps Only*, 25, 31–32, 149, 180–99; ethics of description in, 201–9; ethics of force in, 209–19; ethics of nature in, 189–99; materialist feminism of, 184–85; publication history, 181; race in, 185–86; scientific feminism of, 191–93
— *The Story of an African Farm*, 36, 146n1, 148–49, 180, 217, 218n36
Schuller, Kyla, 19
Schwarz, Daniel R., 227
science: cosmology, 209–10; culture of, 6–7; geology, 109, 117, 131–35, *134, 135*, 137, 204; geometry, 62–64, *64*; histology, 57–59; literature as, 6–7, 29–30; morphological, 96; observational, 95–97; physiology, 93, 193, 204; pseudoscience, 2, 17, 80; zoology (*see* zoology). *See also* ethology; hereditary science; natural sciences; physics; psychology
Scott, Ann, 218
Scott, Sir Walter, 73
secrecy, 84–85
Sedgwick, Eve Kosofsky, 40, 40n62
seeds, 101, 122
selection, sexual, 17–19, 172–73
self-consciousness, 25–26, 27, 140, 142, 164, 240, 243
selfhood, 36, 69–70, 147, 149. *See also* subjectivity
self-repression, 27, 174–76
semiosis: material, 52, 179; nonhuman, 8–9; nonlinguistic, 102
Seneca, Lucius Annaeus, 1n1
Senghor, Léopold Sédar, 196
sensation, 22–23, 77, 81, 85; aesthetic, 205; failures of, 75, 82; in New Realism, 144–46; nonhuman, 75–76; and thought, 207–8. *See also* feeling

separateness, 56, 74, 192, 211, 230
sexism, 182, 184–87
sexuality, 62–63, 152, 154, 168–73; and aesthetics, 205; and reading, 206; representation of, 176; of women, 165–66, 181
Shand, A. F., 3, 11, 35, 109
— "Character and the Emotions," 14
— *The Foundations of Character*, 92
Siebold, Karl Theodor Ernst von, 96
Siegel, Jonah, 112
signification: material, 52, 179; nonhuman, 8–9; nonlinguistic, 102
Signs, Logic of (Lewes), 81, 93–94, 102, 108, 120, 178–79, 233–35
similarity, 110–11, 113
sketch form, 84, 87–89, 202, 217, 228n6, 243; Eliot's use of, 23, 76, 77–79, 90–92; Hardy's use of, 103, 108, 129
skin, 116–20; color, 106–8, 118–20, 121n21
slavery, 193, 194
Smailbegović, Ada, 8, 231
Smuts, Jan Christian, 195
social Darwinism, 32, 172, 182, 190, 203
solids/solidity, 60–64, *64*, *65*, 69–73, 230
soma plasm (*Somatoplasm*), 122–23
soul, 19, 157
specificity, 72–73, 91–92
Spencer, Herbert, 55n16, 99, 111, 172, 190–91
— *First Principles*, 189–90
— *Principles of Biology*, 189–90
Spillers, Hortense J., 120
Spinoza, Benedictus de, 53–54, 159, 160
Spivak, Gayatri Chakravorty, 138–39, 196n21
spontaneity, 6, 16, 223, 228–29, 233, 242
spontaneous generation controversy, 231–33, 235
stability, 45, 64, 67, 123–24
standardization, 110–11, 141
Star, Summer J., 84n11
Stead, W. T., 180
Stein, Gertrude, 228–29, 230
— "Cultivated Motor Automatism; A Study of Character in Its Relation to Attention," 237

— *The Making of Americans*, 37–38, 228, 231, 240
— "Portraits and Repetition," 228–29, 241–42
Steinlight, Emily, 33, 128–29
Stengers, Isabelle, 38–39, 72
Stephen, Leslie, 142n39
stones, 109, 117, 132, 133–35, *134*, *135*
storytelling, 29, 129
structure: atomic, 60, 61–62, 68–69; character as, 71–72; of fiction, 56–57, 139–40; of human body, 57–59; molecular, 48–49, 52–53, 61–62; narrative, 130–31, 217, 237, 242; and plasticity, 55–57
Stubbs, Patricia, 146n1
subject, 21, 25–27
subjectivation, 168
subjectivity, 102, 163, 192n17; vs. character, 12, 16; feminine, 37, 164–65; human, 19, 21; intersubjectivity, 42; as masculinist ideology, 149; nonhuman, 150; and race, 26–27; racialized, 120–21; of readers, 84; and reading, 22–23; of women, 147–48
substance (ontological metaphor), 113
Sully, James, 11, 17, 21–23, 93–94, 95n27
— "George Eliot's Art," 93
— "The Representation of Character in Art," 93
superficiality, 120–21
surfaces: of bodies, 120–21; character, produced on, 90; critique of, 35; vs. depth, 138; mutability of, 106; and outline, 104, 105–6, 121, 140; racialization of, 115–17; in realism, 143; skin, 106–8, 116–20, 121n21; and substance, 135–36
survival of the fittest theory, 189–90
Sydow, Momme von, 123n25
Symonds, John Addington, 169n24

Taine, Hippolyte, 224n4
taxonomy, 71, 85, 95, 228
Taylor, Dennis, 103
teleology, 163, 172, 217, 232; challenges to, 18, 36; in fiction, 4, 34, 129–30, 217, 218
temperament, 92, 133

temporality, 128–29, 135–36, 188n12, 242; geological, 131–32, 133
Theophrastus of Eresus, 79, 85–86, 89, 101
theory: cell, 58, 111, 114, 122–23; ecological, 194–95, 197–98; evolutionary, 131–32, 171–72, 190–91; field, 60–61, 189, 209–10; humoral, 119; of origins of life, 114–16; strong, 40; survival of the fittest, 189–90; weak, 39–40, 40n62, 43, 182, 202. *See also* ethology
theosophy, 169n24
thing in itself (*Ding an sich*), 20, 155, 170, 209, 213, 216
things. *See* object
Thomas, Jane, 112n12
Thomas Aquinas, Saint, 18n29
time, 128–29, 135–36, 188n12, 242; geological, 131–32, 133
Toepfer, Georg, 188n12, 198
Tomkins, Silvan, 40, 40n62
Tondre, Michael, 9, 61
totality, 59n23, 194, 196; of knowledge, 63, 102; refusal of, 84n11; and relationality, 197; and whiteness, 137
touch, 53–54, 56, 208
Tucker, Irene, 119–20
Tyndall, John, 48, 49, 210–12, 234, 236–37; Eliot's reading of, 61n25, 62n27
types, 79, 89n20, 90–92, 91, 223–24; vs. individual, 12–13, 71
typology, 23, 71, 85, 90–92, 228

unity: holism, 190, 193–96; illusory, 134–35; literary, 11; material, 115; social, 196–97; and whiteness, 117, 137. *See also* interdependence
unpredictability, 16, 53, 58, 68, 71, 211, 230

value, 167, 188n13, 240–41
variability, 55–56, 105; of character, 51–53; formal, 55–56; of milieu, 106–7; of surfaces, 106. *See also* continuity
variation, 17–19, 123–24, 129, 131–32, 196, 229; biological, 114–15; and form, 55–56; interdependence, challenged by, 194–95, 196; racial, 109, 115–17, 118–20
Verwey, Jan, 187–88, 198
viscosity, 60, 69–70, 72–74, 114n13, 231
visual art, 112–13, 204–5
vitalism, 232, 237
vitality, 6, 221, 223, 225–26, 241; vs. depth, 225, 227–28; inorganic, 235–36; vs. mechanicity, 38, 227–34, 237
volition: and character formation, 46–47, 157–59; crises of, 146; debates on, 18–20; exclusions from, 161–62; free, 149–50; humans, unique to, 157–58; insufficiencies of, 34; lack of, 20–21, 150; Nietzsche's concept of, 165. *See also* Will (Schopenhauer)
Vrettos, Athena, 21, 46

Walters, Alisha R., 136n34
Ward, Megan, 9–10, 227
Watt, Ian, 5, 221, 222n2
Waugh, Arthur, 144–45, 176, 177
weak theory, 39–40, 40n62, 43, 182, 202
Weismann, August, 111, 122–23, 125n27, 127, 128–29, 135
Westminster Review (journal), 153, 167, 170
Wheeler, William Morton, 187
Whipple, Edwin P., 21
White, Hayden, 153
Whitehead, Alfred North, 192
whiteness, 109, 111, 115–21; and Englishness, 118, 137, 141–42; of femininity, 35, 112; production of, 137–39; protection of, 127–28; restoration of, 141–42; supposed neutrality of, 115, 127; and totality, 137; and unity, 117, 137
will: and character formation, 46–47, 157–59; crises of, 146; debates on, 18–20; exclusions from, 161–62; free, 149–50; humans, unique to, 157–58; insufficiencies of, 34; lack of, 20–21, 150; Nietzsche's concept of, 165
Will (Schopenhauer), 148–49, 154–56; critique of, 156–57; as feminine, 151–

52; grades of, 160–61; matter as, 213–14; and sexuality, 168–70, 172–73; and women, 163–64

women: agency of, 33–34, 146, 147–48; character of, 4n6; circumstance, particular effect on, 33; fallen, 147–48, 161–62, 174–75; as force, 151–52; idealized, 110–11; inferiority, theories of, 155–56; instinct of, 199; misperceptions of, 62–63; mothers/motherhood, 166, 189–90, 191, 200; objectification of, 25; as realists, 202–3; as realist writers, 144–45; self-repression of, 174–76; sexuality of, 165–66, 181; subordination of, 161–62; suppression of, 165–66; and Will, 163–64. *See also* femininity; feminism; New Woman novels

Woolf, Virginia, 217–18, 229; on Schreiner, 185n6
— "Modern Fiction," 217
— "Mr. Bennett and Mrs. Brown," 220, 221
— *A Room of One's Own*, 184–85
— *To the Lighthouse*, 227
Woolner, Thomas, 112n12
Wright, Daniel, 121–22, 141–42
writing, 99; diary, 201–3, 217

Young, Julian, 154–55, 212–13
Young, Kay, 42n1
Young, Robert, 138n35

Zimmern, Helen, 164, 215
Zola, Émile, 29, 30
zoology, 96

www.ingramcontent.com/pod-product-compliance
Lightning Source LLC
Chambersburg PA
CBHW051351290426
44108CB00015B/1967